(RE)THINKING VIOLENCE IN HEALTH CARE SETTINGS

Contents

PART TWO   HORIZONTAL VIOLENCE

PART THREE   PATIENTS' VIOLENCE

List of Figures

List of Tables

Notes on Contributors

Jackie Cook is Senior Lecturer in the School of Communications Studies at the University of South Australia, Australia. Her PhD explored community and talk back radio's place in the capitalist enterprise. Her work has considered masculinity and sport, comedy and sports reporting, cultural and textual analysis of talk back radio, the development of innovative cross disciplinary educational innovations in local communities and Aboriginal communities in Central Australia. Her work is published in cultural and communications studies journals and she is a founding organizer of the international conference *Consoling Passions: Feminism, Soaps and Media Studies*.

Hannah Cooke is Senior Lecturer in the School of Nursing, Midwifery and Social Work at the University of Manchester. She is both a registered general nurse and a sociologist and has practiced as a nurse in both hospital and community settings. She teaches undergraduate and postgraduate nurses and her teaching interests include sociology of health and illness and health policy. She has produced papers on nurse regulation, nursing standards, workplace discipline and patient safety. She has also published sociology texts for nurses as well as a clinical handbook on care of the dying. Her research interests include patient safety, nursing regulation, emotion work and nurses working conditions and working lives.

Cary Federman is the author of *The Body and the State: Habeas Corpus and American Jurisprudence* (SUNY Press, 2006). He has a PhD from the Department of Government, the University of Virginia. Professor Federman has been a Fulbright Scholar at the Faculty of Political Science, the University of Zagreb, Croatia, and at the Institute of Criminology, Faculty of Law, University of Ljubljana, Slovenia. Currently, he is Associate Professor of Justice Studies in the Department of Justice Studies, Montclair State University, United States.

Marilou Gagnon, RN, PhD is Assistant Professor at the School of Nursing, Faculty of Health Sciences, University of Ottawa, Canada. Her doctoral research project explored the experiences of women living with HIV/AIDS who suffer from HAART-induced body shape changes, also known as lipodystrophy. As a doctoral student, she was the recipient of a doctoral research award from the Canadian Institutes for Health Research (CIHR). Marilou has completed her postdoctoral studies with Act-Up Paris and the Simone de Beauvoir Institute (Concordia University, Canada). Her research interests are situated within the field of HIV/AIDS and include topics such as the bodily experiences of Highly Active Antiretroviral Therapy (HAART), the interface technology-body, the chronicity of HIV/AIDS, the politics of HIV/

AIDS and the issues related to the social governance of people living with HIV/ AIDS. As a researcher, Marilou is a member of the University Chair in Forensic Nursing (2009–2014) along with her colleagues who share a common interest in power, discourse, victimology, and the interface between law and health. As a registered nurse, her professional practice is grounded in critical care (emergency nursing care and trauma nursing care) and in HIV/AIDS.

Dave Holmes, RN, PhD is Professor, University Research Chair in Forensic Nursing and Director/Associate Dean, School of Nursing, Faculty of Health Sciences, University of Ottawa, Canada. Dr Holmes's scholarly interests lie in the critique of prevailing orthodoxies and regimes of truth that influence the operations and strategies of the health care apparatus (*dispositif*). His work has been, and continues to be, strongly influenced by those of Canguilhem, Deleuze and Guattari, Foucault, Nietzsche and others writing from a postmodernist/ poststructuralist orientation in health sciences, philosophy, sociology and cultural studies. Within the fields of Public Health and Forensic Nursing, Dr Holmes' work revolves around three definite axes: human rights, power issues in health care settings (total institutions), and nursing epistemology. He is the Editor-in-Chief of *APORIA – The Nursing Journal*, an international peer-reviewed journal.

Jean Daniel Jacob, RN, PhD, is Assistant Professor in the School of Nursing, Faculty of Health Sciences, University of Ottawa, Canada. His doctoral research project explored nursing practice in forensic psychiatry, and more precisely how fear influences nurse-patient interactions in this environment. As a doctoral student, he was the recipient of a doctoral research award from the Social Sciences and Humanities Research Council (SSHRC). His research interests are situated within the field of psychiatry/forensic psychiatry and include topics such as the violence, risk, ethics and the socio-political aspects of nursing practice.

Gloria Hamel-Lauzon, RN, MSc is a Clinical Practice Leader at the Cornwall Community Hospital, Canada. She is a Master prepared healthcare leader with thirty plus years' progressive clinical, administrative and educational experience in acute care and long-term care settings. She has developed expertise in gerontology, wound care and medicine. Her area of responsibilities includes policy development, nursing management issues embracing quality measurement and management, development and implementation of education programs. Her continued personal and research interests revolve around the abuse of the elderly population in health care organizations and management of change in clinical settings.

Sylvie Lauzon, RN, PhD is Professor in the School of Nursing, Faculty of Health Sciences, University of Ottawa, Canada. After more than 10 years of nursing practice, she joined the *Université de Montréal* as professor and then the University of Ottawa as Director of the School of Nursing and later on as Associate Vice-

President (Academic). Her main interests are nursing epistemology and nursing care of older adults and their families.

Tom Mason (1952–2011) was Professor of mental health and learning disabilities at the Faculty of Health and Social Care, University of Chester, United Kingdom. He became External Professor of forensic nursing in 2000 at the University of Glamorgan. His work has had a global influence on forensic mental health and he has attracted almost £1 million pounds in research grants. Tom co-edited and co-wrote 14 books and published over 70 peer reviewed journal articles. His work is used in policy formulation and educational examinations throughout the world and he has been invited to the Harvard University Think Tank to present his work on seclusion and restraints. He was also invited to McGill University (Canada) and the University of Calgary (Canada) to present various seminars on his research. Tom's research interests were related to issues such as the use of nursing models, the decision-making process for restraint interventions, uptake facilities of psychopathic disorders and care planning for offender patients. His research interests were also specifically focused on high security forensic issues such as the management of chronic assaultive behaviour and weapon construction in secure psychiatric services and femicide.

Virginia Mapedzahama is Postdoctoral Fellow in nursing at the University of Sydney, Sydney Nursing School, Australia. She holds a PhD in Sociology from the University of South Australia. She previously worked as a lecturer (sociology) and teaching assistant at the University of South Australia and at the University of Zimbabwe. Her research and scholarly interests include contemporary racism, new African diaspora identities, work–life interaction and non-western feminisms. She is establishing an active programme of research that explores migrant nurse subjectivities and racial violence against migrant nurses. Her current research project applies critical approaches to an investigation of the post-migration and workplace experiences of skilled African migrant nurses working in the Australian health care system.

Barbara Mawn is Professor, Graduate Coordinator, and PhD Director of the Nursing Program at the University of Massachusetts Lowell, United States. She serves as Co-Director for the Center for Health Promotion and Research. Her research focuses on occupational health and health promotion. Dr Mawn served as an investigator on a National Institute Occupational Health and Safety funded project on health disparities and risks among health care workers. In addition she has conducted research on the contextual factors that impact the working conditions of nurses. Dr Mawn also serves as a consultant in the insurance industry with a focus on developing health promotion programs for various industries. In addition to her research in health promotion in various occupational settings, Dr Mawn has also conducted research related to health promotion in chronic disease, including

HIV. Dr Mawn received her PhD at Brandeis University in health policy and a Master's degree from Boston University in Community Health Nursing.

Margaret McMillan is Conjoint Professor within the School of Nursing and Midwifery in the Faculty of Health at the University of Newcastle, NSW, Australia. Through the School's Collaborating Centre for Older Person Care (CCOPC) within the Research Centre for Gender Health and Ageing (RCGHA) Margaret encourages cross disciplinary collaboration on research and scholarly activities which centre on person centered care, practice redesign and capacity building for future generations of health care professionals. Margaret's research over two decades has focused on practice and education issues and practice redesign. Her primary research foci included an elaboration of the *Boundaries for Safe and Therapeutic Practice (the former NSW Nurses Registration Board.* Her translational research has led to significant policy and practice change in nursing care in Australia and internationally through involvement in projects in India, South Africa, Indonesia and The Maldives. Numerous sets of Australian Guidelines for nurses and consumers have been further developed and validated for application to contemporary practice.

Dave Mercer is Lecturer in the Directorate of Nursing at the University of Liverpool, United Kingdom. A mental health nurse, his career spans clinical practice, teaching and research, with a particular interest in the care and treatment of the mentally disordered offender. His chapter is based on the findings of doctoral research, and reflects an ongoing interest in therapeutic approaches to male sexual violence. The greater part of his professional life has been devoted to recognizing and developing the forensic nurse role as a specialist area of practice. Undergraduate and postgraduate degrees in sociology and criminology have informed a critical engagement with the concept of medicalized offending and healthcare practice at the interface of criminal justice and psychiatry. He is co-author and co-editor of three books on forensic mental health practice, has published extensively in peer reviewed professional and academic journals, and contributed to national television programmes in the UK. His contribution to the promotion of quality care in secure settings has resulted in invited keynote presentations at international conferences in Australia (2002) and New Zealand (2003, 2004). In Canada (2000) he received an Achievement Award from the International Association of Forensic Nurses in recognition of 'advancement of the scientific practice of forensic nursing through research and publications'.

Stuart J. Murray is Associate Professor of Rhetoric in the Department of English at Ryerson University, Canada and Assistant Professor of Social and Behavioural Health Science in the Dalla Lana School of Public Health at the University of Toronto, Canada. He received a PhD (2004) in Rhetoric from the University of California at Berkeley, after which he completed a two-year SSHRC postdoctoral fellowship in Philosophy at the University of Toronto. His work is concerned with the constitution of human subjectivity and the links between the rhetoric and ethics of "life," in the multiple ways in which this term is deployed. Current SSHRC- and CIHR-funded research involves a study of ethics in forensic psychiatry settings (prisons) as well as a phenomenological study on the ethics of seclusion in mental health. He has published numerous essays and book chapters, as well as a collected volume edited with Dave Holmes, titled, *Critical Interventions in the Ethics of Healthcare* (Ashgate Publishing, 2009). He is working on a book-length project on the rhetorical dimensions of biopolitics and bioethics after Foucault, tentatively titled, *Thanatopolitics: The Living From The Dead*.

Patrick O'Byrne, RN, PhD is Assistant Professor in the School of Nursing, Faculty of Health Sciences, at the University of Ottawa, Canada. His field of research and clinical practice is public health, particularly in relation to sexually transmitted infections and HIV. As part of this, Patrick has been involved in various Canadian Institute of Health Research and federally funded projects involving marginalized populations, such as, men who have sex with men (gay, bisexual, queer men), teens, and the homeless. He is the Production Editor for *Aporia – The Nursing Journal*.

Amélie Perron, RN, PhD is Assistant Professor at the School of Nursing, Faculty of Health Sciences, University of Ottawa. She holds a PhD from the University of Ottawa and did her postdoctoral fellowship at the University of Sydney Nursing School. She has worked on many research projects in the fields of psychiatry and forensic psychiatry (Canada, France, Australia), as well as in public health (Canada). Her fields of interest include nursing care provided to captive and marginalized populations, psychiatric and forensic psychiatry, power relationships between health care professionals and patients, as well as issues of discourse, risk, gender, subjectivity, politics, ethics, and epistemology. Her clinical practice is grounded in community psychiatry and crisis intervention. She is the Receiving Editor for *Aporia – The Nursing Journal*.

Penny Powers, RN, PhD is Professor of Nursing at Thompson Rivers University, Canada. She has practised nursing in many different areas of nursing practice such as oncology, cardiology, neurology in both the United States and Canada. She received her master's and Ph.D. degrees from the University of Washington in Seattle and has taught nursing in the U.S. and Canada. She has experience as faculty and as a department head for graduate nursing programs. Her scholarship interests include discourse analysis and the effects of climate change on health.

Trudy Rudge, RN, PhD is Professor of Nursing at the University of Sydney, Australia. She is a registered nurse with specializations in trauma and mental health. She has an honours degree in Anthropology from the University of Adelaide and a PhD in nursing from LaTrobe University, Melbourne. Her continuing project is to bring critical perspectives to analyses of nursing and healthcare work. To do this she applies postmodern and poststructural theories such as Foucault, Deleuze,

Kristeva, Žižek and others to discourse analytic modes of enquiry. Professor Rudge (with Dr Sandra West) directs a research group *Society + Work in Nursing*. She publishes analyses of embodiment, spatial analysis, technology studies in nursing and cultures of care in acute and primary health care environments. She has co-edited with Professor Dave Holmes a book entitled *Abjectly Boundless: Boundaries, Bodies and Health Work*, Ashgate, UK (2010).

Shellie Simons received her Bachelor's degree from State University of New York at Plattsburgh and a Master's degree in medical surgical nursing from Boston University, United States. In 2006, she earned a PhD in nursing from University of Massachusetts Boston. She became interested in bullying and lateral violence while completing an internship with the Massachusetts Board of Registration in Nursing. This led Dr Simons to begin her investigation into workplace hostility where she discovered that most of what was written was anecdotal and not research based. This led to her dissertation topic of *Workplace Bullying and the Relationship to Intention to Leav* *the Organization*. Currently, Dr Simons is conducting a qualitative study of nurses who have experienced lateral violence and bullying in order to formulate and test an intervention to deal with this pervasive phenomenon.

Collette Snowden is Program Director of the Communication and Media Management Program at the University of South Australia, School of Communication, International Studies and Language. She was the inaugural Donald Dyer Research Scholar in Public Relations at the University of South Australia. Her doctorate titled *News and Information to Go*, examined the impact of mobile communications on the changing work practices of media professionals. Her research continues to focus on the impact of new technologies and communication processes, especially mobile communications, on public communication and social practices. She is especially interested in the technological transformation of orality and face-to-face communication, and the broader transformation of society and its institutions as a result of changes in language and its transmission.

Teresa (Teri) Stone is Senior Lecturer and Bachelor of Nursing Programme Convenor at the University of Newcastle, NSW, Australia. Teri has qualifications in general and mental health nursing, a BA in psychology, and a master's in health management. Her research interests include verbal aggression, education, clinical supervision, and mental health. She has worked as both clinician and manager in a variety of settings in London, Hong Kong and Australia. Teri recently received a prestigious teaching award; as well as teaching, she works clinically with offenders diagnosed with mental health problems.

Isabelle St-Pierre, RN, PhD is a nurse consultant in health human resources at the Canadian Nurses Association. As part of her work, she has the opportunity to design, develop and implement policies, partnerships and initiatives that support the effective recruitment, retention and deployment of nurses in the Canadian health system in response to population-health and health-system needs. Isabelle recently completed her PhD in nursing at the University of Ottawa. Her research project explored the issue of intra/inter professional workplace aggression from the perspective of nursing managers. Isabelle's background is in occupational health nursing. She worked as an occupational health nurse for a community hospital, a Municipal government as well as a crown corporation of the Federal government. Prior to occupational health nursing, she worked as a public health nurse as well as a staff nurse in intensive care and the emergency department.

Sandra P. Thomas, RN, PhD is Professor and Chair of the PhD Program in Nursing at the University of Tennessee in Knoxville, United States. Her clinical specialization is psychiatric-mental health nursing, and her practice and research have primarily focused on stress, anger, and depression. She conducted the first large-scale, comprehensive study of women's anger. Nurses' anger and horizontal hostility were addressed in her book *Transforming Nurses' Stress and Anger*, now in its 3rd edition (2009, Springer Publishing). Thomas is the editor of *Issues in Mental Health Nursing* and the author of more than 130 journal articles, books, and book chapters. She is a Fellow of the American Academy of Nursing and a Fellow of the Society of Behavioural Medicine. Additionally, she holds memberships in the American Nurses Association, the American Psychological Association, Sigma Theta Tau International, Phi Kappa Phi scholastic honour society, and several psychiatric nursing organizations.

Elizabeth Walsh is a registered general nurse who has worked both for and with HM Prison (UK) Service in clinical, educational and practice development roles since 1995. She completed her PhD in 2007 in which she explored the emotional labour of prison nurses, and has since developed and led a wide range of practice development projects. She has been involved in implementing clinical supervision and reflective practice in offender health care settings; developing prison health care as a learning environment for both staff and students; and has worked closely with non health care custodial colleagues to promote interprofessional working. Liz is currently in post as a Senior Lecturer in Offender Health at the University of Leeds, UK where her work focuses on the support and development of the offender health care workforce through action learning, reflective practice and clinical supervision. She is also currently serving as an elected committee member of the Nursing in Criminal Justice Services Forum at the Royal College of Nursing

Sandra West is Associate Professor, registered nurse and midwife with a clinical background in critical care practice. She has a strong research interest in identifying research-based connections between physiological knowledge and clinical nursing practice. Her research focuses on the physiological and psychological effects of common shiftwork schedules for women and the organization of nursing work within acute care areas, the nursing management of sleep in acute and aged care settings and the biological basis of nursing practices. Methodologically her research spans both quantitative and qualitative approaches and increasingly emphasizes the identification of ritual and the use of evidence-based knowledge within practice.

Elizabeth Mason-Whitehead joined the University of Chester in 2000 where she is Professor of Social and Health Care. Prior to this she was employed by the University of Liverpool where she began her academic career. Elizabeth's clinical background is in nursing, midwifery and health visiting, where she worked for over 20 years. She teaches post-graduate students, supervises Masters' and PhD students, serves on editorial boards and speaks at conferences and professional meetings. Her research interests include stigma, social exclusion, teenage pregnancy and nurse education. Elizabeth has co-authored and edited five books and over twenty research papers.

Cory Woodyatt is currently a research assistant in the School of Nursing, Faculty of Health Sciences, University of Ottawa, Canada. His field of research and clinical practice is public health, particularly in relation to sexual health and sexually transmitted infections. In 2009, Cory travelled to Tanzania, Africa to study extensively on and provide assistance in health clinic services for the prevention, treatment, and control of malaria, tuberculosis, and HIV/AIDS.

Acknowledgements

Dave Holmes, Trudy Rudge, and Amélie Perron would like to acknowledge the financial support of the Faculty of Health Sciences at the University of Ottawa. Thanks to Sébastien Dunn, whose patient work at various stages of the manuscript has been indispensable. Special thanks to Diana Thorneycroft for authorizing the use of her work for the book cover. Finally, we would like to thank Neil Jordan at Ashgate for his precious support.

Foreword

Dave Holmes

This book addresses violence, in all its forms, in the field of health care. I myself experienced violence as a clinician and more recently as a researcher. This is perhaps not surprising since for the past 25 years I have worked in psychiatry and forensic psychiatry, microcosms where organizational, managerial and horizontal violence are endemic, as that of patients may also be in certain instances. Overwhelmingly, however, I experienced organizational violence, a despicable form of violence perpetrated by organizations or members of these organizations against those who are vulnerable: patients and nurses. This violence in health care settings, as well as its trickery, as brought forward by Robert Castel nearly 40 years ago, hides behind the rhetoric of treatment, care and welfare, making this form of violence the most perverse of all.

Although I recognize that nurses may also contribute to institutional violence, in my many years of research in the psychiatric domain, I have observed that they are predominantly objects of (subjugated to) organizational violence as much as the patients they care for. Based on years of funded research in the psychiatric domain, I came to the alarming conclusion that we are obliged to understand the parallels between patients' living conditions and nurses' working conditions. The point here is to derive an overall picture of the institution in order to express a judgment that supports numerous sets of independent empirical data, a judgment about how *all* actors in *all* health care settings may constitute both targets and instruments of various technologies of power.

This personal understanding of violence in health care settings, gathered from years of professional and research experience in psychiatry, forensic psychiatry and public health, was largely influenced by the research of Professor Tom Mason, a leading intellectual in the field of nursing and beyond. The scholarly work and critical reflections of Professor Mason have not only decisively influenced my research, but they also forever transformed my professional practice as a nurse and my way of conceptualizing psychiatric nursing in general and forensic nursing in particular. By way of his numerous scholarly publications including scientific articles, book chapters and books, Tom Mason courageously has embodied throughout his prolific career what Michel Foucault called the specific intellectual [l'intellectuel spécifique]. With access to structures where power and knowledge intersect, and through *parrhèsia*—frank and courageous speech, this intellectual is one who never hesitates to condemn practices and discourses, even risking his own persona and safety, for there is *parrhèsia* when speaking the truth exposes the speaker to significant risks. If there is one lesson that Professor Tom Mason succeeded in teaching me, it is that "the acquisition, and exercise, of power lies at the core of the 'forensic' apparatus by all professional groups (but not necessarily to the same extent by all individuals within them) (…)."

Tom Mason is therefore for me and for many of my colleagues, as well as for my graduate students, a figurehead whose influence will remain for a long time. As far as I am concerned, I cannot find any other influence as decisive in nursing. If the rigor of his work influences mine as well as that of many others, his interventions, continue to have a significant impact in the field of health care. For some, Professor Mason is a heretical figure in the landscape of (forensic) psychiatry and in healthcare more generally. But in devoting himself, throughout the many years of his ongoing career, to the critique of the status quo found in "total" institutions, he has never ceased to challenge the functioning of psychiatric order in all its instantiations, whether in the hospital or the prison.

It is therefore with an inestimable intellectual debt towards Professor Tom Mason that I dedicate this book to a mentor, a colleague and a friend whose work has led me to understand nursing care differently. Thank you, Tom.

Dave Holmes, RN, PhD
Professor and University Research Chair in Forensic Nursing
Director, School of Nursing
Associate Dean, Faculty of Health Sciences
University of Ottawa
Ottawa, Canada
15 June 2011

Introduction
(Re)thinking Violence in Health Care Settings

Dave Holmes, Trudy Rudge, Amélie Perron, and Isabelle St-Pierre

Introduction

Several employers are actively working towards creating healthy and safe workplaces, now that a relationship has been established between patient outcomes and the health of the workforce (Shamian and El-Jardali 2007). As much as possible, safe work environments must be free from violence. Unfortunately, violence in the health sector is omnipresent and often subtle. It has been described as complex problem "rooted in social, economic, organizational and cultural factors" (International Labour Office [ILO], International Council of Nurses [ICN], World Health Organisation [WHO], Public Services International [PSI] 2002: 9). Workplace violence in the context of health care is of mounting importance because there has been an escalation in the frequency and numbers of health care professionals reporting such incidents. However, there is a common belief that the very nature of the work performed by health care professionals places them at risk of experiencing workplace violence (Ferns and Chojnacka 2005, Henry and Ginn 2002, Erickson and Williams-Evans 2000). Statement such as this often implicates patients as the main perpetrators of violence.

This collection sets out to challenge such taken-for-granted and preconceived ideas, and explores ideas about violence that are not commonly in circulation in the literature. In effect, the main objective is to come to terms with forms of violence that are rarely discussed in the scientific or popular literature, and to show how violence is *also* exerted by employers and health care providers against both patients and health care providers themselves. Our goal is to (re)think violence in health care settings to make overt the subtleties, nuances and characteristics of its operations in such a workplace so that formerly hidden and silenced forms of violence are opened up for discussion and analysis.

Several guidelines and position statements have already been developed in an attempt to address the ongoing issue of workplace violence (Registered Nurses' Association of Ontario [RNAO] 2008, 2009, Canadian Nurses Association and Canadian Federation of Nurses Unions 2008, New South Wales Department of Health 2005, International Labour Office [ILO] et al. 2002, Workplace Bullying Project 1997). Yet, health care professionals and stakeholders continue to identify workplace violence as a serious problem (Quality Worklife Quality Healthcare Collaborative [QWQHC] 2007, Shields and Wilkins 2006, Hegney, Plank, and Parker 2003).

Enumerating the Problem: its Prevalence and Categories

While this book's main task is to question the normative approaches to understanding violence in healthcare workplaces, we first want to show the amount of research and effort that has gone into figuring out the dimensions, locations, perpetrators and victims of health workplace violence. As will be seen from the enumeration and prevalence of violence in the healthcare workplace, statistics related to workplace violence are used to confirm the need for action – the need to find solutions to the problem as identified.

For example, a Canadian study of 260 employees (response rate 52 per cent) found that out of 13 occupations studied, nurses were second only to police officers for risk of violence (LeBlanc and Kelloway 2002). Another Canadian study of 8 780 registered nurses by Duncan et al. (2001) found these nurses reporting being the victim of several types of violence including emotional abuse (38 per cent), threat of assault (19 per cent), physical assault (18 per cent), verbal sexual harassment (7.6 per cent), and sexual assault (0.6 per cent). Yet, 70 per cent of these nurses chose not to report the abuse (Duncan et al. 2001). A third Canadian study of about 19,000 regulated nurses by Shields and Wilkins (2006) found that males were more likely than females to experience physical assault (44 per cent compared to 28 per cent respectively) and twice as likely to report such assault, and nurses younger than 45 were more likely to report emotional abuse from a patient (47 per cent) compared to 38 per cent of nurses 55 or older (Shields and Wilkins 2006). In the United States, the Bureau of Labour Statistics reported a rate of 15 injuries from assaults and violent acts per 10,000 workers for those employed in social services and a rate of 25 injuries per 10,000 for nursing and personal care facility workers. These figures compare to an overall injury rate of two per 10,000 workers in private sector industries (Occupational Safety and Health Administration [OSHA] 2004).

Violence in health care settings is not limited to acute care settings, even if the majority of studies on the topic were conducted in these settings. Many health care professionals, mostly staff nurses, from several different types of units are at risk of becoming victims of violence. For instance, intensive care units, general medicine wards, psychiatric wards and emergency departments were all identified as high risk areas for verbal abuse (Öztunç 2006). However, there is still no agreement on whether emergency departments and intensive care units are actually more at risk for workplace aggression than general wards such as medicine (Landy 2005). Violence is also known to be a significant problem in psychiatric facilities (Privitera et al. 2005, Barlow, Grenyer and Ilkiw-Lavalle 2000). Authors found that staff, rather than patients, were more often the victim of both verbal and physical aggression from patients (Daffern, Ogloff, and Howells 2003). As well, aggressive incidents were more likely to be preceded by interpersonal or hospital related antecedents, such as staff refusing a request, and managed by physical interventions such as restraint and medications rather than verbal interactions such as counselling (Shepherd and Lavender 1999). It is research such as this that starts to confront some of the assumptions about violence and certain forms of riskier populations or workplaces. We begin to get a glimpse that violence and its solutions may not lie in simply thinking about the problem as having a single source or origin.

The consequences of workplace violence are far-reaching and include absenteeism related to illness, injury and disability, staff turnover (direct cost); decreased productivity and lower quality of service (indirect cost); and decreased satisfaction at work and decreased moral, decreased commitment towards the organization, and damage to the organization's reputation (intangible cost) (Di Martino 2005, Krug et al. 2002). As well, the ramifications of workplace violence are not only felt by employees and employers but can also affect spouses, children and families in general (Courcy and Savoie 2003). As for the financial cost associated with workplace aggression, Henry and Ginn (2002), citing the work of Jossi (1999), have stated that "combined with other costs such as lawsuits, lost productivity, higher insurance cost and workers' compensation claims, the bottom line figure for workplace violence is an estimated $36 billion U.S. annually" (Henry and Ginn 2002: 481). As such, managing violence in the health sector remains a priority, as seen in the many reports which identify the development of workplace violence prevention programs as organizational priority action strategies for decision-makers and managers to improve quality of worklife for health care professionals as well as quality of care and patient outcomes (Registered Nurses' Association of Ontario [RNAO] 2008, Quality Worklife Quality Healthcare Collaborative [QWQHC] 2007).

The incidence of aggressive acts as well as its management is based on the interaction between: patient (e.g. psychopathology, gender), environment/setting (e.g. size of ward, crowding), interaction/situation (e.g. aversive stimulation, provocation), and staff (e.g. level of education, training in aggression management, attitudes) (Abderhalden et al. 2002). The attitudes and behaviours of staff have been found to be the most important factors affecting patients' aggressive behaviour (Abderhalden et al. 2002). A study exploring differences between patient and staff perceptions of aggression in mental health settings found that staff often perceived patients' illness as the cause of aggression, while patients perceived illness, interpersonal and environmental factors as being equally responsible for their aggression (Ilkiw-Lavalle and Grenyer 2003). As a result, staff believed that change in medication was indicated to deal with the issue, while patients suggested improving staff-patient communication and flexible unit rules to reduce aggression (Ilkiw-Lavalle and Grenyer 2003). As such, strategies identified by staff to respond to acts of patient aggression often included physical interventions such as restraints, medication and seclusion, while strategies identified by patients included counselling (Shepherd and Lavender 1999).

A cyclical model of violence by psychiatric in-patients suggests that nurses' reaction following an act of aggression may contribute to the risk of further aggression (Whittington and Wykes 1994). In effect, since experiencing assault leads to increased stress, such stress may in turn affect nurses' behaviour toward patients. Coping strategies include such behaviours as becoming "confrontive" by over controlling or verbalizing hostility towards patients; or "escape-avoiding" patients by spending as little time as possible in direct communication with them, thus increasing the risk of further aggression (Whittington and Wykes 1994). Conversely, the issue of intra/inter professional aggression does not appear to be reported nor addressed in the psychiatric literature.

More incidents of workplace aggression are also spreading to general wards (Beck 2008, O'Connell et al. 2000). As a result, several studies explored the issue of workplace aggression towards health care staff in relation to their area of practice. Findings from several studies that compared critical care units such as emergency departments (ED) and intensive care units (ICU) to ward units found that certain types of critical care units appear to have a slightly higher rate of aggression. For example, a study of 2 407 Australian nurses (response rate 38 per cent) found that 76.1 per cent of ED nurses, 68.9 per cent of ICU nurses and 63.8 per cent of operating room/day surgery nurses experienced verbal abuse compared to 72 per cent of medical setting nurses and 64.1 per cent of surgical setting nurses (Farrell, Bobrowski, and Bobrowski 2006). The percentage of nurses experiencing physical abuse was also slightly higher in critical care units with 57.5 per cent of ED nurses and 47.1 per cent ICU nurses reporting physical abuse compared to 44 per cent of medical settings nurses and 35.5 per cent of surgical setting nurses (Farrell et al. 2006). While 74.3 per cent of survey respondents identified patients/clients as the most common perpetrators of verbal abuse, patient/client visitors were identified by 35.3 per cent of survey respondents, nurse colleagues by 28.7 per cent, doctors by 27.1 per cent and nurse managers/supervisors by 15.8 per cent (Farrell et al. 2006).

Notwithstanding the significant amount of data pertaining to workplace violence and aggression, as we can see from the above studies, health workers often fail to report incidences ensuring that statistics and prevalence data is unreliable due to much under-reporting (ICN 1999). Several reasons are cited to explain this phenomenon.

Failure to Capture: the Under-reporting of Violence

In putting together this collection on violence in health care workplaces, we noted that as part of our re-thinking, a critique of current approaches to the problem was a necessary first step. While in the section above we outlined many studies of the prevalence and characteristics of violence in healthcare, it was clear that such studies while enumerating the breadth and depth of violence, such approaches failed to develop a reliable picture. One of the reasons for this singular failure, are the numbers of justifications for under-reporting workplace aggression. The justifications include but are not limited to: aggression being perceived as an integral "part of the job"; reporting being considered as not worthwhile because historically nothing was done about it; the fear that the victim will be reprimanded, or accused of negligence or inadequate performance, thus provoking the attack; reporting mechanisms that are both cumbersome and time-consuming; and nurses perceiving a conflict of interest between reporting workplace aggression and being a professional caregiver (Ferns and Chojnacka 2005, Hesketh et al. 2003, Gates and Kroeger 2002, McKoy and Smith 2001, O'Connell et al. 2000, Erickson and Williams-Evans 2000). These numerous explanations suggest a vicious cycle resulting in entrenched, structural failures to approach either full understandings of the situation or to show how systems continue to reproduce violence in healthcare systems across the globe.

Cultures of disclosure in organizations operate to reproduce the conditions for violence. For instance, such situations where under-reporting is encouraged by senior decision-makers because, if the actual number of incidents were known, "administrators would have to respond to pressures to determine why there were so many assaults [and] they would be forced to take remedial action to prevent further incidents of aggression" (Rippon 2000: 454), cultures of silence are promoted. On the other hand, senior managers can be unaware of the real extent of the issue because of lack of reporting from front-line staff and front-line and middle-managers. In the context of understanding attitudes towards a patient safety culture, a study of 15 California hospitals by Singer et al. (2003) serves to parallel this last point. The findings suggest a tendency for front-line workers and middle managers to gloss over patient care problems when briefing senior managers, which in turn made it hard for executives to understand the true state of their organization (Singer et al. 2003). As such, under-reporting plays down the seriousness of the issue of workplace aggression to senior management.

According to ICN (1999), only one-fifth of cases of workplace violence/aggression are officially reported, which serves to confirm the notion of a *code of silence* around reporting incidents of violence. Only in the situation of serious violence does silence become broken. This is attributed to such serious workplace injuries requiring medical attention or involving lost time from work that is required by law to be declared to Workplace Compensation Boards (Rippon 2000), or police and court actions are required. However, Andersson and Pearson (1999) found that allowing low intensity deviant behaviours to prevail by not paying attention to such actions in fact increased the incidence of more serious types of aggressive behaviours. Such research calls for organizations to implement better reporting systems and to encourage staff to report all episodes of workplace aggression. Authors of these forms of organizational cultural analyses believe that monitoring incidents of workplace aggression may be the first steps in identifying trends with which to guide future interventions and educational needs (Clements et al. 2005). Savard (2004) argues that before employees can feel comfortable reporting incidents of workplace aggression, the organization (including the administration) is required to break from the code of silence by taking a clear stance toward violence in the workplace. She suggests, as a first step, the need for a clear policy pertaining to workplace aggression and stresses that management, put simply, do what they say (Savard 2004). What is clear from much of this research into workplace cultures and the reporting of violence is that there are significant barriers to collecting accurate data from merely monitoring violent acts, and that much time is spent on developing strategies that overcome barriers in organizations so that violence no longer goes unreported. However, more concerningly, another important reason for the under-reporting of workplace aggression relates to the lack of a clear definition of the concept.

Naming and Framing: Defining Workplace Violence

The definition of what constitute workplace aggression and violence is contentious to this day. In some instances the terms aggression and violence are used interchangeably, whereas in other instances a clear distinction is made. Current reviews of the terminology suggest that both terms appear to have different meanings whether they are used in English or in French. When used in English, it appears that *aggression* has a broader meaning than violence (Jauvin 2003), with few authors viewing *violence* specifically as the physical expression of aggression (Griffin and Lopez 2005, Mason and Chandley 1999, Newman and Baron 1998). As well, some view the term *violence* as relating more to the area of criminology and criminal justice, and the term *aggression* relating to health care (Chappell and Di Martino 1998). Conversely, when used in French, it is the term "*violence*" that has a broad meaning, while the term "*aggression*" has more of a legal or technical connotation (Jauvin 2003).

Other challenges associated with defining workplace aggression and violence resides in the fact that aggression and violence are often perceived as *emotive topics associated with particular stigma* (Rippon 2000); and as *internal personal constructs with subjective aspects* where the perception of what constitutes violence can vary between groups and cultural settings (O'Connell et al. 2000). A theoretical paper by Waddington, Badger and Bull (2005) reinforces these views and identifies three main reasons as to why the concept of workplace violence is so difficult to define. First, violence can be exhibited in a number of different contexts; in some contexts violence may be acceptable whereas in others it will not be tolerated. Second, participants of a violent episode can give different meanings to their own and others' actions (i.e., objective actions versus subjective responses to these actions). Third, the relationship between the apparent severity of an act of violence and the impact the act has on the victim is often unclear and very complex. For example, verbal aggression could ultimately be more debilitating than physical attack (Waddington et al. 2005). This last point is also paralleled by Engel (2004: 45) who states that "there is no correlation between the extent of physical injury and the degree of psychological injury. People do not have to be physically injured to suffer psychological trauma from a violent episode."

While definitions of workplace aggression and violence may greatly vary in the literature, some factors appear to be consistent, such as: intent on the part of the aggressor, a cognitive process and the behaviour resulting in a physical, psychological or emotional harm (Rippon 2000). However, explicitly including "intent" as part of the definition may create challenges in health care because health care professionals are likely to be the victims of unintentional aggression from patients who are confused, demented or hypoxic (Ferns and Chojnacka 2005) or in physical pain or distress (Ferns 2006), thus making their cognitive process impaired. As well, while factors found in the work environment of employees may potentially elicit aggressive or violent behaviour (ILO et al. 2002), and while common workplace practices (e.g. the measure of time and workload, mandatory overtime) are associated with institutional violence (St-Pierre and Holmes 2008), one would be hard pressed to prove any explicit intention to hurt on the part of the employer (O'Leary-Kelly, Griffin, and Glew 1996), although many definitions of workplace bullying point to the use of high workloads as a form of punishment or harassment by management visited on workers (Workplace Bullying Project 1997). Moreover, as some studies of workplaces have found (Singer et al. 2003, Workplace Bullying Project 1997), how violence in the workplace is defined depends on ones location in the organization. It is not unknown for management to express or excuse bullying by minimising or reducing the severity of an episode of bullying where the worker perceives the same episode as serious. The complexity of the idea of violence means that currently, there is no agreement on a clear definition of what constitutes workplace aggression and workplace violence. As such, definitions and typologies vary considerably from study to study or are completely omitted, resulting in ambiguity, greatly reducing the ability to make inter-study comparisons. In framing the current collection of chapters on violence in health care, we suggest that violence in its various guises requires other forms of analysis and theorization. Clearly enumerating, capturing through categorising and finding a single definition for violence or aggression in health care has not provided a way into its chameleon-like characteristics – hence our move to re-think violence, and to critique its assumed normativity in health care settings.

(Re)thinking Violence in Health Care

For the purpose of this collection the conceptualization of violence will be broad and be largely influenced by the works of critical theorists, notably Michel Foucault, for whom the nexus between violence and power is an instrumental one: that is, violence is an instrument of power. As a consequence, violence means more than inflicting harm or injury (in all their forms) to individuals. It is also a way of looking and constructing these individuals. Drawing together the latest research from Australia, Canada, the UK, and the US, this collection engages with the work of critical theorists such as Bourdieu, Butler, Foucault, Goffman, Latour and Žižek, amongst others, to address the issue of violence in health care settings and theorize its workings in creative and controversial ways. Using a broad range of critical approaches in the field of anthropology, cultural studies, gender studies, political philosophy and sociology, it examines violence following three definite yet interrelated streams: institutional violence and managerial violence against health care workers; horizontal violence amongst health care providers and from health care providers (part of the health care apparatus) towards patients; and patients' violence towards health care providers.

The chapters which make up this collection use explicit theories to account for violence they find in health care settings. In using Foucauldian analyses some authors provide insights into how power and violence intersect in the forensic settings where violence is an instrument of power and the knowledge of groups of professionals and experts in such settings. Goffman's analysis of total institutions is thought to have contributed to how Foucault came to view prisons, school and hospitals – where the organization of a total institution governed all aspects of an inmate's life, as well as of those who were to provide care in such a setting. Indeed the idea of the moral career of a patient has as much to say about the government of care providers in health care as it does the mental health patient in forensic settings. Such forms of analysis lead to explorations of the micro-world of mental health and forensic care, yet speak to the societal structures that make such institutions possible.

A further strong aspect of the volume is the use of theorists such as Butler, Bourdieu, Latour and Žižek whose influence on the works in the book is to explore how violence is constituted in the spaces and interstices of health care settings. For authors using such theoretical approaches it is not that violence is always already a part of such settings but that violence is constituted in the actions, performances or symbolic activities of health care, wherever such practices are located. While Butler and Latour would suggest that violence is not inherent in the forensic or health care setting, but performed or brought into view as a part of a forensic or health network of practices, we can see how violence is potential rather than inevitable in such settings. For structuralist approaches such as Žižek or Bourdieu, violence emerges from the structural relationships and the production of social relations as these intersect with power, symbolic or material that constitutes the relationships in health care settings. In using this range of theoretical perspectives the hope is to expose how violence requires more than merely enumerating, categorising and conceptualisation (or naming), that is working out its grids of specification (Foucault 1972) will always be insufficient. Instead analysis of discourses, texts and talk and practices within social relations are needed to expose more nuanced accounts of the complexities of violence in the social spaces of health care. Moreover, in starting this exploration with an analysis of how institutions and organizations contribute to violence, this collection turns its analysis on its head – starting as such explorations do with interpersonal and specific populations being more problematic than others. Rather, in starting where we do, we suggest the need to look to health care and its organization for how violence is bred in its practices before we turn to explore interpersonal forms of violence in health care.

Part One: Institutional and Managerial Violence

Part one of the collection deals with institutional and managerial violence, that is violence that deploys from various dimensions of institutions, such as administrative rules, policies and procedures, legislative frameworks, their relationship with other institutions, architectural imperatives, and the bureaucratization and *technocratization* of health care work. In the first section of the book, our contributors highlight how organizational and managerial violence are pervasive in health care settings. This collection opens with a most controversial chapter in which Holmes and Murray (the authors) show how behaviour modification programs (BMPs) continue to be in vogue in some "total" institutions, such as psychiatric hospitals, prisons, and penitentiaries. Drawing on the seminal works of Erving Goffman and Michel Foucault, they argue that the continued use of BMPs is not only flawed from a scientific perspective, but constitutes an unethical and violent approach to the management of nursing care for mentally ill offenders. This is followed by Rudge and al.'s contribution looking at the use of migration to address the current deficit in skilled workers in Australia and explore the social relations of difference in health care settings. Using Žižek's (2009) philosophy of objective and subjective violence as the frame of reference the authors examine how the ideological structure of tolerance operates to produce a 'multicultural workplace' that is hostile to skilled migrants. They contend that the ideology of tolerance acts to mask, alienate, and silence those whose daily life is affected by the violence inherent in the smooth running of what is believed to be a multicultural system.

The radical opening chapters of the collection are followed by a sophisticated reflection on blame in nursing and healthcare. Cooke identifies two contrasting narratives which have been used to explain problems in healthcare: "corruption" of care and "bad apple." These two narratives locate responsibility for problems firmly with individual members of staff. She goes on to examine what this tells us about changes both in the boundaries of professional health work and also in the control of professional health work in an age of managerialism (itself an ideology to obtain the smooth running of the system) while also looking at issues of boundary maintenance and control in more depth. For Cooke, these two dimensions of social life are central if we wish to understand how institutional troubles are explained and put to use. The distribution of blame has played a central role in justifying and bringing about changing boundaries of control in healthcare.

In chapter 4, Powers presents the results of a discourse analysis of hospital policies. Using a Foucauldian approach, she examines discourses regarding hospital violence and identifies dominant discourses that pervade policies as well as resisting/resistance discourses. Her analysis sheds light on the effects of discourses on power relations in hospital settings. Studies of power relations in hospitals settings have rarely been published in the health care literature but this type of research in the forensic nursing domain settings have been examined extensively by many researchers.

Amongst them, lies the work of Perron and Rudge (in this collection). Their chapter stands as a renewed way to theorize nursing work in forensic psychiatry. In effect, Perron and Rudge invite readers to a theoretical experimentation seeking to introduce the work of French philosopher Bruno Latour in the health sciences, specifically in nursing. Latour's *Actor-Network Theory* is mobilized in this original chapter to critically examine the violence experienced by psychiatric nurses in an Australian forensic hospital.

As Foucault rightly argued, day-to-day life is often dirty and messy. The last chapter of part one deals exactly with this. Hamel and Lauzon show that nursing ethical considerations are not yet fully integrated in the culture of long term facilities. Although professionally responsible for the quality of the care provided in these institutions, nurses do not always act according to their code of ethics when faced with the ethical dilemma of reporting or not reporting abuse against elderly persons. Hamel and Lauzon's research results are of utmost importance in any settings where vulnerable patients come in contact with nursing staff be they long term care facilities, hospitals, or prisons.

Part Two: Horizontal Violence

In this section of the book, we turn to an exploration of horizontal violence. This section of the collection opens with the provocative work of St-Pierre on intra/inter-professional aggression. The purpose of this chapter is to broaden the understanding of how nurse managers respond to intra/inter-professional workplace aggression. Based on the work of Michel Foucault, it describes violence as an instrument of power and explores the role played by power in instances of intra/inter-professional aggression. The chapter also focuses on some aspects of the social/cultural work environment and how it impacts the ability of nurse managers to deal with such forms of aggression.

Following St-Pierre's contribution, Thomas looks at the interrelationship between horizontal and vertical violence at the hospital in chapter 8. She purports that few authors examine the issue of hospital violence from a critical standpoint, and fewer still consider the effects of violence on nursing student education. Therefore, this chapter examines two distinct, yet interrelated, forms of violence in the hospital setting: horizontal violence between registered nurse peers, and vertical violence from staff nurses to student nurses. Thomas' courageous contribution offers a framework to better understand the complex relationships between these two forms of violence, literally silenced in the nursing literature.

In chapter 9, comes an original account of the rise of violence in HIV/ AIDS prevention campaigns and its implications. Gagnon and Jacob show that while mass media prevention campaigns are widely utilised in the field of HIV/ AIDS in order to raise awareness of health risks and encourage the uptake of desired (healthy) behaviours, violence has now been introduce to achieve these objectives. Their chapter is the result of a critical discourse analysis aimed at examining three HIV/AIDS prevention campaigns launched in 2009–2010. Gagnon and Jacob's work is followed by Simons and Mawn's research on bullying in the workplace. As the literature clearly shows, bullying in the workplace is associated with negative job satisfaction and retention. It has also been found to have adverse effects on the health of employees. Using a qualitative descriptive design, Simon and Mawn examine the stories of bullying among nurses based on actual or witnessed experiences. Their work echoes some of Thomas' conclusions (chapter 8 in this collection) as they demonstrate the extent to which bullying is experienced firsthand and second-hand by nurses, and particularly by vulnerable, newly graduated nurses.

Commonly, nursing practice is conceptualized as a caring process – a therapeutic undertaking in which nurses facilitate rehabilitation, foster skill development, or undertake life-saving techniques. In chapter 11, O'Byrne and Woodyatt explain that nursing interaction with patients can be violent. In effect, in-depth analyses of the intimate exposures that occur during sexual health assessments reveal that these exchanges can be understood as such. This is particularly true when nursing-based sexual health assessments are analysed using Pierre Bourdieu's concept of symbolic violence. This framework allows the authors to understand sexual health assessments as a form of non-physical, yet powerful violence that examines, evaluates, and normalises patients according to set criteria.

The second part of the collection ends with the contribution of Jackie Cook and Collette Snowden which looks at bullying during interpersonal communicative relations through telephone talk. According to Cook and Snowden, telephone contact enacts the talk-relation as a form of interpersonal "chat": a friendly, conversational exchange, with each participant securely inside the relative comfort of their known domestic or professional environment at the point of exchange. Paradoxically, this very form of interpersonal "privacy" permits the deployment of those work-based practices of manipulative control which have evolved within the hierarchies of power built into professional life. Using analytical techniques developed within the Sacksian tradition of *conversation analysis*, this chapter powerfully works to reveal how seemingly casual talk between two individuals can manipulate existing power relations in ways which appear, at least during their enactment, near-impossible to resist. In using common codes that govern interaction and in forms of threat 'talk' understood by both, Cook and Snowden explicate how bullying is difficult to neutralise, taking place as it does in the back-channels, making its control through policy and procedure elusive. They show how to counter such bullying through the use of conversational, yet subversive gambits that are equally personal resisting the power in the conversation and neutralising its personalising operations.

Part Three: Patients' Violence

In the final section, our contributors focus on the violence manifested by patients toward health care providers. However, this exploration is not about violence itself but how its potential has an impact on the development of therapeutic relationships. In these chapters, the authors show how the need to monitor or be alert to the potential for violence may interfere with practices of therapeutic care. In focusing on risk the ability to empathise or to include or exclude some nurses and not others alters the ethics of care in forensic settings. In other research on violence and the nurse-patient relationships, the affects of violence focus on nurse safety and in this last section, we challenge such a focus instead seeking to explore how the potential for violence may alter the characteristics and operation of this relationship.

The third part of the book opens with an important research contribution from Elizabeth Mason-Whitehead and Tom Mason on risk and the use of special observations in mental health practice. The use of special observations in psychiatric practice may be employed as an alternative to more restrictive methods such as the use of seclusion and restraint. Special observations are used for a complex array of signs and symptoms (and risk behaviours) which include suicidal intent, self-injurious behaviour, hallucinatory experiences, and absconding. This chapter reports on research into the use of special observations in both forensic and non-forensic psychiatric settings. A comparative approach was adopted to establish if the perceived risk factors leading to the adoption of special observations were similar in both settings.

In his intriguing and controversial piece, Dave Mercer reports on a portion of his research conducted in a high-secure setting. His chapter focuses on the management of sexual media in the context of a rehabilitative environment for the treatment of detained sexual offenders with a diagnosis of personality disorder. This is a vexed issue which has attracted professional-political attention, and criticism, in the UK. In contrast to a body of empirical research into a causal relationship between pornography and male sexual violence, with little clinical utility, attention is given to the practical problems and challenges faced by practitioners in forensic environments, where decision-making is always a product of competing debates about care or control. Sympathetic to the idea of forensic nursing as a discursive practice the discussion adopts a constructionist approach and suggest that the accounts of forensic nursing staff and offender-patients permit an exploration of the way that individuals position themselves in relation to dominant institutional, and ideological discourses about sex and sexual offending. Mercer concludes that the performative talk of staff and patients contribute to the cultural texturing of a masculine and sexist world in a way that marginalises female nurses, mediates the otherness of inmates and contradicts therapeutic ideals.

Following Mercer's original work, Stone and McMillan undertake an analysis of swearing in health care. Swearing is ubiquitous in a range of health contexts and is under-reported in health care but the implications of swearing are poorly understood by both nurses and managers, who therefore do not appreciate its potentially detrimental effect on the quality of the therapeutic relationship, of which empathy is a core component. The taboo nature of swearing means that the particular circumstances of events involving verbal abuse are not always discussed. The strength of nurses' affective response limits both their range and expression of empathy and the extent of therapeutic engagement with the patient. Implications arise for the nature of the partnership between the nurse and his/her patient. Certain characteristics of the patient or nurse have potential to create a therapeutic gap between the two, leading to a sense of otherness and increasing vulnerability for the patient. The authors conclude with a model which promotes responses to the dilemmas involving complex nurse-patient encounters that may include moments of verbal or other forms of violence.

In chapter 16, Walsh looks at threats to caring in the prison context by exploring the nature of caring for patients in the prison environment where the threat of violence and aggression is ever present, and where nursing practice is set against a custodial philosophy. Anticipated or expected violence and aggression towards both staff and other prisoner patients is illustrated by the clear policies and procedures in place to manage it. In line with Holmes and Murray (chapter 1 in this collection), Walsh shows that prison policies and procedures place control at their core, and are therefore in direct conflict with more therapeutic caring practices that are central to nursing. Walsh argues that clinical supervision might have the potential to both manage emotional labour and develop emotional intelligence and thus, counteracts the effects of custody and care tensions.

Following up on the topics of threat, dangerousness and violence, Cary Federman examines the various methods used to determine criminal dangerousness, especially among serial killers. Many serial killers have never been psychologically assessed while alive. But many have been, usually after capture. This of course presents problems in terms of determining motive and the possibility of repeat offences. Equally problematic is the determination of dangerousness, which is made only in part by interviews. In chapter 17, Federman proposes an overview of the meaning of dangerousness in the criminological and psychological literature as well as an evaluation of the criminal profilers that are used to determine levels of dangerousness among serial killers. The overall objective of his approach is to cast a critical eye on these assessments of danger, principally because such assessments come with assumptions about human nature in general and the criminal in particular that may be nothing more than general pronouncements about the behaviour of a particular subgroup rather than quantify dangerousness, *per se*.

Finally, this collection ends with the reflexive work of Jean-Daniel Jacob regarding nursing work in violent environments, in which the penetration of security imperatives into forensic psychiatric nursing practice is problematized. In the concluding chapter, Jacob presents the results obtained from a qualitative research undertaken in a Canadian medium secure forensic psychiatric unit. He highlights how "security discourses" influence and impede nursing practice, especially the nurse-patient relationship.

Given the content of this collection, we assert that we must (re)think violence in health care settings and continue to find ways to theorise it in alternative and productive ways. Silencing violence, in all its forms will not deter violence or its expression. Furthermore, there is a need to recognize that the multiplication of policies and rules, including those that address issues of violence add further complexity to an already complicated issue; first by making a heavy reporting process even more arduous, and second, by creating new (bureaucratic) technologies that add rigidity to care environments and unintentionally straiten both nurses and patients, thus creating a vicious cycle with the potential to victimize further. The contributors to this collection acknowledge that dealing with issues of workplace aggression and violence in health care is extremely complex and that despite ongoing efforts may be nigh impossible to eradicate. However, the hope is to start a dialogue about these issues and increase awareness, raise debates, theorize ongoing issues, lift prevailing taboos, and recognize the subtle, multiple (and often ignored) forms of violence that pervade institutions that are meant to protect and care for vulnerable populations and the workers who provide their care.

References

Abderhalden, C., Needham, I., Friedli, T.K., Poelmans, J., and Dassen, T. 2002. Perception of aggression among psychiatric nurses in Switzerland. *Acta Psychiatrica Scandinavica*, 106(412), 110–17.

Andersson, L., and Pearson, C. 1999. Tit for tat? The spiraling effect of incivility in the workplace. *The Academy of Management Review*, 24(3), 452–71.

Barlow, K., Grenyer, B., and Ilkiw-Lavalle, O. 2000. Prevalence and precipitants of aggression in psychiatric inpatient units. *Australian and New Zealand Journal of Psychiatry*, 34, 967–74.

Beck, L. M. 2008. Preventing violence in the health care Setting, in *Working Safely in Health Care: a Practical Guide*, edited by Fell-Carlson. New York: Thomson Delmar Learning, 268–90.

Canadian Nurses Association [CNA], Canadian Federation of Nurses Unions [CFNU]. 2008. *Joint Position statement – Workplace Violence*. [Online]. Available at: http://www.cnaaiic.ca/CNA/documents/pdf/publications/JPS95_Workplace_Violence_e.pdf [accessed: 5 December 2010].

Chappell, D. and Di Martino, V. 1998. *Violence at Work*. Geneva: International Labour Office.

Clements, P.T., DeRanieri, J.T., Clark, K., Manno, M.S., and Kuhn, D.W. 2005. Workplace violence and corporate policy for health care settings. *Nursing Economics*, 23(3), 119–24.

Courcy, F. and Savoie, A. 2003. L'agression en milieu de travail: qu'en est-il et que faire? Gestion, 28(2), 19–25.

Daffern, M., Ogloff, J., and Howells, K. 2003. Aggression in an Australian forensic psychiatric hospital. *The British journal of Forensic Practice*, 5(4), 18–28.

Di Martino, V. 2005. A cross-national comparison of workplace violence and response strategies, in *Workplace Violence: Issues, Trends, Strategies*, edited by V. Bowie, B. Fisher, and C. Cooper. Portland: Willan Publishing, 15–36.

Duncan, S., Hyndman, K., Estabrooks, C., Hesketh, K., Humphrey, C., Wong, J. et al. 2001. Nurses' experience of violence in Alberta and British Columbia hospitals. *Canadian Journal of Nursing Research*, 32(4), 57–78.

Engel, F. 2004. *Taming the Beast: Getting Violence Out of the Workplace*. 2nd ed. Montreal, QC: Ashwell Publishing.

Erickson, L. and Williams-Evans, S.A. 2000. Attitudes of emergency nurses regarding patient assaults. *Journal of Emergency Nursing*, 26(3), 210–15.

Farrell, G. A., Bobrowski, C. and Bobrowski, P. 2006. Scoping workplace aggression in nursing: findings from an Australian study. *Journal of Advanced Nursing*, 55(6), 778–87.

Ferns, T. 2006. Violence, aggression and physical assault in healthcare settings. *Nursing Standard*, 21(13), 42–6.

Ferns, T. and Chojnacka, I. 2005. Reporting incidents of violence and aggression towards NHS staff. *Nursing Standard*, 19(38), 51–6.

Gates, D. and Kroeger, D. 2002. Violence against nurses: the silent Epidemic. *ISNA Bulletin*, 25–30.

Griffin, R.W. and Lopez, Y.P. 2005. Bad behavior in organizations: a review and typology for future research. *Journal of Management*, 31(6), 988–1005.

Hegney, D., Plank, A. and Parker V. 2003. Workplace violence in nursing in Queensland, Australia: a self-reported study. *International Journal of Nursing Practice*, 9, 261–8.

Henry, J. and Ginn, G.O. 2002. Violence prevention in healthcare organizations within a total quality management framework. *Journal of Nursing Administration*, 32(9), 479–86.

Hesketh, K., Duncan, S., Estabrooks, C., Reimer, M., Giovannetti, P., Hyndman, K. et al. 2003. Workplace violence in Alberta and British Columbia hospitals. *Health Policy*, 63, 311–21.

Ilkiw-Lavalle, O. and Grenyer, B.F.S. 2003. Differences between patient and staff perceptions of aggression in mental health units. *Psychiatric Services*, 54(3), 389–93.

International Council of Nurses [ICN] 1999. *Guidelines on Coping with Violence in the Workplace*. [Online]. Available at: http://www.icn.ch/guide_violence. pdf [accessed: 5 December 2010].

International Labour Office [ILO], International Council of Nurses [ICN], World Health Organisation [WHO], and Public Services International [PSI] (2002). *Framework Guidelines for Addressing Workplace Violence in the Health Sector*. [Online], Rep. No. 92-2-113446-6. Available at: http://www.icn.ch/ proof3b.screen.pdf [accessed: 5 December 2010].

Jauvin, N. 2003. *La Violence Organisationnelle: Parcours Conceptuel et Théorique et Proposition d'un Modèle Compréhensif Intégrateur.* [Online]. Available at : http://www.csssvc.qc.ca/telechargement.php?id=62 [accessed: 17 October 2010].

Krug, E.G., Dahlberg, L.L., Mercy, J.A., Zwi, A.B. and Lozano, R. 2002. *World Report on Violence and Health.* [Online: Geneva: World Health Organization]. Available at: http://whqlibdoc.who.int/hq/2002/9241545615.pdf [accessed: 23 November 2010].

Landy, H. 2005. Violence and aggression: how nurses perceive their own and colleagues' risk. *Emergency Nurse*, 13(7), 12–15.

Leblanc, M.M., Kelloway, K.E. 2002. Predictors and outcomes of workplace violence and aggression. *Journal of Applied Psychology*, 87(3), 444–53.

Mason, T. and Chandley, M. 1999. The dynamic of violence and aggression, in *Managing Violence and Aggression: a Manual for Nurses and Health Care Workers*, edited by T. Mason and M. Chandley, Edinburg. UK: Churchill Livingstone, 17–33.

McKoy, Y. and Smith, M.H. 2001. Legal considerations of workplace violence in healthcare environments. *Nursing Forum*, 36(1), 5–14.

Neuman, J.H. and Baron, R.A. 1998. Workplace violence and workplace aggression: evidence concerning specific forms, potential causes, and preferred targets. *Journal of Management*, 24(3), 391–419.

New South Wales Department of Health. 2005. *Zero Tolerance Response to Violence in the New South Wales Health Workplace.* Policy Document No. PD 2005 315 ed Employee Relations. North Sydney: Better Healthcare Publications Warehouse.

Occupational Safety and Health Administration [OSHA] (2004). *Guidelines for Preventing Workplace Violence for Health Care and Social Service Workers.* [Online: Rep. No. 3148-01R. U.S. Department of Labor]. Available at: http://www.osha.gov/Publications/osha3148.pdf [accessed: 23 November 2010].

O'Connell, B., Young, J., Brooks, J., Hutchings, J., and Lofthouse, J. 2000. Nurses' perceptions of the nature and frequency of aggression in general ward settings and high dependency areas. *Journal of Clinical Nursing*, 9, 602–10.

O'Leary-Kelly, A., Griffin, R.W., and Glew, D.J. 1996. Organization-motivated aggression: a research framework. *Academy of Management Review*, 21(1), 225–53.

Öztunç, G. 2006. Examination of incidents of workplace verbal abuse against nurses. *Journal of Nursing Care Quality*, 21(4), 360–65.

Privitera, M., Weisman, R., Cerulli, C., Tu, X., and Groman, A. 2005. Violence toward mental health staff and safety in the work environment. *Occupational Medicine*, 55, 480–86.

Quality Worklife Quality Healthcare Collaborative [QWQHC]. 2007. *Within our Grasp: a Healthy Workplace Action Strategy for Success and Sustainability in Canada's Healthcare System.* [Online: Ottawa, Ontario: Canadian Council on Health Services Accreditation]. Available at: http://www.ferasi.umontreal.ca/

eng/07_info/2007%20QWQHC%20Within%20Our%20Grasp.pdf [accessed: 5 December 2010].

Registered Nurses' Association of Ontario [RNAO]. 2008. *Position Statement: Violence Against Nurses: Zero Tolerance for Violence Against Nurses and Nursing Students.* [Online]. Available at: http://www.rnao.org/Storage/45/4013_Violence_in_the_Workplace_Against_Nurses_and_Nursing_Students.pdf [accessed: 5 December 2010].

Rippon, T.J. 2000. Aggression and violence in health care professions. *Journal of Advanced Nursing*, 31(2), 452–60.

Savard, M.F. 2004. Prévention et contrôle de la violence: un modèle, in *Violences au travail*, edited by F. Courcy, A. Savoie, and L. Brunet. Montréal: Les Presses de l'Université de Montréal, 88–106.

Shamian, J. and El-Jardali, F. 2007. Healthy workplaces for health workers in Canada: knowledge transfer and uptake in policy and practice. *Healthcare Papers*, 7, 6–25.

Shepherd, M. and Lavender, T. 1999. Putting aggression into context: an investigation into contextual factors influencing the rate of aggressive incidents in a psychiatric hospital. *Journal of Mental Health*, 8(2), 159–70.

Shields, M. and Wilkins, K. 2006. *Findings from the 2005 National Survey of the Work and Health of Nurses.* [Online: Ottawa, Canada: Statistics Canada; Canadian Institute for Health Information [CIHI]; Health Canada]. Available at: http://www.hc-sc.gc.ca/hcs-sss/alt_formats/hpb-dgps/pdf/pubs/2005–nurse-infirm/2005–nurse-infirm_e.pdf [accessed: 5 December 2010].

Singer, S.J., Gaba, D.M., Geppert, J.J., Sinaiko, A.D., Howard, S.K., and Park, K C. 2003. The culture of safety: Results of an organization-wide survey in 15 California hospitals. *Quality and Safety in Healthcare*, 12, 112–18.

St-Pierre, I. and Holmes, D. 2008. Managing nurses through disciplinary power: a Foucauldian analysis of workplace violence. *Journal of Nursing Management*, 16(3), 352–9.

Waddington, P.A.J., Badger, D., and Bull, R. 2005. Appraising the inclusive definition of workplace violence. *British Journal of Criminology*, 45, 141–64.

Whittington, R. and Wykes, T. 1994. An observational study of associations between nurse behaviour and violence in psychiatric hospitals. *Journal of Psychiatric and Mental Health Nursing*, 1, 85–92.

Workplace Bullying Project. 1997. *Workplace Bullying: Finding Some Answers.* Adelaide: South Australian Working Women's Centre (SAWWC).

PART ONE
Institutional and Managerial Violence

Chapter 1

A Critical Reflection on the Use of Behaviour Modification Programmes in Forensic Psychiatry Settings[1]

Dave Holmes and Stuart J. Murray

Introduction

This chapter examines the management of forensic psychiatric nursing care and the use of behaviour modifications programmes (BMPs) in the discipline and regulation of patient behaviour. As the name suggests, BMPs are schemes designed to improve or correct particular micro-behaviours to bring them into line with macro-social norms and expectations. More euphemistically, they are sometimes called "Rewards Programmes" or "Incentives and Earned Privileges" (Liebling 1999). BMPs are a form of psychological conditioning based on the work of the American behaviourist B.F. Skinner. Theoretically, the patient is (re)socialised through a system of positive and/or negative reinforcement, usually on the basis of a token economy, where "points" (for example) are earned, lost, and can be exchanged for "rewards." Forensic psychiatry settings are "total institutions" that provide the perfect laboratory because environmental conditions can be tightly controlled. In these settings, simple "life rewards" and basic necessities can be offered or withheld as "reward" or "punishment," positive or negative reinforcers. While Gendreau (1996) argues that the most effective ratio of positive to negative reinforcement is 4:1, in total institutions we suspect that the inverse ratio obtains, since operant conditioning extends and adapts the punitive model already in place at the prison. In any case, in these settings it is often difficult to distinguish positive from negative reinforcers in any unequivocal sense (there might be a negative "rewards" scheme, for instance). As we shall demonstrate, even relationships themselves are invested and mobilised as tokens of exchange in the everyday complexities, networks, and discrepancies of prison/hospital life. As nursing staff are enlisted to implement and supervise these programmes, they too become caught in the practical dispositions of power, privilege, and punishment: they become agents of a moral orthopaedics.

---

1   This chapter is a shortened version of the following article: Holmes, D. and Murray, S. 2011. Civilizing the *Barbarian*: A Critical Analysis of Behaviour Modification Programs in Forensic Psychiatric Settings. *Journal of Nursing Management*, 19 (3), 293–301.

Prisons, penitentiaries, and psychiatric hospitals (including their related nexus) are thought to be signs of modernity and civilisation. These institutions help to mediate the individual's relation with state and society, performing managerial roles through sanitary and political techniques, ideally for the benefit of those being managed. While forensic psychiatry settings are meant to provide care for mentally ill offenders, at the same time they are places where captive patients are held against their will and where penal sanctions hold sway. Forensic psychiatric patients therefore exist in limbo, between care and incarceration—between largely incommensurable techniques and objectives. Given their broad social function and legal mandate, in Foucault's sense of the term, forensic psychiatry settings operate as an integrated State apparatus (*dispositif*) that comprises multifaceted and interrelated administrative, social, political, and ethical systems (bringing together the healthcare system and the penal system, for instance). State apparatuses are carefully designed to achieve specific macro-social objectives (treatment, education, punishment, etc.) while being permeated by webs of power relations. Although the macro-social functions of these institutions are publicly known, in this paper we suggest that a critical analysis of BMPs in forensic psychiatry settings will help expose the manner in which institutional power is wielded, calling into question the scientific and ethical basis of the micro-practices we see at work.

This chapter therefore hopes to shed light on the tensions that arise when therapeutic ideals operate within the punitive setting of a prison, when care comes face-to-face with incarceration. The implementation and management of BMPs provides a prime instance where two contradictory ideals collide. Here, we might say that the body of the condemned (in Foucauldian parlance) is doubled: known as "patients" to allied health professionals and "inmates" to correctional staff, a new, apparently neutral, term had to be invented to describe these individuals: "residents." But it is not just the "neutralised" body that is doubled through the various identities or roles that it takes up: the "resident's" body is not just the body of a patient subjected to medical and nursing knowledge and not just the body of a prisoner subjected to incarceration and punishment; while the body of the condemned is undoubtedly the target of a disciplinary apparatus (nursing management, medical science, corrections), the "resident" is also—and perhaps foremost—a member of a society, a social body, a being who shares in the lives of other residents, building relationships with them and with the prison's correctional officers, as well as with allied health staff (indeed, psychotherapeutic rehabilitation requires this). It seems to us that while BMPs *appear* to shore up a resident's autonomy, rational decision-making, or even his individualism and entrepreneurialism, in actuality BMPs target distinctly social behaviours that are relational, value-laden, and that take place in context.

As we argue below, these relations extend beyond the function of "discipline," in Foucault's sense of the term, to treat the population in its generality. Following Foucault, we suggest that this second form of power should be understood as biopolitical, it is power's hold over life itself, and it must be distinguished from disciplinary power:

this technology of power, this biopolitics, will introduce mechanisms with a certain number of functions that are very different from the functions of disciplinary mechanisms. The mechanisms introduced by biopolitics include forecasts, statistical estimates, and overall measures. And their purpose is not to modify any given phenomenon as such, or to modify a given individual insofar as he is an individual, but, essentially, to intervene at the level at which these general phenomena are determined… [R]egulatory mechanisms must be established to establish an equilibrium, maintain an average, establish a sort of homeostasis, and compensate for variations within this general population and its aleatory field. In a word, security mechanisms have to be installed around the random element inherent in a population of living beings so as optimize a state of life. (Foucault 2003: 246)

So we have two axes of bio-power at play: disciplinary power, which takes the individual as its object, and biopolitical power, which takes the life of the population as its means and its end, "life as both its object and its objective" (Foucault 2003: 254). Thus, while BMPs seem to act directly on the individual, in a disciplinary sense, they must also act biopolitically—a dimension that is rarely discussed in the literature. We cannot say that these two axes of bio-power map neatly onto the two management "styles" found in forensic psychiatric settings (i.e., care and incarceration), but rather, that nursing staff in particular find themselves imbricated in both axes of bio-power, just as they find themselves involved in practices associated with corrections, and not just healthcare (the line between "corrections" and "healthcare" is often fluid). BMPs are located at this complex juncture, they provide an allegory for the tensions of prison/hospital life, and so we must complicate this scene in order to give a more just account of the myriad factors at play as well as the ethical implications of BMPs as they feature as part of a treatment plan.

Throughout the 1970s and 1980s, BMPs were used widely in the psychiatric domain after being developed and popularised by psychologists in the post-World War II period (Rothman 1975). Interventions aimed at correcting deviant behaviours were regarded and continue to be regarded (in specific settings) as a "proper use of authority" (Rothman 1975: 17); as a consequence, many total institutions have made BMPs one of their preferred techniques to correct deviance and to reform patients/prisoners. Indeed, we commonly associate total institutions with the use of BMPs. Although this intervention was (and is still to a certain extent) celebrated as *the* new and more humane treatment strategy, critical literature has raised concerns regarding this practice, labelling it as inhumane, debilitating, and infantilising. One professional organisation after another has "recounted the abuses and denounced the barbarisms" (Rothman 1975: 18) of total institutions where BMPs are deployed. Despite this criticism, BMPs continue to be used within psychiatric and correctional settings. Some psychiatrists, psychologists, social workers, and nurses continue to believe that operant conditioning holds the key to effective treatment.

Drawing on Foucault's double understanding of bio-power as disciplinary and biopolitical, coupled with Erving Goffman's sociological analysis of total institutions, we assess the use of BMPs from a political and an ethical standpoint, demonstrating not only how a disciplinary bio-psychiatric model permeates several aspects of the management of nursing care in forensic psychiatry, but also how, in the quest of doing "what is best" for the patients in terms of care and rehabilitation, nurses become part of a machine that harms rather than heals.

Theoretical Framework

In this section we turn to the work of Goffman and Foucault to describe how power operates in forensic psychiatry settings, one instance of what Goffman calls "total institutions." These perspectives offer a strong framework for analysis (Lagrange 1976). Hacking (2004) suggests that Foucault's "archaeology" and Goffman's interpersonal sociology are complementary. Using a "bottom-up" approach, Goffman (1961) studied the internal structure and function of "total institutions" but did not situate it within a larger (macro) perspective. Goffman's micro-sociological perspective is thus useful in describing and analysing social relationships between the many different actors of "total institutions," especially the interactions between staff and patients/inmates.

From a Foucauldian "top-down" or systemic perspective, practitioners such as psychiatrists, psychologists, social workers, and nurses might be understood as bolstering state apparatuses by implementing and providing crucial power/ knowledge in order to shape and transform human material (Ransom 1997). As such, health care professionals working in forensic psychiatry settings are directly involved in what Foucault calls the *discipline* of individuals at the *anatomo-political* level (at the level of the body) (Foucault 1978). The disciplinary system's legitimacy is tied to the scientific knowledge that the apparatus enables, deploys, and produces, in an almost circular fashion. Power and knowledge form a unitary structure: "the Panopticon was also a laboratory; it could be used as a machine to carry out experiments, to alter behaviour, to train or correct individuals" (Foucault 1979: 203). Here we see that discipline works by individualising. Not only are individuals separated from each other, the individual's symptoms and behaviour are observed, taxonomised, classified (according to *DSM-IV* diagnoses, for instance); he is medicated, he is organised (in individual "units" or cells or seclusion rooms, for instance) through the analytical arrangement of architectural space; he is measured against a norm. Discipline, Foucault writes, "tries to rule a multiplicity of men to the extent that their multiplicity can and must be dissolved into individual bodies that can be kept under surveillance, trained, used, and, if need be, punished" (2003: 242). Knowledge and power operate to justify and legitimate one another, forming a practically unitary phenomenon Foucault calls "power/knowledge."

While disciplinary bio-power treats the individual body and "individualises" that body anatomo-politically, as we mentioned above Foucault also points to a second axis of bio-power that he describes as biopolitical—that is, a power that treats the life of *the population or "mass"* more generally, according to weights and measures, the principles of risk-management, statistics and probabilities, management techniques, and policies to control random events, etc., not so much as to discipline individuals but to regulate and regularise a specific group and its social relations. And while disciplinary power is "the easier and more convenient thing to adjust" (Foucault 2003: 250), biopolitics is more subtle and diffuse because it intervenes ontologically, at the level of life itself. Under biopolitics, then, the function of medicine and nursing is regulatory, turning to "public hygiene, with institutions to coordinate medical care, centralize power, and normalize knowledge" (Foucault 2003: 244). What emerges is "a new body, a multiple body, a body with so many heads that, while they might not be infinite in number, cannot necessarily be counted" (Foucault 2003: 245). For an extreme example of biopolitical intervention we might look to eugenics programmes, with their reticulate and capillary vectors of political power and moral duty— intersecting State, biomedical, and popular discourses on race and hygiene, on the high socioeconomic "costs" of preserving the unproductive lives of the weak, the mentally handicapped, the homosexual, the Gypsy, the Jew, and other "life unworthy of life" (*Lebensunwertes Leben*). And ironically enough, it is in the name of "life" that all manner of atrocities can be justified and legitimated. The point here is that biopolitics relies on complex, interrelated, and totalising technologies and techniques, coupled with a deeply moralistic understanding of "life."

In "total institutions," pervasive disciplinary and biopolitical technologies and techniques ultimately strip individuals of agency through a complex and powerful *mortification process*, where they "die" from their old lives and are "re-born" (as it were) into the life of the institution. This process is said to be successful when inmates have internalised institutional rules (Goffman 1961). The mortification process is not a matter of acculturation or assimilation of one group under the auspices of the total institution, but is something more pernicious still. In effect, the forensic psychiatric patient comes into the institution with a specific representation of himself; upon admission, he is stripped of his "domestic" reference schemes and mortified through procedures and standardised plans of care. "In the accurate language of some of our oldest total institutions, he is led into a series of abasements, degradations, humiliations, and profanations of self ... and his self is systematically, if often unintentionally, mortified" (Goffman 1961: 14). The mortification process is a standard(ised) procedure in total institutions epitomised in prisons and psychiatric hospitals. Inmates' personal belongings are taken away from them while institutional substitutes are provided (Goffman 1961). In short, standardised defacement occurs.

The encompassing or "total" character of total institutions is symbolised by the barrier to social intercourse with the outside world that is often built into the architectural design: locked doors, high walls, barbed wire, cliffs and water, open terrain, and so forth. In forensic settings, for instance, almost every aspect of patients' daily life is strictly controlled and monitored. And yet, these are also social environments, which presents another problem for management to devise techniques to control and monitor sociability itself. We have suggested, then, that not only is disciplinary bio-power at play in these settings, but the logics of biopolitical power are pervasive, since the social life of the population is both an object and an objective, always with an eye to rehabilitation and reintegration into the "normal" population, "on the outside." Nowhere is this tension more palpable than in the implementation and management of so-called "scientific" regimens and treatment plans, such as BMPs.

Discussion

It should be relatively easy to see how BMPs strategically deploy an "individualising" disciplinary bio-power, while the biopolitical aspects of this management strategy may seem somewhat more abstract. But BMPs are designed to intervene at the level of a resident's social life, reshaping his social relationships, his sociality in general, and to modify it to fall within the accepted norms of the population at large. BMPs rely on a token economy, an economy of exchange that operates according to the principles of the market economy—so this is a particular kind of socialisation. It is no surprise, then, that Foucault devotes a large part of his lectures on biopolitics (2008) to neoliberal economies, since neoliberalism has become the dominant ideology governing our democratic populations. Forensic psychiatry units are not neutral institutional settings in which care takes place free from the larger influences that operate within society. And it is no surprise that management strategies have silently appropriated the biopolitical logic that governs our neoliberal democracies—where individuals are seduced into seeing themselves as "human capital" within a system that calculates, quantifies, and otherwise measures all manner of human relationships according to the terminology of the "free" market. In Foucault's words, neoliberalism "extends the economic model of supply and demand and of investment-costs-profit so as to make it a model of social relations and of existence itself, a form of relationship of the individual to himself, time, those around him, the group, and the family" (2008: 242). The extent to which we "freely" appropriate this model is questionable, though it is now the "norm"; however, it is worth repeating that the token economies of the forensic setting are imposed absolutely on residents, they are coercive rather than "incentive" programmes, and residents have not been involved in their creation.

Thus, while BMPs might *appear* to "individualise" residents in a positive way, compelling them to be responsible for themselves, to foster a deeply "entrepreneurial" spirit in relation to their own self-management, as well as to better socialise themselves, we must bear in mind that these are not workers freely joining an employee incentive programme, nor are they consumers signing up for a retailer's rewards scheme. Indeed, workers are rewarded for their productivity or outcomes, which might bear little relation (or perhaps even an inverse relation) to their social skills or sociability in general. Similarly, retail rewards schemes are based on a customer's loyalty, and customers are free to shop elsewhere. Here, instead, the residents' social behaviours are being regulated according to a points system that is standardised, one-size-fits-all: the same number of points is lost for the same offence, and these rules apply equally to every resident in the population, while the severity or leniency of enforcement is at times arbitrary. Is this arbitrariness a positive or negative reinforcer? And what are the wider (counter-) therapeutic effects when the interpersonal relationship between nursing staff and residents is shaped "economically," through the threat of punishment and the loss of "rewards"? Will this build trust and confidence in the resident's sociability, or will it not encourage him to "work the system" through the cold, economic calculation of a cost-benefit analysis (something we praise in the business world)? A hegemonic theory of consumption is presumed throughout, and "criminal" activity is redefined as any behaviour that is an "investment," where a certain "profit" is hoped for, but that carries a certain measurable "risk" of penal sanctions understood in economic terms (Foucault 2008: 253).

The management of nursing care, as far as BMPs are concerned, participates in the "building of a world around these minor privileges," according to Goffman, which "is perhaps the most important feature of inmate culture, and yet it is something that cannot easily be appreciated by an outsider, even one who has previously lived through the experience himself" (1961: 50). BMPs therefore cannot and do not work as part of a "care plan" if mental health care involves restoring the patient's sense of autonomy, real or symbolic; BMPs are infantilising, they work through petty privileges. While BMPs allow the forensic psychiatric patient to exercise some control over acquiring rewards and privileges, or avoiding punishments, this infantile world is hardly analogous to the real world, and hence at cross-purposes with "nursing care" if the ultimate objective is "to improve reintegration into the community on release." Any autonomy the forensic psychiatric patient does experience is a false autonomy, since it is clear that his submission to institutional order is total.

Certainly, some will argue that BMPs are therapeutic, even if they are from some perspectives "infantilising." By analogy, one might argue, parents must take some rather unpopular—even punitive—decisions with regard to the care of their children. But in the wider context, in the fullness of time, children come to realise that these decisions are usually loving and protective, guiding the child as she or he develops into a fully autonomous being in her or his own right. It is questionable, however, to what extent the parent-child analogy holds in the context of a prison, where the relationship is between keeper and kept, or in the context of a therapeutic relationship, between a healthcare provider and his or her mentally ill or disordered patient/client. These residents are not children. Where the child grows and learns to interpret a parent's decisions as she or he gains experience in her or his own decision-making processes, the resident lacks that luxury, he has neither the time nor the place to experience something similar; he is apt to experience nursing staff as inconsistent, if not cruel. He will not see beyond the prison's walls. As Foucault writes, "It is not the family, neither is it the State apparatus, and I think it would be equally false to say, as it often is, that asylum practice, psychiatric power, does no more than reproduce the family to the advantage of, or on the demand of, a form of State control organized by a State apparatus" (2006: 16).

Consequently, we must call into question the functional notion of "autonomy" that circulates in the discourse on the effective management of residents in forensic settings and in the use of BMPs to foster ethical comportment amongst residents and in relation to those with whom they share—and will share—a social life. Mainstream biomedical ethics tends to privilege one notion of autonomy as the founding principle of ethics (Beauchamp and Childress 2008). But forensic psychiatry settings are not places where autonomy is encouraged. In effect, as Goffman clearly states, "total institutions disrupt or defile precisely those actions that in civil society have the role of attesting to the actor and those in his presence that he has some command over his world—that he is a person with 'adult' self-determination, autonomy, and freedom of action" (1961: 43). But a critical approach to ethics will delve further still, asking what we mean by "autonomy" as we continue to use the word so freely: a critique would question the ideals of neoliberalism, calculative reason and "rational choice theories," and it would look beyond the kinds of "individuals" produced by disciplinary bio-power to begin, instead, with the intimate and often fragile social relationships without which "ethics" is meaningless, without which it is reduced to just one more management strategy. It is for this reason that we have emphasised the biopolitical valences of BMPs, for it is here, where one intervenes in the life of a population, a life that is first and foremost a shared life, that we must begin again if we hope to imagine an ethics that would be commensurable with the lives of these inmates, patients— "residents"—and the lives of those who care for them. In light of the "life" that is produced biopolitically, we must imagine an ethical life, a life that would be the domain of bioethics.

Conclusion

The popular view of forensic psychiatric patients—and possibly of any other recidivists—is that they merely lack sufficient autonomy and willpower: they do not want to change. But this view ignores the wider forces at play in the formation of the individual; it refuses to begin to take account of the myriad socioeconomic, political, and environmental factors—the conditions—that have contributed to the patient being where he is today. In most cases, these individuals lack infrastructural support, the conditions in and through which an act of sovereign will would seem possible. To speak of these individuals as "autonomous," to hold them to the "principle of autonomy," could itself be regarded as a violent demand, one that might be incomprehensible to someone who lacks the mental and emotional—not to mention financial, institutional, familial, etc.—resources necessary for comprehension. It would be an unethical practice, then, to place this individual in a situation in which "autonomy" is demanded, and, as we stated above, perhaps it is time to question the normative force of this term as desirable in and of itself (for instance, how ethical is the economic model that it presumes?). But it is perhaps worse to place him in an institutional context governed by BMPs. Even if BMPs give the illusion of fostering a sense of autonomy, they understand "autonomy" only in a limited and impoverished sense, and they fail to acknowledge or to begin to redress some of the wider infrastructural conditions of mental illness, crime, and their connections. BMPs represent the perfect example of a bio-psychiatric model that has gone uncontrolled, where symptoms are treated and underlying causes ignored. Not only is this treatment unethical and ineffectual in the real world, not only is its refusal to see the underlying causes tantamount to professional negligence, we assert that this form of "treatment" undoubtedly exacerbates certain forms of mental illness while causing others—what Illich, in his classic text (1976/1995), has called clinical and social iatrogenesis.

"The barbarian ... is someone who can be understood, characterized, and defined only in relation to a civilization, and by the fact that he exists outside it" (Foucault 2003: 195). Civilisation needs its barbarians; indeed, civilisational norms are defined in contradistinction to barbarism, and vice versa—barbarism is civilisation's constitutive outside. Civilised, barbarian, these concepts are deeply related. They are dialogical, even as the latter term is suppressed, silenced, hidden away, and institutionalised to shore up the "naturalness" or evidentiary "goodness" of the first. We might think of these as two populations, governed by two, nevertheless related, sets of tactics, strategies, and knowledges. We hope that this paper has raised some ethical questions concerning the ways that nurses have been co-opted to police the border between these two populations, and to maintain a *cordon sanitaire* in the name of security and effective management—a moral hygienics as much as a moral orthopaedics that seek to instruct and reform observable behaviours. In our analysis of BMPs, we have argued that the "individualising" force of disciplinary bio-power must be understood alongside biopolitical power, which takes life itself as its regulatory object and objective. In one sense, of course it is true that BMPs constitute a form of disciplinary power, producing subjects who turn in on themselves, who internalise the strategies and techniques of surveillance and the so-called scientific "truth" of who they are. But the disciplinary perspective is incomplete because these "individuals" always already find themselves in a shared world with others, and it is here that BMPs wield their greatest—albeit invisible—power to regulate interpersonal behaviour and to intervene in the social lives of others. Ethics must address this "new body" of biopolitics and the complex conditions that authorise, legitimate, and support it. The ethical and political analysis of the forensic psychiatry settings would be incomplete without attention to sociality and relationality—and from here, towards identity and community. This ought to be the domain of bioethics, in the promise of living-together.

References

Agamben, G. 2005. *State of Exception.* Chicago: University of Chicago Press.

Beauchamp, T.L. and Childress, J.F. 2008. *Principles of Biomedical Ethics.* 6th edn Oxford: Oxford University Press.

Foucault, M. 1978. *The History of Sexuality. Volume 1.* New York: Random House.

Foucault, M. 1979. *Discipline and Punish: The Birth of the Prison.* Trans. A. Sheridan. New York: Random House.

Foucault, M. 1997. Governmentality, in *Power: Essential Works of Foucault, 1954–1984*, Vol. 3, edited by J.D. Faubion. New York: New Press, 201–22.

Foucault, M. 2003. *Society Must Be Defended: Lectures at the Collège de France, 1975–1976.* Trans. D. Macey. New York: Picador.

Foucault, M. 2006. *Psychiatric Power: Lectures at the Collège de France, 1973–1974.* Trans. G. Burchell. New York: Picador.

Foucault, M. 2008. *The Birth of Biopolitics: Lectures at the Collège de France, 1978–1979.* Trans. G. Burchell. New York: Palgrave Macmillan.

Gendreau, P. 1996. The principles of effective intervention with offenders, in *Choosing Correctional Options That Work*, edited by A.T. Harland. Thousand Oaks, CA: Sage, 117–30.

Goffman, E. 1961. *Asylums: Essays on the Social Situation of Mental Patients and Other Inmates.* New York: Random House.

Hacking, I. 2004. Between Michel Foucault and Erving Goffman: between discourse in the abstract and face-to-face interaction. *Economy and Society*, 33(3), 277–302.

Illich, I. 1995. *Limits to Medicine, Medical Nemesis: The Expropriation of Health.* London and New York: Marion Boyars.

Lagrange, J. 1976. Foucault et les psy. *Psychanalyse et université*, 4, 704–707.

Liebling, A. 1999. Doing research in prison: breaking the silence? *Theoretical Criminology*, 3(2), 147–73.

Ransom, J.S. 1997. *Foucault's Discipline: The Politics of Subjectivities.* Durham: Duke University Press.

Rothman, D.J. 1975. A historical overview: behaviour modification in total institutions. *Hastings Cent Rep*, 5(1), 17–24.

Acknowledgements

Dave Holmes and Stuart J. Murray would like to thank the Social Sciences and Humanities Research Council of Canada for funding support.

Chapter 2

The Violence of Tolerance in a Multicultural Workplace: Examples from Nursing[1]

Trudy Rudge, Virginia Mapedzahama, Sandra West and Amélie Perron

Introduction

With the acceleration of the global movement of people in the later part of the twentieth Century, many countries have used policies and community-based approaches such as multiculturalism to ease the incorporation of migrants into their societies. This movement of migrants was fuelled by the speed of development in western societies post Second World War and led to an increased need for migrant workers, both skilled and unskilled, to meet these needs. Multicultural policies associated with social practices of tolerance dominate the landscape of such governmental responses both more widely in society but also in specific locations such as the workplace. However, recent forms of analysis seek to problematize the discursive constitution of multiculturalism and attempt to racialize the whiteness of the Australian workplace. We acknowledge that such a position is one amongst many positions available (Ganley 2003: 13) but view it as necessary to expose the effects of racialization in a dominantly white workplace. To do this we draw on data from our research on the experiences of skilled black African migrant nurses working in the Australian healthcare system to expose how within the healthcare workplace, the ideologies of tolerance within multiculturalism constitute a context of violence. Our intention in this chapter is to 'unpack tolerance' (King 1998: 9), that is, we analyse and challenge the notion of tolerance in so far as it is practised and applied in multicultural nursing workplaces. Therefore, the question guiding our analyses is: what purpose does the rhetoric of tolerance serve in a workplace celebrated as multicultural, yet where social interactions are marked by ambivalence and (racial) discrimination?

We do not intend to advocate for intolerance, or non-tolerance. Rather, we aim to expose how, since multiculturalism's inception to guide management of inter-ethnic and race relations, the idea of tolerance initially was its central but now has come to have less utility or application to the practices of multiculturalism. Indeed, there is now strong questioning of this idea, and also a belief that multiculturalism functions

1   This chapter is an extension of a paper presented by the authors at the Annual Australasian Sociological Association (TASA) Conference, Macquarie University, Sydney NSW, December, 2010.

ideologically and rhetorically. In demonstrating how tolerance works to counteract obtaining inclusivity or equity in a multiethnic workplace, we show that it is the tolerator (the person who positions themselves as '*tolerant*') who retains definitional power of what is to be tolerated (Weissberg 1998). From such a perspective we question whether tolerance can be promoted or serve as a guiding principle since it assumes that one is inherently opposed to those who are/need to be tolerated.

We explore Žižek's (2009) ideas to expose how tolerance masks such violence and operates ideologically to silence the racialized 'Other'. Such analysis is necessary, given our contention that the very act of tolerance is experienced by racialized groups as an act of violence. We provide examples of multiculturalism in/action to show how such structures of tolerance erase difference in the workplace, thereby maintaining structural micro-inequities in the nursing workplace. In discussion we highlight that such a situation requires an analysis where whiteness is confronted and show how it combines with tolerance to racialize while leaving the inherent violence of racism unchallenged.

Immigration and Multiculturalism in its Australian Setting

Theories of migration assert that there is interaction between push and pull factors that mobilize either the use of the migrant as a source of skills that are scarce in the recipient country or that the attractions of the receiving country are sufficient to bring migrants from the donor country probably despite significant skill shortages in that donor country (Kingma 2007, Buchan 2002). Such perspectives rely on four essentially economic understandings about the migration of skilled migrants: (i) that skilled workers are global resources that are easily located and mobilized; (ii) there is equivalence in terms of regulatory bodies' recognition of qualifications in similar industries in recipient countries; (iii) there are limitations on the available training opportunities in recipient countries; and (iv) there is a time-lag in addressing shortages through filling or increasing within-recipient country training spaces.

In line with this thinking and because Australia, like other developed countries is experiencing recruitment and retention challenges in its nursing workforce, Australian health care administrators have become increasingly aware that local nursing shortages are concomitant with a 'global nursing shortage' (Buchan 2002) compounding the effects of shortage. Similar to other developed countries, they have sought to manage this shortfall through active skilled migrant recruitment. For example, in 2008–2009 Australia encouraged 2,620 foreign Registered Nurses (RNs) to seek employment here by granting subclass 457 Business (Long Stay) highly skilled migrant visas (Department of Immigration and Citizenship [DIAC] 2010). The success of this initiative is documented by reports categorising RN as the most frequently nominated position for skilled migrants in five of the states and territories of Australian jurisdictions, and second in another two during 2009 (DIAC 2010). The rate of migration-related change is further amplified by the active recruitment of registered nurses by international advertising and home country recruitment initiatives generated by the public and private health care sectors. The Australian nursing workplace thus presents itself as an exemplar of employer-driven nurse migration that has resulted in active overseas recruitment of nurses, and employer-sponsored skilled migration. The notion of employer-sponsored migration is particularly significant because sponsorship involves selection (frequently competitive) that is indicative of economic investment by the employer as well as satisfaction of Australia's criteria for acceptable 'human capital' (Hawthorne 2002: 83). Consequent to this global movement of RNs, the nursing workplace in Australia is also a site of rapid socio-cultural change and increasing cultural diversity.

The direction of current government policies indicates that skilled migration continues to be viewed as an investment in societally required 'human capital' (Hawthorne 2005) and a 'fix' for the predicted deficit in skilled workers (Bowen 2008). Consistent with this position, the integration of highly skilled migrants (those with Bachelor level or above qualifications) into the Australian workforce is perceived from a government perspective as largely unproblematic (Hawthorne 2001). Yet, current analyses of skilled migrant experiences are deficit-driven (in terms of their analyses of the skills migrants bring) and preoccupied with issues such as English language competency, transferability of overseas education and labour force integration (see for example: Ho 2008, Ramsay et al. 2008, Jeon and Chenoweth 2007, Birrell et al. 2006, Hawthorne 2005, Omeri and Atkins 2002). Such research reduces the problematisation of migration to the individual migrant themselves, situating the migrant as '*the*' problem, and fails to expose or challenge the normative assumptions underpinning processes that have formerly been considered solutions and the impact of such processes in what is now a culturally diverse workplace (Berman and Victorian Equal Opportunity and Human Rights Commission 2008).

Yet the changes in Australia's socio-cultural landscape as a result of increased migration affirm Australia's 'status' as a multicultural society, hailed by some as 'one of the most multicultural nations in the world' (Meller 2010: 1). Statistics which show, for example, that overseas born migrants constitute over 25 per cent of the Australian population (Australian Bureau of Statistics [ABS] 2009), and that Australia's migrant population comes from over 200 countries are often cited as proof. Here we make an important distinction, following Jakubowicz (2003: 1), between 'Australia as a multicultural society and as a multicultural polity'. As a multicultural society, Australia is characterized by racial and cultural plurality and Australian multiculturalism is the lived reality of racial and cultural diversity. While some commentators argue that in reality, Australia is a 'multiracial, monocultural' society (Jones cited in Jakubowicz 2003: 1), emphasising the persistence of an Anglo-Australian cultural core, the racio-ethnic diversity that characterizes the Australian population is nevertheless undeniable.

Australia's turn to a multicultural polity (multiculturalism as policy) came in the 1970s as a result of the official, landmark abolition of the 'White Australia' policy. Enacted through the Immigration Restriction Act 1901, the 'White Australia' policy 'aimed at excluding non-white migrants (and was sometimes used to exclude non-British migrants), [doing] so by requiring migrants to pass a dictation test which could be set in any language chosen by a customs officer' (National Centre for Social and Economic Modelling [NATSEM] 2010: 4). Simultaneously, assimilationism which 'encouraged migrants to abandon their culture to become invisible to the majority of Australians and to conform to the Anglo Australian way of life' (Povey 2007: 1), was official policy until the 1960s. However, the significant skills shortages in the post-World War Two period dictated the need for significant immigration policy shifts away from British centred immigration, to immigration from countries whose workers were able to meet Australia's current and projected skills shortages and crucial need for population growth. With increased migration, came racio-cultural diversity and an emphasis on the need for migrants to maintain their cultural identities, with a recognition, as well as public outcry at the inadequacies of assimilation policies. The formulation of multicultural policy in the 1970s was therefore a reflection of Australia's concern for its social harmony enacted through 'the tolerance of cultural and linguistic diversity, which reflected a growing understanding of the importance of language to ethnic self-identification' (Povey 2007: 2).

Theoretical Framework: Žižek on Violence and Tolerance

In exploring the debates about multiculturalism, violence and tolerance we use Žižek's (2009) model for exploring violence in advanced globalized capitalism. Using Lacanian psychoanalytical theory and a neo-Marxist structural analysis of capitalism he shows that violence has different faces, mobilizes complex systems of belief and is used to control as well as mobilize populations in support of the requirements of global capital. Žižek's approach challenges and troubles dualistic thinking and is therefore deconstructive. He identifies the violence inherent in the systems as *objective violence*, and explains the paradox of contemporary society as stemming from its focus on what he terms *subjective violence* which is experienced, observed and enacted on individual victims by perpetrators. He argues that objective violence is hidden just as simultaneously it hides and mystifies the systemic causes of subjective violence in the relationships of global capitalism (Žižek 2009). Moreover, *objective violence* is misrecognized and normalized; whereas *subjective violence* is noisy, riotous and a perturbation of the norm. For Žižek, each form of violence is not to be viewed as an opposite pole; rather each is implicated and implicit in the activities and operations of the other. Objective and subjective violence operate together to form the façade of the smooth running system and its underpinning beliefs.

The Violence of Multicultural Tolerance

Žižek (2009) suggests that discourses of production do not operate transparently, rather capitalism (in its transnational, global formation), along with its supporting ideology of multiculturalism, act to mask alienation or racism produced in the social relations of production. As Žižek highlights, these relations allow only personal responses to such structural effects – the political is personal. Hence, Žižek's (2009) approach discloses how violence sustains the social relations of advanced capitalism through emotional and language structures combining their effects. He reveals how psychoanalytic theories expose how unconscious motivations, resident in the imaginary and language (through the symbolic order), combine to construct ideologies that mystify how violence works through policies such as multiculturalism.[2] Moreover, a psychoanalytic approach explicates the issues facing nurses and others in their day-to-day work where the affective realm is hidden behind ideological structures of tolerance and disavowal of conflict and anxieties in the work place (Rudge and Holmes 2010, Evans 2010, Holmes et al. 2006).

Where the notion of difference is contentious, Žižek's exploration of the social relations in contemporary society has significance. With accelerating global movements of people, the metropolitan centre has experienced pressure from the many different groups within its boundaries. In such a situation, anti-immigration movements have found a voice because, as Žižek argues, 'the main parties now found it acceptable to stress that immigrants are guests who must accommodate themselves to the cultural values that define the host society – it is our country, love it or leave it' (2009: 35). In setting such boundaries, a source of potential conflict and societal disunity is the very size of large metropolitan conurbations where many people are strangers and 'strange' to each other. Žižek alerts us to how transnational capital rests on this movement of people, the establishment of an hierarchy of migrants, and also upon a symbolic threat from those excluded from 'metropolitan' wealth to 'worry' and make uncomfortable those who live in its metropolitan centres (Žižek 2009, see also Bauman 2007, Hage 1998).

While metropolitan populations recognize their own status as well as the vulnerability of those outside the metropole, it is important for those living in its bounds that they are not disturbed by that vulnerability – living in the centre is associated with the right to *not* be harassed. A salient feature of 'the metropolitan' is to promote distance and also to mark neighbours as distinct from 'us'. However, such distancing becomes problematic as media produce a continuous stream of news and opinion that makes what is distant appear close, and even crucial in the event of a disaster that requires our attention and focus, and perhaps our resources. Our globalized networked world brings its sense of urgency to much of what happens (Žižek 2009, Bauman 2004, Castells 1996). Our differences therefore seem both more *and* less obvious.

Through Lacan, Žižek stresses how language and its use in the symbolic realm is central to the violence that others. Language others through a process of extracting essences, that is essentialising, denaturing and concretizing meanings

---

2   There is a long history of combining psychoanalytic with structural and critical analyses. Habermas and Adorno are two critical theorists who have found the works of Freud useful to explore how the unconscious might work through communications. Žižek uses Lacan because of his relevance in the analysis of text, discourse and language in the symbolic.

assigned to experiences and the social relations that experiences are built upon. Žižek also highlights the way the Judeo-Christian tradition (and perhaps other religions too) bolsters racist and sexist beliefs because such beliefs set up 'the Other'. He argues that not recognising this feature perpetuates symbolic violence in the veiled discussions about who, or who not, to include in a society. Moreover, these discussions are always censored and modulated and in censoring how things can be talked about preserve the objective violence of the system (Žižek 2009: 86). Žižek (2009: 87) asserts that 'the truth of globalisation [is]: the construction of new walls safeguarding prosperous Europe from the immigrant flood' (see also Bauman 2004, 2007).

From this perspective, multiculturalism is an ideological formation and a set of 'new walls' which are central to the operations and modes of production of global capitalism where those who are excluded are now as likely to be inside a national boundary as they are external to it. In the metropolitan centre, the need for immigration from countries of varying degrees of difference to each centre so as to meet short and medium term workforce shortages has made more urgent the accommodation of difference – with the assumption that differences *always already* brings about conflict and diminishing social cohesion in any polity. As seen in the section on immigration into Australia, such assumptions fuelled and made necessary a raft of governmental policies and agencies to manage the insertion of these 'strangers' (see Bauman 2004, Schutz 1967). Such discourses frame achievement of social cohesion through controlling those admitted to a polity, in earlier times in Australia such framings led to the much maligned 'White Australia Policy'. Hence, societal level policies are mobilized to manage this multiplicity of cultures rubbing up against each other under the workforce requirements of global capital.

Žižek maintains that ideologies of multiculturalism are central to the smooth operation of contemporary capitalism, and therefore part of the *objective* violence of the system, rather than the solution to *intercultural, subjective* violence. In rushing to solutions, the problem is misapprehended as the need to take the *politics* out of ethnicity through situating ethnicity outside of political remit. Such a move has resulted in the culturalization of politics – modern society in an ethnic foment that misplaces the problem on the stranger (Žižek 2009). This means that rather than there being a reduction of the noise arising from issues of violence and aggression in relation to the *stranger as neighbour and also as Other*, a paradoxical response occurs. The racialized Other is central to the maintenance of the status quo, an object of multiculturalism's focus. In such a figuring the migrant is the problem rather than the alienation, oppression and social discrimination resulting from the structures of global capital.

Parallel to this culture as a concept is de-clawed. Rather than culture being understood as publicly shared rules and laws governing cultural practices, culture is figured merely as a set of individualized private attitudes, beliefs, or ways of living that are de-politicised and naturalized, unchanging and universal to a particular 'culture'. The politics of multiculturalism uses this declawed version of 'culture' to structure the solutions put forward to deal with obtaining order. Difference is both problematized and also viewed as the solution through the sanctioning of some forms of cultural differences (for example, Harmony Days, multiethnic dining precincts and food courts, legal acts that constitute how difference is to be both maintained and ameliorated). Multiculturalism thus works in the metropolitan centre through ideologies of individualism and tolerance (within limits) of '*Othered*' cultures – yet tolerance and autonomy remain contingent on making the *right choice* where such a choice aligns itself with that of the tolerator. Moreover, such differences play out as the clash of western versus 'Othered' cultures figured as a clash between civilizations, with some cultures more civilized (and hence more worthy) than others. As Žižek (2009: 125) highlights:

> To modern Europeans, other civilizations are caught in their specific culture, while modern Europeans are flexible, constantly changing their presuppositions... One can, of course, argue that, in a way, the Western situation is even worse because in it oppression itself is obliterated and masked as free choice.

In the analysis of the black highly skilled migrants' experiences in the multicultural workplace that follows, we suggest how free choice, oppression and tolerance operate to constitute a context of violence in the healthcare workplace.

The Interview Study

The overall aim of the study was to examine how skilled African migrant nurses working in Australia forge social and professional identities within their transnational, cross-cultural existences. The core of the research was sociological analysis of the interpretation by migrant nurses of their cross-cultural nursing experiences, the negotiation of professional nursing and diasporic identities, and how such negotiations go towards informing the construction of their identity as nurses.

This study was an interview study of 14 RNs (13 females, one male) ranging in age from 30–47 years old. Participants were initially recruited into the study through the lead author's personal networks (see Bourdieu 1996) as well as through a process of snowballing from students enrolled in a university course. Participants had all been recruited under the category of skilled migrant from sub-Saharan African countries such as Zimbabwe, Botswana and South Africa. All worked in the public and private hospital sectors, aged care residential facilities and agency nursing in a large metropolitan city in Australia. They all had more than five years' experience as RNs in their country of origin as well as more than one year working in Australia at the time of the study. Many of the nurses had left very senior positions in their country of origin and a few had temporarily come to Australia on their own leaving husbands and children behind.

All participants chose a pseudonym for the purpose of the study. The second author undertook all interviews for the study following institutional ethics approval.

While sharing similar ethnic background to the participants, she was not from the same professional background. From our shared perspective, the interview relationship was able to 'reduce as much as possible the symbolic violence which is exerted' (Bourdieu 1996: 19) in the social and power dynamic of the research interview as located usually.

Multiculturalism In/Action

The following sections show how the hostility of the multicultural workplace was experienced by the participants when beginning their work. Surprising to the participants was hostility came from those who had migrated recently before them and also from groups with a longer tenure who continued to 'other' the newer migrant workforce – particularly if they were recognisably different from them. Despite institutional policies on tolerance and non-violent communications, we can see from the following interview excerpt that much is made of 'difference' by all involved.

> We were finding it very hard because we were being victimised by all sorts of races in terms of colleagues: Australians, the Filipinas, because there's a huge population of Filipina nurses here in Australia too. Some of them recruited from the Philippines, some of them trained here, and there's also the Chinese, there's a big group of Chinese registered nurses. Some of them have trained here, I don't know if there's any who have come from China, but, we did feel that, we were being prejudiced, because they didn't really embrace us as colleagues. So it makes you wonder: where do I, how do I fit in? When you come to work and someone asks you: why are you coming here [chuckles] in big numbers? Then you start wondering. I remember this lady who said: why does the company keep recruiting them? Because at our particular workplace, [there] must have been 5 of us that came periodically, over a period of 2 months, and so they probably were comfortable with the first one, and then the second one came, then the third one came, then the fourth one, I was probably the fifth one so I copped it a little bit because they were starting to ask: why are you coming in big numbers?... I remember saying to this girl. "I wouldn't expect that from you, you are not even Australian [pause]. You must have come from somewhere else, there is something that pressured you to come here, so whatever it is that pressured you, it's the same thing that pressured me, and I'm not employed by you, I'm employed by the company, if you've got issues, go and consult the company, but don't ever say that in my face!". So at that early stage we started to build our own walls, to protect ourselves, so that you don't get bruised... (Taurai)

This participant describes her place in the hierarchy of the latest group of migrants, all of whom are categorized as a group who signify to others (many of whom immediately preceded them) 'a rush' of people 'coming in big numbers'. A nurse from the Philippines sees the fifth black nurse from 'Africa' as one too many. The participant's attempt to locate herself as a non-white immigrant and therefore 'like' her interlocutor does not seem to have been successful, or a position easily 'tolerated' or accepted even by those who are themselves visibly different migrants from other countries. As Hage (1998) points out racism is not only a set of practices enacted towards those who are more recognisably 'the Other'. Variations and subtleties occur where, in reverse racism, the white person defines for 'Others' what is acceptable; and a black nurse from 'Africa' is surprised by racism as not only emanating from 'white' people.

In a workplace such as the participants describe, it is clear that racializing attitudes and beliefs are reproduced and sustained despite the laws, procedures and policies that are meant to address them and to change how these workplaces 'work'.[3] While the view expressed by the Filipina nurse in the excerpt above is established as exclusionary by the participant, the covert practices of denial, hostility, exclusion and avoidance are less easy to characterize.

Tolerance, Power and the Dominance of Whiteness

Hage writes that 'multicultural tolerance, like all tolerance, is not, then, a good policy that happens to be limited in its scope [instead] it is a strategy aimed at reproducing and disguising relationships of power in society' (1998: 87). As the objective violence embedded in ideologies of tolerance depoliticize culture, such operations allow the depoliticization of whiteness, absolving the dominant white worker from questioning their part in the maintenance of micro-inequities of the workplace. A discourse of tolerance gives power to those who are positioned as tolerant, leaving racial hierarchies in place.

Tolerance was another matter altogether for one participant. In the following excerpt, she explores her experience of multicultural Australia where the numbers of cultures and people from other countries encountered as part of everyday nursing work meant that nurses were more likely to erase difference as the range of differences were too difficult to negotiate. In this participant's view tolerance amounted to a failure to enact or take notice of how difference might *matter*, to nurses or patients.

> It's like trans-cultural nursing, we have patients they're different cultures probably. Everywhere, everyday you have probably more than 3 backgrounds on the ward, as patients. So it's really hard to say I have to learn the cultures, so the best thing is just mainstream, whatever patients are expected, it's easier for

---

3   In Australia, there are laws and policies such as Occupational Health and Safety Laws, Zero Tolerance policies against violence and aggression; Anti-discrimination Acts and various Acts under the Human Rights and Equal Opportunity Commission that set appropriate workplace behaviours.

nurses, but not to teach them like this is Arabic, or this is Armenian, or this is, you know, because there are so many. So obviously I think mainstream is best. Just to teach the standard Australian whatever, if it's Australian nursing, that's ok. (Natsai)

When such differences are unacknowledged, even by those who would prefer to have their difference noted, then it is clear that such a location is 'white washed-out' (Reitman 2006), as differences between staff and among staff, and differences between and among patients, are consistently avoided. In such a situation, hierarchies are maintained (Hage 1998) and those denying, yet using colour to situate knowledge, remain in positions of power.

Just joking and other hostilities

As we note above, there are many moments of awkwardness and insensitivity recorded in the interviews and moments of frank hostility provided as evidence of the racism of the healthcare workplace. Kuzie related a story of joking behaviour by a surgeon. While jocular behaviour is meant to be non-offensive it is clear in what follows that this was no joke to her:

> In the workplace, it was very difficult to prove yourself that you are worthy, that you can do something. People look at you and they say: oh you are coming from Africa, and they think there's nothing good from Africa. You really have to prove yourself that you are worthy. I remember one time I was the scrub nurse, I was scrubbing, my runner was African as well, then the anaesthetic nurse was another dark person, so when the surgeon came, the anaesthetist came, he looked at us and said: Oh my God, it very dark here, can someone switch on the lights. I got really offended by that, because what he meant was: how come there are all dark people here. I got really offended that I went and spoke to the manager, I told the manager: look, I don't take such comments, I don't want this. So she changed me, and moved me from there, and she said she spoke to him. (Kuzie)

From the perspective of the 'joker', making fun of 'colour' is a way to reduce his discomfort at finding himself 'being' the minority, and needing to re-negotiate his challenged, unsettled identity and social place through the double actions of the 'joke'(Santa Ana 2009). On the surface, such jokes are the 'prime' tolerance, but jokes also mask violence suggesting the hostility towards 'black' people who are unacceptably taking over the operating suites. Freud most famously developed a grammar of joke-telling that acknowledged the layering of meaning, the play of ambiguity and the unconscious motivation for 'the joke' (Douglas 1966/2002). The play of double meanings are central in such 'joking' interactions, but much like 'the sexual tease' of sexual harassment, joking about colour *racializes* the non-white Others (Yieke 2004). If Kuzie was to respond directly it means that *she* makes the impropriety of his joking obvious, makes trouble for *herself* as a subordinate to a powerful other, and makes *overt* the racism and violence embedded in his joke. Moreover, in moving her from this surgeon's lists the management make *the black nurse* into both a victim and '*the*' problem.

Tolerance and Discrimination: The disguise for racial discrimination

> Since this nation was a multicultural nation I expected people to really want to know about these African nurses who are coming who are new to them but then nobody would do that. They would just look at us with – I don't know what was in their minds but it was not acceptance at all. They wouldn't accept us which was a hitch in our settling [in here]… That took a long time to get over. Because you had to really watch your back when you are working which is not supposed to be according to me… it took us quite long to settle in because of those little things. (Imbai)

When tolerance is the embodiment of discrimination and hierarchy, it follows then, that in a multicultural workplace the discourse and practice of tolerance also functions to disguise the existence of racial discrimination. As one participant commented:

> The issue of racism… at my workplace, wherever you go there's actually literature to conscientize people that racism, intimidation and bullying is not allowed but it is done in such a way that even if you were to decide to take it up, you can't prove it [pause]…. You can realise that a lot of racism is done against me but you – if you are to take it to Court, you can't prove it because it's not openly done… (Tete)

What is significant about this excerpt is that it confirms firstly, Hage's (1998) contention that discourse about tolerance does not take power away from the tolerator, rather it reinforces their power. In such a case, the tolerator's power to discriminate against the non-white nurse is magnified. Secondly, tolerance does not stop discrimination, it merely changes its face, making it more subtle, so subtle that it becomes confined to small acts of confrontation or omission that ultimately add up to continuous affronts about ones colour or difference (accent, lifestyle, way of dressing) that continually position the nurses as inferior until proved otherwise – everyday racism (Essed 1991). Little was done to prepare the workplace for the arrival of the black migrant nurses. Instead there is a complete denial (a position afforded through tolerance and erasure of difference) of the difference of the black nurses who were recruited into a workplace where erasure of the experience of racism for those experiencing it is silenced by an *always already* tolerant workplace.

> When they recruited, they probably did not do their homework well; they should have researched a bit more, and prepared themselves for this big chunk of nurses

coming from Africa. And they should have done the groundwork, so that they could prepare even the people who are here. They should have informed them that we've got a big number of African nurses who are coming in, but they are competent, they know what they are doing, instead of us being brought here to become part of the workforce and work for the nation, but also to be victimised, because this is going to be a chip on our shoulder for the rest of our lives... which [is] sad. (Taurai)

That was my first experience in [unit name]: Day one, I did the showering quietly. I'm like: "why am I doing this?" Day 2, I did, and the 3rd day I'm thinking: this is going to be a permanent thing, so instead of doing the showering I said: "Can I come into your office and see you?" – To the DON. [Director of Nursing] Then I went into her office and said: "the job description doesn't say I do showering coz in a nursing home a registered nurse doesn't do showering, showering is done by AINs. [Assistants in Nursing]. In the hospitals the registered nurses do showering, right?" And the DON then said: "oh, it's because you are a bit too many on the floor!" So, why employ us? Why are you employing us? If I'm going to do showering, take me to a nursing home where there is a shortage of registered nurses, then I'll do the job that I trained for, the job that I agreed to come and do, the job that was on the job description, the job description that I signed and the contract that I signed. (Taurai)

As Taurai reflects on her situation, she can see that her ability to perform as a RN is being questioned as she is being kept from the work she has been recruited to do. She is provided with what she determines is a poor excuse, particularly as she knows there are shortages of RNs in the facility. The first excerpt highlights the paradox inherent in many skilled migrants' entry into what is putatively a multicultural and tolerant workplace. This participant highlights how tolerance works in such locations to leave no space or place for recording the lack of tolerance evident in the in/action of multiculturalism and its ideology of tolerance.

Repressiveness of Tolerance

In analysing the idea of tolerance and its operation in a multicultural society, the study's participants (in)formed the use of Žižek's model of violence in this chapter by indicating how the *objective* violence of tolerance figured in the social relations of their workplaces. Weissberg (1998: 8) comments how the meaning of tolerance has changed from its conception as 'putting up with the objectionable' to a meaning that something is irretrievably bad and unworthy. He goes on to highlight how 'judgmentalism inheres in the concept; disapprobation is intrinsic... it is impossible, by definition, to be tolerant in a world of complete worthiness' (Weissberg 1998: 8). It is clear that the RNs in this study struggled as to how to attain worthiness in their workplace. Moreover, their understandings about tolerance and multiculturalism are paradoxical, imbued with a longing to belong as much as to be recognized as different (Povey 2007). In an Australian multicultural society, many immigrants recognize the positive associations with tolerance, and also how these dominate to obscure the violence of racism from those who do not experience it (Wemyss 2006: 236).

In Australian healthcare workplaces, multiculturalism uses tolerance ideologically. It places limits on certain types of speech, making some behaviours compulsory and compliant to the ideal of multiculturalism – while obscuring how these black nurses experience the judgmentalism and disapprobation emanating from their racialization. The instances of reproduction of racialized distrust are peppered throughout their interviews. What is clear is that the tolerant, multicultural workplace (dis)locates immigrants in solving its workforce shortages. What is perhaps less well recognized is that the more such locations are under duress, the more workers are 'expected to seek biographical solutions to systemic contradictions' (see also Žižek 2009, Bauman 2004: 51).

The core of Australian multiculturalism is its structural belief that places Anglo-Australian culture (although it is not accurate to speak of this as a monoculture) at the apex, retaining dominance over the cultural economy. Other cultures (and races) are acceptable if they accept the dominant order and do not challenge this hierarchy (Jakubowicz 2003: 80). However, and this is where Žižek's critique on tolerance, violence and multiculturalism assists, the idea of tolerance becomes harder to sustain as multiculturalism increasingly comes under fire as mere political correctness which is stopping free speech and interfering in social relations. In such a situation, calls for tolerance rather than questioning the power of those who tolerate, contribute to the reproduction of power relationships (Wemyss 2006: 227).

Moreover, multiculturalism is not 'set', particularly as discourses used to define it emanate from such disparate positionings as human rights, equity and social justice, and a politics of cohesion mobilized to reduce conflict due to human and essentialized responses to difference figured as race (Solomos 1998: 47). Compounding these variations in expressing the 'multicultural', the concept is inherently contradictory in both conceptual and political terms. In Australia, multiculturalism is firstly a location for the *struggle for equality* by minorities who are excluded; and secondly, is an *affirmation of cultural difference* through claims to ethnic and racial authenticity. Therein, lay its difficulties (Solomos 1998: 48). Immigrants who have linked together to survive racism and marginalisation are accepted to the extent that they have an associated right to claim 'cultural differences'. Multiculturalism as a historical and contextual practice is singularly constituted in the processes of migration and figures in the struggles between the universal, the transcendent and the fixedness of 'cultural' particularities (Žižek 2009).

Racialization occurs through a politics of whiteness evident in the data of our study – where blackness came to be central to the identity marker imposed on the skilled migrant nurses recruited to work in Australia. Within an ideology of tolerance and multiculturalism it becomes impossible to question identity politics, or the use of human rights or other responses affording a direct response to the violence of tolerance. Tolerance is an attitudinal response to a structural issue – and Žižek would suggest that this is why it is doomed to fail as a solution. In failing to address the direct causes of racism, it instead inflicts the violence of tolerance on those who experience racism and are racialized by their difference from the dominant group.

Conclusion

In a paper on the violent confrontations needed to take apart colonialist histories, Thomas (2007: 229) suggests how the wounds inflicted by colonialism are 'wounds of embodiment *and* wounds of consciousness' (emphasis added). In our analysis of violence in the multicultural healthcare workplace, the embodiment of blackness and the wounds of everyday racism (Essed 1991) enacted through institutionalized racism intersect across the bodies and consciousness of highly skilled black African nurses. The use of a framework that challenges the ideology of tolerance within multiculturalism affords a perspective on their transition that confronts the reproduction of racism and exclusion and its violent effects. Such views suggest how acts of tolerance are inherently violent and contradictory, leaving the black migrant nurses with strong recollections of their racialization.

In such a situation, it is little wonder that the ideas behind multiculturalism and tolerance provide less credible ways to think about Australian society. A strong political and governmental response to the potential for culturally-based conflict obtained a focus on achieving cohesion before much else. The in/action we discovered as inhering to multicultural ideologies playing out in the healthcare workplace merely led to blaming any conflict on 'the migrant', hence maintaining the violence of racism. A Žižekian analysis exposes that when violence is *objective* and experienced as *subjective*, 'naturalized' exclusionary outcomes for visibly different migrants are anything but natural and instead reproduce the dominance of 'whiteness' in the Australian healthcare workplace.

References

Australian Bureau of Statistics [ABS]. 2009. Migration, Australia, 2007–2008, ABS Cat No. 3412.0

Bauman, Z. 2007. *Liquid Times: Living in an Age of Uncertainty.* Cambridge: Polity.

Bauman, Z. 2004. *Wasted Lives: Modernity and its outcasts.* Cambridge: Polity.

Berman, G. and Victorian Equal Opportunity and Human Rights Commission. 2008. *Harnessing Diversity: Addressing Racial and Religious Discrimination in Employment*. Melbourne: Victorian Equal Opportunity and Human Rights Commission.

Birrell, B., Hawthorne, L. and Richardson, S. 2006. *Evaluation of the General Skilled Migrant Categories*. [Canberra: Dept. of Immigration and Multicultural Affairs]. Available at: http://www.immi.gov.au/media/publications/research/gsm-report/ [accessed: 20 January 2011].

Bourdieu, P. 1996. Understanding. *Theory, Culture & Society*, 13(2), 17–37.

Bowen, C. 2008. Address to the Committee for Economic Development of Australia about the Federal Government's plan for meeting the growing demand for skilled labour. Available at http://www.minister.immi.gove.au/media/speeches/2008/ce080627.htm [accessed: 18 January 2011].

Buchan, J. 2002. Global nursing shortages. *British Medical Journal*, 324(7340), 751–2.

Department of Immigration and Citizenship (DIAC). 2010. *Subclass 457 Business (Long Stay) State/Territory Summary Report 2008/09* Report ID BR0008, Canberra: AGPS.

Douglas, M. 1966/2002. *Purity and Danger*. London: Routledge.

Essed, F. 1991. *Understanding Everyday Racism: An Interdisciplinary Theory*. California: Sage Publications.

Evans, A. 2010. Distasteful, disgusting and frightening, yet compelling: anxiety and abjection in hospital nursing, in *Abjectly Boundless: Bodies, Boundaries and Health Work*, edited by T. Rudge and D. Holmes.Farnham: Ashgate, 199–212.

Ganley, T. 2003. What's all this talk about whiteness? *Dialogue*, 1(2), 12–30.

Hage, G. 2003. *Against Paranoid Nationalism: Searching for Hope in a Shrinking Society*. Annandale: Pluto Press.

Hage, G. 1998. *White Nation: Fantasies of White Supremacy in a Multicultural Society*. Annandale: Pluto Press.

Hancock, B.H. 2005. Steppin' out of whiteness. *Ethnography*, 6(4), 427–61.

Hawthorne, L. 2001. The globalisation of the nursing workforce: barriers confronting overseas qualified nurses in Australia. *Nursing Inquiry*, 8(4), 213–29.

Hawthorne, L. 2002. Qualifications recognition reform for skilled migrants in Australia: applying competency-based assessment to overseas-qualified Nurses. *International Migration*, 40(6), 55–91.

Hawthorne, L. 2005. Picking winners: the recent transformations of Australia's skill migration policy. *International Migration Review*, 39(3), 663–96.

Ho, C. 2008. Chinese nurses in Australia: Migration, work and identity, in *The International Migration of Health Workers*, edited by J. Connell. New York: Routledge, 147–62.

Holmes, D., Perron, A. and O'Byrne, P. 2006. Understanding disgust in nursing: abjection, self, and the other. *Research and Theory for Nursing Practice: An International Journal*, 20(4), 305–15.

Jakubowicz, A. 2003. Multiculturalism is the Australian way of life. Paper presented at 'Auditing Multiculturalism: the Australian empire a generation after Galbally', Annual Conference of the Federation of Ethnic Community Councils of Australia, Melbourne, 4 December.

Jeon, Y. and Chenoweth, L. 2007. Working with a culturally and linguistically diverse (CALD) group of nurses, *Collegian*, 14(1), 16–22.

King, P.T. 1998. *Toleration*. New edition. London: Frank Cass Publishers.

Kingma, M. 2007. Nurses on the move: a global overview. *Health Research and Educational Trust*, 42 (3 (part II)), 1281–98.

Meller, C. 2010. Foreword, In *Calling Australia Home: The Characteristics and Contributions of Australian Migrants,* AMP and National Centre of Social and Economic Modelling (NATSEM) Income and Wealth Report, Issue 27, November 2010.

NATSEM. 2010. *Calling Australia Home: The Characteristics and Contributions of Australian Migrants*. AMP NATSEM Income and Wealth Report, Issue 27, November 2010.

Omeri, A. and Atkins, K. 2002. Lived experiences of immigrant nurses in New South Wales, Australia: searching for meaning. *International Journal of Nursing Studies,* 39, 495–505.

Povey, E. 2007. Longing to belong and the paradoxes of multiculturalism. Annual Conference of The Australasian Sociological Association. Auckland, New Zealand, 4–7 December.

Ramsay, S., Barker, M. and Shallcross, L. 2008. Counterproductive forces at work: challenges faced by skilled migrant job-seekers. *International Journal of Organisational Behaviour*, 13(2), 110–21.

Reitman, M. 2006. Uncovering the white place: whitewashing at work. *Social and Cultural Geography*, 7, 267–82.

Rudge, T. and Holmes, D. 2010. *Abjectly Boundless: Bodies, Boundaries and Health Work.* Farnham: Ashgate.

Santa Ana, O. 2009. Did you call in Mexican? The racial politics of Jay Leno immigrant jokes. *Language in Society*, 38, 23–45.

Schutz, A. 1967. *The Phenomenology of the Social World.* Translated by G. Walsh and F. Lehnert. Evanston: Northwestern University Press.

Solomos, J. 1998. Beyond racism *and* multiculturalism. *Patterns of Prejudice*, 32(4), 45–62.

Thomas, G. 2007. On psycho-sexual racism and Pan-African revolt: Fanon and Chester Himes. *Human Architecture: Journal of the Sociology of Self-Knowledge*, Summer, 219–30.

Weissberg, R. 1998. The abduction of tolerance. *Society*, Nov/Dec, 8–14.

Wemyss, G. 2006. The power to tolerate: contests over Britishness and belonging in East London. *Patterns of Prejudice*, 40(3), 215–36.

Yieke, F. 2004. Sexual harassment in the workplace: a case for linguistic and sexual politics? *Journal of Cultural Studies*, 6(2), 175–96.

Žižek, S. 2009. *Violence: Six sideways reflections.* London: Profile.

Chapter 3

Changing Discourses of Blame in Nursing and Healthcare

Hannah Cooke

Introduction

In this chapter, I will be considering the uses of blame in contemporary healthcare organisations looking at changes in United Kingdom (UK) nursing and health policy discourse as a case study. Some similar changes have taken place in other countries although the trajectory of change in the UK has been striking in its rapidity. I will look in particular at changes in the distribution of blame as they affect nurses. I will also consider the ways in which changes in the distribution of blame have been instrumental in effecting changes in the boundaries of the nursing profession, as well as justifying increased managerial control of health care professionals. Different explanations of trouble place blame in different places and these narratives have played a central role in effecting changes in frontiers of control in healthcare. Firstly, I will look at the different explanations which have been used at different times to explain poor care. I will argue that these changing narratives reflect wider changes in the power structures of healthcare organisations. I will then consider how this change of narrative has influenced changes in the professional regulation of the health professions as well as changes in the control and disciplining of nurses. I will then consider the work of Mary Douglas on risk perception and blame. I will outline the ways in which her ideas can be applied to the distribution of blame in nursing to help us to understand what blame tells us about changing patterns of control and responsibility in healthcare.

Managerialism and the Declining Power of the Professions

Any consideration of the use of blame in contemporary healthcare organisations has to be understood in the context of changing frontiers of control between managers and professionals. Recent commentary on the changing fortunes of the professions has noted a decline in professional autonomy and the increasing power of corporate management and state bureaucracy in relation to professional groups. Thus according to Freidson (2001: 197) there has been an assault on the credibility of professions which is 'economically inspired and reflects the material interests of both private capital and the state'. This carries the risk that the professions will be transformed into merely technical workers, allowing employers to routinise and standardise professional work in order to better control the professional workforce and reduce its costs. Such technical workers will lose the moral authority of professionalism and in particular the professionals' independence of judgement and the ability to serve what Freidson (2001: 222) calls 'transcendent values' such as public service, equity and the impartial pursuit of professional knowledge independent of economic considerations.

Recent critiques of professionalism have advanced the argument that the professions need external regulation because they no longer have the moral authority to control their errant members. In the UK scandals involving rogue or incompetent health professionals have been mobilised in order to advance these critiques (see for example Kennedy 1981, 2001). Strong (1992) noted that the growing contemporary attack on medicine and the professions mirrored the attack on medicine launched by the utilitarians in the early nineteenth century. This inaugurated an era of 'therapeutic nihilism' and arguably we are experiencing a similar period today. We can thus detect the long shadow of those utilitarian architects of the Poor Laws, Jeremy Bentham and Edwin Chadwick, in contemporary healthcare. 'Therapeutic nihilism' is accompanied by a dominant preoccupation with cost utility. Strong (1992) suggests that 'therapeutic nihilism' also represents the 'encirclement' of medicine by rival empires, in particular 'Law and Capital'. He notes, for example that Kennedy's (1981) critique of medicine was 'little more than legal imperialism in populist clothing' whilst also noting that the financial corporations see challenges to medical dominance (and state welfare) as offering new opportunities for profit.

What Dingwall (2001) has called 'atrocity stories' played an important part in the era of 'therapeutic nihilism'. Similarly, media 'spectacles' of errant health professionals (McGivern and Fischer 2010) have had a critical role to play in recent changes in UK healthcare. Next, I will consider the ways in which our understandings of poor care and poor performance amongst health professionals have changed over the last 30 years, and I will outline the implications of the different discourses about poor performance that have emerged.

Moral Panics

Recent public concern about poorly performing health professionals has reflected a dominant explanation of misfortune in terms of 'character'. Such concerns have at times amounted to a 'moral panic'. The term 'moral panic' implies an increase in publicity about a particular issue with heightened expressions of (moral) concern. There are also some indications that expressions of concern are both volatile and disproportionate (Goode and Ben Yehuda 1994, Cohen 1972). Goode and Ben Yehuda suggest that 'moral panics' result in large part from the activities of 'moral entrepreneurs' who have something to gain from their creation. Moral entrepreneurs may have highly personal motivations for their campaigns such as the relatives of crime victims or victims of medical mistakes. However, a different type of moral entrepreneur may have more instrumental motivations, such as career advantage, in the case of some self appointed 'experts'. Moral enterprises may also emerge in the form of organisations that can profit from regulatory expansion. McGivern and Fisher (2010) describe this as the growth of the 'blame business'. We can therefore see the 'moral panic' surrounding the 'problem' health professional as furthering the interests of particular groups, enterprises and individuals. The 'blame business' may also direct blame away from the top of healthcare organisations. For politicians and managers it both places blame elsewhere and justifies redefining the frontiers of control between them and health professionals.

Rules of Pessimism

In 1985, Stimson wrote an analysis of the 'impaired physician' movement in the United States. His analysis foreshadowed many recent events in UK healthcare particularly those following the recent scandal and subsequent public inquiry about the Bristol heart surgeons accused of poor performance and high death rates (Kennedy 2001). Stimson suggested that there had been a move within US medicine from a 'rule of optimism', which assumed that most doctors practised with propriety and that a system of high trust was justified, to a 'rule of pessimism'. A 'rule of pessimism' views all doctors as potential problems and justifies low trust systems of surveillance and control. Such a change within medicine inevitably impacts on other health professionals. Stimson argued that whilst a 'rule of optimism' successfully promotes high standards amongst the vast majority of professionals, it is ill-equipped to deal with the persistent deviant. On the other hand a 'rule of pessimism' may have negative consequences for the majority, by imposing intrusive and time consuming regulation. This undermines confidence and trust in competent and ethical practitioners.

Stimson argued that calls to tighten professional self regulation and move towards a 'rule of pessimism' were related to the attempts of the state and corporations to reduce the costs of care. He describes this change as part of the 'corporate bureaucratisation of medicine and consequent managerial scrutiny of medical care'.

What is singular about recent concern about the 'problem' or 'under-performing' health professional is that the move to a 'rule of pessimism' and consequent pre-occupation with individual pathology has occurred precisely at the moment when the structural pressures on healthcare institutions have been at their most intense. We may consider this ironic. We may also wish to consider the possibility that such an irony is not accidental. I will now consider the ways in which narratives of healthcare problems have changed before considering the reasons for these changes.

The Narrative of the 'Corruption of Care'

Before considering current explanations of misfortune in healthcare, I will go back to an earlier period in the history of healthcare and consider a narrative of health service problems which is now, to a large extent, overlooked.

In the UK, a series of hospital scandals in the 1960s and 1970s revealed the deficiencies of institutional care (Martin 1984). Similar scandals took place during this period in many other parts of the world including the US, Canada, Australia and New Zealand (see for example Brunton 2005). Public inquiries during this period revealed a stark picture of negligent and impoverished care of long stay patients reminiscent of the nineteenth century workhouse system. The dominant narrative to explain these problems was one which saw institutions as essentially harmful.

During the 1960s a number of influential studies had highlighted the dysfunctions of institutional life. Goffman's (1961) study of 'total institutions' described such institutions as stripping individual inmates of dignity and self identity through a process he described as the 'mortification of the self'. 'Total institutions' would come to be seen as essentially damaging and oppressive rather than as benign or charitable. During this period the psychiatrist Barton (1966) described a range of pathologies associated with incarceration in institutions such as apathy, submissiveness and a loss of individuality. He termed this syndrome institutional neurosis. This narrative of institutional harm helped to accelerate the large scale decarceration of inmates from state institutions such as mental hospitals and geriatric hospitals which began with the creation of a new generation of anti-psychotic medication in the 1950s (Scull 1977).

A look at the accounts of hospital scandals during this period shows that explanations of error, neglect and abuse focus primarily on institutional factors. For example, the Inquiry into South Ockenden Hospital (South Ockenden Inquiry 1974: 3) found 'overcrowding, staff shortages and lack of facilities' to be major factors in the deterioration of patients. The Inquiry also highlighted the physical and professional isolation of the long-stay institution. Martin (1984) suggests that these inquiries revealed the problem of the 'corruption of care'. He defines this as:

> the fact that the primary aims of care – the cure or alleviation of suffering – have become subordinate to what are essentially secondary aims such as the creation and preservation of order, quiet and cleanliness (86–87).

Essentially, then, Martin sees the corruption of care as a problem of goal displacement. Organisations had lost sight of their fundamentally caring purposes and were motivated by goals related to institutional order. In these circumstances:

> Care becomes impersonal, regimented and orientated towards the performance of routines, rather than the quality of life enjoyed by the patients (Martin 1984: 87).

Martin (1984) listed a number of management failures which he believed were implicated in the corruption of care. These are summarised below:

- Staff at all levels was allowed to become intellectually and professionally isolated.
- There was a failure of senior staff, at both technical and moral levels, to set standards of care and to display them in their own work.
- Managers were insensitive to the need for staff to obtain some degree of job satisfaction from their work.
- There was a conspicuous failure of will and determination on the part of senior staff to act positively when confronted with weaknesses in their organisation.
- There was victimisation of those who by drawing attention to failures of care are seen as 'rocking the boat' or threatening the professional reputations of those in charge.

Martin suggested that institutional pressures led to personal corruption. Once individuals had condoned the corruption of care by not speaking out against it they 'can never enforce standards for fear of their own misdeeds coming to light'. Thus, the 'intense pressures' of institutional life create a 'subculture of delinquency' that allows abuse to flourish. According to Martin, ill treatment may sometimes be due to the 'cruelty and weakness' of individuals but it always involved situations in which 'an unsuitable person was given the wrong tasks, with inadequate training and leadership' (Martin 1984: 97).

Wardhaugh and Wilding (1993: 7) later extended Martin's analysis of the corruption of care in a paper written in response to a series of scandals in local authority care. Their central thesis was that the corruption of care occurs in situations in which 'usual moral inhibitions' are weakened and moral concerns 'neutralised'. In particular they viewed bureaucratisation as particularly negative in its effects leading to depersonalisation and corruption. Their analysis thus closely mirrored Bauman's (1989) analysis of Nazi bureaucracy.

They also suggested that the corruption of care is 'closely connected with the balance of power and powerlessness in organisations' and that the 'particular pressures' which lead to the corruption of care include the contradiction between 'the rhetoric of policy' and 'the sharp reality of practice' (Wardhaugh and Wilding 1993: 16). They remarked:

> Policy is built up of fine words but the reality of what is provided for these groups denies their truth. The work is wrapped round with high sounding terms such as care, reform, rehabilitation but the resources and facilities made available convey to staff the low value which society puts upon their work and upon their clients. Official aspirations and standards are therefore deprived of legitimacy (Wardaugh and Wilding 1993: 14).

They argued that 'management failure' underlies the corruption of care. Management is distant, fails to set standards and goals are displaced from care to institutional efficiency. Innovation and criticism are stifled. Accountability is unclear and front line staff are 'left to get on with things'.

Analyses of the corruption of care centre on the problems of institutions themselves. Power relations are central and particularly the sense of powerlessness experienced by front line staff. Most particularly, this analysis highlights the risk of goal displacement from caring to institutional self-preservation. In this situation both staff and patients are seen as objects to be manipulated – as less than fully human.

During my own research health service managers voiced the belief that the corruption of care was something associated with the past and with 'old fashioned' custodial regimes which had now been 'modernised' (Cooke 2002). Yet Macintyre (1985: 74) has suggested that the authority claims of contemporary management rest on a claimed expertise in 'the manipulation of human beings into compliant patterns of behaviour'. Further Macintyre criticises the moral 'character' of contemporary management which treats human beings as ends to be manipulated in the service of bureaucratic corporations, whether public or private. His arguments have some similarities to Sennett's (1998) description of the 'corrosion of character' in contemporary work organisations. In contemporary healthcare the primacy of institutional preservation is expressed in new forms but expressed none the less and thus contemporary managerialism may not offer the solution to the corruption of care. Indeed, the unanswered question which this analysis raises is whether 'new public management' (Hood 1991) with its regimes of inspection and measurement has simply created new forms of goal displacement. Power (1997) has identified the dangers of such forms of goal displacement in his analysis of the growth of audit society and the building of new worlds of risk management (Power 2004).

Power's analysis describes the unintended consequences of the spread of accountancy based systems and processes into all areas of social life so that they become empty 'rituals of verification'. Whereas old institutional regimes placed a value on institutional order within static regimes, new forms of goal displacement place value on compliance with targets, success in league tables and increased productivity through faster throughput of patients (the imperative to move patients through the system 'sicker and quicker'). In applying Wardhaugh and Wilding's analysis to contemporary settings we could predict a relocation of the 'corruption of care' to new settings such as those concerned with preventing admissions or accelerating discharge (emergency or medical admissions departments for example).

The Narrative of the 'Bad Apple'

The critique of institutional life which underpinned the inquiries of the 1960s and 1970s helped to accomplish the dismantling of many large scale state institutions. Scull (1977) linked this era of 'decarceration' to fiscal pressures on the state in an era of post industrial economic restructuring just as the era of incarceration in the nineteenth century could be linked to industrialisation and the imposition of the new labour disciplines of mills and factories. Institutional inquiries continued into the early 1980s but then began to dwindle in number. During the 1980s most long stay care was relocated from the state sector to private and not for profit care facilities. As Stanley and Manthorpe (2004) note these latter sectors are less open to public scrutiny and criticism than state institutions. Furthermore within state institutions in the UK there has been a move away from independent judicial inquiries towards internal inquiries or inspections/inquiries by government appointed regulators (Stanley and Manthorpe 2004).

During the 1990s attention shifted towards an individual professional's deviant behaviour with a series of inquiries focusing on the reckless, incompetent (Kennedy 2001) or predatory behaviour (Smith 2004) of individual professionals. This led to a shift in focus from institutional failing towards the personal and moral failings of individual care professionals.

A shift in focus towards a 'bad apple' model, which located problems in deviant individuals from whom institutions must seek protection, took two forms. Firstly, individuals might have problems of 'conduct' and the 1990s saw a considerable growth and elaboration of the discourse addressing abuse by professionals and carers. This discourse was given further impetus by the murderous behaviour of Dr Harold Shipman and the subsequent inquiry into his crimes (Smith 2004). Secondly, individuals might have problems of 'competence'; this discourse initially centred mainly on the medical professional and the 'incompetent doctor'. It followed a number of well-publicised failures in medical care, with the case of the Bristol heart surgeons being the most prominent (Kennedy 2001).

The 'bad apple' model was given considerable prominence in UK nursing as a result of the Beverly Allitt case in which a nurse working in a children's ward was responsible for several child deaths. The central explanation for Allitt's homicides was the diagnosis of Munchausen by Proxy although this diagnostic label has subsequently been the subject of considerable controversy (Kaplan 2008). The recommendations of the Clothier inquiry into the Allitt case focussed almost exclusively on the protection of the institution from the 'determined miscreant' heightening the focus on 'malevolence' as an explanation of adverse events (Clothier 1994).

These recommendations were reiterated in the report into the case of Amanda Jenkinson convicted of tampering with equipment in an intensive care unit. The Bullock Report (1997) focused on methods of screening that would prevent 'miscreants' from entering nursing (as a postscript to this report, Amanda Jenkinson, after several years in prison, was exonerated by the Court of Appeal in 2005. The Court also ordered that her nurse registration be reinstated). Similarly, the Clothier report recommended that individuals who had received treatment or counselling for mental health problems should not be allowed to enter nursing.

The Allitt and Jenkinson cases had a decisive influence on the management of nursing problems by promoting the idea that 'malevolence' was an important cause. This idea did not, however, occur in a vacuum but against a background in which the 'bad apple' model was already gaining considerable ground as an explanation for a wide range of healthcare problems. 'Bad apples' could have problems of 'conduct' or 'competence' thus accounting not only for abuse but also for errors, omissions and 'variations' in the outcomes of care. The term 'variation' in care marked the rise of audit culture in healthcare with numerical indicators gaining increasing prominence in imputations of poor care and abuse. As Stimson had suggested the move towards a 'rule of pessimism' was already well under way prior to Allitt.

According to Stimson, the impaired physician movement medicalised the issue of the 'problem' doctor. Stimson saw that medicalisation had allowed the medical profession as a whole to retain control of the management of the 'problem' doctor, whilst conceding some shifts in the boundary of control in favour of corporate management. This compromise imposed quite draconian controls on the individual 'problem' doctor as the price that the profession was prepared to pay for retaining overall control of its errant members. The profession at that time conceded a move to a 'rule of pessimism' and in return was allowed to retain its jurisdiction over the 'impaired' physician. We will see however that although UK nursing has indeed moved to a rule of pessimism, its ability to retain professional jurisdiction over its own members with 'performance problems' is somewhat open to question.

The Narrative of Professional Closure: Rationalising Managerial Control

The increasing dominance of the bad apple model has been supplemented by a narrative which holds the professions almost entirely responsible for any failures in care by health professionals. Older narratives of institutional corruption are supplanted by narratives in which the institution held culpable is not a hospital or healthcare organisation but the professions, their associations and regulatory bodies. Individual cases of poor performance dominated health service enquiries from the 1990s onwards and were explained by a failure of professional bodies to effectively screen, educate, supervise and regulate their members. Professional socialisation was represented as something suspect which encouraged professionals to look after their own and conspire against outsiders, particularly clients. Mistakes and poor performance had too often been managed 'behind closed doors' according to the critics of professionalism.

Managers in particular argued that the professions were 'tribal' in their allegiances. This epithet was used by managers to refer disparagingly to the professions in Strong and Robinson's (1990) ethnographic account of the conflicts surrounding introduction of 'general management' to the UK National Health Service (NHS). By the mid-1990s this pejorative epithet had entered official policy discourse and it is echoed in the Bristol enquiry when Kennedy suggests that medicine has too often been characterised by a 'club culture' (Kennedy 2001). Much of the discourse of this period represents medicine as secretive and self-serving, as critics of the profession sought to build a case for the reform or abolition of professional self-regulation. Thus according to one newspaper medicine had a 'traditional secretive culture' and self regulation had an 'unhappy history' (quoted in Abbasi 1998: 1599).

One influential study during the 1990s reproduced this critique of professional 'tribalism'. Rosenthal (1995) drew inspiration from early work by Eliot Freidson (1980) explicitly building on a theoretical tradition which saw professional autonomy as essentially problematic. Her study involved interviews with managers and doctors and drew on many of the ideas central to new public management discourse particularly as expressed in the growing literature on risk management. She criticised medicine for managing its problems 'behind closed doors' and she saw the solution to medical incompetence to lie in greater managerial scrutiny, greater 'transparency' of professional boundaries and greater codification of professional work. Rosenthal rejected any arguments in favour of professional discretion and judgement, suggesting that medicine could largely be reduced to technical work which could be standardised and codified to eliminate variation. Codification via the creation of procedures and protocols would allow professionals to be more effectively audited and any variations subject to sanction. She argued that discretion within the health professions could and should be eliminated and she suggested that any justification of variation on grounds of professional uncertainty was invalid with 'growing empirical evidence that clinical practice may not be as uncertain as is generally believed' (Rosenthal 1995: 108).

Rosenthal's work reflected the views of many members of the growing patient safety movement who saw codification of health work as the best way to ensure patient safety. I have discussed elsewhere the tensions and contradictions within the patient safety movement between the call to codify and routinise professional health work and the call to create an open learning culture in which professionals are encouraged to continually reflect on and improve their practice (Cooke 2009). In the UK recent evidence has suggested a growing bureaucratisation, particularly of nursing work (McDonald, Harrison, and Waring 2005) as healthcare organisations become increasingly dominated by corporate management whilst also having to respond to an increasingly crowded regulatory environment. As Power (2004: 56) has noted excessive regulation can lead to a preoccupation with blame avoidance so that risk management practices become 'essentially amoral, inward looking and self-referential' and thus risk management can become decoupled from clinical realities.

Changes in Professional Regulation

I have outlined some changing discourses about problems and failures in care within the health services during the late twenty first century. I will now briefly outline the cascade of changes in professional regulation in the UK which resulted from this change in the understanding of problems in care.

I have alluded at various points to the influence of recent scandals in healthcare which have influenced the move to a 'rule of pessimism' in the UK. Following these scandals new guidelines were laid down for the management of the 'problem' doctor following a consultation paper in 1999 (DOH 1999). This recommended the setting up of the National Clinical Assessment Service to manage and treat 'problem' doctors. The proposals explicitly affirmed a model of individual pathology closely following the model created by the 'impaired physician' movement in the United States. The definition of 'poor clinical performance' was given a wide remit:

'Poor clinical performance can be associated with errors or delays in diagnoses, use of outmoded tests or treatments, failure to act on the results of monitoring or testing, technical errors in performance of a procedure, poor attitude and behaviour, inability to work as a member of a team or poor communication with patients... Poor doctors cannot excuse their failings by blaming others '(DOH 1999: 13–14).

Although initially reforms gave the medical profession control of their errant members these proposals were only the start of a sequence of changes to medical regulation which increased state control over professional regulation (DOH 2008). Amongst changes to medical regulation were an increase in lay representation with members no longer chosen by the profession but appointed by a government appointment board. In addition a new meta-regulatory body was created called the Council for Healthcare Regulatory Excellence (CHRE) to oversee the regulation of all health professions through standard setting, audit and the power to appeal cases in which it considered that a health professional regulator hay body been 'unduly lenient' (but not unduly harsh).

The changes to the regulation of nursing followed a similar pattern to changes in medicine. However nurses did not have access to the National Clinical Assessment Service and at a local level disciplining largely remained in the hands of managers.

The government commissioned a firm of management consultants, JM Consulting (1998) to recommend on the regulation of nursing and as a result of their recommendations the new Nursing and Midwifery Council (NMC) replaced the United Kingdom Central Council for Nursing (UKCC) in 2002. The NMC was to be a more streamlined body with parity of lay representation (DOH 2001). As with medicine, members were appointed by a government appointments commission to the new council. The new council was warned not to be 'overly sympathetic' to professionals but to work in partnership with employers. Senior managers were heavily represented on the new council (even 'lay' representatives are often non executive directors or chairs of NHS boards).

The UKCC had been partially elected and had sometimes made itself unpopular with employers by raising concerns about the environment of care particularly in relation to the nursing home sector (Davies 2002). In my own study senior managers interviewed were highly critical of UKCC panels, sometimes describing them as 'idiots'. Managers felt that if they had sacked a member of staff they expected the UKCC to back their decision. Managers also described themselves as 'incensed' at being questioned about staffing levels and staff training during hearings and a common remark about professional conduct panels was 'how dare they question me' (Cooke 2002). Clearly their voice had been listened to in the report that led to the reform of nursing regulation which claimed that the UKCC did not have the confidence of 'stakeholders' (JM Consulting 1998). A greater range of sanctions were available to the new NMC when dealing with cases of nurses accused of breaches of professional conduct (now renamed 'fitness to practice'). Furthermore the standard of proof in fitness to practice cases was to be reduced from a criminal to a civil standard of proof. This made a great deal more evidence admissible in fitness to practice cases and in particular allowed more evidence collected by employers in their disciplinary hearings to be admitted to regulatory hearings.

There has been a continued steady increase in complaints against nurses to the NMC with 2899 complaints in 2009–2010 compared to 1627 in 2000–2001, the last year of the UKCC (NMC 2010a, UKCC 2001). The greatest number of complaints is made by employers and changes in the nature of complaints may reflect changes in employment practices. For example recently dishonesty has become the most common reason for sanctions in cases heard by the NMC. Many of these cases involve disputes about sickness absence and allegations regarding nurses 'moonlighting'. This may reflect the recent period of fiscal tightening in healthcare with nurse sickness absence having been prominently identified as a target for future cost savings. Thus employment disputes which would formerly have been dealt with at a local level are now prominent in cases heard before the nursing regulator. By contrast in 2000–2001 patient abuse was the leading reason for cases heard against nurses and midwives.

The NMC has overseen many changes to professional regulation in its short history. It has received some negative media attention being accused of undue leniency and subject to criticism from the CHRE (2008). It now operates with 'fitness to practice' rules which are highly codified and bureaucratised in order to meet the demands of the CHRE and government scrutiny (NMC 2004). The most recent controversy to hit the NMC has been their treatment of a whistle-blower. On this occasion they were accused of undue harshness rather than undue leniency. Margaret Heywood was struck off for co-operating with investigative journalists in the covert filming of poor care and abuse in 2009. After a public outcry Heywood was later reinstated in a deal between the NMC and the Royal College of Nursing who had begun legal action against the NMC.

Subsequently the NMC has issued guidance for nurses on whistleblowing (NMC 2010b). This outlines a five-step procedure for nurses to raise concerns. Nurses are reminded of their professional responsibility to raise concerns about poor care. They are required to first inform their line manager and then escalate their concerns within the organisation first verbally and then in writing. Once they have exhausted the procedures within their organisation they are required to report the matter to a regulator. It is only after this step has failed that nurses can go public with their concerns. The NMC's own consultation highlighted the fact that many nurses were afraid to speak out for fear of victimisation and yet their procedure offers a daunting series of hurdles for nurses to tackle if they choose to raise concerns to an unsympathetic or defensive management. The NMC seems to be operating in an extremely constrained legal and regulatory environment and one has to wonder whether it has the independence to strike an appropriate balance between organisational interests and public protection. This, in part, results from the fact that the prevailing narrative to explain poor care is still the 'bad apple' model and thus employers and regulators see whistleblowing as what in the US is known as a 'snitch law' (Stimson 1985). This is the obligation on professionals to report colleagues for mistakes and malpractice rather than an obligation to raise concerns about organisational or management failings. Thus the reforms of professional regulation have largely ignored cultures of blame within healthcare organisations and the possibilities for institutional corruption that such cultures engender.

Blaming Nurses

I have suggested that the 'bad apple' model has predominated in recent years in health care and that this has drawn attention away from institutional failings and institutional corruption. Recent increases in disciplinary activity against nurses are seen in official discourse as evidence of the success of a more stringent regulatory system which has become more effective in removing unfit, incompetent or malevolent nurses from the profession. In this section I will consider the limited evidence available on the management of disciplinary cases against nurses at a local level and what they tell about the ways in which blame is apportioned in nursing.

A small number of studies of disciplinary actions in nursing have been undertaken in the United States. These have been small scale, mainly qualitative studies. Supples (1993) interviewed staff nurses and managers about the management of the 'substandard or incompetent' nurse. Nurses were offered either a punitive or a helping response. Managers' social judgements influenced the offer of a helping response described by Supples as judgements of 'workability' and 'worthiness'. Managers judged that 'workable' nurses had shown remorse and a willingness to comply with managers' remedial practices. 'Worthy' nurses were judged to be 'good workers', they 'pulled their weight' and possessed useful skills. Supples suggested that organisational pressures affected judgements of 'worthiness' and 'workability' and thus these had a decisive influence on outcomes for nurses who had made mistakes. La Duke (2000) interviewed New York nurses who had been disciplined and concluded that many had received little support and had been unable to represent their side of the case; shame and guilt often prevented nurses from obtaining adequate representation. She concluded that nurses often bore responsibility for systemic failures (La Duke 2000).

Similarly a study by Rosettie (1989) found that nurses were harshly penalised with the lowest grades of nurse receiving the harshest penalties. More recently a quantitative study of disciplinary cases against nurses by US state boards over a ten-year period has shown a 65 per cent increase in cases during this period with older nurses, male nurses and lower grades nurses being at higher risk of disciplinary action (Kenward 2008). Another recent study in Australia by Pugh (2009) found that disciplinary action for errors had devastating psychosocial and professional consequences for nurses and that system issues were often implicated in nursing errors particularly where these were isolated incidents in an otherwise unblemished career. Similarly Johnstone and Kanitsaki (2005) suggested that deliberations in

Australian disciplinary cases against nurses were punitive and thus substantially at odds with models of good practice for the management of clinical errors. In a qualitative study in the UK Murray (2005) also showed that suspension had devastating psychological consequences and frequently ended a nurses professional career irrespective of whether he or she was found guilty or innocent. Thus there is a growing body of evidence that discipline is inconsistent, negative in its consequences and that nurses are too frequently being blamed for system deficiencies.

In the UK cases dealt with by the regulatory body have shown a steady increase as noted earlier however data on the conduct of disciplinary cases at a local level is extremely limited. There has been some disquiet expressed about employers' behaviour in disciplinary cases in UK healthcare particularly in respect of doctors. Tomlin (2003) expressed the view that doctors were frequently unfairly treated and that procedures for suspending health professionals lacked any natural justice. He also alleged that whistle-blowers were particularly at risk of unfair suspension. The high cost of doctor suspension led to an investigation by the National Audit Office (NAO 2003). This investigation led to the finding that suspensions were used inconsistently and were too often a 'knee jerk' reaction by NHS managers. The NAO also conducted a national survey which showed that 53 per cent of all NHS suspensions involved nurses who were more likely to be suspended than other groups. Outcomes of nurse suspension were shown to be poor with almost one third of suspended nurses being dismissed and a similar number choosing to resign or retire from the profession.

My own qualitative case studies of disciplinary cases in three NHS organisations found a high level of variability between organisations in their propensity to discipline nurses, with some organisations having very high levels of disciplinary activity whilst others rarely disciplined nurses (Cooke 2006a). I found that disciplinary cases were poorly conducted and that managers could rarely give a clear rationale for their decision to discipline, which as the NAO noted was frequently a 'knee-jerk' response to an adverse incident. Cases were carried out in an atmosphere of hostility and distrust and outcomes were overwhelmingly negative. Although managers claimed that the purpose of discipline was to 'effect an improvement in performance' there was little evidence that this occurred, with discipline frequently leading either to exclusion from the workplace, resignation or long-term sick leave.

My study also found some evidence of scapegoating of individual nurses often involving poorly managed organisational change (Cooke 2007). Reasons given by managers for disciplinary cases were variable but many cases did not involve any suggestion of harm to patients. Nurses were particularly likely to be disciplined for what managers called 'attitude problems'. These attitude problems did not involve nurses' communications with patients but rather a tendency to criticise the organisation or its management which was interpreted as insubordination or 'management bashing'. Nurses experienced discipline as arbitrary but I found that disciplinary activity tended to occur in waves and to be related to wider organisational factors. Factors which contributed to waves of disciplinary activity included the appointment of new managers, periods of work intensification, management restructuring and downsizing, and finally moral panics in the media about deviant health professionals (Cooke 2002).

Thus the theme of much research on the disciplining of nurses has been its inconsistency but studies also show the recent increase in disciplinary activity against nurses which seems to be a continuing trend. This raises the possibility that nurses have become victims of a growing blame culture in healthcare. Recent surveys in the UK have suggested an increasing proportion of nurses are victims of some form of bullying. For example the Royal College of nursing membership survey in 2000 found that 17 per cent of the nurses had been bullied at work in the previous 12 months but by 2006 this had increased to 23 per cent. A further survey in 2009 showed wide variations according to setting with 30 per cent of NHS hospital nurses reporting that bullying was a problem in their place of work (RCN 2009). This series of surveys has also strongly indicated that disabled and ethnic minority nurses are particularly vulnerable to bullying. This variation in trends strongly suggests that bullying is an organisational problem and Lewis (2006) argues that despite many studies which interpret bullying as a personality issue there is strong evidence that organisational factors play an important part in the creation of bullying and blaming cultures.

In the next section I will consider a theoretical model which may help to understand the growth of blame cultures in contemporary health care.

A Cultural Theory of Blame

Mary Douglas was an anthropologist who looked at how the ways in which we see the world are shaped by culture. She also believed that culture in its turn was shaped by social structures particularly power structures. For Douglas it was axiomatic that 'in all places at all times the universe is moralised and politicised' (Douglas 1992: 4). In later life she turned her attention to cultural perceptions of risk. She was concerned with understanding the ways in which institutional cultures filter perceptions of risk and how the allocation of blame is used to reinforce existing power structures.

Douglas criticised the risk management industry believing it was naïve in its assumption that risk could be calculated numerically or that an increase in bureaucratic regulation could bring greater safety. She argued that disasters are invariably turned to political account and thus risk perception is always influenced by political and cultural factors. In essence when something goes wrong; 'someone already unpopular is going to be blamed' (Douglas 1992: 4).

Douglas was thus concerned to understand how blame was systematically used in the micro politics of institutions. According to Douglas blaming has three latent functions: it explains disasters; it justifies allegiances, and it stabilises existing institutional regimes. Within a politically stable regime blame tends to fall on the weak or on the victim of misfortune but in a less stable regime blame pinning may involve a battle between rival factions. Douglas was concerned then with the way in which blame stabilises existing power structures within institutions or social groups.

Douglas introduces a two-dimensional typology of institutions. The first of these is the strength of boundaries and social cohesion which she refers to as 'group'. The second of these is the degree of hierarchy and the degree to which 'social categories' are imposed on individual members of an institution. She refers to this as 'grid'. She produces a fourfold typology based on these two dimensions.

Isolate high grid, low group	**Bureaucracy** high grid, high group
Market low grid, low group	**Clan** low grid, high group

According to Douglas blame will fall in different places in each of these four institutional types. In a market, misfortune is recruited in a power struggle between potential leaders. Douglas says that the forces invoked to explain misfortune would be 'fetish power' – the personal or charismatic qualities of the leader or of a rival faction. In a bureaucracy blame will tend to travel downwards and misfortune is attributed to a failure to follow rules. In a clan blame falls on outsiders or involves allegations of treachery; misfortune is used to suppress dissidence and strengthen the boundaries of the group.

Douglas' fourth category is characterised by high grid and low group. In this circumstance individuals find themselves isolated and facing the competitive pressures of the marketplace yet these are combined with the rules and hierarchies of a bureaucracy. Douglas described individuals in this category as 'isolates' and she said that their powerlessness and isolation would lead to fatalism. In response to recent changes in the nature of workplaces other authors have recently attempted to develop the category of high grid, low group further. In an important early study of workplace deviance Mars (1984) distinguished jobs with these characteristics as 'donkey jobs', a term which he borrows from Nichols and Beynon (1977). Donkey jobs tend to tie people to a particular time and place of work and limit their interaction with fellow workers'. These jobs are therefore characterised by 'isolated subordination', and 'donkey jobs' are among the most vulnerable and powerless.

Later authors have considered the ways in which Douglas' cultural theory can be used to understand contemporary changes in public sector organisation. The category which she refers to as 'isolation' nicely describes the organisational hybrids that have been created by the introduction of 'managed markets' into public bureaucracies. This category can also be used to understand the loss of professional identity that has accompanied the growth of managerialism in healthcare. In short we may be in danger of replacing professional health work with 'donkey jobs' Bellaby and Lawrenson (2001) applied Douglas' model in an analysis of the effects of audit on higher education and the health service. They particularly wanted to explore the impact of audit cultures on patterns of responsibility and blame in contemporary public sector organisations. Bellaby and

Lawrenson characterise low group, high grid as a condition of 'fragmentation'. They describe fragmentation as follows:

> It resembles the 'mass society' that is the centre of attention of the tradition of critical theory developed by the Frankfurt School. Such a society contains inequalities of power and resource, but lacks mediating forms of communal and corporate life. Weak boundaries and strong lines encourage those on the inside to see threats (if any) as coming from above or below in the social scale rather than from outside (Bellaby and Lawrenson2001).

Threats stem from the 'pervasive sense of being under resourced and working at the edge of capacity'. There is a tendency to blame those above and below and an increasingly pervasive 'blame culture' and a culture which is also 'risk averse'.

In my own work I found similar pressures and I used the term 'seagull management' to describe the culture of the organisations that I studied. Nurses described their managers thus:

We have seagull managers here, they fly in from a great height, make a lot of noise, drop a lot of crap, then they fly off again.

The organisations that I studied were characterised by a distant management who nevertheless subjected nurses to occasional and unpredictable periods of microscopic scrutiny in response to perceived problems which managers saw a need to 'crack down' on. Relationships with managers were frequently poor and the management culture was characterised by distrust and defensiveness. Blame was pervasive but was inconsistent and unpredictable. It was this inconsistency and unpredictability that frequently fuelled the culture of fear that prevailed in many clinical areas. Nurses were often fatalistic about the risk of blame as Douglas predicted. The term 'fragmentation' could be readily be used to describe the environments that I studied. There was a loss of social cohesion in clinical teams as nurses were frequently moved about the organisation. Nurses no longer felt secure in their professional identities as managerial demands were seen to take precedence over professional concerns and judgements. Nurses were thus frequently fearful of being held accountable for circumstances which they could not control (Cooke 2006b).

In a recent meta analysis of 204 workplace ethnographies, Roscigno et al. (2009) found that 'workplace incivilities' (which they describe as negative treatment of workers which threatens their safety and integrity) are rooted in 'organisational chaos'. Organisational chaos is particularly strongly associated with management bullying and bears strong similarities to the organisational context which I have previously referred to as 'fragmentation' and which my informants referred to as 'seagull management'. Chaos implies ineffective management and poor coordination of work. It is often produced by work intensification and downsizing where managers demand 'heroic efforts' from the workforce' to cope with cost pressures but reward these with job insecurity and worsening pay and conditions. In the absence of incentives to reward the extra efforts demand of the workforce, managers use threats and scapegoating to secure compliance and it is frequently the weakest members of the workforce who are singled out for punishment and blame. As Hutchinson and colleagues have noted (2006), too often nursing authors have seen workplace bullying as a personality issue This paper has argued that bullying, conflict and blaming in healthcare workplaces often have institutional roots. Institutional changes in the management and regulation of nursing have made nurses more vulnerable to being bullied and blamed. They have also diminished nurses' ability to defend professional values and standards.

Conclusion

In the last 20 years health policy discourse has turned away from a consideration of problems of institutional corruption and abuse and has emphasised instead the individual accountability of front line health workers, stressing instead that poor case and abuse are due to 'bad apples' within the professions. In the last 10 years in the UK nurses have seen professional self regulation replaced by state directed bureaucratic regulation (Waring et al. 2010) in which the interests of corporate management plays an increasingly dominant role. Sennett (2006) has described a decline in social capital in the professions and we can see this process at work in nursing as the profession becomes increasingly fragmented and loses its independence. The theories of Mary Douglas illuminate the links between this process of fragmentation and the growing culture of blame in healthcare. There is no convincing evidence that this erosion of professional identity protects patients but it certainly creates a fearful workforce who does not feel empowered to speak up about threats to their professional standards. Freidson (2001) says it is in the realm of institutional ethics that the professions most need to assert their independence from the bureaucratisation and marketisation of care and yet nursing's ability to do so seems to be extremely limited. Increasingly we are seeing the weakest and most vulnerable members of our profession allowed to carry away blame for systemic weaknesses in the organisation of care. We are not yet wise to the new forms of the corruption of care which the contemporary pressures of healthcare are producing and yet recent scandals should give us clues to what these are (Healthcare Commission 2009).

The question we now have to ask ourselves is whether we are prepared to see the institutional roots of poor care left unchallenged or whether we reassert the moral authority of our profession by asserting our right to judge practice ethics on the basis of professional rather than bureaucratic values?

References

Abbasi, K. 1998. Butchers and Gropers. *British Medical Journal*, 317, 1599.
Barton, R. 1966. *Institutional Neurosis*. Bristol, UK: Wright and Sons.
Bauman, Z. 1989. *Modernity and the Holocaust*. Cambridge: Polity.

Bellaby, P and Lawrenson, D. 2001. *Audit and Risk-Averse Management in the Public Sector: A Comparison of Trends in the NHS and Higher Education in the UK.* Paper presented at the Work, Employment and Society (BSA) conference, University of York.

Brunton, W. 2005. The place of public inquiries in shaping New Zealand's national mental health policy 1858–1996. *Australia and New Zealand Health Policy* 2.24.

Bullock, R. 1999. *Report of the Independent Inquiry into the Major Employment and Ethical Issues Arising from the Events Leading to the Trial of Amanda Jenkinson.* Nottingham: North Nottinghamshire Health Authority.

Clothier, C. 1994 .*The Allitt Inquiry.* London: HMSO.

Cohen, S. 1972. *Folk Devils and Moral Panics.* London: McGibbon and Kee.

Cooke, H. 2002. *Disciplined Nurses: A Case Study Approach Unpublished PhD thesis.* University of Manchester.

Cooke, H. 2006a. Examining the disciplinary process in nursing: a case study approach. *Work, Employment and Society*, 20(4), 687–707.

Cooke, H. 2006b. Seagull management and the control of nursing work. *Work Employment and Society*, 20(2), 223–43.

Cooke, H. 2007. Scapegoating and the unpopular nurse. *Nurse Education Today*, 27(3), 177–84.

Cooke, H. 2009. Theories of risk and safety what is their relevance to nursing? *Journal of Nursing Management*, 17(2), 256–64.

Council for Healthcare Regulatory Excellence (CHRE). 2008. *Special Report to the Minister of State for Health Service on the Nursing and Midwifery Council CHRE London.*

Davies, C. 2002. Registering a difference: changes in the regulation of nursing, in *Regulating the Health Professions*, edited by J. Allsopp and M. Saks. London: Sage.

Department of Health (DOH). 1999. *Supporting Doctors, Protecting Patients.* London: DOH.

DOH. 2001. *Establishing the New Nursing and Midwifery Council.* London: DOH.

DOH. 2008. *Trust Assurance and Safety.* London: DOH.

Dingwall, R. 2001. Contemporary legends, rumours and collective behaviour:some neglected resources for medical sociology. *Sociology of Health and Illness*, 23(2), 180–202.

Douglas, M. 1992. *Risk and Blame:Essays in Cultural Theory.* London: Routledge.

Freidson, E. 1970. *Profession of Medicine: A Study in the Sociology of Applied Knowledge.* London: Dodd & Mead Co.

Freidson, E. 2001. *Professionalism: The Third Logic.* Cambridge: Polity Press.

Goffman, E. 1961. *Asylums: Essays on the Social Situation of Mental Health Patients and Other Inmates.* New York: Doubleday.

Goode, E. and Ben-Yehuda, N. 1994. *Moral Panics:the Social Construction of Deviance.* Oxford: Blackwell.

Healthcare Commission. 2009. *Investigation into Mid Staffordshire NHS Foundation Trust.* London: Healthcare Commission

Hood, C. 1991. A public management for all seasons? *Public Administration*, 69(1), 3–19.

Hutchinson, M.,Vickers, M., Jackson, D., Wilkes, L. 2006. Workplace bullying in nursing: towards a more critical organisational perspective. *Nursing Inquiry*, 13(2) 118–26.

J.M. Consulting. 1998. *The Regulation of Nurses, Midwives and Health Visitors*. Bristol: J.M. Consulting.

Johnstone, M. and Kanitsaki, O. 2005. Processes for disciplining nurses for unprofessional conduct of a serious nature: a critique. *Journal of Advanced Nursing*, 50(4), 363–71.

Kaplan, R. 2008.Savonarola at the stake: the rise and fall of Roy Meadow. *Australasian Psychiatry*, 16(3), 213–15.

Kennedy, I. 1983. *The Unmasking of Medicine*. London: Granada Publishing.

Kennedy, I. 2001. *Learning from Bristol: The Report of the Public Inquiry into Children's Heart Surgery at the Bristol Royal Infirmary 1984–1995*. London: HMSO.

Kenward, K. 2008. Discipline of nurses: a review of disciplinary data 1996–2006. *JONA's Healthcare Law Ethics and Regulation*, 10(3), 81–4.

La Duke, S. 2000. The Effects of professional discipline on nurses. *American Journal of Nursing*, 100(6), 26–33

Lewis, M. 2006.Nurse bullying: organizational considerations in the maintenance and perpetration of health care bullying cultures. *Journal of Nursing Management*, 14, 52–5.

Macintyre, A. 1985. *After Virtue:a Study in Moral Theory*. London: Duckworth.

McDonald, R., Waring, J., and Harrison, S. 2003. Balancing risk, that is my life: the politics of risk in a hospital operating department. *Health Risk and Society*,7(4), 397–411.

McGivern, G. and Fischer, M. 2010. Medical Regulation, spectacular transparency and the blame business. *Journal of Health Organisation and Management*, 24(6), 597–610.

Mars, G. 1984. *Cheats at Work: An Anthropology of Workplace Crime*. London: Allen & Unwin.

Martin, J.P. 1984. *Hospitals in Trouble*. London: Blackwell.

Murray, R. 2004. *Researching the Lived Experience of Nurses Suspended from the Workplace*. Unpublished PhD Thesis. University of Manchester.

National Audit Office. 2003. *The Management of Suspensions of Clinical Staff in NHS Hospital and Ambulance Trusts in England*. London: HMSO.

Nichols, T. and Beynon, H. 1977. *Living with Capitalism: Class Relations and the Modern Factory*. London: Routledge & Kegan Paul.

Nursing and Midwifery Council (NMC). 2010a. *Fitness for Practice Annual Report*. London: NMC.

Nursing and Midwifery Council (NMC). 2010b. *Raising and Escalating Concerns: Guidance for Nurses and Midwives*. London: NMC.

Power, M. 1997. *The Audit Society: Rituals of Verification*. Oxford: University Press.

Power, M. 2004. *The Risk Management of Everything: Rethinking the Politics of Uncertainty*. London: Demos.

Privy Council. 2004. *The Nursing and Midwifery Council (Fitness to Practise) Rules Order of Council 2004*. London: HMSO.

Pugh, D. 2009. *A Substantive Theory to Explain How Nurses Deal with an Allegation of Unprofessional Conduct*. Unpublished PhD thesis. RMIT Australia.

Roscigno, V., Hodson, R., and Lopez, S. 2009. Workplace incivilities: the role of interest conflicts, social closure and organizational chaos. *Work, Employment and Society*, 23(4), 747–73.

Rosenthal, M. 1995. *The Incompetent Doctor: Behind Closed Doors*. Buckingham: Open University Press.

Rosettie, G.A. 1989. *A Study of Professional Misconduct of Registered Professional Nurses in New York State for the Years 1976 through 1986*. Thesis (Ed. D.). State University of New York at Albany.

Royal College of Nursing (RCN). 2009. *Past Imperfect, Future Tense: Nurses Employment and Morale in 2009*. London: RCN.

Scull, A. 1977. *Decarceration*. New Jersey: Prentice Hall.

Sennet, R. 1998. *The Corrosion of Character*. New York: Norton and Co.

Sennet, R. 2006. *The Culture of the New Capitalism*. Yale University Press.

Smith, J. 2004. *Shipman Inquiry Fifth Report: Safeguarding Patients Lessons from the Past-Proposals for the Future Command Paper Cm 6394*. London: HMSO.

South Ockenden Hospital Inquiry. 1974. *Report of the Committee of Inquiry into South Ockenden Hospital*. London: HMSO.

Stanley, N. and Manthorpe, J. 2004. *The Age of The Inquiry*. London: Routledge.

Stimson, G. 1985. Recent developments in professional control: the impaired physician movement in the United States. *Sociology of Health & Illness*, 7(1), 140–65.

Strong, P. 1984. Viewpoint: the academic encirclement of medicine. *Sociology of Health & Illness*, 6(3), 339–55.

Strong, P. and Robinson, J. 1990. *The NHS – Under New Management*. Buckingham: Open University Press.

Supples, J. 1993. Self-regulation in the nursing profession: response to substandard practice. *Nursing Outlook*, 41(1), 20–24.

Tomlin, P. 2003. The Suspensions scandal. *Journal of Obstetrics and Gynaecology*, 23(3), 221–7.

UKCC. 2001. *Professional Conduct Annual Report*. London: UKCC.

Wardhaugh, J. and Wilding, P. 1993. Towards an explanation of the corruption of care. *Critical Social Policy*, 13(1), 4–31.

Waring, J., Dixon-Woods, M., and Yeung, K. 2010. Modernising medical regulation: where are we now? *Journal of Health Organisation and Management*, 24(6), 540–55.

Chapter 4

Hospital Policies Regarding Violence in the Workplace: A Discourse Analysis

Penny Powers

Introduction

Nurses everywhere experience violence in their place of work at some time. For many nurses, violence has long been considered "just part of the job" (Chapman and Styles 2006: 245), but the level of violence in the hospital workplace is increasing, especially in the U.S. (Rintoul, Wynaden, and McGowan 2008, Stirling, Higgins, and Cooke 2001), despite the fact that workplace violence in general in the U.S. has been falling since 1994 (NIOSH 2006). In a review of the literature on violence in the emergency department, Stirling, Higgins, and Cooke (2001) conclude that the majority of violence is performed by young males, at night, involving alcohol or street drugs, and various conditions such as diabetes, head injuries, psychopathology, and waiting times. In a survey of violence in Emergency departments in the U.S. (Behnam, Tillotson, and Davis 2008), the authors randomly selected 65 from the 140 accredited emergency medical residency programs in the U.S. At least one hospital workplace violence incident in the previous 12 months was reported by 78 per cent of respondents and 27 per cent reported more than one type of violent incident. The most common type of workplace violence was verbal threats (75 per cent) followed by physical assaults (21 per cent), confrontations outside the hospital (5 per cent), and stalking (2 per cent). Hospital security was available in almost all settings and 38 per cent of hospitals screened for weapons. Forty percent (40 per cent) of the sample hospitals had metal detectors. Only 16 per cent of the sample hospitals provided violence training to staff, and less than 10 per cent provided defensive training. Workplace violence was reported equally between males and females and was more common in large EDs with yearly visits over 60,000 patients.

Four World Health Organization reports on workplace violence prevention programs (Sethi et al. 2004, Richards 2003 Di Martino 2003, Wiskow 2003) addressed common aspects of workplace violence prevention programs in many different countries, providing model policies, evaluation instruments and form letters. The number of Medline articles identified using the search terms *workplace violence* has gone from none in 1970–1974 to 193 in 2000–2004 (NIOSH 2004) and 407 on October 24, 2011. The human costs of workplace violence in the hospital are high (Wiltenburg 2007, Brookes 1997) including both physical injuries and psychological effects. Efforts to address the situation have been proposed, including increasing the influence of nurses on hospital policies (Chapman and Styles 2006) the development of empowerment strategies for nurses (Higgins and MacIntosh 2010), the use of Tasers® in the hospital setting (Ho, Clinton, Lappe, Heegaard, Williams, and Miner 2011, the use of metal detectors in hospitals (Behnam, Tillotson, and Davis 2008), seclusion rooms for patients (Chan and Chung 2005), patient contracts (Forster, Petty, Schleiger, and Walters 2005), better employee hiring screening procedures (Gates and Fitzwater 2003), and prosecuting patients who assault staff (Coyne and 2002). Several further suggestions from the literature were reviewed by Stirling, Higgins and Cooke (2001) and included closed circuit television, police officers in the emergency room ER, or emergency department (ED) alarms linked to police stations, personal violence alarms on staff members, security dogs, background checks on job applicants, and restraint training for staff.

Policies in acute care hospitals reflect the concern with escalating violence. As a related body of documents with effects on power relationships, hospital policies are a good candidate for a discourse analysis. Conceptualizing hospital policies as a discourse allows an in-depth analysis of the effects (Shaw 2010). This chapter will present the results of a discourse analysis of general hospital policies regarding violence in the facility from selected medical hospitals (excluding psychiatric hospitals) in Canada, the U.S. and U.S. territories (including Veterans Hospitals), the U.K., Australia, and Norway.

Method

Discourse analysis is a philosophical approach to the analysis of a body of knowledge in the tradition of critical social theory (Powers 2001). Discourse is defined for the purposes of this study as a systematically integrated body of knowledge that can include text, social institutions, images, spoken words, symbols and behaviour. Discourses arise from other discourses in the context of a set of situational factors and discursive necessities that are usually discoverable in retrospect. Discourses have a history, precipitating events, people who contribute to the functions, effects and lifetime of the discourse. Some discourses last a very long time, include many revisions and adjustments and involve many people, such as the discourse of mathematics. Some discourses have a very short but intense life and low long term influence, such as the discourse of phrenology. It is sometimes difficult to detect the point at which one discourse has completed the evolution to another discrete discourse, or to detect when the influence of a discourse is at its peak or its end.

The term *discourse analysis* was originally used to describe a variant of computational linguistics, a way of analyzing text linguistically with symbols to indicate specific grammar, meaning and syntax (for example, see: Jazayery, Polome, and Winter 1976). Discourse analysis is now performed in many different ways, depending on the theoretical tradition and discipline involved (see: Phillips and Jorgensen 2002, Barker and Galasinski 2001, Wodak and Meyer 2001, Titscher, Meyer, Wodak, and Vetter 2000, Wood and Kroger 2000, Fairclough 1995). In this chapter, I use the method described in Powers (2001) which is based on the philosophical approach of Michel Foucault, Rawlinson (1987) and post-modern feminism. In this method, the analysis is mainly concerned with the effects of the discourse on power relations within the social context in which the discourse operates. The analysis produces interpretive claims that are based on a description of the genealogy, the structural analysis, and the power analysis of the particularly situated discourse. Results may or may not be applicable to other discourses, and other analyses may be equally useful in informing the transformation of oppressive conditions. The evidence to support the interpretive claims of a discourse analysis is presented in three sections: genealogy, structural analysis, and power analysis.

According to Rawlinson (1987: 376), Foucault was interested in the historical emergence of a system of rules for the construction of meaningful statements, justifications, concrete material realities and procedures for determining truth and falsity in a discourse. The genealogy explicates the historical conditions that made the discourse possible; how the discourse went about constructing the right to pronounce truth in some part of human experience. A genealogical approach uncovers the way

> the epistemological and the political, knowledge and power, are ineluctably intertwined, so that truth is not so much discovered (…) as produced according to regular and identifiable procedures that determine in any given historical situation what it is possible to say, who is authorized to speak, what can become an object of scientific inquiry, and how knowledge is to be tested, accumulated, and dispersed (Rawlinson 1987: 373).

The structural analysis consists of three axes: the axis of knowledge; the axis of authority; and the axis of value or justification (Rawlinson 1987). The axis of knowledge explores the system of concepts and rules of the discourse, the styles of statements and theoretical strategies. The axis of authority examines the rules for who is allowed to speak in this discourse, what systems are in place for education, reproduction and advancement of the discourse, and how the right to pronounce truth is managed internally. Analysis in the axis of value or justification includes the systems of regulation and the technologies of power, and how the deployment of the discourse on the bodies of actual human beings is justified.

In the power analysis, relationships of power are identified that are either supported or not supported by the discourse. Dominant discourses within the discourse being analyzed are identified. Discourses that resist the dominant discourses are also identified. Resistant discourses are alternative speaking positions for people that provide ways of acting and speaking that may or may not support the dominant way of thinking. Dominant and resistant discourses are acknowledged in order to demonstrate that some situations of power relations are preferable to others. However, individual readers may choose their own subjectivities and speaking positions from the analysis. Not all discourse analysts include preferential claims.

In naming and describing resistance to power, the analysis may trigger the process of co-optation by the dominant discourse to control the level of resistance. Marginalized voices may be raised and then silenced. A discourse analysis assumes that people can be deceived about their oppressive situation, but does not assume that the analysis can identify what is actually going on in the real world. The discourse analysis is one possible interpretation of the development and use of privilege.

Data Collection

The data for this study consisted of 23 hospital policies collected over a period of four months in 2010. Some policies applied to one hospital and some were blanket policies that applied to a large system of hospitals. Some were available online and others were requested from specific countries, states or provinces.

Analysis

Genealogy

Violent physical action has traditionally been viewed as a criminal act, subject to prosecution as assault under the law. Society reserves the right to deal with violence through the rule of law. The term *workplace violence* is relatively new. Violence in hospitals was originally discussed in the literature as physical assault on staff by psychiatric patients and was considered a well-known occupational hazard (British Medical Journal 1971). Predicting violent behaviours has a research history in the social sciences going back to the 1950s, when statistical prediction was noted to be superior to unaided clinical judgement (Meehl 1954). Factors that have been successfully used to predict violence are age, sex, past antisocial and violent conduct, aggressive childhood behaviour, and substance abuse (Harris and Rice 1997).

Before the term workplace violence,, the terms occupational homicide, occupational violent crime, murder at work, and fatal occupational injuries were used. The earliest references in English to the term *workplace violence* in academic publications, legal decisions and newspapers were found in an article on Ante-Bellum labour in the U.S. South (Grimstead 1985), which referred to workplace violence on farms and factories at the time; and in an article discussing fatal occupational injuries of women workers in Texas in the year 1987 (Davis, Honchar, and Suarez 1987) which referred only to fatalities among women at work. The U.S. National Institute for Occupational Safety and Health (NIOSH), part of the U.S. Centers for Disease Control (CDC), began keeping statistics on national workplace traumatic injury deaths in 1988 (NIOSH 2006). Canadian statistics were first compiled in 2004 (Stats Can 2007). An article in the Journal of Occupational and Environmental Medicine (Hales, Seligman, Newman, and Timbrook 1988) referred to workplace violence but did not include hospitals.

In the late 1980s and early 1990s, the U.S. postal service, the nation's second largest employer, suffered a rash of violent incidents involving firearms, beginning with the case of a part-time letter carrier facing dismissal from his job who went to the Edmond, Oklahoma Post Office on August 20, 1986 and killed 14 people, then killing himself. This incident, among others, led to the phrase, "going postal" which remains in popular use today. Scholarly publications began to use the term *workplace violence* beginning in 1992 with the analysis of post office violence. Early research consisted mainly of surveys of facilities to determine the extent of workplace violence. The next common type of research was a study of common characteristics of perpetrators and pre-assaultive clinical symptomatology (Distasio 1994). In the late 1990s there were more articles regarding prevention, risk and treatment. Presently, the most common type of research on workplace violence is a prevalence survey.

According to Taft and Nanna (2008), hospital policies come from three sources, organizational, public, and professional. In the present case of hospital policies on workplace violence, all three sources are represented. U.S. governmental regulations were put in place in the early 1990s to require employers to take more of a role in addressing workplace violence, including prevention. The U.S. Department of Labour Occupational Safety and Health Administration (OSHA) issued general workplace violence guidelines in 1993 and introduced hospital specific guidelines in 1996, revised in 1998 (Barish 2001). In addition, a body of case law began to accumulate (Speer 1997), making it clear that employers were expected to make reasonable efforts to keep their workplace free of violence.

The earliest workplace violence guidelines in Canada were initiated by British Columbia in 1993 (Barish 2001). The guidelines required a risk assessment, staff education, and reporting of incidents to the Worker's Compensation Board (Barish 2001). In 2003, the Registered Nurses' Association of Ontario (RNAO) received funding from the Ontario Ministry of Health and Long-Term Care to develop evidence-based best practice guidelines that could be used to "create healthy work environments" (RNAO 2009).

In 1993, NIOSH issued an alarm regarding the rising incidence of what was called "homicide in the workplace." In 1996, NIOSH defined workplace violence to include non-fatal injuries: "physical assaults and threats of assaults, directed toward people at work or on duty" (NIOSH 1996). In 2004, NIOSH expanded its definition of workplace violence to include four categories: criminal intent, customer-client, worker on worker, and personal relationship (NIOSH 2004).

The Canada Centre for Occupational Health and Safety (CCOHS 2010) presently defines workplace violence as:

...any act in which a person is abused, threatened, intimidated or assaulted in his or her employment. Workplace violence includes:

- **threatening behaviour** – such as shaking fists, destroying property or throwing objects.
- **verbal or written threats** – any expression of an intent to inflict harm.
- **harassment** – any behaviour that demeans, embarrasses, humiliates, annoys, alarms or verbally abuses a person and that is known or would be expected to be unwelcome. This includes words, gestures, intimidation, bullying, or other inappropriate activities.
- **verbal abuse** – swearing, insults or condescending language.
- **physical attacks** – hitting, shoving, pushing or kicking.

Rumours, swearing, verbal abuse, pranks, arguments, property damage, vandalism, sabotage, pushing, theft, physical assaults, psychological trauma, anger-related incidents, rape, arson and murder are all examples of workplace violence.

Workplace violence is not limited to incidents that occur within a traditional workplace. Work-related violence can occur at off-site business-related functions (conferences, trade shows), at social events related to work, in clients' homes or away from work but resulting from work (a threatening telephone call to your home from a client) (CCOHS 2010).

In December, 2009, the province of Ontario enacted Bill 168, the *Occupational Health and Safety Amendment Act (Violence and Harassment in the Workplace)* that came into effect on June 15, 2010. Employers are required to maintain policies to address workplace violence and harassment and to assess the risk of violence in its workplace. *Workplace violence* in Bill 168 is defined as: (a) the exercise of physical force by a person against a worker, in a workplace, that causes or could cause physical injury to the worker, (b) an attempt to exercise physical force against a worker, in a workplace, that could cause physical injury to the worker, (c) a statement or behaviour that it is reasonable for a worker to interpret as a threat to exercise physical force against the worker, in a workplace, that could cause physical injury to the worker (Legislative Assembly of Ontario 2009).

The Occupational Health and Safety Administration (OSHA) in the U.S. Department of Labour provides the following definition of workplace violence: "Workplace violence is violence or the threat of violence against workers. It can occur at or outside the workplace and can range from threats and verbal abuse to physical assaults and homicide" (OSHA 2002: 1). OSHA compliance officers can cite employers who allow opportunities for violence to persist. OSHA recommends that every facility develop a policy on violence and provide education to employees with regard to a zero-tolerance for violence, including a pledge that all incidents will be investigated. OSHA also recommends extra lighting, alarm systems, employee badges, escort services, keeping vehicles in good repair, not carrying money on your person, and a buddy system for people who must enter a situation in which they feel unsafe (OSHA 2010).

The National Health Service in the UK developed a Zero Tolerance campaign against workplace violence in 1999 and has re-launched the campaign several times in the years since (Gabe and Elston 2008). Penalties for violent behaviour include patients being refused treatment. The UK definition of workplace violence comes from the European Commission: "any incident where staff are abused, threatened or assaulted in circumstances related to their work, involving an explicit or implicit challenge to their safety, well-being or health" (Wynne et al. 1997, cited in Steinman 2003: 3).

All re-definition efforts are moves of power. In a concept analysis of workplace violence, Ventura-Mandangeng and Wilson (2009) reported finding no universally accepted definition of workplace violence. These authors argue that this situation results in the under-reporting of the phenomenon. The spread of similar definitions of workplace violence has allowed an industry in workplace violence prevention to arise in order to provide assistance to employers with policy development, employee education, security, insurance, legal aid, violence prevention workshops, de-briefing services for victims and co-workers, risk assessment services, and post-traumatic stress counseling (Podolak 2000). Through various associations and social research firms, the industry lobbies governments, elected officials, the public, and civil servants.

In the area of professional input in policies, all nursing organizations now have position statements on workplace violence. The International Council of Nurses defines workplace violence as "Incidents where staff are abused, threatened or assaulted in circumstances related to their work, including commuting to and from work, involving an explicit or implicit challenge to their safety, well-being or health" (ICN 2002). The Occupational Health and Safety Council of Nova Scotia defines workplace violence as, "the attempted, threatened or actual conduct of a person that endangers the health or safety of an employee, including any threatening statement or threatening behaviour that gives an employee reasonable cause to believe that the employee is at risk of injury" (Nova Scotia Department of Environment and Labour 2006: 3).

It is not clear where the first hospital policy on workplace violence was developed because it was most likely an internal document that is not currently available. Workplaces that have experienced an incident of violence are more likely to have policies in place than workplaces that have not experienced such an event (Gates and Fitzwater 2003). The first law regarding hospitals and workplace violence was passed in 1993 in California. The law required hospitals to develop a plan to prevent violence in the facility and to educate staff regarding the phenomenon. The law provided for inspections of facilities and reporting of incidents.

It is clear that the previously existing discourses on assault in hospitals, occupational violent crime, traumatic injury deaths at work, etc., combined with very public cases of the murder of co-workers, led governmental agencies to respond to what was called an *epidemic* (Kinney and Johnson 1993). The development of a term like *workplace violence* plus the initiation of governmental legislation and regulations to address what was perceived as a growing problem points to the beginning of an organized discourse. The new discourse that was formed combined some elements from law, public health, occupational medicine, occupational health and safety, psychology, and risk management. Workplace violence became a concern that had to be dealt with in some portfolio within the hospital organization. In addition, the topic could also be studied by academics that might also be available to do consulting work for hospitals working to develop a wide range of approaches such as awareness workshops, risk assessment tools, and the development of policies. In 2008, the Joint Commission in the U.S. that accredits hospitals issued two new leadership standards that required hospitals to have a code of conduct for staff (Joint Commission 2008). Accreditation Canada required hospitals to prevent violence in 2011.

The physical, bodily space created by the discourse of hospital workplace violence policies consists of the physical bodies of people in the hospital at any one time. The bodies are now re-defined by the discourse as being *at-risk* of violence – a condition that must be identified and addressed by the hospital itself, in response to laws and regulations. A new dimension of responsibility is thus created by the discourse. Before the development of the discourse, people were considered to be responsible for their own security. Your co-workers might come to your aid in a violent situation out of concern for your safety, but the organization was not responsible for taking any kind of preventative or follow up action in the case of violence. Since the development of the discourse, hospitals are required to actively create a culture of non-violence among staff. Hospitals are required to provide awareness training; policies to be followed, actions to be taken before, during and after an incident, and penalties exist for not doing so.

The discourse emerged on the surfaces of the previously existing discourses of occupational injuries and fatalities, assault while at work, occupational violent crime, and hospital risk management. These relatively small discourses were available, academic work had been done, statistics were kept, but there was no impact on policy at any level. The social context of people being murdered in post offices in the U.S. in the 1980s and 1990s generated calls for OSHA to do something (Thomas 1992). A 1996 book by Michael D. Kelleher was titled, *New Arenas for Violence*, as though violence had not happened in places of employment before then. Such pressure caused U.S. governmental agencies to consolidate all of the previous work under the term *workplace violence* and take action. As a result, the previous terms gradually disappear from the literature, except in publications from Australia, where *occupational violence* continues to be used. Everyone today presumably understands what workplace violence means. It is now a topic that generates policies and headlines, appears on CV's and websites, and makes careers possible through the availability of grants to study the phenomenon. In short, a significant amount of money circulates as a result of the discourse.

The formation of this discourse served the interests of the hospitals in that they were protected from lawsuits and fines from governmental agencies by having approved policies and procedures in place. A publication from the Norfolk County, Massachusetts District Attorney's Office in 2007 stated that the benefits of workplace violence prevention programs were: "employees will feel safer, more severe forms of violence will be less likely to occur, and expensive and embarrassing incidents may be avoided" (Norfolk District Attorney's Office 2007: 28). If employees take actions in accordance with the policies, the institution is protected. If employees take action not in accordance with the policies, the institution is still protected from lawsuits because they have taken all reasonable precautions. The discourse served the interests of employees in that there are policies to refer to in seeking protection and redress, for example in the case of horizontal workplace violence. Members of the public could be reassured that hospitals knew about the problem and were doing something. Seeking to artificially manage the creation of a certain prescribed culture in an institution may not ultimately be in the interests of the employees, however. More will be said about this in the power analysis.

Media outlets now have a category of story called *workplace violence* that members of the public understand is a story about an incidence of a certain phenomenon. Statistics can be kept regarding the phenomenon, so trends can be interpreted. Institutes and corporations are able to provide consultation regarding violence prevention programs, training and retraining programs, aggression management programs, interpersonal skills training, deterrence consulting, debriefing and security (Stirling, Higgins, and Cooke 2001) (for examples, see: http://workplaceviolencenews.com/ and http://noworkviolence.com/).

Academics have benefited by the description of a new field of power/ knowledge in which to perform research and pronounce truth. The victims of workplace violence have a term to use when discussing the incident so that people can understand it as a specific incidence of a category of events that happen at work. It is now more socially acceptable to speak about workplace violence in nursing than it was in the 1980s.

It is not clear in this sample whether the interests of perpetrators are considered within this discourse. The voice of the perpetrator is only represented in the policies as an objectified "other" whose characteristics are to be used to identify someone else who is similar enough to be suspicious. Getting help for people who commit violent acts is not the purpose of these policies. It is also not clear whether the interests of women specifically are considered by the discourse because women tend to include behaviours in their definitions of violence that are not included in the hospital policies. More will be said about this in the power analysis.

Structural Analysis

The second part of a discourse analysis is the structural analysis. In this section, claims are made regarding how the discourse presently functions. The claims are grouped in the following three categories: 1) the axis of knowledge, 2) the axis of authority and 3) the axis of value or justification.

The Axis of Knowledge

The objects of the discourse on workplace violence in hospital policies are the individual incidents of violence that happen to people in the facility. These incidents are now defined by policies, not by individuals, nor by a consensus of individuals, or legal precedent, or social context. It is not workplace violence unless the policy says it is. The incidents that fit the definition are now the subjects of the discourse of the policies, including some types and excluding others. The process of definition is used by hospitals to create the subjects of the discourse, the incidents of workplace violence, from the objects in a social context, an event that happens within the context of work or work-related spaces. Defining workplace violence creates a discursive field, a turf, for the institution that now claims the power to define and address this issue in its own way. If an issue is quickly defined and addressed in a coordinated effort, then the entire discourse can be added to that group's intellectual turf. Competing definitions then have less power to claim the knowledge-producing properties of a newly acknowledged region of human experience.

The discourse of hospital policies defines people in the facility as potential victims or potential perpetrators. People are now defined as *at-risk* of some condition. The discourse determines what types of evidence can be used to identify events that can be classed as workplace violence and what action is to be taken, by whom, and along what time line. Competing discourses have less of a chance to set the agenda because they have a late start at defining the important issues.

The discourse is spread from hospital to hospital by federal and international guidelines, industry associations, conferences, and consultants. Hospitals are required to have these policies in place and they hire consultants to help them develop policies that will satisfy the governmental and accreditation requirements. Therefore, policies are very similar. Many policies state that the goal is "zero tolerance" for any type of violence in the facility. Violence is defined in slightly different ways in the policies, following the most generally accessible definitions quoted above, from OSHA to the European Commission. The main type of discursive language used by the policies is the business language of risk reduction. The problem has now been defined and addressed by the corporate world in the same manner as other risks to the smooth functioning of the facility. The issue of violence in the hospital workplace will be *managed*. The voice of management literature is the dominant voice present in the policies.

The responsibilities of major stakeholders, management, staff, and patients are delineated in the policies. The major responsibilities lie with management. Screening and risk assessment procedures are the first step, sometimes called workplace security analysis or worksite analysis. Workplaces are then structurally adapted to provide more security; this is sometimes called engineering control measures. The structural measures include moving desks, making doors lockable, installing windows in doors, curved mirrors to see around corners, staff washrooms separate from visitor and patient washrooms, TV monitoring of high-risk areas, increasing lighting and installing panic alarms. Pro-active educational programs are prescribed to include management and staff. Posters and reminders are distributed. Staff education and regular required re-training sessions are scheduled. Class topics include risk factors, characteristics of aggressors, policies that need to be followed and forms that need to be completed.

The policies follow a standard format. They usually begin with principles or a pledge of zero tolerance for violence. Legal and accreditation requirements are usually listed. Employees are required to report any violent situations on the proper form within a certain time period to their supervisor who will keep a detailed log. Records must be kept and incidents tracked to monitor trends. The investigation procedure for each incident is specified. Post-incident and emergency procedures are described, such as critical incident de-briefing. Regular evaluation of the policy is discussed.

Changing work practices are often described in great detail. Sometimes called administrative and work practice controls, these changes to the work culture are extensive, necessitating a complete change in the way an employee goes about her or his work. This is sometimes referred to as a cultural change in work habits. Examples include:

- Establish lines of instant communications with local police and provide them with maps of the facility;
- Establish a trained response team for emergency situations;
- Increase the number of security guards;
- Reduce waiting times for patients and be more reassuring to those who must wait to be treated;
- Monitor patients with a history of gang affiliation or violence;
- Prohibit employees from working alone in high risk areas;
- Work with aggressive patients in a public area;
- Prohibit staff from performing intimate physical examinations alone;
- Provide badges to staff that display only last names;
- Recommend that staff wear no jewellery and carry no pens or keys.

The business language of risk management is also used to determine the processes, strategies and styles of statements in the policies. This language is available for anyone to learn. The American Society for Health Care Risk Management declares Healthcare Risk Management Week every year. The society was formed in 1980 to draw together risk managers from hospitals all over the U.S. Organizations work with governments to develop model policies that can be used by individual hospitals, and collaborate with others to publish handbooks to be used to develop policies. This type of early work determines the discursive language that will be used for the entire life of the discourse.

The discourse of the hospital policies does not use epidemiological and medical language that is used in academic literature, such as *epidemic*, *treatment*, and *prevention*. The rules of evidence and styles of theoretical statements for the generation of knowledge in the discourse therefore consist of business language of risk management. This language uses business models and processes for developing knowledge in the field. Risk management language focuses on reducing a corporation's level of exposure to adverse events (e.g. loss of revenue, lawsuits, bad public relations) by using such tools as *creating a risk-aware culture, measuring and monitoring risk, creating buy-in, mitigating risk, and managing risk.*

For example, as the discourse of hospital policies becomes more complex, tracking mechanisms become inevitable. In Canada, the province of British Columbia employs the WHITE™ system, the Workplace Health Indicator Tracking and Evaluation computerized reporting system, providing "healthcare stakeholders with comparative performance indicators on workplace health and safety" (Gilligan and Alamgir 2008). This system is used to compile data for statistical purposes and to monitor workers' compensation claims. The database collects information on all individual health care workers in the province, including incident tracking and investigation, immunization schedules and follow-up, case management, sickness, absences, long term disability, biological, physical and chemical exposures, training and education, and baseline health and communicable disease history. The database does not take into consideration the experience of employees or their assailants. The system is self-described as a surveillance system, a term that would delight Michel Foucault.

The structure of the discourse has increased in complexity over time. There are classification systems for the subjects of the discourse, such as the NIOSH (2004) taxonomy, which classifies workplace violence into four types: criminal intent, customer on staff, personal relationship, and worker on worker. Another classification system for workplace violence in health care was described by Wiskow (2003) in the ILO/ICN/WHO/PSI Joint Programme Working Paper. Hospital policies most often define violent situations as applying to anyone in the hospital, but examples are most often related to client or patient aggressors. It is clear that the policies assume that violent situations can be avoided and if not avoided, then managed, like any other risk to the organization. The term *management* is deliberately used instead of *control* because of the "potentially pejorative connotations" of the latter (Heilbrun 1997: 348). Therefore, violence and its outcomes are addressed by the science of risk management, something already familiar to large organizations.

Forms and procedures for supporting and counselling victims of workplace violence are specified in hospital policies. Relevant sections begin with the moment following a violent event. What happens during the violent episode is not discussed. Nothing is said regarding what happens to the aggressor, unless it happens to be a peer or supervisor, in which case both are treated as victims and debriefed and counselled. In the National Health System of the United Kingdom, violent patients can be refused further treatment, but what happens during or immediately after the violent incident is not addressed.

Another area in which the policies are relatively silent is evaluation. Some policies dictate that the program will be evaluated every year, or every three years, but none say exactly how the policies will be evaluated. Staff satisfaction surveys were found in only one case.

The Axis of Authority

The axis of authority addresses the rules for who is and is not allowed to speak, what they can and cannot say and the systems for education, association and advancement. Since the dominant discourse is that of risk management, one cannot contribute to the discussion on policies unless one can speak the language of risk reduction. Hospital risk managers maintain membership in associations, attend conferences and publish articles in professional and academic journals. In some hospitals, risk managers are part of upper levels of management. In other hospitals, risk management duties reside in the human resources department. Any discourse that functions in such a complex manner has effectively co-opted other ways of speaking about the subjects of the discourse. The events of violence that occur in hospitals now have a label and their management is located within hospital bureaucracy. Funding for prevention and management is typically included in the budget and risk managers are considered the authorities on the subject. None of the policies I examined describe any retribution for any other department's handling of violent incidents, but it was clearly not necessary. All policies, procedures and communication on the topic of workplace violence come from the risk management department.

The discourse is preserved, transmitted and disseminated at conferences and in journal articles and by government agencies that produce model policies. The only speaking position available is that of a risk manager or a consultant to risk managers. Academics who study violence in the hospital workplace have not been able to contribute to policies that are in force in actual hospital settings.

The Axis of Value or Justification

The axis of value or justification addresses how the discourse justifies its power, knowledge and technologies. The discourse justifies itself by citing evidence of its successful reduction of workplace violence. For example, it has been reported that the incidence of hospital workplace violence in California emergency departments dropped by 48 per cent after the enactment of the California Hospital Safety and Security Act of 1995 (Casteel et al. 2008). Given the many and competing definitions of hospital workplace violence, it may be difficult to generalize this finding.

There may be some question regarding how to justify the cost of addressing hospital workplace violence based on outcomes. It might be difficult to compare the reduction or increase in hospital violence in relation to the cost of maintaining policies because of incommensurate definitions of the phenomenon and the difficulty of identifying all costs associated with continuous staff training and engineering modifications. The cost of maintaining the discourse in health care facilities is borne by the public domain through government assistance. The result is that there is no incentive to keep costs down.

Power Analysis

The third part of this discourse analysis, the power analytic, identifies the dominant and resistance discourses and their effects. The power analytic focuses on the following questions: whose interests are furthered by the continuation of the discourse? What dominations are established, perpetuated or eliminated, and is there evidence for the co-optation of other discourses?

Dominant Discourse

As seen earlier, the dominant discourse in the policies is that of risk management. This conclusion is further supported by the observation reported earlier that only one hospital policy focused on what happens during a violent episode. The discourse of risk management is not about what happens between people in a violent altercation; it is about managing the factors that lead up to the situation and what happens afterwards. When management addresses the risk of something happening that has detrimental outcomes for the organization, the approach is to prevent it and, to manage the effects on the organization. There are strategies to this approach that have been developed for other threats to risk that are now used in the case of violence. Management policies remain dominant over any other approach to workplace violence because the discourse was co-opted early and specific terms were assigned. Hospital staff may be consulted for the purpose of defining terms and suggestions for changes to the workplace, but the nuances of their responses are lost in risk management language. There may be a risk that such a complex system of reporting and de-briefing prevent workers, such as nurses, to report incidents or participate in de-briefing.

Resistance Discourses

Discourses are multiple and offer competing ways of constructing knowledge for people to identify with and use (consciously or unconsciously) as a way of enacting, embodying, or performing meaning in a situation (Gavey 1997). One resistance discourse found in the literature, but not in the policies examined here, is that of patient rights. Paniagua, Bond and Thompson (2009) argue that a zero tolerance policy toward violence interferes with patients' right to express legitimate anger at poor care. However, hospital policies do not address the rights or opinions of those who commit violent acts.

Another resistance discourse is that of ethics. A few hospital policies included pledges with respect to the ethical treatment of individuals, to sensitivity, respect and fairness. These words do not come from the risk management literature, but are found in the discipline of health care ethics. Such pledges are not common, but do represent another way to think of management's responsibility to maintain a safe place to work.

There is a resistance discourse among female practising nurses that avoids the usual language of workplace violence in favour of another that is more emotionally loaded. In one study, female nurses specifically asked the researcher not to use such words as abuse, violence, mobbing or bullying (Hockley 2000). The nurses used terms such as *hamstrung, walking through a minefield* and *bitch*. Hockley (2000: 28) noted that nurses "described an event and left it to the researcher to name." This behaviour results in under-reporting workplace violence because nurses do not name the incident using the accepted words of management. Such powerlessness is described by Belenky and colleagues (1986) as subjective knowing. This type of knowing views truth as residing inside the person, rather than abstract, objective academic knowledge. None of the policies or definitions used in this study included these terms. It is not clear how common is their use by female nurses, or whether another researcher would obtain similar results. It is interesting to note that the voice of the male nurse is absent in the discourse on hospital workplace violence.

The effect of the dominant discourse is to provide an overwhelming speaking position that leaves other ways of describing the situation unavailable to participants. Changing policies thus becomes very difficult. Nurses have low rates of involvement in the development of policy at any level (Taft and Nanna 2008) and it does not seem likely that the approach to violence in the hospital could be changed.

Whose interests are supported by the continuation of this discourse? Researchers can continue to study the subject, health care facilities can use the results to educate employees on methods to prevent violence, and victims can continue to receive support from people who specialize in treatment of the ongoing after effects of the incidents. The discourse can expand and secure its influence and the public can feel assured that problems are dealt with in clinical research settings using scientific methods. Subsequently, employees generating resistance discourses, those who are located outside the normal range of behaviour can be identified and targeted with normalizing strategies designed to uphold the status quo of power relations. Public discussions of moral and ethical issues and social context are thus avoided.

Other agents who benefit from the continuation and expansion of this discourse include consulting corporations specializing in the prevention, treatment, insurance, and legal aspects of hospital workplace violence. Recommendations in research studies include strong leadership, documentation and system requirements, support groups, debriefing sessions, task forces, staff training, mandatory reporting and changes in individual nurses (Levin, Hewitt, and Misner 1998).

Follow-up after violent events is always cited as crucial to the well-being of the organization. While writing this chapter, I received a flyer in my university mailbox from a U.S.-based company advertising courses in the management of violent situations in a nearby city. Such courses include introductory seminars, comprehensive workshops, and instructor certification programs, plus on-site training specialists. These types of seminars make it clear that the burden of identifying and managing risk in potentially violent situations is on the health professional because nurses are social agents of governmentality (Holmes, Perron, and Savoie 2006). Risk management is a top-down policy that uses fear to increase control over staff (Gabe and Elston 2008). What happens *during* a violent incident is left to staff to work out for themselves. Self-discipline is thus a form of regulation (Ruhl 1999). The dominant discourse ignores the experience of individual nurses in favour of totalizing general narratives, the effect of which is to "write ourselves into a web of obedience" (Bail et al. 2009: 1457). Oppression of individual nurses is thus perpetuated at the same time as nurses are being encouraged to seek outside support (e.g. courses). There is a dual message here – fend for yourself then fill out the forms.

Finally, there is no input of voices from individual nurses or perpetrators except as self-confessing research subjects. The interests of perpetrators are generally ignored except as sources of clues for identifying potential violent situations (Distasio 1994) and in those cases when the perpetrator is also a staff member, as described above.

Limitations of the Study

No declaration is made for the absolute truth or *generalizability* of the claims made through discourse analysis. As with any method of inquiry, competing claims are possible regarding the same discourse by another analyst. The selected policies all came from developed countries, certainly creating a bias. It is hoped however that this work will raise readers' consciousness and inform the work of those within the discourse in order to reduce oppression and support alternate speaking positions. It is also possible that the analysis may have unintended consequences or not reach the audience to which it is addressed.

Conclusions

Understanding the power relations in any discourse enables participants and observers to reproduce or resist such discourse. This analysis has demonstrated that the discourse of hospital workplace violence has been co-opted by the discourse of hospital risk management. The result is that other speaking positions are unavailable to hospital staff and the public. Other discourses that resist the dominant discourse on this topic have been identified. Discourse analysis encourages discussion regarding the advantages and disadvantages of available speaking positions and their effect on power relations. Some discourse analysts refrain from expressing a preference of one discourse over another. Michel Foucault chose this position. Other analysts base their preference on whether or not oppression is perpetuated.

The important point is that the issue is raised for dissemination and consideration. Other analyses are welcomed, and discussion should be stimulated.

References

Bail, K., Cook, R., Gerdner, A., and Grealish, L. 2009. Writing ourselves into a web of obedience: a nursing policy analysis. *International Journal of Nursing Studies*, 46, 1457–66.

Barish, R.C. 2001. Legislation and regulations addressing workplace violence in the United States and British Columbia. *American Journal of Preventive Medicine*, 20(2), 149–54.

Barker, C. and Galasinski, D. 2001. *Cultural Studies and Discourse Analysis: A Dialogue on Language and Identity.* Thousand Oaks, CA: Sage.

Behnam, M., Tillotson, R., and Davis, S. 2008. Research forum abstracts: violence in the emergency department: a national survey of emergency medicine resident and attending physicians. *Annals of Emergency Medicine*, 52(4), Supplement 1, 172.

Belenky, M.F., Clinchy, B., Goldberger, N.R., and Tarule, J.M. 1986. *Women's Ways of Knowing: The Development of Self, Voice, and Mind.* New York: Basic Books.

Brookes, J.G. 2009. The impact of violence on emergency department staff. *Emergency Medicine*, 9(2), 117–21.

Casteel, C., Peek-Asa, C., Nocera, M., Smith, J.B., Blando, J., Goldmacher, S., O'Hagan, E., Valiante, D., and Harrison, R. 2009. Hospital employee assault rates before and after enactment of the California hospital safety and security act. *Annals of Epidemiology*, 19(2), 125–33.

CCOHS (n.d.). *Violence in the Workplace.* [Online]. Available at: http://www. ccohs.ca/oshanswers/psychosocial/violence.html [accessed: 23 July 2010].

Chan, C.C., and Chung, C.H. 2005. A retrospective study of seclusion in an emergency department. *Hong Kong Journal of Emergency Medicine*, 12(1), 6–13.

Chapman, R., and Styles, I. 2006. An epidemic of abuse and violence: nurse on the front line. *Accident and Emergency Nursing*, 14, 245–9.

Clements, P.T., DeRanieri, J.T., Clark, K., Manno, M.S., Kuhn, D.W. 2005. Workplace violence and corporate policy for health care settings. *Nursing Economics*, 3(23), 1–10.

Coyne, A. 2002. Should patients who assault staff be prosecuted? *Journal of Psychiatric and Mental Health Nursing*, 9(2), 139–45.

Davis, H., Honchar, P.A., and Suarez, L. 1987. Fatal occupational injuries of women, Texas 1975–84. *American Journal of Public Health*, 77(12), 1524–7.

Di Martino, V. 2003. Relationship between work stress and workplace violence in the health sector. An ILO/ICN/Who/PSI Joint Programme Working Paper: Geneva.

Distasio, C.A. 1994. Violence in health care: institutional strategies to cope with the phenomenon. *The Health Care Manager*, 12(4), 1–34.

Doyle, L.M. and Klein, M.C. 2001. Comparison of two methods of instruction for the prevention of workplace violence. *Journal of Nurses in Staff Development*, 17(6), 281–93.

Fairclough, N. 1995. *Critical Discourse Analysis: the Critical Study of Language*. New York: Longman.

Forster, J.A., Petty, M.T., Schleiger, C., and Walters, H.C. 2005. Know workplace violence: developing programs for managing the risk of aggression in the health care setting. *Medical Journal of Australia*, 183(7), 357–61.

Gabe, J. and Elston, M.A. 2008. We don't have to take this: zero tolerance of violence against health care workers in a time of insecurity. *Social Policy & Administration*, 42(6), 691–709.

Gates, D., Fitzwater, E., and Salazar, M.K. 2003. Linking practice and research. Dealing with workplace violence – strategies for prevention. *American Association of Occupational Health Nurses Journal*, 51(6), 243–45.

Gilligan, T. and Alamgir, H. 2008. Bridging the knowledge gap: an innovative surveillance system to monitor the health of British Columbia's health care workforce. *Canadian Journal of Public Health*, 99(6), 478–82.

Grimsted, D. 1985. Ante-bellum labor: violence, strike and communal arbitration. *Journal of Social History*, 19, 1. Available at: http://www.jstor.org/stable/3787916 [accessed: 11 August 2010].

Hales, T., Seligman, P.J., Newman, S.C., and Timbrook, C.L. 1988. Occupational injuries due to violence. *Journal of Occupational and Environmental Medicine*, 30(6), 483–7.

Harris, G.T., and Rice, M.E. 1997. Risk appraisal and management of violent behavior. *Psychiatric Services*, 48(9), 1168–76.

Heilbrun, K. 1997. Prediction versus management models relevant to risk assessment: the importance of legal decision-making context. *Law and Human Behavior*, 21(4), 347–59.

Higgins, B.L., and MacIntosh, J. 2010. Operating room nurses' perceptions of the effects of physician-perpetrated abuse. *International Nursing Review*, 57, 321–27.

Ho, J.D., Clinton, J.E., Lappe, M.A., Geegaard, W.G., Williams, M.F., and Miner, J.R. 2011. Introduction of the conducted electrical weapon into a hospital setting. *The Journal of Emergency Medicine*,.41(3), 317–23. doi:10.1016/j.jemermed.2009.09.031.

Hockley, C. 2000. Violence among nurses in the workplace. *Collegian*, 7(4).

Holmes, D., Perron, A.M., and Savoie, M. 2006. Governing therapy choices: power/knowledge in the treatment of progressive renal failure. *Philosophy, Ethics, and Humanities in Medicine*, 1(12).

ICN 2002. *Framework Guidelines for Addressing Workplace Violence in the Health Sector.* [Online]. Available at: http://www.icn.ch/images/stories/documents/

pillars/sew/sew_framework_guidelines_for_addressing_workplace_violence. pdf [accessed: 26 June 2010].

Jazayery, M.A., Polome, E.C., and Winter, W. 1976. *Singuistic and Literary Studies in Honor of Archibald A. Hill: Vol I: General and Theoretical Linguistics.* Amsterdam: Johns Benjamins Publishing Company.

Joint Commission 2008. *Sentinel Event Alert: Behaviors that Undermine a Culture of Safety.* [Online]. Available at: http://www.jointcommission.org/ SentinelEvents/SentinelEventAlert/sea_40.htm [accessed: 6 August 2010].

Kelleher, M.D. 1996. *New Arenas For Violence.* Santa Barbara, California: Praeger Publishing.

Kinney, J.A., and Johnson, D.L. 1993. *Breaking Point: the Workplace Violence Epidemic and What to Do About it.* Charlotte, North Carolina: National Safe Workplace Institute.

Legislative Assembly of Ontario 2009. *Bill 168, Occupational Health and Safety Amendment Act (Violence and Harassment in the Workplace).* [Online]. Available at: http://www.ontla.on.ca/web/bills/bills_detail.do?locale=en&BillI D=2181&BillStagePrintId=4499&btnSubmit=go [accessed: 11 August 2010].

Levin, P.F., Beauchamp, J.B., and Misner, S.T. 1998. Insights of nurses about assault in hospital-based emergency departments. *Image: Journal of Nursing Scholarship,* 30(3), 249–54 .

Meehl, P.E. 1954. *Clinical Versus Statistical Prediction: a Theoretical Analysis and a Review of the Evidence.* Minneapolis: University of Minnesota.

NIOSH 2004. *Workplace Violence Prevention Strategies and Research Needs.* [Online]. Available at: http://www.cdc.gov/niosh/docs/2006-144/pdfs/2006-144.pdf [accessed: 2 August 2010].

Norfolk District Attorney's Office 2007. *Protecting our Caregivers from Workplace Violence.* [Online]. Available at : http://www.mass.gov/da/norfolk/PDF%20 Brochures/Copy%20of%20Workplace%20Violence.pdf [9 September 2010].

Nova Scotia Department of Envionment and Labour 2006. *Strategic Directions: Addressing the Risk of Workplace Violence in Nova Scotia.* [Online]. Available at : http://www.gov.ns.ca/lwd/healthandsafety/docs/ WorkplaceViolenceConsultation.pdf [accessed: 24 June 2010].

OSHA 2002. *Workplace Violence Fact Sheet.* [Online]. Available at http://www. osha.gov/OshDoc/data_General_Facts/factsheet-workplace-violence.pdf [accessed: 5 August 2010].

Paniagua, H., Bond, P., and Thompson, A. 2009. Providing an alternative to zero tolerance policies. *British Journal of Nursing,* 18(10), 619–23.

Phillips, L. and Jorgensen, M.W. 2002. *Discourse Analysis as Theory and Method.* Thousand Oaks, CA: Sage.

Podolak, A. 2000. Is workplace violence in need of refocusing? *Security Management,* 44(6), 152.

Powers, P. 2001. *The Methodology of Discourse Analysis.* Sudbury, MA: Jones and Bartlett.

Rawlinson, M. 1987. Foucault's strategy: knowledge, power, and the specificity of truth. *Journal of Medicine and Philosophy*, 12(4), 372–95.

Richards, R. 2003. Management of workplace violence victims. An ILO/ICN/WHO/PSI Joint Programme Working Paper. Geneva: World Health Organization.

Rintoul, Y., Wynaden, D., and McGowan, S. 2009. Managing aggression in the emergency department: promoting an interdisciplinary approach. *International Emergency Nursing*, 17, 122–7.

RNAO 2009. *Preventing and Managing Violence in the Workplace*. Toronto: Registered Nurses Association of Ontario.

Ruhl, L. 1999. Liberal governance and prenatal care: risk and regulation in pregnancy. *Economy and Society*, 28(1), 95–117.

Sethi, D., Marais, S., Seedat, M., Nurse, J., and Butchart, A. 2004. Handbook for the documentation of interpersonal violence prevention programmes. Department of Injuries and Violence Prevention, World Health Organization: Geneva.

Shaw, S.E. 2010. Reaching the parts that other theories and methods can't reach: how and why a policy-as-discourse approach can inform health-related policy. *Health*, 14(2), 196–212.

Speer, R.A. 1997. The legal implications of workplace violence: planning can prevent harm, liability. *Women Lawyers Journal*, 83(2), 13–19.

Stats Can 2007. *Study: Criminal Victimization in the Workplace*. [Online]. Available at: http://www.statcan.gc.ca.ezproxy.tru.ca/daily-quotidien/070216/dq070216a-eng.htm [accessed 16 August 2010].

Steinman, S. 2003. *Workplace Violence in the Health Sector – Country Case Study: South Africa.* [Online: Joint Programme on Workplace Violence in the Health Sector. Geneva: International Labour Office, International Council of Nurses, World Health Organization and Public Services International]. Available at: http://www.who.int/violence_injury_prevention/violence/interpersonal/en/WVcountrystudysouthafrica.pdf [accessed: 24 August 2010].

Stirling, G. and Higgins, J.E. 2001. Violence in A&E departments: a systematic review of the literature. *Accident and Emergency Nursing*, 9, 77–85.

Taft, S.H., and Nanna, K.M. 2008. What are the sources of health policy that influence nursing practice? *Policy, Politics, & Nursing Practice*, 9(4), 274–87.

Thomas, J.L. 1992. Occupational violent crime: research on an emerging issue. *Journal of Safety Research*, 23(2), 55–62.

Titscher, S., Meyer, M., Wodak, R., and Vetter, E. 2000. *Methods of Text and Discourse Analysis*. Thousand Oaks, CA: Sage.

Vanwiltenburg, S.L. 2007. Workplace violence against registered nurses: an interpretive description. Unpublished master's thesis from the University of British Columbia.

Ventura-Madangeng, J. and Wilson, D. 2009. Workplace violence experienced by registered nurses: a concept analysis. *Nursing Praxis in New Zealand*, 25(3), 37–50.

Wiskow, C. 2003. *Guidelines on Workplace Violence in the Health sector: Comparison of Major Known National Guidelines and Strategies: United Kingdom, Australia, Sweden, USA (OSHA and California)*. [Online: An ILO/ICN/WHO/PSI Joint Programme Working Paper. World Health Organization: Geneva]. Available at: www.who.int/entity/violence_injury_prevention/violence/interpersonal/en/WV_ComparisonGuidelines.pdf. [accessed: 30 August 2010].

Wodak, R. and Meyer, M. 2001. *Methods of Critical Discourse Analysis*. Thousand Oaks, CA: Sage.

Wood, L.A., and Kroger, R.O. 2000. *Doing Discourse Analysis: Methods for Studying Action in Talk and Text*. Thousand Oaks, CA: Sage.

Wynne, R., Clarkin, N., Cox, T., and Griffiths, A. 1997. *Guidance on the Prevention of Violence at Work*. Luxembourg: European Commission DG-V.

Chapter 5

Exploring Violence in a Forensic Hospital: A Theoretical Experimentation

Amélie Perron and Trudy Rudge

Introduction

We would like to start by stating that when this study was first conducted, violence was not identified as an issue requiring investigation in the context of forensic psychiatry. The objectives of the study were to examine role tensions and professional relationships in a newly established Australian forensic hospital[1]. Nurses were formally identified as the leading professional group to run the units of this facility and this entailed the consolidation of some aspects of their professional practice with the concomitant redefinition or disappearance of others. Furthermore, we were not familiar with the work of Latour and Actor-Network Theory (ANT). In other words, ANT did not constitute a theoretical underpinning that allowed us to frame our study. Rather, the decision to explore ANT for the purpose of this research was made *post facto* in light of the complexity in which nurse participants found themselves in their day to day practice.

Our use of ANT was to explore how violence constituted the forensic network. Much research into nursing in such locations positions violence as central partly due to the nature of the population of patients in such a setting. In using ANT we are seeking to explicate how various forms of violence are brought about by the type of network, for instance, violence such as interpersonal conflict, aggression, bullying, self-deprecation, disparagement in staff to staff interactions. In using ANT, this provides a frame to show the way nurses are enrolled in the network, how they associate with other actors (including other health professionals, patients, security measures, risk management policies, professional standards, wider public, the controversial creation of the FH, nursing's long history of defining its purpose, etc.) and leads nurses to both experience and perpetuate these forms of violence in their day-to-day forensic work.

---

1   This study was undertaken while the first author was a visiting postdoctoral fellow with Sydney Nursing School at the University of Sydney.

Background

Scientific literature about forensic psychiatric nursing abounds and systematically reports on the ongoing difficulty for nurses to harmonize two contradictory aspects of their work: caring for mentally ill inmates while also enacting custodial practices and policies in order to manage risk and aggression. In correctional and forensic settings, nurses play a pivotal role in improving patients' mental health through counselling and teaching activities (e.g. problem solving and coping skills, management of pharmacological regimens). Yet in forensic psychiatry, patients are typically perceived as dangerous, violent, and manipulative (Weiskopf 2005). Such representations induce distrust and even suspicion, and may shape nurse-patient relationships and the provision of care.

Nurses practising in correctional and forensic settings are located at the intersection of care and control. Delivering health care to inmates must be carefully balanced against the need for security. Nurses' responsibilities are dictated by these paradoxical mandates which may lead to confusion regarding priorities in the provision of ethical care and patient advocacy (Bernheim 2000). Furthermore, individualized and empathetic care is deemed risky in correctional and forensic settings, and typically results in reprimands and even harassment (Perron and Holmes 2011, Weiskopf 2005). Subsequently, some have questioned the feasibility of caring for inmates in an environment intended to confine, control and punish (Wright 1980). For this reason, and because inmate health outcomes are typically lower than the general population's (Australian Institute of Health and Welfare 2010), new models of psychiatric care provision to offenders have been developed in order to promote a therapeutic (often hospital-based) culture that is more balanced against a custodial culture. This study takes place in one such setting recently established as a free-standing hospital independent from prison administration.

The Study

The study was conducted in a newly built high-risk forensic hospital near a large city in Australia. It provides care to formal forensic patients as defined in the Mental Health Act. The hospital caters to male and female patients as well as young adults and adolescents. It provides intensive inpatient mental health program in acute, subacute, chronic and rehabilitation units. Nurses constitute its largest professional group and are responsible for the provision of clinical care and security interventions. Beside nurses, the multidisciplinary team includes psychiatrists, psychologists, occupational therapists, diversional therapists, dentists and mental health workers. Nurses at the forensic hospital come from various backgrounds. Some have worked at a nearby jail before transferring to the forensic hospital. Others come from mainstream psychiatric facilities, while others have no mental health background (e.g. critical care, paediatrics).

The units are only staffed with health professionals; no corrections or security agents are present. Security agents control the main entrance to the hospital but are not authorised to enter the premises. All health professionals must therefore undergo training in aggression and violence management and are expected to manage situations involving aggressive episodes. Security-related interventions are therefore carried out by health professionals. Interestingly, as we shall see later, this role has somehow befallen the nurses exclusively.

The goal of the study was to examine mental health nurses' perspectives and discourses in a high-security forensic psychiatry facility; to describe the way nurses manage this type of practice environment and harmonize their various, and at times conflicting, obligations; to examine challenges as well as resources; and to explore the contribution of research to support nurses' practice. The lead author carried out the recruitment and data collection which spanned three months. Ethical approval was obtained from the relevant institutions. Fourteen registered nurses were recruited for this study (six females, eight males) based on their interest to participate. Every participant had the opportunity to seek further information about the study. The purpose of the research was clarified as well as confidentiality issues. Participants signed a consent form, chose a pseudonym, and filled a short demographic questionnaire. Individual interviews were conducted in private offices on the units and lasted between one and two and half hours. All interviews except one were audio recorded and transcribed. Observation was also carried out on two acute and one chronic wards, between five and 14 hours a week (day, late evenings and weekends); it was however limited to the nursing station as the researcher could not circulate without a staff member. As most staff-staff interactions took place in the nursing station, observation was nonetheless informative and it confirmed many situations reported by participants.

The purpose of this study was to explore nurses' role in working in and managing a new forensic facility. Although professional roles and tensions were initially the object of inquiry, conflict and violence were not originally identified as a focus but surfaced, in various forms, as prominent issues for the participants. Because of this emergence, led by the participants themselves, and because of the complexity of this new practice setting, ANT appeared as an appropriate and innovative approach to frame nurses' perceptions and to understand the intricacies of nursing relationships and representations that make up the social space of the forensic hospital.

Actor-Network Theory (ANT)

ANT is an anti-essentialist approach developed by Bruno Latour and Michel Callon to understand how networks form and perform social phenomena, their occurrence, their meanings, their representations, and their effects. ANT sets forth a relational materiality: "Actor network theory is a ruthless application of semiotics. It tells that entities take their form and acquire their attributes as a result of their relations with other entities. In this scheme of things entities have no inherent qualities" (Law 1999: 3). Various concepts are central to ANT. It is impossible to define all of them here but a review of the main ones is necessary for the purpose of our discussion.

Network is defined as a "group of unspecified relationships among entities of which the nature itself is undetermined" (Callon 1993: 263). Networks are the result of associations and interactions between various entities. Such entities can be human, non human (objects), or semiotics. Importantly, Latour insists that these entities carry no essential differences between them; such differences are an artefact, a product generated by and through networks themselves. This leads to a point of contention for many sociologists: according to Latour, one needs to "inquire about the agency of all sorts of objects" (2005: 76). Objects are part of the collective, they carry action across the network, and as such, they should be examined on the same level as human actors with whom they associate.

Translation is a key concept of ANT. Translation is the process through which networked entities are attributed roles, and are distributed. Translation refers to the way identities and subjectivities are formed, and interactions are governed:

> By translation we understand all the negotiations, intrigues, calculations, acts of persuasion and violence, thanks to which an actor or force takes, or causes to be conferred on itself, authority to speak or act on behalf of another actor or force (Callon and Latour 1981: 279).

Translation occurs through four stages: *problematization* – a primary actor identifies a problem and as such establishes itself as indispensable. Other actors who will make up the solution are also identified, and identities, interests and goals are established); *interessement* – recruitment of other actors who will assist the primary actor(s) in solving the issue; *enrollment* – all roles are defined and actors formally accept to be part of the process: and *mobilization* – the primary actor serves as a spokesperson and further mobilizes public interest.

Translation can provide networks with both stability and durability by ensuring networked entities are aligned and coordinated. This in turn crystallizes collective understandings and meanings associated with particular phenomena, and standardizes actions. Van Loon (2005: 41) states that "For Latour, networks are not all-powerful uncontested systemic forces but (...) rather fragile achievements, prone to collapse and disorder. It is the doubling of power and fragility." The links that hold a network together can be material (e.g. biochemical bonds, roads) or semiotic (e.g. rumours, research accounts, spiritual beliefs, symbols). Regardless of their nature, these links are needed to stabilize the network and make it functional.

Associations are key to understanding the way the social works. Latour argues that the social is not to be understood as a sort of backdrop or context according to which phenomena are to be investigated and understood. Rather, "the social" is constituted of multiple, ongoing and complex associations and dissociations between various human and non-human entities. As such, group formations and their study are considered one of the first foundations of a "sociology of associations." Latour is not interested in groups (such as nurses, ethnic minorities, or parents) and does not subscribe to the norm that groups are fixed and stable units. Nor is he interested in specific concepts, such as race or power. He suggests instead to focus on "the study of associations between different materials and relations through which orders and hierarchies are made (and unmade) and through which society is held together and made durable" (Ruming 2009: 454). In other words, he seeks to focus on group *formation* instead of group *existence*, and to understand the way social effects or social processes are the result of a myriad of such associations. This is a radical shift from "traditional" sociology. Latour is highly critical of the sociological tradition according to which one uses a particular concept or phenomenon (e.g. power) as a starting point to explain various social processes when in fact "power" is the phenomenon to be explained: "[Sociologists] have simply confused what they should explain with the explanation. They begin with society or other social aggregates, whereas one should end with them" (Latour 2005: 8).

Actants and *actors* are often used interchangeably in ANT literature, including in the present chapter in order to simplify this overview of ANT. Actors designate agents that enter an association with other actors. ANT reconsiders "relationships as an open ended set of interactions where the actors (…) do not pre-exist the relationships; the actor is generated in and by these relationships" (Cordella and Shaikh 2006: 9). A stable network means a greater number of enrolled actors. Actors are central in shaping social phenomena. While one is tempted to define them as a source of action, Latour cautions that a source of action is difficult, if not impossible, to pinpoint mainly because there are multiple locations from which action unfolds, retreats and circulates:

> the word actor directs our attention to the complete dislocation of the action, warning us that it is not a coherent, controlled, well-rounded, and clean-edged affair. By definition, action is *dislocated*. Action is borrowed, distributed, suggested, influenced, dominated, betrayed, translated. … it represents the major source of uncertainty about the origin of action (Latour 2005: 46).

An actor is *made* to act by, and therefore it relies on, a complex assemblage of other actors and relationships (a network) that make actions possible. A clock, for instance, is an actor in its own right because it can mobilize a range of heterogeneous entities to do certain things (for instance, to build it, make it accurate using the atomic clock, use it to organize a national transport system, or coordinate business meetings or a surgical intervention), thus generating movements, meanings, goals and representations. Importantly, the network of entities mobilized around a clock is hermetic, because its connections are stable and rarely questioned or challenged by those who use this clock, let alone recognize how they are brought into associations with others who are mobilized by its effects.

Actors may be human beings, objects, symbols, concepts or gossip. They include those entities that have been explicitly and decisively excluded from social action by traditional sociology because of their supposed lack of agency. Yet Latour argues adamantly that any 'thing' that changes, inhibits, creates, or transforms something is an actor. "Actor" is then defined as something that "makes a difference" by carrying any social action forward and taking it further, without being burdened with issues of intentionality. This delivers another blow to the idea that society and social affairs are exclusively shaped by social forces or social processes (e.g. power) that support, bring together and hold, in and of themselves, the social body (Latour 2005).

Through ANT, the "social" is subjected to a radical ontological shift; it now refers to

> a movement, a displacement, a transformation, a translation, an enrollment. It is
> an association between entities which are in no way recognizable as being social
> in the ordinary manner, *except* during the brief moment when they are reshuffled
> together' (Latour 2005: 64–5).

Latour's (1993: 10–11) perspective challenges and deconstructs various traditional dualisms that are prized by Modern thinkers: nature/culture, society/technology, human/non human, material/virtual, in their quest to "purify" each domain and construct them as separate. Modernity comes with a set of practices, including a set of "purification" practices with "creates two entirely distinct ontological zones: that of human beings on the one hand; that of nonhumans on the other." Latour (1993) however suggests that this purification process has never been achieved and that, therefore, "we have never been modern."

Using the example of power, Latour argues that "it's so important to maintain that power, like society, is the final result of a process and not a reservoir, a stock, or a capital that will automatically provide an explanation. Power and domination have to be produced, made up, composed." We believe this is highly relevant for the examination of other social effects, such as violence. Examining the intricacies of what we term the "forensic network" is useful to understand how violence comes into being, is experienced within the network, and becomes an actor in its own right.

Breeding Conflict and Violence in the Forensic Network

Role definition is especially critical in light of the current push (in Australia and elsewhere) to make any care facility multidisciplinary in nature. Negotiating role boundaries is integral to interactions within the network; it constitutes a common source of conflict and tensions for nurses who feel that their expertise is devalued, encroached upon or relegated to security:

Sophie: We've employed all these OT's and psychologists and they do the groups… It makes me angry, the nurses used to do these activities… I resent the fact that they come in and do what nurses used to do.

Eli: I've had quite a heated exchange with the art therapist, she tried to tell me about medication, and I said "Look, I don't tell you how to finger paint so you don't tell me about medication…", and we need to be very weary of the blurring of the lines. It's nice being multidisciplinary and everybody has the same approach, but let's just stick to what we do. It's good that they let us know "In my group he wasn't so good and I think he's decompensating," that's great, that's good information but leave it at that.

Nurses report being heavily involved in running therapy and skill acquisition groups up until allied health staff were hired:

Sophie: Us nurses would list everything that patients were going to get out of the group and I would speak to the patients about that… and I don't think the psychologists and the OT's do the groups as well as the nurses did, I really don't think they do … It's just another slap in the face, not feeling valued.

Eli: One thing that was also brought up was the groups, which has been taken from the nursing staff to the OT staff. [Doctor X], a consultant who is very keen to having nurses running groups, because, you know, that's what we do, that's what we did and we're not just here as security staff for the OT's and that has to be made very clear, and I'm quite happy saying that this is, at the end of the day, a nurse-led unit.

As Eli alludes to, most participants strongly resent the fact that the role redistribution has left nurses mostly in charge of "the dirty work":

Damien: What I understood about psychiatric or mental health nursing was, it's watered down, it is grossly eroded to what it was. When I started, we ran the groups, we were the social workers, we were the OT, we were the psychologists, and we were "it."

Researcher: So what is nursing left with?

Damien: They're left with custodial behaviour, that's what they do.

Chris: We're meant to be a multidisciplinary team and it just seems the nurses do a lot of the dirty work … The value of the nursing opinion, even though it's required, no, it's not there.

Becky: The best defined part of [nurses' role], it's the security part… as usual the nurses are the cannon fodder, the persons that are expected to manage the aggressive people. Allied health staff do all of the training for aggression management, the physical techniques, the steps of de-escalation, the importance of good relationships, communication, behavioral emergencies. All of them do that, yet none of them act as part of our response team, none of them will jump in unless they're explicitly told to. Yet there's the nurses, expected to dash around and … I'm sick of us always being the ones that are responsible for it and no one else.

This sense of disparagement towards psychiatric nurses is echoed by other participants' in various ways:

> *Eli:* We've got nurses here who aren't trained in any way in psychiatry at all, and I think that's wrong… one or two nurses in orientation apparently asked how to do their mental status exam!… I think it says that… the value goes down, our value goes down.
>
> *Mandy:* People used to put down psych nurses … there is a nurse I know, said that mental health nurses are the lowest of the low… I said "you know what lady, it takes a specialist to work in this area."

Nurses carry this disparagement with them as they bear the stigma of being a psychiatric nurse and working with a highly stigmatised population.

As seen earlier, role negotiation and definition is a powerful act in ANT because it is a crucial step to generate consensus and stabilize the forensic network. It is also a politically and emotionally charged process, even among nurses, as evidenced by the tense reactions of those who feel pressured into playing a more prominent security role mainly because of their gender, age and fitness level:

> *Thomas:* Half of the nurses are really unfit, some can't run one lap around the hospital, more than half of the nurses here are females, some of them have a bodyweight of 40 kg. I can't possibly ask them to restrain a 150 kg man, so this creates problems. If the same strong boys are the primary respondents all the time, it's discrimination. We are all getting the same salary, you know what I mean?

Paradoxically, while nurses who fit this ideal feel pressured and discriminated against in situations requiring physical interventions, those who do not typify this profile report similar feelings:

> *Sophie:* I did my fair share of restraining and stuff, but because I can't do it anymore, I just feel that I'm not valued.

Tensions around role definition are also evident in the reactions of agents who have been explicitly excluded from the new forensic hospital:

> *Mandy:* We went to the cafeteria for lunch and the guards saw the new faces, they asked where we were from, I said from the forensic hospital. Oh, wow, it was the worst thing to say! This woman, a corrections officer, said, "I see you've come to get your head kicked in." She's pointing her finger at me, "Do you realize you need us? Well, we hope you fall flat on your face and when you do,

[*slams hand on table*] we'll be there to take over. Because one day you could be attacked by a prisoner and we'll just look the other way."

Several nurses reported incidents such as the ones above and spoke of the multiple forms of conflict and even bullying brought on by the dominance of nurses' security role in the formation of the forensic network. Many former prison nurses spoke of the prevailing "love-hate" relationship between nurses and correctional agents and how the new forensic hospital allowed them to move to a "healthier," "less toxic," workplace. Such a move implied new associations and interactions with health- and therapy-driven professionals and policies, as well as offenders redefined as *patients*. However, the move alone into a new structure was not enough to end the animosity and start anew:

> *Fiona:* Something that has been addressed in the interaction with each other here is a little tiny bit of aggression in the tone used, sort of borderlining onto bullying… It pretty much was normal in the prison. The way we interacted with each other was at times aggressive. The officers with us, us with the officers, nurses with the nurses, officers with the officers. And it just… it permeated you.

This speaks to the way actions (e.g. bullying) are carried forward and sustained from one setting to the next, despite a clear new direction meant to break from prison culture.

The creation of the forensic hospital has generated heavy controversy. Nurses speak about the way this negatively affects them by eliminating room for error and creating a climate of uncertainty and suspicion. This intensifies the scrutiny under which they find themselves and further constrains their practice:

> *Fiona:* I think basically [administrators] are just being paranoid so there's a blanket thing… They're just being overcautious. They want to cover their backs, they don't want anything happening, no incidents! Because they've got the state government on their back so you've got all this political stuff going on. [The forensic hospital] is in the spotlight, it's in the spotlight big time!
> *Eli:* There's more scrutiny out there now, there's more outside people looking in, the ombudsman, everybody is here to question what we do.

As a result, nurses become objects of surveillance themselves, which translates into a culture of blame perpetuated by managers and nurses alike:

> *Eli:* I can understand management monitoring nurses, but nurses trying to dob each other in, you know, that's how it's perceived. I think monitoring is a very nice way to put it, but really, you're spying on me, and once that starts, that's a downward slope.

> *Bryce:* One thing that I found, when I first came here, was, a huge blame culture... it's so easy to blame somebody else for somebody's human error and the finger pointing that goes on is unnecessary.
> *Eli:* There are so many things in place so that if someone is not performing, you must make a note of it, or if someone's made a mistake, you must do an incident report and it's a culture of catching people, almost, blaming.
> *Chris:* It's to do with the nurses... there is still a culture of blame and I think it more or less comes down to us.

Because the forensic hospital is a new facility, it is still evolving and working out how best to fulfil its mandate. Participants described current policies as necessary to provide some structure to the running of the unit but also as very restricting and creating constraints and tensions where human experiences are concerned:

> *Damien:* I've looked at the policy and I would go, "Here we go, another monumental library of policies" and I think that's the sad thing in this state modern health... it's policy, policy, policy. And it would be more intense in here.
> *Bryce:* There are the black and white policies and procedures. But there's always grey when you're dealing with humans and you need to have grey, and yet, in this environment, the black and white seems to prevail.

These excerpts exemplify the way non human entities, such as policies and procedures, commission particular types of representations and behaviours within the forensic hospital. These quotes are congruent with ANT's claim that objects or ideas can instigate actions and interactions (e.g. among staff or between staff and patients) as much as humans can; as such they are equal actors because they bend, regulate, and standardize nursing practice.

Participants report significant confusion related to the fact that policies are still being developed as the hospital evolves and establishes itself. This confusion is described as resulting in nurses doubting themselves and experiencing loss of confidence, some despite their vast experience:

> *Jasmine:* There's more management here. It's ok if responsibilities are well defined but there's still confusion sometimes... you need to double check because information is missing. You feel you're not doing your job right, you feel foolish.
> *Bryce:* You'll have one nurse unit manager on the shift with a set of rules and the nurse unit manager on the next shift will have his own, and that can cause some real irritating issues. And I think that's where staff just become confused and irritated and end up trying to do the right thing but end up in shit.

Participants go on to report that this climate of confusion has detrimental effects on the way nurses associate and interact with each other, despite the fact that they operate within what is meant to be a hospital culture:

Melinda: If we give patients tolerance, we have to give ourselves tolerance and I think that nurses are notoriously bad at fostering the young, supporting younger nurses, they tend to demoralize them and hate them and spit them out sometimes. *Chris:* One of the issues I have with nurses is that they're very quick to bait others... I just find that there's an awful lot of that... they turn on each other very quickly and in here it's consistent.

"Strong personalities" are clearly identified as problematic, and some nurses reported being belittled, hassled, and bullied by nurse colleagues.

Kevin: There are many clinical managers so they all make decisions, so as a nurse, working here, you cannot fully use your skills or knowledge, because if they make a decision, they don't agree with you, you have to listen to them. *Mandy:* You've got an ongoing issue with staff, if it's two strong personalities, they just don't talk, there's a degree of bullying. *Eli:* We've got some quite strong willed, quite opinionated people, quite strong personalities, and at some point, that's going to have effects.

In order to "counter" strong personalities, nurses need to develop a personality of equal strength. The problem and the solution thus become blurred, as "strong personalities" sustain and breed each other, making nurses' relationships highly reciprocal:

Mandy: It takes a very strong person to work in a setting like this... if people get you down, don't let them get on top of you. What I found is, working in this setting has made me a very strong person.

In this study, it repeatedly came to our attention that violence among nursing staff was prevalent and constituted a disabling and distressing experience for many participants. Violence (in any form) is an important component of human interactions because it can motivate strong relationships (by stressing the need for effective teamwork) or it can create tensions, therefore displacing (and multiplying) the locus of violence:

Mandy: I found that there was so much negativity with the nurses which projected onto the patients.

Some participants suggest that these issues are likely to arise out of any forensic environment. This may be explained by the fact that, given its mandate to provide care for mentally ill offenders, it is likely to enrol the same actors and generate the same type of associations no matter where it gets formed:

Mandy: It doesn't matter what city you work in, and even what country you live in because same staff, different country, basically.

> *Becky:* It was so exciting, like, wow, the potential is just amazing! And unfortunately what they did was pretty much just shift the same old shit into a new building, and they really missed an opportunity to put people into positions of authority that would change the culture, and it was a shame.

This leads to an important aspect of the way networks get formed and for what purpose. Actors create a particular space in the network, one, in this case, that can be constituted as "therapeutic" and "also clinical." However, nurses' relocations into the forensic network have led to the creation of a "secure" space that duplicates largely a correctional model of forensic psychiatry because it translates much of the same interests, symbols, and representations into its current location. While nurses were deemed an appropriate group to staff the hospital because of their combined clinical and therapeutic competences, knowledge and skills, it seems "security" and "control" have remained the *modus operandi* through and by which associations acquire meaning and further enrollment occurs, thus leading to "missed opportunities" for the materialization of a new, therapeutically-driven, ethos.

On the Enrollment and Associations of Forensic Nurses

The inception of the forensic hospital has created noteworthy unrest because its security is deemed insufficient. Its creation is an ambiguous (and controversial) event, contingent upon discursive articulations by powerful players who either celebrate it as a therapeutic, technological, and architectural achievement, or dismiss it as a naïve and risky experiment. Credibility of its practices is integral to making the forensic hospital viable, especially where public perceptions are concerned. For example, there is a view among many stakeholders that the hospital is not punitive enough as an environment to rehabilitate offenders. The following participant describes how public anxiety and pressure seep into the hospital and govern nurses' attitudes towards patients:

> *Bryce:* We need to address that psychological issue of: Why do I feel the need to punish these people? Why is it that I have this overwhelming desire, is it something that I adopt as a community pressure? Is it community pressure that requires me to inflict punishment? Is it that I'm adopting the position of the victims that requires this level of punishment on these people?

Here, a non-tangible entity, such as public opinion, becomes a full-blown actor in the forensic network because it may precipitate punitive or custodial behaviours on nurses' part as well as constitute hospital culture.

As a primary actor in the forensic network, the state government holds tremendous power to "set an agenda and a cultural tone" (Manning 2002: 658). This is all the more important since the creation of the forensic hospital is a controversial and problematic event. Specific actors (in favour of the project) thus need to be enrolled in the network (professional groups, academic agents, etc.) while others must be neutralized (opposing interest groups, media agents, members of the wider public). The professional base of the hospital is a pivotal component to lend further credibility. Nurses are considered useful by administrators because they embody the values and the skills needed to deliver therapeutic, patient-centered interventions balanced with security. Nurses' experiences within this new workplace gravitate around this professional feature which governs how roles and responsibilities are distributed across the hospital.

The forensic nursing role is described as follows:

> *Becky:* Clinically, you've got to have those generic mental health skills, you've got to be able to engage with someone, establish a rapport, do a good mental status assessment, be holistic on your care planning, talk, be able to engage with someone about their hopes and goals, look at some fairly realistic goals and the change to help them get there, recovery focus... but I guess what makes it a specifically forensic nursing job, is you need to actually go there and talk about the offence.
>
> *Melinda:* We actually have to get the ability and the language to bring [the offence] into conversations and to start addressing it... You set things to work on that are real and have value for the patient and you don't instil false hope... looking at the skills deficits and helping the person to own those and work with those.
>
> *Kevin:* These patients need mental, physical, spiritual care, they have a history, many have no family support so they need more support, not just medication. Counselling is also very important. You need to sit and talk with them for 10 or 20 minutes... spend time with them. Sometimes no intervention is the best intervention... these patients are very special, they don't just have mental health problems, they have behavioural problems, substance abuse, so you have to be flexible.

The security aspects constitute a major focus of nurses' statements and many discussed the difficulty of harmonising their roles:

> *Chris:* Strip searching patients for matches and stuff like that, I can't justify in my head, it just unbalances everything. One moment you're trying to build a relationship and the next you're required to completely put that aside and be a very different person ... it's just hard, you have to change roles very quickly.

Participants stressed the importance of being weary of safety issues but also stressed that security interventions were not punitive but remained therapeutically focused.

Nurses recruited by the forensic hospital have to accept the roles that are defined for them in order to make the hospital functional. This entails an important transformation to integrate security-related functions (e.g. cutlery counts, searches, restraining and/or secluding patients):

> *Chris:* It was a huge concern when I came here and realized there was no
> security… It's above and beyond what I went to university for. I feel like it's a
> corrections officer's job to do that.

Latour argues that networks and actors continuously need a high level of alignment
and convergence of goals and interests. This is equally true of developing and
more established networks.

> *Melinda:* I think that, A, you have to have your goals with where the institution
> is going, B, you have to have people who are interested in driving it there and C,
> you have to have your own vision and your own values. I think you have to have
> some self awareness of what sort of professional or operator you want to be,
> where you would like your practice to go and whether that could fit within the
> boundaries of what the institution is setting up. And if not, you need to move on.

Consequently, nurses who reject the assignment of security roles cannot be
enrolled in the network:

> *Fiona:* A lot of nurses refused to do it [act as the security team]. They didn't
> really think it through, about what the ramifications were of coming here and
> how our role would change and I think a couple of nurses actually went back
> to the prison because they didn't feel that that was a part of their role as nurses.

Through security-driven functions, nurses are allocated a specific location within
the forensic hospital network, one that rests on, and generates, a particular
understanding of risk management. Where risk and violence are raised as significant
concerns, they are typically discussed as patient traits, and as originating "within"
them and their offence:

> *Bryce:* Because these people have committed a crime they need to be punished
> in some way, although we see them as patients and even so this is a forensic
> hospital, *(Deep voice, taps finger on table)* "They've still committed the crime
> and we've got to remind ourselves every handover what that crime was."
> *(Normal voice)* It was recently introduced that during handover, the index
> offence had to be cited. The clinical managers brought that in… because of the
> new staff and the need to impress on them the need for security and to maintain
> the level of security, that by introducing the index offence into the handover, you
> would stress the level of risk.

We argue that the process described by Bryce is part of establishing a common
understanding, a consensus around the level of risk (defined by the index offence)
and ensuring that nursing interventions with "risky individuals" are consistent,
which is crucial to maintaining convergence and stability within the network.

Interestingly, nurses themselves are identified as posing a risk (actual or potential) to the organisation and participants report being treated accordingly:

Mandy: Sometimes treatment from the [security] staff out there is horrendous, almost to the point where I feel they're treating us like criminals.
Kevin: Because here security is high, as a staff I feel we are locked up too.
Damien: Whether it's a maximum security or a medium security or a minimum security hospital, it's still a permanent staff and you're working in a hospital. Why should you be subjected to this constant barrage of steel doors and cameras and X-rays, it's ridiculous!

The configuration of the forensic network requires a particular set of associations among its various actors. Following participants' experiences, it is clear that these associations lead to specific interactions that generate various forms of violence, described as discrimination, conflict, self-deprecation, disparagement, bullying, and coercion. However, given the hospital's mandate, its "cutting-edge" quality and the population it cares for, the question arises as to whether the types of representations and priorities that it generates predictably produce violent practices that are directly experienced by nurses. The following discussion explores this point further.

Discussion

Using ANT in public health, Van Loon (2005: 40) describes a "junctural zone" where various actors meet, including (in our study) diagnostic categories, state laws, public anxiety, community pressure to "punish" offenders, safety regulations, psychiatrists, the media, politicians, stereotypes and assumptions about mental illness, suspected brain anomalies, surveillance technologies, violence, patient charts, and particular legal categories such as *non criminally responsible*. The forensic hospital brings all of these entities together into a forensic network configuration. This configuration, if 'assembled' and 'connected' effectively, will provide, through social, legal, economic, and political clout, meaning and significance to the hospital and its workforce.

The forensic hospital configures its staff as much as its staff configures it through formal and informal assumptions about "forensic work," especially forensic nursing work. In this regard, ANT contributes to the current theories on power because it takes into account the mechanics of power through and by which associations and interactions are mobilized, stabilized, and made durable. Power is not considered to be a form of ownership, but rather a form of influence reflected in the number of entities that are enrolled in the network.

Violence in a forensic setting may originate from various sources and forensic patients are typically the 'usual suspects' of violent behaviours. However, given the way the forensic network is itself linked to other networks (e.g. media representations of criminality, public opinion, etc.), it is difficult (impossible, we argue) to pinpoint precisely where violence begins and where it ends. What we see instead is that these particular network configurations make possible the manifestation of bullying and violent behaviours as well as their spread through interactions with other (human and non-human) actors. As seen earlier, policies and nurses alike may be vectors of violence, namely in the shape of discrimination, exclusion, suspicion, and blame.

The hospital was created in order to address mental health care provision to disordered offenders who are deemed dangerous and violent. Paradoxically, the way all elements of the network associate and interact with one another has created a space in which one of nurses' greatest concern is not patients and their dangerousness, but other matters such as public scrutiny, discrimination among allied health staff, the devaluing of nurses' knowledge, and policies in the making. This aspect supports Latour's claim that non human entities constitute actors of the same importance as humans. They mediate and make possible multiple and ongoing social (possibly violent) processes; they are therefore more than mere "social props."

Despite their highly dynamic nature, networks develop and sustain stability and durability over time. "Younger" networks, such as the selected setting, are likely then to rely on existing structures (e.g. ideas, persons, policies) in order to grow and establish themselves within and alongside other networks. In this particular case, it seems that traditions and representations derived from prison-based practices and culture have made their way into collective representations and management of risk and violence, despite a desire to deploy professional practices that are more consistent with a therapy and treatment ethos. This is particularly felt by nurses, who identify issues around security as problematic in several ways. The informal attribution of security roles, in particular, engages nurses in a way that detracts them from care interventions, despite the fact that the forensic hospital is meant to be led by nurses. It appears as though nurses mobilize a certain idea of "security" as it is imposed onto them, making "security" yet another powerful actor in the forensic network. We argue that nurses engaged in being "therapeutic" are unsupported in this role. Participants describe the devastating effects of this shift as hostility between and within groups. Indeed, "risk" and its management have mobilized a "security" network through the mobilization and concretization of the ideas of dangerousness and violence, rather than the planned "therapeutic network" of government policy and strategy.

We argue, contentiously perhaps, that violence is inherent to the forensic network. Violence is a recurring theme in the construction and understanding of forensic psychiatric work. It is typically signified as a trait 'inherent' to forensic patients who integrate the network because of (violent) criminal behaviours. Interestingly, participants in this study did not discuss patient violence but described instead the way violent practices pervade the forensic hospital and are sustained through current policy and public controversy around the safety of this model of care and treatment. Violence, then, can be seen as a force, a concept, a symbol that is fluid, flexible, and easily mobilized, displaced and relocated throughout the network, through ongoing processes of translation and enrollment. As discussed throughout this chapter, violence pervades the network, and it may travel along its multiple connections. This is so because an array of various entities is mobilized and translated into the network around the need to manage risk, aggression and violence, rather than the construction of a therapeutic space (in which nurses had a designated clinical role to play). Violence is therefore a central actor in the way the network is organized, acquires meaning and functionality, and operates as part of the social body. Because of this central position, we suggest that violence constitutes a powerful stabilising force of the forensic network despite its potential to disturb and dislocate social spaces.

Final Remarks

This study has allowed us to explore the constitution of violence in a new forensic facility, but it has also enabled a discussion using new theoretical constructs that may be useful to nursing as practice, research, and discipline. ANT is a highly dynamic perspective and we believe it can engage with more complexity than interpersonal, institutional or structural perspectives on violence, conflict, and aggression.

It is clear from our data that issues around bullying and violence were pivotal for our participants. Through participants' accounts, they appear to be a powerful driving force across the network and they reflect the political nature of nursing work in forensic psychiatry. Experiences of violence are certainly not unique to this forensic environment; however this setting does imply particular entities or events that become actors themselves (e.g. controversy, newness of the facility, public opinion on crime and justice, etc.).

Nurse participants also expressed positive work experiences in the new hospital, including a focus on health/therapy instead of custody/punishment, productive relationships with patients, potential for teamwork and growth, and a chance at changing the culture. However, violence turned out to be a very disabling and thwarting reality for many, namely because it was prevalent yet normalized into the work environment itself. The forensic network is thus a relational configuration through which conflict, aggression and violence travel. Paradoxically, this new forensic hospital is both part of the solution and part of the problem to risk and violence: it constitutes a zone for the (re)production of order but also a site of struggle, where various meanings of particular contingencies (for example, mental illness, aggression) may conflict and therefore mobilize different levels of concerns, priorities, and interventions. It creates a zone where "risky" individuals (offenders) are grouped and confined (removed from society), but also where violence may be more likely to erupt in various, subtle, and dislocated forms.

References

Australian Institute of Health and Welfare. 2010. *The Health of Australia's Prisoners 2009*. Cat. no. PHE 123. Canberra: AIHW.

Bernheim, J.C. 2000. Éthique et prison. *Éthique Publique – Revue Internationale d'Éthique Sociale et Gouvernementale*, 2(1), 171–76.

Callon, M. 1993. Variety and irreversibility in networks of technique conception and adoption, in *Technology and the Wealth of Nations: The Dynamics of Constructed Advantage*, edited by D. Foray and C. Freemann. New York: Pinter Publishers, 232–68.

Callon, M. and Latour, B. 1981. Unscrewing the big Leviathan: how actors macrostructure reality and how sociologists help them to do so, in *Advances in Social Theory and Methodology. Toward an Integration of Micro and Macro Sociologies*, edited by K.D. Knorr-Cetina and A.V. Cicourel. Boston: Routledge & Kegan Paul, 277–303.

Cordella, A. and Shaikh, M. 2006. From epistemology to ontology: challenging the constructed truth of ANT. *London School of Economics and Political Science Department of Information Systems Working Paper Series*, 44.

Latour, B. 1993. *We Have Never Been Modern*. Cambridge, MA: Harvard University Press.

Latour, B. 2005. *Reassembling the Social: An Introduction to Actor-Network Theory*. New York: Oxford University Press.

Law, J. 1999. After ANT: complexity, naming and topology, in *Actor Network Theory and After*, edited by J. Law and J. Hassard. Oxford, UK: Blackwell Publishing, 1–14.

Manning, N. 2002. Actor networks, policy networks and personality disorder. *Sociology of Health and Illness*, 24(5), 644–66.

Perron, A. and Holmes, D. 2011. Constructing mentally ill inmates: nurses' discursive practices in corrections. *Nursing Inquiry*, 18(1), 1–14.

Ruming, K. 2009. Following the actors: mobilising an actor-network theory methodology in geography. *Australia Geographer*, 40(4), 451–69.

Van Loon, J. 2005. Epidemic space. *Critical Public Health*, 15(1), 39–52.

Weiskopf, C.S. 2005. Nurses' experience of caring for inmate patients. *Journal of Advanced Nursing*, 49(4), 336–43.

Wright, K. 1980. A re-examination of correctional alternatives. *International Journal of Offender Therapy and Comparative Criminology*, 24, 179–92.

Chapter 6

Nurses' Failure to Report Elder Abuse in Long-Term Care: An Exploratory Study

Gloria Hamel-Lauzon and Sylvie Lauzon

Introduction

According to a World Health Organisation report (Krug, Dahlberg, Mercy, Zwi, and Lozano-Ascencio 2002), elder abuse (EA) is one of the leading global public health issues and societal problems of our time. This phenomenon may become even more important in the future given the aging of the population which is defined by the augmentation of the proportion aged 65 years and its increased risk of frailty. Indeed, it is estimated that over 6 per cent of the aged population are victims of some form of abuse whether they live alone, with others in the community or in residential facilities (Cooper, Selwood, and Livingston 2008) and it is well documented that dependency on others for care is linked to EA (Bonnie and Wallace 2003).

Defined as the "(a) intentional actions that cause harm or serious risk of harm, whether or not harm is intended, to a vulnerable elder by a caregiver or a person who is in a trust relationship with the elder or (b) failure by a caregiver to satisfy the elder's needs or to protect the elder from harm" (Lachs and Pillemer 2004: 1264), EA is definitely a phenomenon that occurs in many forms.

Context and Background

Experts in the domain (Burgess et al. 2005, Daly and Jogerst 2001, Lachs and Pillemer 1995) agree on five types of abuse. *Physical abuse* consists of an intentional act resulting in injuries. Rough behaviours involve the use of physical restraints or inappropriate use of medication. *Psychological abuse* includes all actions perpetrated with the purpose of causing moral or emotional distress. It can include verbal threats, insults, derogatory comments, intimidation, infantilization or condescendence. *Financial exploitation* is expressed by misappropriation of funds or belongings. *Sexual abuse* can be described as all sexual actions committed without consent such as rape, sexual touching and exhibitionism. Finally, *neglect*, which can be active or passive, is the caregiver's failure to provide the care required by the elderly person's condition. Active negligence consists of purposely avoiding essential tasks such as mouth care, ignoring a bedridden patient or refusing to answer the call bell, whereas passive negligence relates to insufficient knowledge to provide proper care to the patient (Cario 2005, Bonnie and Wallace 2003, Namiash 2000).

A systematic review of 49 studies conducted all over the world concluded that more than 6 per cent of the older general populationreportbeing victim of abuse (Cooper, Selwood and Livingston 2008) and several local surveys (Bonnie and Wallace 2003, Hawes 2003, Ens 2002) indicate that long-term care (LTC) facilities are not exempt from this inexcusable situation despite their precise mandate to ensure the well-being and dignity of all residents. In the Province of Québec, all LTC institutions are bound by strict provincial legislation that obliges them to state clearly their commitment to high-level care in a home-like environment. LTC facilities are also provided with guidelines for the development of each resident's care plan. Care is to be given and monitored according to the best clinical studies available and in complete respect of the residents' rights. Staff is expected to constantly improve the quality and safety of residents' health. However, despite the existence of clear mandates as well as specific guidelines and expectations, abuse of the elderly residents is still present in LTC facilities.

Reviews of medical files (Allen, Kellet, and Gruman 2003) and interviews with nurses (Georgen 2004, MSSS 2004, CNO 2004) suggest that almost half of the residents have suffered at least one episode of abuse and that a high percentage of nurses witness abuse of elderly residents. There is also ample evidence that nurses under-report the abuse they witness (Almogue, Weiss, Marcus, and Beloosky 2010, Levine 2003, Harrel et al. 2002, Glendenning and Kingston 1999). Moreover, Gray-Vickerey (2005) believes that for each case reported, five are not. Yet, all nurses working in LTC must adhere to a code of ethics and are professionally accountable for the protection of this particularly vulnerable population (OIIQ 2002). They have the legal and moral obligation to report incompetent, illegal or unethical acts supposedly done for the patients' safety and well-being (Malmedal, Hammevold, and Saveman 2009, Baker and Heitkemper 2005, Miller 2005, Neno and Neno 2005, OIIQ 2000).

Nurses' failure to report the abuse they witness in LTC facilities is still poorly understood. Probably because of the very sensitive nature of the phenomenon, whistleblowing studies are few in number and have been conducted mostly in the community and in acute care settings. They do however shed some light on the topic. First, nurses may be unable to recognize abuse when it occurs. Saveman, Norberg, and Hallberg (1992) observed that nurses (n = 21) experienced uncertainty and ambiguity in the presence of elder abuse and a recent study among physicians and nurses (Cooper, Selwood, and Livingston 2008) reported a lack of confidence in defining, identifying and reporting abuse. Second, some authors contend that the duty of whistleblowing creates a dilemma for nurses torn between their patient advocacy role and their loyalty towards their peers and the organisation in which they work (Firtko and Jackson 2005, Bec 2000, CNA 1999). According to Glendenning and Kingston (1999), nurses may be insufficiently prepared to face this kind of dilemma. It is our contention that this shortcoming combined with learned helplessness, which occurs frequently among health professionals, may increase nurses' feeling of incompetency, thus contributing to their sense of hopelessness and lack of initiative.

Third, nurses fear the potential negative impact of whistleblowing: legal involvement, reprisals and even ostracisation (Amolgue et al. 2010). Wilmot (2000) asserts that employers often react punitively to reports of abuse, accusing staff of being disloyal. A study conducted among nurses (n = 40) showed they indeed suffered from the hostile and even punitive reactions of their employer. Waters (2008) found that 38 per cent of the nurses (n = 752) who reported abuse experienced severely negative professional consequences and 64 per cent thought that their organisation would not have supported them had they been the object of reprisals. Finally, since nurses who report abuse may experience health-related problems, their choice not to report might avoid such a negative consequence. A study conducted with a non-random sample of 35 whistleblowers from various healthoccupations showed stress-related symptoms such as sleep disorders, panic attacks, anxiety, suicidal thoughts and feelings of guilt and uselessness (Lennane 1993). Vanbergeik and Sarmiento (2006) who analyzed the experience of teachers reporting child abuse (n = 28) also observed severe emotional problems including burn-out, a sense of helplessness and failure, anxiety and frustration. Similarly, Macdonald and Ahern (2002) observed negative emotional effects in people who reported abuse, but also noted comparable reactions in people who witnessed abuse but failed to report it.

Although informative, current knowledge is far from explanatory as to why nurses who witness elder abuse in LTC facilities fail to report it, despite their ethical and legal duty to do so. A deeper understanding of the phenomenon is urgently needed, especially given the expected increase in the number of LTC facilities. Improved knowledge could provide the guidance and support necessary not only to report elder abuse, but also to reduce the problem and eventually prevent it. A step in that direction is the present exploratory study, the aim of which is to describe the factors related to nurses' failure to report elder abuse they have witnessed in LTC.

Method

An exploratory design with a grounded theory approach was chosen to conduct this research. Two main reasons guided this choice. First, this specific method can enhance the understanding of phenomena for which there is very limited knowledge (Strauss and Corbin 1998) such as the one of interest in this case. Second, from an epistemological point of view, grounded theory has a very strong heuristic value because its theory-generating potential comes from an emic perspective and can also provide guidelines to future interventions (Strauss and Corbin 1998).

Sampling Strategy

Participants were selected through the snowball technique as suggested by Faugier and Sargeant (1997) when the topic at stake is highly sensitive. Poupart (1997) adds that this is also a particularly useful approach to reach participants and to increase sample diversity. The first step consisted in meeting separately with two executive directors of long-term care associations who knew the health network well and could identify the Chief Nursing Officers likely to collaborate in the study. Then, two Chief Nursing Officers of long-term care facilities located in the Montreal metropolitan region were identified and contacted. They were informed of the general context and purpose of the study along with their expected role in identifying potential participants; both agreed to take part in the process. They were then given sealed letters of information to distribute to potential participants who would meet the following criteria: (a) to be a registered nurse or a nursing assistant, (b) to have worked in a long-term care facility for at least six months, (c) to have witnessed elder abuse and (d) to be fluent in French or in English. These letters comprised detailed information on the purpose of the study, the inclusion criteria, the data collection process, the special ethical considerations related to anonymity and confidentially, and the means to contact the investigator. Nurses who expressed interest were met and interviewed at the time and place of their choice and assigned pseudonyms. They were also asked to pass the letter of information along to other nurses. Consistent with the grounded theory approach, sampling was stopped when saturation was achieved. In all, seven participants were interviewed.

Description of the Sample

All participants (n = 7) were female and employed full-time. Four were registered nurses with administrative responsibilities and three were registered practical nurses. Only one had a university degree. Five were in the 35–44 age group, the two others were older. The participants had an average length of experience in LTC of 27 years.

Data Collection and Analysis

After signing the informed consent, each participant was met by the investigator, first author of this chapter (Hamel-Lauzon), through a single, face-to-face, semi-structured, audio-taped interview that lasted from 60 to 90 minutes. Semi-structured interviews were chosen because they provide flexibility and allow for confidence-building and commitment from participants. Each interview started with an open question on elder abuse and on the participant's personal experience of not reporting what they had witnessed; it ended with the investigator summarising the most salient information. Because of her nursing background, the investigator was able to remain alert and responsive to emotional outbursts throughout the interview. Consistent with the grounded-theory approach, data analysis started immediately after the first interview using Paille's six-step process (1994), but without reaching the theorization stage. Interviews were audiotaped for subsequent verbatim transcription by the investigator. Data from each interview were then coded and categorized to identify and define the themes. Themes were discussed with a panel of experts composed of three doctorally prepared nurses and refined until agreement was reached among all members. Data collection continued until saturation of emerging issues was reached. Finally, definitions were written for each theme.

Results

Eight themes or factors, some including sub-themes, emerged from the analysis: (a) Negative past experiences, (b) Taking control attitude, (c) Feelings of role ambiguity (d) Organizational inertia, (e) Culture of silence, (f) Severity of abuse, (g) Desensitization, and (h) Constraining social relationships at work. Themes were further classified into three categories underlining their source: personal factors, environmental factors and person-environment interaction factors (Table 6.1).

Table 6.1   Emerging Categories, Themes and Sub-themes

Personal Factors	Environmental Factors	Person-Environment Interaction Factors
Negative past experiences	Organizational inertia A prevailing "Kill the messenger" culture Lack of clearly defined internal policies Lack of actual or perceived support Union blockage	Perceived severity of abuse
Taking control attitude Managing care by monitoring Teaching and awareness raising Providing care "in lieu of"	Culture of silence Fear of reprisals Racial blackmail	Desensitization
Feeling role ambiguity		Constraining social relationships at work Pernicious friendship Unconditional collaboration

Personal Factors

This category refers to factors that are inherent to nurses themselves. They are linked to their personal experience or to others' experience that they have internalized, as well as their own behaviours and perceptions. It comprises three themes.

Negative Past Experiences

Implicitly or explicitly, all participants referred to their own, or to their colleagues' negative experience with regard to elder abuse reporting; some discussed the issue at great length. They underlined the fact that reporting abusive behaviours involved a highly demanding and extremely stressful process that usually ended in turmoil. In retrospect, they believed that the consequences and multiple ramifications of reporting abuse were not worth the trouble, given the lack of satisfactory outcomes and, for this reason, they would not consider going through the process again.

> Anna: I believe this is why many people fail to report. It's hell (…) and it's been hell for me for the last two years. Everything has been going wrong since.
> Bertha: It's useless. There is no use in making a report. Why? Because it took so long and the employer did nothing. There are absolutely no consequences to reporting abusive behaviours.

Taking Control Attitude

Although participants did not explicitly referred to a code of ethics, they all stressed the importance of nursing values and expressed their strong belief that residents' safety and protection were of the utmost importance. During the interviews, they all underlined their responsibilities in assuring their patients' well-being and protecting them from mistreatment. They recognized the fact that they did not report abuse but instead decided to take the matter into their own hands and stop the abuse or a potential abuse. This taking control attitude was expressed in three different ways.

Managing Care by Monitoring

Some participants put in place a strategy of strict supervision of nursing staff, specifically when they were made aware or themselves observed inappropriate care and/or abusive behaviours towards residents. They considered that monitoring staff members and the care they provided was an acceptable autonomous nursing intervention which reduced their psychological discomfort to a tolerable level and prevented them from taking further steps toward disclosure. Therefore, to be consistent with their values, nurses increased their level of supervision either by watching the nurses more closely or assigning other staff members to do the monitoring.

Diana: When I know that someone is problematic, it requires a lot of energy on my part, I never give up. I constantly keep an eye on that person, and yes, at some point, it becomes really exhausting. I then ask the nursing assistant to watch over that person just in case he or she becomes impatient, abrupt or blunt. It is exhausting.

Teaching and Awareness Raising

Few participants chose to provide the abusive staff member with information, guidelines and directives to help prevent repeating unacceptable behaviours toward residents. They used readily available documentation or resorted to their own knowledge and experience in a spontaneous fashion. These actions were not planned but thought of at the moment of witnessing and responding to an inappropriate act. Hence, with this strategy, reporting was not an option.

Diana: I found information on the Internet and brought it to the staff member who could then learn about the patient's disease and its related behaviours [...] this reduced the tension associated with the care of this patient.
Cora: The patient does not like to be washed. He may become aggressive and then he strikes the health care aid. The health care aid has sometimes squeezed the patient's arm and, yes, this is violence. I then asked the health care aid on which side he stood to wash the patient and since he was on the wrong side, I gave him some tips.

Providing Care "in lieu of"

Interviews revealed that some nurses replaced staff members who refused to provide care in a safe and professional manner. However, they added that this strategy soon became overwhelming and was not sustainable.

Elena: The patient wants to go to the toilet but the health care aid refuses to bring him at the time the patient asks because it interferes with the aid's daily routine. Sometimes, I need to step in and bring him to the toilet myself.

Feeling Role Ambiguity

Some participants believed that their responsibility to report abuse was limited by their position in the organisation. They discussed the power of the hierarchy and the feeling that their role in reporting was linked to their status. One participant also shared her experience as union advisor and admitted she felt torn between her moral duty to report a colleague and her union responsibility to defend or protect that same colleague.

Anna: There are limits to what you can do. If the Head Nurse does not go further, it's not my responsibility; I'm not the boss.

Fiona: It also depends on your role. I once was a union representative, responsible for defending the staff's rights. Even if this role did not mean that I was excused from also defending the patients' rights, sometimes it was difficult to settle between the two. I remember meeting with nurses to tell them that they needed to be careful, because things could go further up.

Environmental Factors

This second category relates to contextual elements that are imposed on nurses by their practice setting and its prevailing culture. All participants discussed at length the contextual elements that convinced nurses not to report abuse. Two themes came to light as a result of the analysis: the organizational inertia towards abusive behaviors and the presence of a culture of silence.

Organizational Inertia

This environmental factor is connected to the absence or perceived absence of specific measures provided by the organisation or by the union to deal with abusive behaviours. It comprises four different sub-themes.

A Prevailing "Kill the Messenger" Culture

A majority of participants told of perceived hostility on the part of their immediate supervisor when they attempted to report a caregiver's inappropriate behaviour toward a resident. They testified that supervisors became critical of nurses who wanted to report abuse. They even questioned the nurse's judgment. This uncomfortable situation eventually brought to an end the reporting of abuse, even among nurses who were planning to do so.

Anna: When I report the caregiver, I feel that my supervisor believes I am exaggerating. She can say things like: "I know you don't like her and now you are going to tell me bad things about her."

Diana: I did my report on a nurse who was wrong, but it was as if I was the one who had wrongly behaved … as if I was the one who started everything … I felt it would turn against me.

Lack of Clearly Defined Internal Policies

All participants claimed that guidelines and policies for abuse-reporting were either inexistent or insufficient in their facilities. They all referred to the concept of "zero tolerance" of abuse in their respective institutions, but added there were no concrete measures to implement it. Several reported they were uncertain as to what should be reported and how to proceed when witnessing or hearing about abuse. They also revealed there were no known measures to protect the whistleblower.

> Anna: If there is a clear policy, I am not aware of it. We all know that here, it's zero tolerance. We all know that we should report abuse, the employer talks at length about it, but beyond and above words, it's a complete vacuum, there is definitely no clear guidelines.

Lack of Actual or Perceived Support

Most participants stated that the lack of well-known and clearly defined policies made them feel that they were left on their own to handle a complex problem. Implicitly or explicitly participants revealed that support was notably insufficient and constituted a strong deterrent to reporting an abusive event. Some commented on the importance of receiving emotional support to protect their psychological integrity, given that reporting could have negative consequences on their well-being.

> Anna: After she reported a colleague, a friend told me she never received any kind of support from the hospital or from her supervisor. She told me she would never report again because of this lack of support.

Union Blockage

Interviews revealed a sort of union blockage as one of the most important constraints to reporting abuse. Some participants perceived unions as the dominant constituent in LTC facilities because they use their intimidating power to protect abusers.

> Anna: Abusers always have the union to protect them, because it is almost impossible to fire someone. You need to build a very strong case and it takes years. Even if employers want to get rid of abusers, they can't, because they have to face the union.

Culture of Silence

This theme refers to the tacit agreement that seems to prevail among staff members to remain discrete and keep quiet when abusive behaviours occur. This culture of silence needs to be understood as a means of maintaining the status quo on the unit. Indeed, results in the present study suggest that caring and highly-motivated staff members are not popular. This seems to divide staff into two antagonistic groups, the "oppressors," composed of health care aids, and the "oppressed," nurses, each ostracizing the other. The "oppressors," including both the abusers and their supporters, dominate the "oppressed" who tend to become passive. Two sub-themes are imbedded in this culture of silence.

Fear of Reprisals

All participants mentioned reprisals awaiting those who report abuse and all expressed their fear of retaliation from the dominating group. They referred to the "tough" or "strongheaded" members of the group who actually control the unit by using several strategies such as intimidation, harassment and threats to impose silence.

> Elena: The one who reported abuse has been threatened by the abuser who mentioned how some of the rough people on the unit could do things to her. Yes, some people will never report abusive behaviours because they are scared of what could happen to them, it is sure.
>
> Diana: A couple of years ago, I witnessed a nurse being physically assaulted by a nursing assistant who told the nurse to let her alone.

Racial Blackmail

Two participants discussed at length the increasing number of health care workers coming from diverse ethnic backgrounds and the resulting racial blackmail. This refers to the fact that some workers, when involved in interpersonal conflicts or accused of any form of abuse by a supervisor or a peer from another ethnic background will cry racism. Hence, to avoid any accusation of racism, staff will keep silent when confronted with abuse.

> Fiona: It was not racism, I would have acted exactly the same way with a person of my race. She told me that she would denounce me to Human Rights, so I stopped telling her when she was doing something wrong.
>
> Anna: It is very difficult to address the situation when the nurse is from another culture, because right away you are accused of racism.

Person-Environment Interaction Factors

This category comprises three themes that show a definite link between the personal and environmental factors that discourage nurses from reporting abuse. These three themes emerge from nurses' perceptions that are influenced by their work environment.

Perceived Severity of Abuse

This theme relates to the nurses' perception of the gravity of the abuse on residents' general well-being. As there is no classification system to determine the severity of the elder abuse, it is left entirely to the nurses' clinical judgment, which is informed by their knowledge and experience. Interviews revealed that nurses seemed to evaluate the severity of abuse using two discrete and very arbitrary classes: (a) very severe and unacceptable; (b) less severe. The first class includes physical abuse with actual or potential injuries, the second, all other forms of reprehensible actions. Nurses admitted they would be inclined to report actions they considered very severe. Perceived severity of abusive behaviour would then become a criterion for deciding to report or not to report and very severe abusive actions, a threshold that would definitely call for reporting. Such subjective assessment could lead to an underestimation of abuse.

> Elena: I have seen patients being moved roughly, but they were not injured.
> Diana: Sure, there are things I would not tolerate, like a patient that would be force-fed to make her stop talking, it's not like someone who would talk roughly to a resident.

Desensitization

This category is characterized by a loss of sensitivity, a decline of commitment and a lack of purpose on the part of nurses, all changes that gradually alter their judgement. Data suggest that when care is based on rigid routines, abusive behaviour can gradually become part of that routine, thus altering the nurses' judgment of what actions may be qualified as normal. Minimizing inappropriate care or abusive behaviours and their consequences on residents' life can lead to less empathy towards abused elders and more tolerance of abusers' behaviour. Desensitized nurses will not be likely to report abuse.

> Cora: Once, the health care aid entered the room where the patient was sleeping. I don't understand what happened, but as the patient would not wake up, she threw a glass of water at her face. I am sure she did not want to hurt him.
> Elena: I didn't do anything because I thought it was part of the routine.
> Anna: This was not alarming. Nobody was hurt. Do we wonder how things can affect residents? For us, it becomes so natural, I guess we get used to it.

Constraining Social Relationships at Work

This category includes all social relationships that are identified in the working environment as an attempt to buy social peace on the unit or to prevent any potentially destabilizing situation among staff. Anything that jeopardizes the nature or quality of these relationships inherently prevents some people from reporting abusive behaviours as the following two sub-themes indicate.

Pernicious Friendship

Closeness and a sharing of common space can lead to the development of social relationships between people regardless of their status, roles, or hierarchy. However, these relationships may become pernicious when they prevent or prohibit reporting abusive behaviours.

> Fiona: I have friends at work but I need to keep a certain distance with co-workers. It helps to remain more objective and sometimes to report abuse.
> Gracia: Authority is not authority when you are a friend of the person who has it. If you are close with the boss, if you eat together and so on, then it becomes harder to make remarks and even more to report.

Unconditional Collaboration

Data indicate that collaboration is of the utmost importance in LTC. Participants revealed that when trying to please others and to maintain the "social peace," they come to ignore their own sense of ethics and moral obligations including their duty to report abusive behaviours. Some participants explained that they lowered their practice standards in order to avoid problems with their team, to keep a good spirit of collaboration and to maintain good relationships with others.

> Fiona: It is hard to report because you want to keep your team on your side.
> Cora: One often works with the same people. Let's say that 80% of the time, they're nice, funny and give you a hand when you need them, but for the rest of the time, they're rough. Then, you tend to excuse them. But, if you work with people only once in a while, it's easier to report them.
> Diana: It's normal to have bad days, people may go through difficult times and they may not see that their behaviour changes.

This section on results would however be incomplete without briefly mentioning the moral and emotional distress experienced by all participants while taking part in the study. Some were in tears, others moved uneasily on their chair and avoided eye contact, some even admitted being disappointed in themselves as human beings. In short, they all expressed some form of distress when talking about abuse and all confided they had never before discussed the topic with others.

Conclusion

This exploratory study led to the identification of eight mutually exclusive factors involved in nurses' decision not to report elder abuse witnessed in LTC facilities. Although consistent with existing knowledge, the evidence gathered using a grounded theory approach is now providing substantial new information about this decision-making process that is closely associated with ethics. If fear of reprisals (Waters 2008, Strausser and Fulmer 2007, Kitchen, Richardson, and Livingston 2002), lack of know-how (Glendenning and Kingston 1999), and role ambiguity (Saveman, Norberg, and Hallberg 1993) have been earlier identified in nurses' failure to report abuse, the results of this study provide a larger, richer and more refined set of elements. Results indicate that unless nurses judge the abusive actions as being very severe, they will not report violent or negligent behaviours. Having lost faith in the reporting process and being fearful of retaliation, they generally feel alone and helpless in the face of abuse, feelings that are usually exacerbated by an organisational culture that does not value the reporting of abusive behaviour, even less the taking of corrective action. Concomitantly, nurses are not always clear about the extent of their own professional responsibilities when witnessing abuse; role ambiguity, especially in environments where close relationships and collaboration are valued, along with a perceived lack of clear guidelines and support on the part of senior administration prevent nurses from reporting abuse. However, witnessing abuse and keeping silent about it are generally painful and emotionally distressing. Hence, unless completely desensitized, nurses will try to reduce their discomfort and live up to some of their standards by taking the matter into their own hands, at least for a while. They will educate, monitor and even replace the abusers, thus convincing themselves that they need not to report abuse. From these results, four major findings will be discussed.

First, it seems quite obvious that ethical considerations are not yet fully integrated in the culture of LTC facilities. Although professionally responsible for the quality of the care provided in these institutions, nurses do not always act according to their code of ethics when faced with the ethical dilemma of reporting or not reporting abuse. Failure to report elder abuse is indeed the result of a highly emotional decision-making process which is, in itself, an ethical dilemma where safety and protection values for patients conflict with self-preservation for nurses. This is consistent with Varcoe et al. (2004), who state that nurses facing ethical dilemmas do not always make decisions according to the highest moral standards. These authors contend that before making the decision to report or not to report, nurses will calculate the report's possible impact on residents and on themselves as well. Results of this study also indicate that nurses are not fully aware of the professional standards that are supposed to guide their practice nor do they know the exact procedure to follow in case of abuse. This strongly suggests that nurses are ill-prepared to deal efficiently with ethical dilemmas, an observation also noted by Firtko and Jackson (2005). Basic nursing curricula and continuing education programs should enable nurses to recognize all types of abuse and to understand the professional and ethical standards that guide nursing practice. As well, clear guidelines and specific procedures should be made available on all LTC units. The number of abuse cases and the measures taken to prevent even more cases should be publicly known and included in the institution's annual report.

Second, emotional distress is overwhelmingly present among nurses who choose to remain silent. The concept of "moral distress" has been developed to explain the emotional turmoil experienced in situations where an ethical dilemma becomes significant (Wilkinson 1987/1988, Jameton 1984). This emotional or moral distress seems to be felt before, during and after reporting abuse, as well as in the absence of reporting. It is experienced throughout the entire decisional process. Mitchell (2001) refers to "moral residue" as the psychological scars that may persist indefinitely despite the nurses' use of cognitive strategies to reduce their distress. Participants started to doubt themselves and felt left alone after they witnessed abusive actions and had to decide what to do. Reminiscing about these situations was difficult for most participants even long after the dilemma had been experienced, which seems consistent with the concept of moral residue. The reality is that some nurses must simply learn to live with their moral distress since they have too much to lose if they break their silence. They learn to cope psychologically as best as they can. However, such situations, if prolonged, could lead to depression, guilt, burnout, feelings of helplessness, resignation and, in some cases, to desensitization. Several authors have also reported that moral distress among the nursing staff negatively influences the quality of patient's care (Zuzelo 2007, Corley 2002, Wilkinson 1987/1988). The challenge is then to engage units in an ethical dialogue and, most importantly, to bring them to recognize elder abuse in LTC. Strategies could include creating opportunities to discuss the ethical practice in interdisciplinary forum and nurses' committees. Only then, the lifelong moral residue experienced when witnessing elder abuse without reporting could become a significant source of insight and a learning opportunity. In fact, from an ethical perspective, this could lead to a better understanding of patients' needs.

Third, failure to report abuse is obviously a complex and multifaceted phenomenon where several personal and environmental factors interact. While nurses are health care professionals who must take full responsibility for their actions or omissions, they are also only one group in a much larger system that has its own functioning. A policy of "zero tolerance" may prevail in LTC, but the genuine commitment to eradicate abuse and to implement concrete measures to enforce this policy are lacking. Results of the present study indicate that nurses who want to practice according to their moral values and who are highly dedicated to meeting residents' needs are often ostracized; they find they must resort to "engaging in a battle" with a larger group of health care workers who spend most of their time with residents and therefore have greater influence on the residents' daily lives. Once again, continuing education using case studies, open communication between administration and union representatives, the valuing of health care workers' contribution to health care delivery are concrete measures that could induce a culture of excellence in LTC.

Lastly, the work organisation in some LTC facilities seems to be conducive to abuse. Indeed, Teeri, Leino-Kilpi, andVälimäki (2006) suggested a sixth type of abuse which they called *systemic violence*. According to these authors, systemic violence refers to the internal or inherent functioning of institutions that insist on rigid schedules in their supposed effort to satisfy elderly residents' basic needs. For instance, residents have to wake up according to a non-flexible routine and eat at hours that not only ignore their particular needs, but also allow for so little time that mealtime becomes unsafe and the residents force-fed. In such environments residents must follow all the rules for the well-being of the organization until they gradually lose their sense of personal identity. Back in 1968, Goffman coined the term "total institution" where "a large number of residents are placed in the same situation ... with rules that are explicitly addressed." Institutions have definitely improved in the last 40 years and efforts have been continually made to instil a culture of personalised care in home-like environments but much more needs to be done. From political leaders to each staff member on LTC units, every single level of the health care services should work toward ensuring abuse-free environments. Are Ministries of Health and LTC senior administrations prepared to go down that road or are we as a society sustaining a masquerade of "political correctness"?

References

Allen, P.D., Kellet, K., and Gruman, C. 2003. Elder abuse in Connecticut's nursing homes. *Journal of Elder Abuse & Neglect*, 15, 19–42.

Almogue, A., Weiss, A., Marcus, E.L., and Beloosky, Y. 2010. Attitudes and knowledge of medical and nursing staff toward elder abuse. *Archives of Gerontology and Geriatrics*, 51(1), 86–91.

Baker, M.W., and Heitkemper, M.M. 2005. The roles of nurses on inter-professional teams to combat elder mistreatment. *Nursing Outlook*, 53, 253–59.

Bec, J. 2000. Le devoir de divulgation – Le *whistleblowing*: une éthique de la loyauté. *Téléscope*, 7(2). www.enap.ca/observatoire/docs/telescope/volumes6-11/2000-juin-vol7num2.pdf.

Bonnie, R.B., and Wallace, R.B. (eds). 2003. *Elder mistreatment: Abuse, Neglect and Exploitation in an Aging America*. Washington, DC: The National Academies Press.

Burgess, A.W., Brown, K., Bell, K., Ledray, L.E., Faan, S-A., and Poarch, J.C. 2005. Sexual abuse of older adults. *American Journal of Nursing*, 105(10), 66–71.

Canadian Nurses Association (CNA). 1999. *Déontologie pratique : témoin je me tais/témoin, je dénonce; le dilemme éthique de la dénonciation*. Ottawa: CNA.

Cario, R. 2005. L'aîné victime : approche victimologique. *Info PV*, 5–11.

College of Nurses of Ontario (CNO). 2004. La prévention des mauvais traitements infligés aux clients. Fact Sheet.

Cooper, C., Selwood, A., and Livingston, G. 2008. The prevalence of elder abuse and neglect: a systematic review. *Age and Ageing*, 37, 151–60.

Corley, M.C. 2002. Nurse moral distress: a proposed theory and research agenda. *Nursing Ethics*, 9, 636–50.

Daly, J.M., andJogerst, G. 2001. Statute definitions of elder abuse. *Journal of Elder Abuse & Neglect*, 13, 39–57.

Ens, I. 2002. Les mauvais traitements à l'égard des aînés en établissement. Public Health Agency of Canada: http://phac-aspc.gc.ca/nefv-cnivfviolencefamiliale/html/ageinstitutions_f.html. [accessed: 28 February, 2006].

Faugier, J., and Sargeant, M. 1997. Sampling hard to reach populations. *Journal of Advanced Nursing*, 26, 790–97.

Firtko, A., and Jackson, D. 2005. Do the ends justify the means: nursing and the dilemma of whistleblowing. *Australian Journal of Advanced Nursing*, 23(1), 51–6.

Glendenning, F., and Kingston, P. 1999. *Elder Abuse and Neglect in Residential Settings: Different National Backgrounds and Similar Responses*. New-York: The Haworth Press.

Goergen, T. 2004. A multi-method study on elder abuse and neglect in nursing homes. *The Journal of Adult Protection*, 6, 15–25.

Goffman, E. 1968. *Asiles: éudes sur la condition sociale des malades mentaux.* Paris: Les Éditions de Minuit.

Gray-Vickrey, P. 2005. Elder abuse: are you prepared to intervene? *LPN*, 1(2), 38–43.

Harrel, R., Toronjo, C.H., Mclaughlin, J., Oavlick, V.N., Hyman, D.D., and Bitondo Dyer, C. 2002. How geriatricians identify elder abuse and neglect. *American Journal of the Medical Sciences*, 323(1), 34–8.

Hawes, C. 2003. Elder abuse in residential long-term care setting: what is known and what information is needed?, in *Elder Mistreatment: Abuse, Neglect and Exploitation in an Aging America*, edited by R.B. Bonnie and R.B. Wallace, Washington, DC: The National Academies Press, 446–500.

Jameton, A. 1984. *Nursing Practice: The Ethical Issues*. Englewood Cliffs, NJ: Prentice Hall.

Kitchen, G., Richardson, B., and Livingston, G. 2002. Are nurses equipped to manage actual or suspected elder abuse? *Professional Nurse*, 17, 647–50.

Krug, E.G., Dahlberg, L.L., Mercy, J.A., Zwi, A.B., and Lozano-Ascencio, R. (eds). 2002. Abuse of the elderly (123–43). *World Report on Violence and Health*. Geneva : World Health Organisation.

Lachs, M.S., and Pillemer, K. 2004. Elder abuse. *The Lancet*, 364, 1263–72.

Lachs, M.S., and Pillemer, K. 1995. Abuse and neglect of elderly persons. *The New England Journal of Medicine*, 332(7), 437–43.

Lennane, J. 1993. Whistleblowing: a health issue. *BMJ*, 307, 667–70.

Levine, J.M. 2003. Elder neglect and abuse: A primer for primary care physicians. *Geriatrics*, 58(10), 37-44.

McDonald, S., and Ahern, K. 2002. Physical and emotional effects of whistleblowing. *Journal of Psychosocial Nursing and Mental Health Services*, 40(1), 14–27.

Malmedal, W., Hammervold. R., and Saveman, B.E., 2009. To report or not to report? Attitudes held by Norwegian nursing home staff on reporting inadequate care carried out by colleagues. *Scandinavian Journal of Public Health*, 37, 744–50.

Miller, C.A. 2005. Elder abuse: the nurse's perspective. *Clinical Gerontologist*, 28(1/2), 105–33.

Ministère de la Santé et des Services sociaux (MSSS). 2003. *Un milieu de vie de qualité pour les personnes hébergées en CHSLD: Orientations ministérielles.* Québec: MSSS.

Mitchell, G.J. 2001. Policy, procedure, and routine: matters of moral influence. *Nursing Science Quarterly*, 14, 109–14.

Nahmiash, D. 2000. Les mauvais traitements et la négligence à l'égard des personnes âgées, in *Psychologie clinique de la personne âgée*, edited by P. Cappeliez, P. Landreville and J. Vézina. Ottawa: Les Presses de l'Université d'Ottawa, 197–216.

Neno, R. and Neno, M. 2005. Identifying abuse in older people. *Nursing Standard*, 20(3), 43–7.

Ordre des infirmières et infirmiers du Québec (OIIQ). 2000. *L'exploitation des personnes âgées*. Mémoire présenté à la Commission des droits de la personne et des droits de la jeunesse dans le cadre de sa consultation générale sur le sujet en titre. http://www.oiiq.org/uploads/publications/memoires/mem_exploitation_pa.html. [accessed: 3 March 2006].

Ordre des infirmières et infirmiers du Québec (OIIQ). 2002. *Code de déontologie des infirmières et infirmiers*. http://oiiq.org/infirmieres/lois_reglements_pdf/I-8-r-4.1.pdf. [accessed: 28 February 2006].

Paillé, P. 1994. L'analyse par théorisation ancrée. *Cahiers de recherche sociologique*, 23, 147–81.

Poupart, J. 1997. L'entretien de type qualitatif: considérations épistémologiques, théoriques et méthodologiques, in *La recherche qualitative: enjeux épistémologiques et méthodologiques*, edited by J. Poupart, J-P. Deslauriers, L-H. Groulx, A. Laperrière, R. Mayer, and A.P. Pires. Boucherville: Gaëtan Morin, 174–209.

Saveman, B-I., Hallberg, I.R., and Norberg, A. 1993. Identifying and defining abuse of elderly people, as seen by witnesses. *Journal of Advanced Nursing*, 18, 1393–400.

Strauss, A., and Corbin, J. 1998. *Basics of Qualitative Research*. Thousand Oaks, CA: SAGE.

Strausser, S.M., and Fulmer, T. 2007. The clinical presentation of elder neglect: what we know and what we can do. *Journal of the American Psychiatric Nurses Association*, 12, 343–9.

Teeri, S., Leino-Kilpi, H., and Välimäki, M. 2006. Long-term nursing care of elderly people: identifying ethically problematic experiences among patients, relatives and nurses in Finland. *Nursing Ethics*, 13, 116–29.

VanBergeijk, E., and Sarmiento, T.L.L. 2006. The consequences of reporting child maltreatment: are school personnel at risk for secondary traumatic stress? *Brief Treatment & Crisis Intervention*, 6(1), 79–98.

Varcoe, C., Doane, G., Pauly, B., Rodney, P., Storch, J.L., Mahoney, K., McPherson, G., Brown, H., and Starzomski, R. 2004. Ethical practice in nursing: working the in-betweens. *Journal of Advanced Nursing*, 45, 316–25.

Waters, A. 2008. Nurses fear their concerns about care will be ignored. *Nursing Standard*, 22(37), 12–13.

Wilkinson, J.M. 1987/88. Moral distress in nursing practice: experience and effect. *Nursing Forum*, 23(1), 16–29.

Wilmot, S. 2000. Nurses and whistleblowing: the ethical issues. *Journal of Advanced Nursing*, 32, 1051–7.

Zuzelo, P.R. 2007. Exploring the moral distress of registered nurses. *Nursing Ethics*, 14, 344–59.

PART TWO
Horizontal Violence

Chapter 7

Foucault and the Nexus between Violence and Power: The Context of Intra/Inter Professional Aggression

Isabelle St-Pierre

Introduction

I have worked in the field of occupational health nursing for almost 15 years. As part of my work in the hospital sector, I had the opportunity to observe the effects of an unhealthy work environment on employees. I saw nurses burn out and leave the profession. I also witnessed how workload, role ambiguity and competition can lead to conflict and aggression. These observations combined with the experience I acquired working in health care institutions have stimulated my interest in exploring the issue of workplace aggression and more specifically intra and inter professional aggression. Instinctively, I perceived a relationship between power, power games and aggression. My readings of Michel Foucault's work, particularly *Discipline and Punish* and *The Subject and Power*, allowed me to better understand how power is insidious and everywhere and the need to question "normal" organizational dynamics. As a result, it is increasingly important to address the issue of power and challenge the *status quo* when dealing with intra/inter professional aggression.

Intra/Inter Professional Aggression

Intra-professional aggression is also referred to as nurse to nurse aggression, horizontal violence, intra-staff aggression and bullying. Most often, intra-professional aggression is psychological rather than physical and is often covert rather than overt. Examples of types of aggression include: rudeness, abusive language, humiliation in front of others, others failing to speak up for someone in his/her defence, denied access to opportunities, stealing credit for someone's work, being refused help to perform necessary tasks, excessive scrutiny of one's work, spreading malicious rumours about someone and unjustified criticism (McKenna, Smith, Poole, and Coverdale 2003, Farrell 1999).

While aggression by "other" health care professionals is gaining momentum with the thrust towards collaborative practices, physicians are still identified in the literature as the main perpetrator of inter professional aggression towards nurses. Verbal abuse appears to be the most common type of aggression perpetrated by physicians and includes: abusive anger, ignoring, condescension (Manderino and Berkey 1997), as well as judging, criticizing, accusing and blaming (Oweis and Diabat 2005). While mentalities regarding nurse-physician relationships and the role of nurses have changed tremendously over the years, there is still an inherent conception that the nurse's role includes executing physician's orders, resulting in nurses' expertise being devaluated and hierarchal rapports maintained (Fédération des infirmières et infirmiers du Québec 1995). Nurses report being concerned about the tolerance of administrators towards physicians' disruptive behaviours as well as the lack of support from executive physicians in dealing with such behaviours (Rosenstein 2002).

Prevalence of Intra/Inter Professional Aggression

The prevalence of reported cases of intra/inter professional aggression is alarming. In effect, findings from the Canadian component of a large international study involving Canada, the United States, England, Scotland and Germany found that of the 8,780 registered nurses from Alberta and British Columbia that took part in the study (response rate 51 per cent), 46 per cent of respondents experienced one or more types of violence in the last five shifts (Duncan et al. 2001). While patients were the main source of physical assaults, hospital staff (physicians and nursing co-workers) were the main source of non-physical violence (e.g. emotional abuse and verbal sexual harassment), especially in critical care areas (not including emergency departments) (Hesketh et al. 2003). More specifically in critical care settings, physicians were responsible for 31.2 per cent of all instances of emotional abuse while nursing co-workers committed 25.5 per cent. Physicians were also responsible for 43.7 per cent of all cases of verbal sexual harassment while nursing co-workers for 9.9 per cent. As well, of all critical care nurses sampled (n=1439), 14 per cent reported being emotionally abused by a co-worker in the last five shifts (compared to 7.7 per cent of nurses from all other specialties combined), and 2.2 per cent of critical care nurses reported being sexually harassed by a co-worker (compared to 0.8 per cent of the rest of the nurses) (Hesketh et al. 2003).

A second Canadian study of about 19,000 regulated nurses (registered nurses, licensed practical nurses and registered psychiatric nurses) across the country (response rate 80 per cent) found 12 per cent of all nurses reporting emotional abuse by a nurse co-worker and 8 per cent by a physician (Shields and Wilkins 2006). Notwithstanding the large amount of data pertaining to the issue workplace aggression, including intra/inter professional aggression, it is estimated only one-fifth of cases are officially reported (International Council of Nurses [ICN] 1999).

Explanations for the Prevalence of Intra Professional Aggression

The literature suggests many explanations for the prevalence of nurse to nurse aggression. A common theory is that horizontal violence is the product of nursing being an *oppressed discipline* where nursing is part of a strict hierarchy and nurses are made to feel inferior. As a result, nurses become hostile and aggressive towards their peers or subordinates because they cannot fight back their oppressor (Longo and Sherman 2007, Leiper 2005, Thomas 2003, Farrell 2001).

However, others have criticized this view as falling short of an adequate reason to explain horizontal violence and have presented other explanations such as: *disenfranchising work practices* (where a nurse might annoy her peers if she regularly fails to fully complete her tasks during her shift); *low self-esteem or potency* (where nurses may feel that they or their work are undervalued compared to other groups); *generational and hierarchical abuse* (where more senior nurses believe that they have "earned the right" to abuse others including more junior nurses or students); *clique formation* (where a subgroup marginalize those who are not part of the clique); *aggression breeding aggression* (where aggression is seen as part of the job and staff may mimic aggressive behaviours); *actor-observer effects* (where nurses view their own negative behaviour as related to factors outside of their control, making them unaccountable for their behaviour); and *easy targets* (where new nurses and students become the aim of aggressors because they lack the personal and professional resources to challenge such practices) (Leiper 2005, McKenna et al. 2003, Randle 2003, Farrell 2001).

Power as an Alternative Explanation for Intra/Inter Professional Aggression

As stated at the beginning of this chapter, I believe that issues of power can be the root cause of numerous instances of intra/inter professional aggression. As such, the work of Michel Foucault around disciplinary power offers a rich theoretical perspective to help broaden the understanding of intra/inter professional aggression. This chapter will now explore how power (or power struggles) is often the basis for many instances of intra/inter professional aggression.

Disciplinary Power

The most important phenomena that accompanied industrialization is, according to Foucault (1975), the birth of a mechanism of power which served to control others; a discipline that regards individuals as both objects and instruments of its exercise. Discipline therefore produces bodies that are submissive, useful and obedient, "docile" bodies (Foucault 1977). Consequently, Foucault considers discipline as a new political anatomy where the impact of discipline increases the body's utility, while the political influence reduces the body to a position of obedience.

According to Foucault (1975), discipline is in fact the art of distribution. To this end, discipline proceeds to the distribution of people in space in order to derive maximum advantages and minimum inconveniences. Through the use of time, discipline also exerts a form of dominance by the exhaustive control of activities and by the continuous extraction of more available moments from time. Thus appear a new demand to which discipline must respond; "to construct a machine whose effect will be maximized by the concerted articulation of the elementary parts of which it is composed. Discipline is no longer simply an art of distributing bodies, of extracting time from them and accumulating it, but of composing forces in order to obtain an efficient machine" (Foucault 1977: 164). In summary, discipline creates from the bodies it controls four types of individuality composed of four characteristics: "it is cellular (by the play of special distribution), it is organic (by the coding of activities), it is genetic (by the accumulation of time), it is combinatory (by the composition of forces)" (Foucault 1977: 167).

Holmes and Gastaldo (2002) explain that for Foucault, the chief function of disciplinary power is to "train" individuals to enhance their productive potential and make optimal use of their capacities. Thus aside from the disciplinary practices outlined above, three disciplinary techniques constitute the core of disciplinary power: hierarchical observation, normalizing judgment and examination. Each is examined.

Hierarchical Observation

Foucault (1977) describes the exercise of discipline as a mechanism that coerces by means of observation. Those at the top of the power structure can monitor all activities by means of an omnipresent and insidious system of surveillance (Dzurec 1989). Similar to the panopticon[1], the perfect disciplinary apparatus allows a single glance to continually see everything while remaining invisible, thus giving it multiple, automatic and anonymous power. Disciplinary power is then "both absolutely indiscreet, since it is everywhere and always alert, since by its very principle it leaves no zone of shade and constantly supervises the very individuals who are entrusted with the task of supervising; and absolutely 'discreet', for it functions permanently and largely in silence" (Foucault 1977: 177).

Normalizing Judgement

Foucault (1977) states that a micro-penal mechanism based on the non-observance of rules is at the heart of every disciplinary system . Normalizing judgement involves the upholding of established doctrines where non-conforming activities

---

1   The panopticon a model prison that functioned as a round-the-clock surveillance machine, was introduced around 1787 by Jeremy Bentham. The design of the prison ensured that prisoners never knew whether they were being monitored or not thus resulting in prisoners self policing for fear of being watched.

are punishable and conforming activities are rewarded. As such, disciplinary punishment is essentially corrective and has the function of reducing gaps. Corrective effects involve expiation and repentance and are obtained through training (*dressage*).

In terms of normalizing judgement, two opposite poles define performance: negative and positive. As such, discipline punishes by demoting to a lower rank and rewards by promoting to a higher one. . The rank itself is a form of punishment or reward. As such, "the perpetual penality that traverses all points and supervises every instant in the disciplinary institutions compares, differentiates, hierarchizes, homogenizes, excludes. In short, it normalizes" (Foucault 1977: 183).

Like surveillance, normalization becomes an important instrument of power at the end of the classical age. In an effort to institute normality, standardized education has introduced for medicine and generic norms of health were established for hospitals (Foucault 1977). Additionally, membership in a homogeneous social body contributes to the classification, hierarchization and distribution of ranks. "In a sense, the power of normalization imposes homogeneity; but it individualizes by making it possible to measure gaps, to determine levels, to fix specialities and to render the differences useful by fitting them one to another" (Foucault 1977: 184). In other words, as a result of measurement, the norm introduces the shading of individual differences in an attempt to standardize people and practices.

Examination

For Foucault (1977), examination brings together both hierarchical observation and normalizing judgement and is highly ritualized. Knowledge becomes a form of power, where examination measures "levels of knowledge or skill" and imposes "diagnostic labels" (Dzurec 1989: 72). Examination thus serves to decide and establish *the truth*. According to Foucault (1977: 185), the "visible brilliance" of examination comes from the superimposition of power and knowledge. Examination is thus the technique by which power permits the objectification of its subjects.

Foucault (1977) explores how hospitals became places for regular observation where patients were (and still are to this day) in a state of continuous monitoring and perpetual examination. Simultaneously, physicians gained power over religious staff who were reduced to subordinate roles, the position of the "nurse" was created and the hospital became a place of training (Foucault 1977). "The well-disciplined hospital became the physical counterpart of the medical discipline; this discipline could now abandon its textual character and take its references not so much from the tradition of author-authorities as from a domain of objects perpetually offered for examination" (Foucault 1977: 186).

Registration and documentation accompany examination, and the resulting documents make is possible "to classify, to form categories, to determine averages, to fix norms" (Foucault 1977: 190). As such, examination and documentation have two purposes: they allows people to maintain their individual features and own aptitudes and abilities; and they make possible via the birth of a comparative system, the description of groups and the calculation of gaps between individuals. As a result, each individual becomes a "case" that can be "described, judged, measured, compared with others, in his very individuality; and it is also the individual who has to be trained or corrected, classified, normalized, excluded" (Foucault 1977: 191).

According to Foucault (1975), discipline marks the reversal of the political axis of individualization. Consequently, in a disciplinary regime, as power becomes more anonymous, those on whom it is exercised tend to be more strongly individualized. For Foucault (1977: 193), "the transition from historic-ritual mechanisms for the formation of individuality to the scientifico-disciplinary mechanisms ... is the moment when a new technology of power and a new political anatomy of the body were implemented."

Relationship between Power and Knowledge

Foucault argues that knowledge is inextricably linked to power, and explores the power/knowledge relationship through the concept of discourse (Cheek 2000). According to Foucault, discourse both sanctions and restricts the production of knowledge by allowing certain ways of thinking while excluding others (Cheek 2000). Foucault (1977: 27) believes that knowledge is intrinsic to the exercise of power as illustrated by this statement:

> Perhaps we should abandon the belief that ... the renunciation of power is one of the conditions of knowledge. We should admit rather that power produces knowledge (and not simply by encouraging it because it serves power or by applying it because it is useful); that power and knowledge directly imply one another; that there is no power relation without the correlative constitution of a field of knowledge, nor any knowledge that does not presuppose and constitute at the same time power relations.

Consequently, "every development of knowledge fosters an increase in specific forms of power, and conversely, any expansion of specific power required an increase in specific forms of knowledge" (Chambon, Irving and Epstein 1999: 275). Cheek (2000) applies Foucault's conception of power/knowledge to explain the current status of the nursing profession. According to Cheek (2000), the way nurses and nursing as a profession is currently portrayed is directly related to powers and practices that gave value to certain aspects of nursing while excluding others. As a result, the dominant discourse in health care with its associated norms and values is what is shaping nursing and nurses (Cheek 2000).

Another significant contribution of Foucault's analysis of power lies in his belief that power is not merely oppressive but also productive. "In fact power produces; it produces reality; it produces domains of objects and ritual of truth"

(Foucault 1977: 194). Thus power produces knowledge which operates as a form of lens through which one comes to recognize oneself and others. As such, by taking up and rejecting certain identities, one normalizes his/her own behaviour and that of others, making knowledge an integral part of the regulatory process (Mason 2002).

Violence as an Instrument of Power

For Foucault, "where there is power there is resistance" and "resistance is never in a position of exteriority in relation to power" (Foucault 1976: 127). As such, resistance can be compared to a chemical catalyst that brings to light power relations (Foucault 1982), where power could be identified through the manifestations of forms of resistance (Chambon, Irving and Epstein 1999). Mason (2002) explains that violence can engender practices of resistance; and that the perceived risk of violence is enough to exert a subtle governing influence over victims or potential victims of violence.

For Foucault (1982), while violence (and consent) do not constitute the basic nature of power, they certainly are instruments of it. "Obviously, the bringing into play of power relations does not exclude the use of violence any more than it does the obtaining of consent; no doubt the exercise of power can never do without one or the other, or both at the same time" (Foucault 1982: 789). Accordingly, violence only emerges at those points where power is under threat, as the practice of violence is used in the exercise of power (Mason 2002).

Mason (2002) argues that if violence is to be theorized through Foucault's concept of power, then violence needs to be both an oppressive and a productive practice. Accordingly, on one hand, violence can be described as a form of oppression used by power when it's more subtle strategies fail – a form of struggle between power and resistance (Mason 2002). On the other hand, violence is said to be productive as it generates knowledge: knowledge embodied by violence which makes it oppressive (e.g. pain, fear, danger); and knowledge which contributes to the identification of possible targets and perpetrators of violence (Masson 2002).

Power, Violence and Institutions

Foucault views institutions as instruments of power "where power becomes embodied in techniques, and equips itself with instruments and eventually even violent means of material intervention" (Caputo and Yount 1993: 9). The notion of power, knowledge and resistance can easily be applied to employment practices, labour management conflicts and labour inequalities where divisions of labour often result in struggles and conflicts.

Obedience through disciplinary practices is also central to the production of power in organizations (Clegg 1998). For example, surveillance is not limited to direct control but can include "cultural practices of moral endorsement, enablement and suasion, to more formalized technical knowledge" (Clegg 1998: 38) such as computer monitoring or continuous and intensive administrative scrutiny of managerial decisions (McKinlay and Starkey 1998). For example, the intensification of the administrative gaze can be attributed to the promise of "rational" decision making based on notions of efficiency and bureaucracy, as confirmed by the power of "facts and numbers" (McKinlay and Starkey 1998). Recently, using a Foucauldian framework, common workplace practices found in health care institutions such as constant monitoring of time, measurement of workload and mandatory overtime were demonstrated to be associated with institutional violence to provide an alternate and critical perspective to a well known and well documented problem (St-Pierre and Holmes 2008).

Power to Explain Intra/Inter Professional Aggression

The three main techniques described by Foucault (1977) under *disciplinary power* can serve to explain intra/inter professional aggression. First, through the use of *hierarchical observation*, nurses are watched by their peers, physicians, and clients; and must remain accountable to the team, their managers and ultimately their regulatory body (St-Pierre and Holmes 2008). One is thus coerced by mean of observation. Second, Foucault's description of *normalizing judgement* helps us further understand the power of normalization. In effect, by imposing homogeneity, normalizing judgement serve to individualize by identifying gaps. If the nurse deviates too often from the norm, he/she will more than likely be reprimanded, punished and excluded; and will become the target for surveillance and intervention (Gastaldo and Holmes 1999). The nurse then risks becoming what Girard identified as a *scapegoat*, where she will be excluded from the group in an attempt to bring back social order and peace (St-Pierre and Holmes 2010). While non-conforming activities are punishable, the contrary is also true and conforming activities will often be rewarded. Finally, *examination* is a tool to assess individual characteristics and skills against those considered mandatory by the profession (Dzurec 1989). The superimposition of power and knowledge thus permits the objectivation of subject. Once again, a deviation from the norm is typically viewed as negative, undesirable and needing correction (St-Pierre and Homes 2008).

It is important to remember that for Foucault, power is two-fold: it is productive (thus seen as positive) and repressive (thus seen as negative). Using the three disciplinary techniques described above, productive power "produces" individual subjects (subjectivation), and by means of political technologies such as dressage, repressive power ensures obedience. In the case of nurses, productive power is used throughout their training to "create" health care professionals who will deliver effective patient centered care. However, upon entering the workforce, nurses are quickly confronted with the reality of the milieu where difficult working conditions and an unhealthy work environment prevail. As such, there is often a marked discordance between what the nurse was thought in school and what is now expected of her/him. A different subject is then created (again using disciplinary techniques specific to each work environment). Confronted by this dilemma, the nurse can become destabilized and her/his suffering can be manifested by anger and aggression. The nurse can also decide to resist and not conform to the demands of the workplace. In this context, resistance can be interpreted as a form of retaliation or aggression against the system.

Nursing Managers and Power – Results

Findings from my recent study involving 23 nursing managers working in acute care or psychiatry support the premise that power plays a role in intra/ inter professional aggression (St-Pierre 2010). For example, managers reported instances where they witnessed victims of verbal aggression immediately assert themselves to the perpetrator at the time of the incident. These people not only diffused a potentially explosive situation, but by directly confronting their colleague they levelled the playing field and ended up having a better rapport with the person following the incident (perpetrator was more respectful following a polite challenge). Conversely, managers have also witnessed instances where victims had not called colleagues on their behaviour and as such have given them a "permission slip" to continue.

Nursing managers also discussed power in the context of leadership. More specifically, participants at the psychiatric hospital witnessed how informal leaders were able to take on unofficial leadership roles when front line managers were removed as a cost cutting measure. Unfortunately, these informal leaders were not always positive, helpful and effective leaders. In effect, some people came to power not because of their qualifications, but because the environment became ruled by the strongest.

Hierarchy

Hierarchy was also identified by several nursing managers as contributing to inter professional workplace aggression. While many organizations are still considered very hierarchical, hierarchy was even more pervasive in the past. For example, the following passage from a participant alludes to how history contributed to hierarchy which in turns contributes to aggression.

> So everyone had their place more so in history, or historically had their place, and so whenever any were trying to break that mould, in my opinion, often resulted in aggression (22–2).

The perception of hierarchy can also contribute to people/profession feeling devalued and subjugated. In effect, some health professionals perceive themselves and their profession powerless and at the bottom of the totem pole, leaving them feeling that they have nothing to contribute to the team because their views will not be heard or taken seriously. This was referred to by one participant as "academic arrogance" where people with higher education or a higher "status" because of their education did not perceive that lower "status" colleagues could contribute to the team. These "superior" professionals made their beliefs known by openly dismissing any comments or contributions made by "inferior" people. As a result, some participants felt that inter professional aggression was related to some disciplines perceiving of themselves as above others. The following passage from a participant demonstrates how some professionals perceive it to be part of a nurse's job to take "crap".

> There is still I think a perception of OK, you are here 24/7 and, like you're the nurse and that's the drudge and you have to take that crap from patients and staff, because pretty much that's what you're here for (21–3).

Conversely, while some participants were aware that the nursing profession was not always highly regarded, they felt that nurses had an active role to play in promoting themselves and their contribution. One manager believed that this could be achieved by nurses actively taking part and speaking up during medical rounds.

Physicians were specifically identified by several participants as actively contributing to the hierarchy issue, with some physicians perceiving themselves to be above other health care professionals and expecting to be treated accordingly. As described by one participant, some physicians think rather highly of themselves.

> Depending on the professions involved, there are some physicians who, hum, for lack of a better word, think they're God (laugh), and what they say goes, and have a very abrupt manner (21–5).

Similarly, a number of managers knew of physicians who were aware of their aggressive behaviour but who also felt that they had the right to act that way since their behaviours did not impact patients. Participants also reported that some physicians perceived that the physician shortage gave them *carte blanche* to be aggressive as the organization would not confront them with the issue for fear of losing them. The following excerpt describes how employees were, and to an extent still are, afraid to confront physicians about their bad behaviour because physicians may just threaten to leave and the organization would then have a bigger problem on their hands.

> But of course nothing ever happened 'cause people were afraid to approach the physicians and actually deal with them … Like if you say that to me then I'll just leave and then what will you do? There's a physician shortage and who do you think you are to tell me what to do, and you know that kind of a thing. Like they

were sort of a law under themselves, and I must add in here that that's changed quite a bit right now (21–5).

The issue of physician recruitment was particularly true for one site located in a small town where recruiting and retaining physicians was even more challenging. Thankfully, participants at that site reported that the culture was slowly changing and that physicians were getting better at seeing themselves as members of a team rather than the person in charge.

A few participants reported that for some seniority amounted to status (hierarchy). Consequently, some employees perceived junior employees as being less credible and less deserving of privileges than senior ones. In effect, for these employees credibility and privileges come hand in hand with seniority. A manager who was new to the organization reported finding it difficult to manage employees who had been working for the same employer for decades. She explained that these employees acted as if they knew the organization and she did not, and sometimes made derogatory comments showing that they did not respect her as a manager.

Similarly, another manager who was much younger than the majority of her staff felt that her authority was often challenged because of her age. The same manager also perceived that she had limited credibility with seasoned nurses because she did not prove herself as a staff nurse before becoming a manager – "but I know that you have people on the floor who don't think that I've put in my time in order to be in this [manager's] position" (21-1). Participants who worked for the same employer for a long time, who started as front line staff and were promoted to a managerial position, spoke to the challenge of managing former peers. These managers felt the additional burden of having to ensure that decisions were fair so staff did not perceive favouritism towards friends.

Agendas

Some participants attributed instances of professional aggression as being related to personal agendas. The following passage describes how issues are sometimes lost to people's personal agendas.

> People have agendas, and that's what I think steers a lot of ... people's behaviours. It may not be discussing the issue for the issue. It will be discussing an agenda against the issue (22–5).

Hidden agendas were also attributed to concealed competition between employees and to individuals wanting to be recognized as moving forward or as being successful even if at the detriment of others. In these instances, hidden agendas can undermine team work and team cohesion. Some participants provided concrete examples of hidden agendas such as physicians verbally attacking staff and managers when not getting what they wanted because they did not want their statistics to be affected and reflect poorly on them; as well as members of a management team deliberately sabotaging meetings and the collective efforts of a working group to prevent delivery of an important document.

Politicizing Relations

Power is said to be most pervasive in "total" institutions such as forensic psychiatric institution where there is an "agenda" of social control (Holmes and Federman 2006). Total institutions were defined by Goffman (1968: 41) as "a place of residence and work where a large number of people in similar situation, live cut off from the larger society for a considerable period of time, lead a recluse life together where modalities are explicitly and meticulously regulated". "Inmates" living in total institutions have tightly scheduled daily activities imposed from above through a system of explicit and formal rules which are enforced by a body of officials (Goffman 1968). As such, in these institutions employees are often in a position of formal power over "inmates" who need to request permission to be allowed simple acts such as smoking, shaving or even using the telephone. Consequently, these "total" institutions have a different conception of and relationship with power.

Fundamental differences were identified between the two organizations included in this study. For example, the psychiatric hospital appeared to still be guided by medical hierarchy where psychiatrists were still perceived as superior to other health care professionals and where many front-line employees were still afraid to discuss/confront issues with psychiatrists. While the psychiatric hospital was attempting to change its culture, there was still evidence of reluctance to hold psychiatrists accountable for their bad behaviours, especially at one site. The fact that the psychiatric hospital was once an asylum and is rooted in history dating back a century might serve to partially explain the ongoing medical dominance and resulting power struggles.

Hospitals are known to be hierarchical organizations. The current study identified hierarchy as an element of power. The "traditional pyramid of hierarchical power" was defined by DiPalma (2004: 298) as:

> A series of horizontal levels of authority that are broader at the base and narrow toward the peak. The pyramid does not merely stand on its base with a single point of power at the top. The bureaucratically organized pyramid of hierarchy is strengthened by the support of horizontal stacks of authority controlled from the top down to the base. Through its tidy lines of authority and communication, hierarchy offers comfort and clarity.

As such, hierarchy can be described as both a *structure* and *process* where "the shape of the structure will influence the processes that are possible within it" (DiPalma 2004: 299). Vredenburgh and Brender (1998: 1338) explained that there are a lot of incentives that make people want to abuse power in organization, incentives such as reward and status acquisition as well as autonomy.

> Power represents the currency in organizations that allows individuals and groups to gratify needs and attain goals. In addition, institutionalized forms of power constitute a primary source of privilege and prestige in a democratic society.

The study findings substantiate the assessment that hospitals are hierarchical organizations. The evidence of hierarchy continuing to play a role in relationships remains prevalent today and is made visible within health care organizations by the position physicians and most especially specialists hold. As other health care professionals struggle to have their disciplines recognized and advanced, the dominant disciplines push back in an attempt to maintain their positions creating conflict and aggression (St-Pierre and Holmes 2010a).

A Canadian study by Salhani and Coulter (2009) explored the micro political struggles of nursing to gain professional legitimacy and therapeutic space amidst a new era of collaborative practice on a psychiatric unit. The study found intra-professional struggles within nursing where nurses with different academic degrees (baccalaureate versus masters) and non degree nurses had different loyalties and interests resulting in tensions. The study also identified inter-professional struggles between nursing and non-nursing professionals (such as psychiatrists, social workers, psychologists, occupational therapists and chaplains) arising from nursing's attempt to gain professional autonomy and expand its professional jurisdiction.

The current study identified hidden agendas as an instrument of power. In effect, while it is possible to observe how some people appear to repeatedly sabotage initiatives, it is often harder to understand the reason for such behaviours. In this study, hidden agendas were framed in the contexts of competition and rivalry whereby certain individuals were identified as willing to go to great lengths to move personal agendas forward and achieve success. While people with hidden agendas may be successful in attaining their goal(s), they may do so at great cost to themselves and others. Their reputations might be tarnished and they may be identified as non-team players. Moreover, their peers may distrust and disrespect them, knowing that when collaboration is needed, they may not be able to count on them. Finally, the overall perception of organizational justice may be blemished as a result of hidden agendas for "an organization" may be portrayed as being competitive and dishonest.

Conversely, it is important to validate intent when hidden agendas are suspected. In effect, some individuals can be perceived as sabotaging initiatives because of a hidden agenda when in fact they may be only displaying an inability to cope with change. While the end result remains the same (i.e. the initiative is undermined), these people cannot be described as being malicious. They are attempting to maintain status quo to protect themselves.

The above example also raises the issue of formal versus informal power, referred to as *legitimate power* by French and Raven (1959). While people attempting to sabotage an initiative are not always in a position of legitimate or formal power, they can however hold enough informal power to be able to derail a project. In some instances, people with informal power (e.g. informal leaders) can in fact have more power and influence then individuals who hold legitimate/formal power (e.g. manager). In the context of change management, it is therefore important to have informal leaders included in the decision making process so they understand the reason for the change and buy into it. Otherwise, they may work hard behind the scenes to derail the project, hence the perception of having a hidden agenda. On the other hand, not everyone has the power to sabotage an initiative. People who do not hold either formal or informal power will have limited influence on others. In effect, people with little credibility or power tend not to have many followers.

Conclusion

While not specifically in the context of workplace aggression, the concept of power has repeatedly been researched and a plethora of books and articles exist on the subject. Additionally, Michel Foucault's conceptualization of power is also well documented in the literature. This chapter contributes to the body of knowledge pertaining to workplace aggression and power by providing a fresh look at the role power plays in some instances of intra/inter professional aggression. The awareness that power games and power struggles may be at play in the context of intra/inter professional aggression provides not only a new understanding of the issue, but can also offer novel solutions to a widespread problem.

It is my hope that as we continue to explore, denounce and work on addressing the many facets of intra/inter professional aggression, we will observe an improvement in other related outcomes such as a reduction in nursing attrition, in absenteeism, and in burnout. Positive relationships at work can also lead to satisfaction at work and increased productivity. These all contribute to a better workplace which should ultimately positively influence patient outcomes, something that is dear to every nurse.

References

Caputo J. and Yount, M. 1993. Institutions, normalization, and power, in *Foucault and the Critique of Institutions*, edited by University Park. Pennsylvania: The Pennsylvania State University Press, 3–23.

Chambon, A., Irving, A., and Epstein, L. 1999. *Reading Foucault for Social Work*. New York: Columbia University Press.

Cheek, J. 2000. *Postmodern and Poststructural Approaches to Nursing Research*. Thousand Oaks, California: Sage Publication Inc.

Clegg, S. 1998. Foucault, power and organizations, in *Foucault, Management and Organization Theory*, edited by A. McKinlay and K. Starkey. Thousand Oaks, California: Sage Publications, 29–48.

DiPalma, C. 2004. Power at work: navigating hierarchies, teamwork and webs. *Journal of Medical Humanities*, 25(4), 291–308.

Duncan, S., Hyndman, K., Estabrooks, C., Hesketh, K., Humphrey, C., and Wong, J. et al. 2001. Nurses' experience of violence in Alberta and British Columbia hospitals. *Canadian Journal of Nursing Research*, 32(4), 57–8.

Dzurec, L. 1989. The necessity for an evolution of multiple paradigms for nursing research: a poststructuralist perspective. *Advances in Nursing Sciences*, 11(4), 69–77.

Farrell, G.A. 1999. Aggression in clinical settings: nurses' views – a follow-up study. *Journal of Advanced Nursing*, 29(2), 532–41.

Farrell, G.A. 2001. From tall poppies to squashed weeds: why don't nurses pull together more? *Journal of Advanced Nursing*, 35(1), 26–33.

Fédération des infirmières et infirmiers du Québec [FIIQ]. 1995. La violence au travail, ça blesse. Québec: Fédération des Infirmières et Infirmiers du Québec.

Foucault, M. 1975. *Surveiller et Punir: Naissance de la Prison*. Paris: Éditions Gallimard.

Foucault, M. 1976. *Histoire de la Sexualité I: la Volonté de Savoir*. Paris: Éditions Gallimard.

Foucault, M. 1977. *Discipline and Punish: the Birth of the Prison*. New York: Vintage Books: A division of Random House Inc.

Foucault, M. 1982. The subject and power. *Critical Inquiry*, 8(4), 777–95.

French, J. and Raven, B.H. 1959. The bases of social power, in *Studies in Social Power*, edited by D. Cartwright. Institute for Social Research, 150–67.

Gastaldo, D. and Holmes, D. 1999. Foucault and nursing: a history of the present. *Nursing Inquiry*, 6(4), 231–240.

Goffman, E. 1968. *Asiles: Études sur la Condition Sociale des Malades Mentaux*. Les Éditions de Minuit. Paris, France.

Hesketh, K., Duncan, S., Estabrooks, C., Reimer, M., Giovannetti, P., and Hyndman, K. et al. 2003. Workplace violence in Alberta and British Columbia hospitals. *Health Policy*, 63, 311–21.

Holmes, D. and Federman, C. 2006. Organizations as evil structures, in *Forensic Psychiatry: Influences of Evil*, edited by T. Mason. New Jersey: Humana Press, 15–30.

Holmes, D. and Gastaldo, D. 2002. Nursing as means of governmentality. *Journal of Advanced Nursing*, 38(6), 557–65.

International Council of Nurses [ICN]. 1999. *Guidelines on coping with violence in the workplace*. [Online]. Available at: http://www.icn.ch/guide_violence. pdf. [accessed: 5 December 2005].

Leiper, J. 2005. Nurse against nurse: how to stop horizontal violence. *Nursing*, 35(3), 44–5.

Longo, J. and Sherman, R.O. 2007. Leveling horizontal violence. *Nursing Management*, 38(3), 34–7, 50–51.

Manderino, M.A. and Berkey, N. 1997. Verbal abuse of staff nurses by physicians. *Journal of Professional Nursing*, 13(1), 48–55.

Mason, G. 2002. Violence: an instrument of power, in *The Spectacle of Violence: Homophobia, Gender and Knowledge*. New York: Routledge, 118–35.

McKenna, B.G., Smith, N.A., Poole, S.J., and Coverdale, J.H. 2003. Horizontal violence: experiences of registered nurses in their first year of practice. *Journal of Advanced Nursing*, 42(1), 90–96.

McKinlay, A. and Starkey, K. 1988. The velvet grip: managing managers in the modern corporation, in *Foucault, Management and Organization Theory*, edited by A. McKinlay and K. Starkey. Thousand Oaks, California: Sage Publications, 111–24.

Oweis, A., and Diabat, K.M. 2005. Jordanian nurses perception of physicians' verbal abuse: findings from a questionnaire survey. *International Journal of Nursing Studies*, 42, 881–8.

Randle, J. 2003. Bullying in the nursing profession. *Journal of Advanced Nursing*, 43(4), 395–401.

Rosenstein, A.H. 2002. Nurse-physician relationships: impact on nurse satisfaction and retention. *American Journal of Nursing*, 102(6), 26–34.

Salhani, D. and Coulter, I. 2009. The politics of interprofessional working and the struggle for professional autonomy in nursing. *Social Science & Medicine*, 68(7), 1221–8.

Shields, M., and Wilkins, K. 2006. *Findings from the 2005 national survey of the work and health of nurses*. [Online: Ottawa, Canada: Statistics Canada; Canadian Institute for Health Information [CIHI]; Health Canada]. Available at: http://www.hc-sc.gc.ca/hcs-sss/alt_formats/hpb-dgps/pdf/pubs/2005-nurse-infirm/2005-nurse-infirm_e.pdf. [accessed: 30 August 2007].

St-Pierre, I. 2010. Understanding the management of intra/inter professional aggression: a critical nursing ethnography (Unpublished doctoral dissertation). Ottawa: Author.

St-Pierre, I. and Holmes, D. 2008. Managing nurses through disciplinary power: a Foucauldian analysis of workplace violence. *Journal of Nursing Management*, 16(3), 352–9.

St-Pierre, I. and Holmes, D. 2010. Mimetic desire and professional closure: toward a theory of intra/inter-professional aggression. *Research and Theory for Nursing Practice: An International Journal*, 24(2), 57–72.

Thomas, S.P. 2003. Horizontal hostility: nurses against themselves: how to resolve this threat to retention. *American Journal of Nursing*, 103(10), 87–8.

Vredenburgh, D. and Brender, Y. 1998. The hierarchical abuse of power in work organization. *Journal of Business Ethics*, 17(12), 1337–47.

Chapter 8

Examining Nurse-to-Nurse Horizontal Violence and Nurse-to-Student Vertical Violence through the Lens of Phenomenology

Sandra P. Thomas

Introduction

"I'm a female Southerner, trained from birth to be passive-aggressive. You can cut them, but don't let them know they're bleeding until they look down and see it" – Female RN, participating in study by Smith, Droppleman, and Thomas (1996).

"She purposely attacked me, embarrassing me in front of others, humiliating me, trying to make me look incompetent" – Male RN participating in study by Brooks, Thomas, and Droppleman (1996).

These excerpts from interviews conducted by my research team depict nurses mistreating other nurses, being "mean to our colleagues" in the words of Fudge (2006). Although it is estimated that 80 per cent of nurses have such experiences (Lewis 2006), scholars contend that the meanness is "hidden" (Vessey, DeMarco, Gaffney, and Budin 2009), shrouded from view like "the elephant in the room" (Sincox and Fitzpatrick 2008), and underreported (Hutchinson, Vickers, Jackson, and Wilkes 2006a). Considering the plethora of recent literature about nurse-to-nurse maltreatment, it seems the "secret" is out. Dozens of articles have been published, documenting the phenomenon or dispensing advice about coping with it. Authors such as Sellers, Millenbach, Kovach, and Yingling (2009/2010) say that we must call the phenomenon by name before we can begin to eradicate it. This admonition begs the question: What should we call this phenomenon?

Naming the Phenomenon

Many terms for nurse-to-nurse maltreatment are available. In older literature, it was usually called horizontal hostility or horizontal violence (HV). For example, Muff wrote eloquently about the phenomenon of horizontal violence in 1982. Perhaps "violence" was an unfortunate choice when initially naming the phenomenon, because it conjures up images of actual physical attack. The interpersonal meanness between nurses seldom involves physical attack. Nurses wound each other with words, and with more subtle indicators of hostility such as giving someone a cold shoulder or spreading gossip (Thomas 2009). Research demonstrates that this nurse-to-nurse hostility is more distressing than the abusive behavior of physicians (which is also widespread) (Farrell 1997: 1999).

In recent years, new labels for HV have emerged. "Disruptive behavior" is a label that gained currency following a 2005 paper by Rosenstein and O'Daniel. Clark (2005) used the term "incivility" to describe disruptive behaviors in nursing education, generated by attitudes of faculty superiority and student entitlement. The terms "lateral violence," "bullying," and "mobbing" came into prominence in the literature of the past decade, most notably in European and Australian papers (Stanley, Martin, Nemeth, Michel, and Welton 2007, Hutchinson, Vickers, Jackson, and Wilkes 2006b, Fornes, Reines, and Sureda 2004, Stevens 2002, Einarsen 2000, Quine 1999, Turnbull 1995). "Bullying" and "mobbing" originally referred to abusive behavior of groups rather than individual workers, although "bullying" seems to have become an umbrella term in recent literature (Vessey et al. 2009). Research by an Australian team showed that bullies often form alliances and engage in repeated acts that, over time, destroy their victims' self-confidence, morale, and productivity (Hutchinson et al. 2006b, Hutchinson et al. 2006c).

Metaphors for HV

Colorful metaphorical language is used to describe the HV phenomenon, such as "a blight" (Dulaney and Zager 2010) and "professional terrorism" (Farrell 1997). Broome (2008) called perpetrators of horizontal violence "sharks," and Hutchinson et al. (2006b) called alliances of nurse bullies "wolves in a pack." Victims of HV have been called "squashed weeds" (Farrell 2001). The metaphor of *cannibalism* came into nursing discourse with the oft-cited paper by Meissner (1986) in which the phrase "eating our young" was used. Meissner was referring to faculty treatment of nursing students. Likewise, Jarratt (1981: 10) was referring to abusive faculty behaviors when she wrote: "The 'we' who were being mistreated or misunderstood then, are the 'they' of today." Missing from this literature about intergenerational transmission of abuse were actual research reports of *staff nurse abuse of students*, a gap which our 2009 study (Thomas and Burk) addressed. In that paper, we asserted that the term "vertical violence" should be used for these cases, because student nurses are undeniably lower in the institutional hierarchy than their staff nurse abusers. This distinction is seldom made, however. For example, Rowe and Sherlock (2005) titled their article "Stress and Verbal Abuse in Nursing: Do Burned Out Nurses Eat Their Young?", but perusal of the article revealed that the researchers did not investigate nurses "eating our young." The verbally abusive behaviors occurred between nurse peers, not between staff nurses and students. (The careful reader also notes that RN burnout was an implied cause of the verbal abuse, but burnout was not measured in the study).

The Link between HV and Staff Nurse Attrition

Noted Censullo (2008: E12), "no other profession, beyond soldiering or security, demands that its professionals save lives and concurrently take verbal and physical abuses." Censullo construes an inhospitable work environment as a breach of the caring ideology that motivates individuals to enter nursing: "It is not natural that individuals who strive to heal and/or empower others should be so vilely abused and undefended." She argues that breach of ideology is a cause of the worldwide nursing shortage, i.e., quitting is the only ideologically compatible solution if the breach cannot be eliminated. Research supports Censullo's argument: Studies across the globe indicate that workplace abuse is a major cause of staff attrition (Vessey et al. 2009, Stevens 2002). New graduates are particularly vulnerable to the destructive impact of HV (Vessey et al. 2009). According to Griffin (2004), as many as 60 per cent of new graduates leave their first position within six months because of HV. In the study by Vessey et al. (2009), 15 per cent of bullied nurses who resigned did so without even having a new job lined up. Leaving a unit does not necessarily relieve psychological trauma, however. Memories of mistreatment can linger for years. One survey respondent was so traumatized that she gave away the uniforms that she had worn when working on the dysfunctional unit (Dulaney and Jacobs 2010).

The Why Question—Why Do Nurses Engage in Maltreatment of One Another?

Among the early explanations of HV—which still provoke debate—is that proffered by Rodgers (1982). She proposed that the hostile interactions between nurse peers could be attributed to *envy*. She explained that human envy, in the psychoanalytic tradition, originates in the early mother-baby relationship. The breast is the first object of envy, and consequently, woman is the first person envied. Nursing, as a female-dominated profession, evokes the image of the nursing mother. According to Rodgers' argument, the profession is "vulnerable to angry, envious, destructive, though perhaps largely unconscious, impulses of the many others with whom we deal—patients, as well as physicians and other colleagues."

Other authors sought to explain women's inhumanity to other women, a phenomenon that is not confined to nurses. Chesler (2001) compiled countless examples of undermining, manipulation, and cruelty inflicted by women upon other women. Although Chesler's explanation of the behavior was derived from psychodynamic theory, she also acknowledged the influence of patriarchal culture. Women—especially those performing "women's work" such as nursing—

are devalued in a patriarchal culture, and internalize the culture's judgment of their inferiority. According to this argument, women cannot view their female colleagues as valuable (and presumably cannot treat them with respect). In support of Chesler's claim, female nurses in our studies often referred to other nurses with derogatory terms such as "dizzy Lizzies," "dingbats," and "bad apples." It is hard to imagine male professionals, such as doctors or lawyers, speaking of colleagues in this way.

Gender differences in expression of anger and aggression are often considered when seeking the etiology of HV in nursing. There is a sizeable literature on differences between women and men in aggression (see Thomas 2006 for a summary of this literature). In brief, overt aggression generally feels good to men because it conforms to gender role socialization for masculinity and confers rewards of power and control over others (Campbell 1993). Traditional socialization for femininity, on the other hand, inculcates an entirely different attitude: anger and aggression are ugly, unfeminine, and ineffective (Brown and Gilligan 1992). Growing girls learn to present a façade of niceness, stifling negative emotions. Anger leaks out in passive-aggressive acts towards other girls, such as giving "the silent treatment." This is called "relational aggression" in the developmental literature (e.g., Crick and Grotpeter 1995). Authors such as Dellasega (2005) portray the continuation of relational aggression into adulthood in books such as "Mean Girls Grown Up: Adult Women Who Are Still Queen Bees, Middle Bees, and Afraid-to-Bees."

Depending upon an individual nurse's uptake of gender role socialization, and his or her cultural heritage, conformity to these gender norms will vary. It is not known to what extent contemporary nurses adhere to stereotypical conceptions of "masculinity" and "femininity" and whether horizontal violence can be attributed to the predominantly female composition of the nursing workforce. I contend that female gender is not a sufficient explanation of HV in nursing, however, because our research showed that HV is not confined to females (Brooks et al. 1996). Both male and female nurses gave, and received, overt verbal attacks. Both men and women chose to suffer in silence after incidents of HV. Both described relationships with coworkers that had been completely severed.

More plausible, in my view, are the etiological arguments relying on Freire's (2000) oppressed group model, such as that of Roberts (1983). Roberts (1983) contended that nurse-to-nurse maltreatment was no different than the behavior of other oppressed groups who fight amongst themselves because they cannot vent their anger and frustration upward toward their superiors. She supported her argument by comparing nurses (lower in the hospital hierarchy than physicians and administrators since the time of Nightingale) to colonized Africans, Jews, and African Americans.

Although some will argue that today's nurses are less oppressed than the nurses of earlier generations, there is no dispute that the HV phenomenon continues to exist. Ample evidence has been produced by researchers of many nationalities (Yildirim and Yildirim 2007, Hutchinson et al. 2006a, Lewis 2006, Rowe and Sherlock 2005, Daiski 2004, McKenna, Smith, Poole, and Coverdale 2003).

Reports of the phenomenon exhibit a depressing similarity. Little new insight is gained from reading study after study. It seems nonproductive to simply continue documenting the existence of horizontal violence.

Taking a Fresh Look Through the Lens of Phenomenology

The multiplicity of labels for nurses-to-nurse abuse has hampered attempts to synthesize the extant literature. For example, Lindy and Schaefer (2010) deplored the scarcity of research on the phenomenon of "negative workplace behavior" - still another label that has been introduced. Yet studies have been conducted for decades under the general umbrella of HV or the other concept labels that we have just reviewed. I contend that the phenomenon has not changed during my 50 years in nursing. It is only our discourse about it that seems to shift from decade to decade. While there is disagreement about the proper label for the phenomenon, there is agreement on its destructive impact on individual nurses and on unit morale and its direct correlation with failure to retain new graduates.

Viewing the phenomenon of HV from the perspective of existential phenomenology may allow us to see it freshly (Merleau-Ponty 1962). Phenomenological philosophy asserts that person and world form a Gestalt; they co-construct one another. If person and world co-construct one another, how can person be understood as a discrete entity separately from world, and how can world be grasped without consideration of the unique perceptions of the persons intertwined with that world? In this chapter, I return to my research data, gleaned from in-depth, face-to-face phenomenological interviews with nurses (Thomas 2009, Shattell, Andes, and Thomas 2008, Brooks et al. 1996, Smith et al. 1996,) to seek a new understanding of horizontal violence. I will use the term horizontal violence to refer to staff nurse to staff nurse aggression and vertical violence to refer to abusive behavior of staff nurses toward student nurses. My research has included non-hospital settings, but here I concentrate on the hospital because the hospital is still the major place of employment for nurses. The hospital constitutes a unique work environment. Ostensibly devoted to the humane activities of curing and caring, our studies show that hospitals may be experienced as dehumanizing, cold, and even cruel (Thomas 2009, Shattell et al. 2008, Shattell 2002).

Perception is the Key to Understanding

For French philosopher Maurice Merleau-Ponty (1962), phenomenology was a way to evade the abstract constructions and manipulations of science and return to simple descriptions of human involvement with the world that could lead to new understandings. Researchers who employ phenomenological methodology accomplish this descriptive enterprise through eliciting the *perceptions* of their research participants. Perception provides "a direct experience of the events, objects, and phenomena of the world. Unlike thinking and language, which deal with ideas and representations of the world, perception always concerns an ongoing transaction between person and world" (Thomas and Pollio 2002: 14).

Merleau-Ponty brought the figure-ground concept from German Gestalt psychology into his work. He pointed out that perception of any phenomenon has a figure-background structure: what stands out as distinct, commanding our awareness, is *figure*; what is less prominent at the moment (but nevertheless still there) is *ground*. For example, to a woman in labor, uterine contractions become her sole focus (i.e., become figural in her consciousness). Contextual elements, such as the relationship with her spouse, the time of the day, the color of the walls in the labor room, recede from her perceptual awareness. She is dimly aware of persons coming and going, asking her questions and checking her progress. Only episodically do these persons become figural. If she has requested an analgesic, the slowness of the nurse will become figural in her perception.

The Four Existential Grounds

The phenomenological researcher must report both central and contextual aspects of human experience. There are four existential grounds. Using the terms of Munhall (2007), these contextual grounds are corporeal, temporal, relational, and spatial. In our own textbook, we simply say Body, Time, Others, and World (Thomas and Pollio 2002). Obviously, these contexts of lived experience are all interconnected and contribute to making sense of the data we collect from our research participants. As noted by Merleau-Ponty (1962: 365):

> But if we rediscover time beneath the subject, and if we relate to the paradox of time those of the body, the world, the thing, and others, we shall understand that beyond these there is nothing to understand.

In the following sections of the chapter, we immerse ourselves in the perceptions of nurses regarding the four existential grounds of their day-to-day work life. We listen to their words, and the words of patients, extracted from phenomenological research interviews. We undertake this exploration because the phenomenon of nurse-to-nurse violence must be understood within its contextual grounds.

World of the Hospital

Hospitals have evolved from "houses of mercy" in the Byzantine era to "houses of rehabilitation" in the Renaissance era to "houses of dissection and cure" in the eighteenth and nineteenth centuries to today's "houses of high technology" with their sophisticated monitors and computer systems (Risse 1999). Sometimes I fear that my old article predicting the death of hands-on nursing may yet come true, as technology becomes ever more dominant (Thomas 1980).

When we consider what the world of the hospital is like, we reflect on both the physical appearance of the place, and the deeper meaning of lived experiences of the hospital. First, we examine appearance. Architects of modern hospitals aimed for a clean and sterile look with little attention to aesthetics. Consequently, hospitals were often drab and prison-like, with concrete walls and few windows to admit natural light and views of nature. Corridors were noisy and crowded, furniture was institutional, and seldom were nurses provided with a private place for respite from the pressures of the unit. In recent years, there has been a movement to make hospitals look more like places of healing.

While newly built hospitals are often more pleasing in general appearance (e.g., greater attention to décor, large windows permitting views of garden greenery), human experiences within their walls are often dehumanizing and distressing—for both patients and nurses. *Confinement* was a major theme in Shattell's (2002) phenomenological study of the world of the hospital ("You're shut up in here"). Both patients and nurses experience the environment as restricting their freedom (Shattell et al. 2008). Patients are *ordered* to enter the facility; nurses are *ordered* by doctors to enact certain treatments. The response to orders is to obey, not to question. Orders, rules, and regulations dictate much of what nurses do in their daily work. For example, nurses in our studies resented being ordered to do unnecessary tasks, such as documenting skin integrity every shift on ambulatory patients (Shattell et al. 2008).

Another figural theme in Shattell's study was the patient's ever-present sense of *insecurity* and impending danger (Shattell 2002). "There is no 'simple' procedure or 'minor' hospitalization" (Adkins, cited in Thomas 2009). The ultimate danger, of course, is death itself.

No matter how aesthetically pleasing hospitals could ever become, they are still places of pain and death. Patients are grappling with profound existential questions. Nurses cannot help but be deeply affected by working in such a world. Merleau-Ponty noted that the world "invades" us. Nurses are invaded by the sights of mutilated and burned bodies, the smells of vomitus and tarry stools, the sounds of bereaved parents crying in anguish (Gunther and Thomas 2006). Inexplicably, some patients die after routine surgery, leaving care providers to wonder why, and whether anything could have been done differently (Gunther and Thomas 2006). Remediation of a hospital's oppressive architectural features, although welcomed by patients and nurses alike, cannot ever obliterate the heaviness of the enterprise taking place within its walls.

Body

Reading Merleau-Ponty's (1962) writings on the body is revelatory. For Merleau-Ponty, the body is the fundamental category of human existence. It is the unwavering vantage point of perception, giving meaning to the spaces through which it moves and the objects that it uses. Merleau-Ponty called attention to the difference between the "body object" that is palpated and dissected by medicine and the "body subject" that is the body of the patient's personal experience. Hospital nurses, even if imbued with a view of the body as sacred, are called upon by the system to perform their bodily ministrations in a task-oriented and time-pressured way—a way that leaves patients feeling like objects on an assembly line and nurses feeling frustrated and discouraged.

What nurses do to patients' bodies violates normal social rules regarding intimate bodily contact. Patients' bodies are exposed to us and they lie vulnerable before us. Noted Lawler (1993: 83), "nurses have a degree of access to bodies and a need to know about the body that is incomparable to any other group." Nurses, in fact, have amassed a vast knowledge of the body, and expertise in providing physical care and comfort measures. It takes an astute observer to notice the first indication of a pressure sore forming on a heel. It is an artful act to know exactly how to change a patient's position and place every pillow in the best way. In the following account of a bed bath (sometimes considered a lowly procedure), a cardiac patient attests to its healing effect:

> The bath was a thoroughly visceral experience and the relation to the nurse, too, had that quality of utter physicality. Somehow, she seemed to sense the threshold of my body's tolerance for pain and touch ... [After the bath] I simply felt so much better, physically better in a way that was indeed experienced as healing ... "physical healing." The nurse touching me had a peculiar effect: I was allowed to be myself and feel my own body again." (van Manen 1998: 8).

Unfortunately, expert provision of physical care is not valued by society. Nurses' work is considered "dirty work." As Lawler's (1993: 221) research showed, nurses can talk about their "dirty work" only with other nurses, because society forbids discussion of bodily functions: "things which nurses do are considered dirty and they make people feel uncomfortable." Demoralizing and degrading depictions of nurses in the media perpetuate public devaluation of the profession. On many popular television programs, "nurses are generally just dim or disagreeable servants... [who] fetch things for physicians and clean up patient messes" (Summers 2010: 18). Not only does society devalue body work, but nurses themselves internalize the societal devaluation. Nurses in our studies often referred to their work as "scut work" or "taking care of the petty things" (Thomas 2009: 101).

We cannot leave the topic of body without considering the nurse's own body. Enduring through work shifts as long as 12 hours, the nurse's tired body may ache for a rest. The back, the shoulders, the feet may begin to hurt. Yet the well-ingrained nursing norm of self-sacrifice ("Good nurses work until they drop") prevents the nurse from taking restorative breaks. Sheer fatigue is perhaps an unacknowledged contributor to horizontal violence, because it precipitates irritation and short tempers.

Time

We humans experience time from a particular perceptual viewpoint. According to Merleau-Ponty (1962), time is not a system of objective positions but a mobile setting that moves toward and away from us. Depending upon the activity in which we are immersed, time can be perceived as fast or slow. In Western societies, people are very oriented to clocks and calendars. Speed and efficiency are highly valued. Time seems to be parceled out somewhat stingily—we say that there is "never enough" of it, and we hurry to get things done "in time." Perceptions of time by hospitalized patients and nurses are very different (Shattell et al. 2008). For the patients, the passage of time is excruciatingly slow, punctuated at brief intervals by fleeting glimpses of doctors and ministrations of caregivers (Shattell et al. 2008, Radley and Taylor 2003, Shattell 2002). In Radley and Taylor's study (2003), patients photographed objects that were perceived as meaningful to their experience of hospitalization. One patient photographed the ward clock to show that "time stands still."

In contrast, time is perceived by nurses as flying. Throughout the Western world, the nursing shortage has led to higher nurse-patient ratios. More is demanded from the sturdy souls who remain on the job. The corporatization of the healthcare delivery system in the United States, and various restructuring and reengineering measures in other countries, have escalated time pressures experienced by nurses, especially those working in profit-driven hospitals. Speaking of her experience as a new graduate, one of our study participants said, "I really felt like a robot, you know, that somebody just pressed a button and said 'go'… I just felt overwhelmed. I jumped from one room to the next trying to meet the patients' needs" (Smith et al. 1996: 28).

Time becomes a tyrant that hospital nurses decry because they feel they cannot give patients proper care, as shown in this excerpt from our data:

> "I knew the stuff I was taught to do, but I did not have time to do it…. It is like
> a rat race. We are here to push pills and drugs, but no time to do patient care….
> It seems I always fall behind on time and that makes me angry…. It is like you
> are pulled in 20 different directions" (Thomas 2009: 15).

Study participants felt that hospital management expected Supernurses. The absurdity of management's expectations was captured perfectly by this study participant:

> "I think of the fairy tale Rumpelstiltskin, where they would put the person in the
> room full of straw every night and say 'produce gold.' That's how I feel" (Smith
> et al. 1996: 28).

Other People

Connections with Others allow humans to transcend their existential aloneness. Merleau-Ponty (1962) wrote about the intersections of his path and the paths of Others: "My own and other people's [paths] intersect and engage each other like gears." He was more optimistic about interpersonal relationships than other existential philosophers such as Sartre or Heidegger, speaking of the potential for deep dialogue in which common ground could be discovered between Self and Other (Thomas and Pollio 2002). He wrote inspiringly about the recognition and affirmation from those who are our fellow travelers in life's journey (Thomas 2005). However, recognition and affirmation from fellow nurses were strikingly absent from our studies of hospital nurses (Brooks et al. 1996, Smith et al. 1996, Thomas 2009). Nurses were angry because they were always being told what they were doing wrong. No one noticed or mentioned what they were doing right. For example, "Sue" believes that she is doing some good things that make a difference, but "nobody will remember it" (Smith et al. 1996: 26). "Bob" described the way his critical nurse manager would walk through the unit "like a stick stirring up rattlesnakes," getting all of the nurses "in an uproar and tense...pointing out all these small things" (Thomas 2009: 19). The longing for support from management and coworkers was profound and poignant, as shown in these verbatim quotes from our data:

> "One of the biggest voids in my life is peer support" (Thomas 2009: 20) "I have never seen where nurse administrators will be your advocate. They sell you down the tubes. They have totally lost sight of the nursing side. And you shouldn't be at sides or at war" (Thomas 2009: 19).

Staff Nurse to Staff Nurse Horizontal Violence

Being scapegoated and unfairly accused by other nurses was a particularly galling form of HV to our study participants. Often the accusation was made behind the nurse's back. For example, a nurse is reported to the manager and reprimanded for an infraction. The manager protects the identity of the accuser, preventing the nurse from taking any productive action. The injustice of the unfair accusation rankles. The sniper is hidden from view. This type of HV was the most common form reported in a recent survey of critical care nurses (Alspach 2008). As one critical care nurse succinctly stated, "I stand accused and know not the accuser" (Alspach 2008: 18). For one male RN, this type of workplace abuse replicated a childhood experience of unjust accusation (Brooks et al. 1996: 13).

Abuse inflicted by peers in the presence of other individuals was humiliating. Powerless to mount an effective response, one man admitted, "I stood there and took it. It's kind of like kicking a dog, and the dog never runs off." Nurses in all of our studies described a form of HV that is perhaps the epitome of powerlessness:

inability to achieve a hearing for one's concerns. "Joy" explains, "I am most angry at the lack of being heard, that what I need and what I want does not matter…You are a nonentity…Everybody does not have to agree with me, but I would like the courtesy of being heard" (Smith et al. 1996: 29).

Metaphors used by female nurses in our 1996 study (Smith et al. 1996: 24) depicted a *war zone* ("It's like an armed camp") in which they were frequently under assault: "I become very fatigued by having to do all these battles;" "There is character assassination." Other military terms in common nurse parlance included "on the firing line," "in the trenches," and "turf battles." The institutional hierarchy was depicted with the military term "chain of command."

To be sure, combatants in the war zone were not all nurses. Verbal assaults were perpetrated by physicians and patients as well as by peers. In response to the assaults, nurses engaged in counterattacks (both overt and covert) and also turned impotent anger on themselves.

In a subsequent study of male nurses (Brooks et al. 1996) the work environment was similarly described as hostile. Like the female nurses in the previous study, military language predominated: "It was rapid-fire;" "I was getting flak;" "I went in with loaded guns;" "You have to fight for what you get" (Brooks et al. 1996: 6). Descriptions of nurse-to-nurse maltreatment in our data included violent words, like "cutting" and "needling," that connote painful wounds.

For both female and male nurses, events of workplace abuse that had occurred many years earlier were recalled in vivid detail. Neither female nor male nurses had effective strategies for management of their negative emotions. Residual anger and pain often lingered for weeks, months, even years. The theme "old baggage" from a 2010 phenomenological study (Lindy and Schaefer) corroborates the continued inability of nurses to resolve conflicts. Confrontation of a bully was rare in our studies, and the theme "they just take it" depicted continuing passivity of victims in Lindy and Schaefer's (2010: 288) data. Speaking of one bully, a study participant stated, "It's just how she is." This reminded me of the resignation exhibited by our own study participants. They wished for someone or something to deal with the bully and/ or improve the adversarial work climate, but they could not envision themselves taking action to accomplish this.

Staff Nurse to Student Vertical Violence

To a beginning student nurse, the staff nurse on the hospital unit is an extremely important Other—both a role model and a teacher of clinical skills. Therefore, it was disheartening when we found egregious maltreatment of junior students by staff nurses in our 2009 study (Thomas and Burk). Descriptors of RN behavior included "condescending, overbearing, rude, sarcastic, disrespectful, patronizing, and degrading" (Thomas and Burk 2009: 228). Severity of the vertical violence incidents ranged from discourteousness and rudeness to scapegoating and public criticism similar to that seen in our studies of nurse-to-nurse HV. Here are just three examples:

- The nurse belittled me in front of my colleagues and the patient to whom I was delivering care.
- The nurse lashed out at me because the room was not up to her standards, although it was only 8 AM, and we had only been there for an hour.
- The nurse approached me…and asked why I had not given the 0900 meds. I was not scheduled to give meds … The nurse turned to my patient and said, 'The student forgot to give you your meds, so now they are late' (Thomas and Burk 2009: 229).

Thus, the Other not only failed to welcome the novice nurses but also mistreated them, hampering their learning and undermining their fragile confidence.

Reflections on These Data

The ugliness of nurse-to-nurse maltreatment in our data suggests a variety of interpretations. Shall we presume that this interpersonal violence is simply a pathology of individual nurses? Do our data suggest that the nurses mainly lack self-esteem, manage anger poorly, or engage in passive aggression because they lack assertiveness? After all, in our own data, as well as other literature, some individuals are "bad apples," and every barrel contains a few bad apples that spoil the bushel (Smith et al. 1996). Alternatively, HV is viewed as a pathology of the group—specifically, the "oppressed group," as exemplified in the papers by Roberts (1983: 2000). This view still places blame for the abusive behavior on nurses themselves. Allegedly, the remedy is "empowerment" (Laschinger, Wong, McMahon, and Kaufmann 1999). Standard advice includes urging nurses to become more assertive and to firmly refuse victimization. The nurse must learn to swim with sharks and never bleed when injured (Broome 2008). This genre of nursing literature might be described as the "Buck up, be strong, and be proud" literature. Perhaps I have contributed to it myself with my book *Transforming Nurses' Stress and Anger* (Thomas 2009), in which I urge nurses to use their anger for empowerment.

While I have no argument with initiatives to promote individual empowerment, the fact remains that decisions that profoundly affect the welfare of the nurse are made by Others who are higher in the hierarchy. Our study participants consistently reported little influence over important decisions about safe staffing and resource allocation, even when they possessed the most accurate knowledge of what was needed (Thomas 2009). Nursing is, in fact, a classic example of an occupation in which there is high demand for performance but low decision authority. Such occupations typically generate substantial worker anger. As early as 1997, researchers demonstrated that women in high-demand-low-control jobs often displayed negative emotionality that was directed toward their supervisors and coworkers (Williams, Barefoot, Blumenthal, Helms, Luecken, Peiper et al. 1997). More recent findings by Johnston, Jones, McCann and McKee (2008) are consistent. Using computerized ecological momentary assessment, the researchers studied demand, control, and negative emotions of hospital nurses during 3 work days. The combination of high demand and low control was associated with the highest scores on the measure of negative affect. Negative affect was also high when nurses desired more control but had little. Will empowering staff nurses be sufficient when they still have no seat at the decision-makers' table and no control over many aspects of their work life?

Conclusion

Based on the foregoing analysis, drawing insights from phenomenology, I conclude that we have given disproportionate attention to nurses' own "pathology." We have failed to take a comprehensive look at all of the contextual grounds of the phenomenon of HV. Given the aforementioned heavy strain on the nurse's Body, the tyranny of Time, and a work World that is like a "war zone," should it be surprising that conflict with Others is frequent? During the decades of blaming nurses for our own "meanness" to colleagues, scant attention has been given to the hospital world and its omnipresent pressure-cooker atmosphere and demand for Supernurses. "Stressful" is too mild an adjective to capture this workplace environment of heavy pressure. Bartholomew (2006: 74) points out that nurses, situated at the bottom of the hierarchical ladder, feel "the *total weight* of all the pressures from above."

Phenomenological philosophy reminds us that person and world are inextricably linked. The lived experiences of nurses cannot be adequately understood without full cognizance of the world that "invades" them. Hospitals meet all of Stokols' (1992) criteria for conflict-prone organizations, i.e., rigid ideologies, non-participatory organizational processes, absence of shared goals, existence of competitive coalitions, and uncertainty stemming from economic changes. Conflict between nurses' goal of giving excellent patient care and a hospital's mandate to remain a financially viable business inevitably produces a power struggle (Bartholomew 2006). This is not a struggle that nurses are winning: "to do one's best and not achieve the primary goal of nursing—accomplishing what is best for a patient—is just not enough. Failure to meet this obligation results in moral distress" (Gunther and Thomas 2006: 375). Both moral distress and job dissatisfaction are widespread (e.g., Aiken et al. 2001), yet hospital executives "are in a state of denial about nurse dissatisfaction" (Nelson 2007: 19).

The research of Hutchinson, Wilkes, Jackson, and Vickers (2010) demonstrated a direct relationship between organizational factors and bullying behaviors of staff. Organizational characteristics were actually *antecedents* of bullying. Legitimate organizational processes and procedures were misused. The organizations not only tolerated, but rewarded, bullying. Many health care organizations actually cultivate a culture of "shame and blame." This appeared to be the case at one West Coast hospital where I conducted a workshop. Nurses there complained of an epidemic of snitches writing one another up for infractions. Betrayal by one's own peers was particularly painful.

Improving the nursing work environment must become a priority. A systematic literature review by Schalk, Bijl, Halfens, Hollands, and Cummings (2010) revealed a variety of interventions that have been implemented to improve the environment, e.g., adoption of primary nursing, shared governance, social support training, stress inoculation training, nursing practice quality circles, training of supervisors to give positive feedback, and an "educational toolbox," designed to improve nurses' teamwork. Most of these interventions had mixed effects, and nearly every study had design weaknesses. The authors concluded that there is an urgent need for well-controlled and sufficiently powered studies of work environment interventions. Research regarding specific interventions to address HV is especially needed, because it is almost nonexistent.

It is imperative that nurses in leadership positions assume more responsibility for improving the climate of the workplace. Conflict among a work team has direct effects on job satisfaction (Cox 2003). Corroborating our own research findings, Vessey et al. (2009: 303) found that nurse managers were often part of the problem, not part of the solution: "nurse managers were most often implicated as engaging in or condoning bullying activities." When bullying is occurring, hospital leadership must take definitive steps to change the culture. Nursing turnover, which had reached 28 per cent at one hospital, was significantly reduced after workshops were held and anti-bullying practices were instituted (Stevens 2002). Sellers et al. (2009/2010) drew from Bourdieu's (1977) *Theory of Practice* to suggest that leaders can change the "habitus" behavior of those within the work unit: "the leader has capital with which to reward members for their behavior." Anthony et al. (2005: 153) assert that the nurse manager can become the "chief retention officer," managing relationships and helping new nurses assimilate into the team via coaching and mentoring. Faculty can encourage students to report abusive incidents and support them in confronting the abusers; RN mistreatment of students should never be excused on the basis of "stress" or "workload" (Thomas and Burk 2009). New graduates can be taught a cognitive technique to cope with horizontal violence that proved to be effective in a study by Griffin (2004).

Although I have emphasized measures to improve the toxic nursing work environment, this does not preclude introspection and self-assessment by each individual nurse. Horizontal violence cannot be extinguished until we all commit ourselves to its eradication. There is no shortage of self-help articles (e.g., Broome 2008) and books about transforming conflictual relationships with peers (e.g., Thomas 2009, Bartholomew 2006). The American Nurses Association Code of Ethics points out that "the nurse is responsible for contributing to a moral environment that encourages respectful interactions with colleagues, support of peers, and identification of issues that need to be addressed... Acquiescing and accepting unsafe or inappropriate practices, even if the individual does not participate in the specific practice, is equivalent to condoning unsafe practice" (2001: 21).

Acknowledgements

The author would like to acknowledge the members of my research teams over the past 15 years and the nurses who shared their stories with us. I am also grateful to Teresa Heaton for her assistance with literature searches.

References

Aiken, L., Clarke, S. Sloane, D., and Sochalski, J. 2001. An international perspective on hospitals' work environments: the case for reform. *Policy, Politics, and Nursing Practice*, 2, 255–63.

Alspach, G. 2008. Lateral hostility between critical care nurses: a survey report. *Critical Care Nurse*, 28, 13–19.

American Nurses Association. 2001. *Code of Ethics for Nurses with Interpretive Statements*. Washington. DC: American Nurses Association.

Anthony, M., Standing, T., Glick, J., Duffy, M., Paschall, F., Sauer, M., Sweeney, D., Modic, M., and Dumpe, M. 2005. Leadership and nurse retention: the pivotal role of nurse managers. *Journal of Nursing Administration*, 35, 146–55.

Bartholomew, K. 2006. *Ending Nurse-to-Nurse Hostility: Why Nurses Eat Their Young and Each Other*. Marblehead, MA: HCPro.

Bourdieu, P. 1977. *Outline of a Theory of Practice*. Cambridge: Cambridge University Press.

Brooks, A., Thomas, S.P., and Droppleman, P. 1996. From frustration to red fury: a description of work-related anger in male registered nurses. *Nursing Forum*, 31(3), 4–15.

Broome, B.A. 2008. Dealing with sharks and bullies in the workplace. *The ABN Journal*, 28–30.

Brown, L., and Gilligan, C. 1992. *Meeting at the Crossroads: Women's Psychology and Girls' Development*. Cambridge, MA: Harvard University Press.

Campbell, A. 1993. *Men, Women, and Aggression*. New York: Basic Books.

Censullo, J.L. 2008. The nursing shortage: breach of ideology as an unexplored cause. *Advances in Nursing Science*, 31(4), E11–E18.

Chesler, P. 2001. *Women's Inhumanity to Women*. New York: Thunder Mouth's Press/ Nation Books.

Clark, C. 2008. The dance of incivility in nursing education as described by nursing faculty and students. *Advances in Nursing Science*, 31(4), E37–E54.

Cox, K.B. 2003. The effects of intrapersonal, intragroup, and intergroup conflict on team performance effectiveness and work satisfaction. *Nursing Administration Quarterly*, 27, 153–63.

Crick, N.R., and Grotpeter, J.K. 1995. Relational aggression, gender, and social-psychological adjustment. *Child Development*, 66, 710–22.

Daiski, I. 2004. Changing nurses' disempowering relationship patterns. *Journal of Advances Nursing*, 48(1), 43–50.

Dellasega, C. 2005. *Mean Girls Grown Up: Adult Women Who Are Still Queen Bees, Middle Bees, and Afraid-to-Bees*. Hoboken, NJ: Wiley.

Dulaney, P., and Jacobs, D. 2010. We hear you! Lateral violence is (unfortunately) going on right here in South Carolina. *The South Carolina Nurse*, 17(2), 1, 4.

Dulaney, P., and Zager, L. 2010. Lateral violence: it's time to stop this blight on our profession. *The South Carolina Nurse*, 17(1), 1.

Einarsen, S. 2000. Harassment and bullying at work: a review of the Scandinavian approach. *Aggression and Violent Behavior*, 4, 379–401.

Farrell, G. 1997. Aggression in clinical settings: nurses' views. *Journal of Advanced Nursing*, 25, 501–08.

Farrell, G. 1999. Aggression in clinical settings: a follow-up study. *Journal of Advanced Nursing*, 29, 532–41.

Farrell, G. 2001. From tall poppies to squashed weeds: why don't nurses pull together more? *Journal of Advanced Nursing*, 35, 26–33.

Fornes, V.J., Reines, F.J., and Sureda, G.C. 2004. Mobbing in nursing: a pilot study. *Revista ROL de Enfermeria*, 27, 8–10, 13–16.

Freire, P. 2000. *Pedagogy of the Oppressed*. New York, NY: Continuum.

Fudge, L. 2006. Why, when we are deemed to be carers, are we so mean to our colleagues? *Canadian Operating Room Nursing Journal*, 24(4), 13–16.

Griffin, M. 2004. Teaching cognitive rehearsal as a shield for lateral violence: an intervention for newly licensed nurses. *Journal of Continuing Education in Nursing*, 35, 257–63.

Gunther, M., and Thomas, S.P. 2006. Nurses' narratives of unforgettable patient care events. *Journal of Nursing Scholarship*, 38, 370–76.

Hutchinson, M., Vickers, M., Jackson, D., and Wilkes, L. 2006a. Workplace bullying in nursing: towards a more critical organizational perspective. *Nursing Inquiry*, 13, 118–26.

Hutchinson, M., Vickers, M., Jackson, D., and Wilkes, L. 2006b. Like wolves in a pack: stories of predatory alliances of bullies in nursing. *Journal of Management and Organization*, 12(3), 235–51.

Hutchinson, M., Vickers, M. Jackson, D., and Wilkes, L. 2006c. They stand you in a corner, you are not to speak: nurses tell of abusive indoctrination in work teams dominated by bullies. *Contemporary Nurse*, 21, 228–38.

Hutchinson, M., Wilkes, L., Jackson, D., and Vickers, M. 2010. Integrating individual, work group, and organizational factors: testing a multidimensional model of bullying in the nursing workplace. *Journal of Nursing Management*, 18, 173–81.

Jarratt, V. 1981. Why do nurses eat their young? *The Arkansas State Nursing Association Newsletter*, 1(2), 4, 10.

Johnston, D.W., Jones, M.M., McCann, S.K., and McKee, L. 2008. Determinants of negative affect in nurses during the working day: the role of demand, reward, control, and desire for more control. *Annals of Behavioral Medicine*, 35, S123.

Laschinger, H., Wong, C., McMahon, L., and Kaufmann, C. 1999. Leader behavior impact on staff nurse empowerment, job tension, and work effectiveness. *Journal of Nursing Administration*, 29(5), 28–39.

Lawler, J. 1993. *Behind the Screens; Nursing, Somology, and the Problem of the Body.* Redwood City, California: the Benjamin/Cummings Publishing Company.

Lewis, M. 2006. Nurse bullying: organizational considerations in the maintenance and perpetration of health care bullying cultures. *Journal of Nursing Administration*, 14(1), 52–8.

Lindy, C., and Schaefer, F. 2010. Negative workplace behaviors: an ethical dilemma for nurse managers. *Journal of Nursing Management*, 18, 285–92.

McKenna, B., Smith, N., Poole, S., and Coverdale, J. 2003. Horizontal violence: experiences of registered nurses in their first year of practice. *Journal of Advanced Nursing*, 42(1), 90–96.

Meissner, J. 1986. Nurses: are we eating our young? *Nursing*, 16(3), 51–3.

Merleau-Ponty, M. 1962. *The Phenomenology of Perception (trans. C. Smith).* London: Routledge & Kegan Paul.

Muff, J. 1982. *Women's Issues in Nursing: Socialization, Sexism, and Stereotyping.* Prospect Heights, IL: Waveland Press.

Munhall, P.L. 2007. *Nursing Research: a Qualitative Perspective.* 4th edition. Boston: Jones & Bartlett.

Nelson, R. 2007. U.S. hospitals need staffing makeover. *American Journal of Nursing*, 103(2), 19.

Page, A. 2004. *Keeping Patients Safe: Transforming the Work Environment of Nurses.* Washington, DC: National Academies Press.

Quine, L. 1999. Workplace bullying in NHS community trust: staff questionnaire survey. *British Medical Journal*, 318, 228–32.

Risse, G.B. 1999. *Mending Bodies, Saving Souls: a History of Hospitals.* Oxford, UK: Oxford University Press.

Roberts, S.J. 1983. Oppressed group behavior: implications for nursing. *Advances in Nursing Science*, 5(7), 21–30.

Roberts, S.J. 2000. Developing a positive professional identity: liberating oneself from the oppressor within. *Advances in Nursing Science*, 22(4), 71–82.

Rodgers, J. 1982. Women and the fear of being envied. *Nursing Outlook*, 30, 344–7.

Rosenstein, A., and O'Daniel, M. 2005. Disruptive behavior and clinical outcomes: perceptions of nurses and physicians. *American Journal of Nursing*, 105(1), 55–64.

Rowe, M., and Sherlock, H. 2005. Stress and verbal abuse in nursing: do burned out nurses eat their young? *Journal of Nursing Management*, 13, 242–48.

Schalk, D., Bijl, M., Halfens, R., Hollands, L., and Cummings, G. 2010. Interventions aimed at improving the nursing work environment: A systematic review. *Implementation Science*, 5: 34.

Sellers, K., Millenbach, L., Kovach, N., and Yingling, J. 2009/2010. The prevalence of horizontal violence in New York State Registered Nurses. *Journal of the New York State Nurses Association*, 20–25.

Shattell, M. 2002. Eventually it'll be over: the dialectic between confinement and freedom in the world of the hospitalized patient, in *Listening to Patients: a Phenomenological Approach to Nursing Research and Practice*, edited by S.P. Thomas and H.R. Pollio. New York: Springer, 214–36.

Shattell, M., Andes, M., and Thomas, S.P. 2008. How patients and nurses experience the acute care psychiatric environment. *Nursing Inquiry*, 15(3), 242–50.

Sincox, A., and Fitzpatrick, M. 2008. Lateral violence: calling out the elephant in the room. *Michigan Nurse*, 81 (3), 8–9.

Smith, M., Droppleman, P., and Thomas, S.P. 1996. Under assault: the experience of work-related anger in female registered nurses. *Nursing Forum*, 31(1), 22–33.

Stanley, K., Martin, M., Nemeth, L., Michel, Y., and Welton, J. 2007. Examining lateral violence in the nursing workforce. *Issues in Mental Health Nursing*, 28, 1247–1265.

Stevens, S. 2002. Nursing workforce retention: challenging a bullying culture. *Health Affairs*, 21, 189–93.

Stokols, D. 1992. Conflict-prone and conflict-resistant organizations, in *Hostility, coping and health*, edited by H.S. Friedman. Washington, DC: American Psychological Association, 65–76.

Summers, S. 2010. The truth about nursing: organization founded to monitor media portrayals of nurses. *Tennessee Nursing Extra*, 2(1), 16–20.

Thomas, S.P. 1980. The adventures of Joey in patientland...a futuristic fantasy. *Nursing Forum*, 19, 350–56.

Thomas, S.P. 2005. Through the lens of Merleau-Ponty: advancing the phenomenological\approach to nursing research. *Nursing Philosophy*, 6, 63–76.

Thomas, S.P. 2006. Cultural and gender considerations in assessment and treatment of anger-related disorders, in *Anger-related disorders: A practitioner's guide to comparative treatments*, edited by E. Feindler. New York: Springer, 71–95.

Thomas, S.P. 2009. *Transforming Nurses' Stress and Anger: Steps Toward Healing*. New York: Springer.

Thomas, S.P., and Burk, R. 2009. Junior nursing students' experiences of vertical violence during clinical rotations. *Nursing Outlook*, 57, 226–31.

Thomas, S.P., and Pollio, H.R. 2002. *Listening to Patients: a Phenomenological Approach to Nursing Research and Practice*. New York: Springer.

Turnbull, J. 1995. Hitting back at the bullies. *Nursing Times*, 91, 24–7.

van Manen, M. 1998. Modalities of body experience in illness and health. *Qualitative Health Research*, 8, 7–24.

Vessey, J.A., DeMarco, R., Gaffney, D., and Budin, W. 2009. Bullying of staff registered nurses in the workplace: a preliminary study for developing personal and organizational strategies for the transformation of hostile to healthy workplace environments. *Journal of Professional Nursing*, 25, 299–306.

Williams, R.L., Barefoot, J.C., Blumenthal, J.A., Helms, M.J., Luecken, L., Pieper, C.F. et al. 1997. Psychosocial correlates of job strain in a sample of working women. *Archives of General Psychiatry*, 54, 543–8.

Yildirim, A., and Yildirim, D. 2007. Mobbing in the workplace by peers and managers: mobbing experienced by nurses working in health care facilities in Turkey and its effect on nurses. *Journal of Clinical Nursing*, 16, 1444–53.

Chapter 9

The Rise of Violence in HIV/AIDS Prevention Campaigns: A Critical Discourse Analysis

Marilou Gagnon and Jean Daniel Jacob

Introduction

Mass media prevention campaigns are widely utilized in the field of HIV/AIDS to raise awareness of health risks and encourage the uptake of desired (healthy) behaviours (Noar, Palmgreen, Chabot, Dobransky and Zimmerman 2009). Such campaigns have beenan integral part of prevention efforts since the beginning of the HIV/AIDS epidemic, mainly because they are considered cost-effective interventions to communicate health globally while encouraging behavioural change locally (Noar et al. 2009).The use of shock or scare tactics to design HIV/AIDS prevention campaigns has been widely criticized over time by scholars and activists. Many of these refer back to the "Grim Reaper Campaign" launched by the Australian government in 1987 to illustrate how these tactics have detrimental effects on people living with HIV/AIDS (Lupton 1994). In recent years, there has been a call for more persuasive ways of raising awareness about HIV/AIDS (now considered a chronic illness) and producing high impact messages to remind mass audiences of sex-safe practices. As a result, fear (Gagnon, Jacob and Holmes 2009) and disgust (Pezeril 2011) have resurfaced in HIV/AIDS prevention campaigns but with greater focus on threats posed by HIV – and people living with HIV/AIDS.

We have recently engaged in the critical examination of three HIV/AIDS prevention campaigns that were launched in Luxembourg (2009), Germany (2009) and Canada (2010).The purpose of this paper is to engage readers with the use of violence in these campaigns and its broader implications. To set the stage, we introduce and describe each of the prevention campaigns. Then, drawing on a poststructuralist perspective, we critically examine how these prevention campaigns produce new meanings around HIV, new understandings of HIV transmission, and new representations of people living with HIV/AIDS. Finally, we expand on the extensive (and unforeseen) use of violence in these campaigns and its overall implication in the fight against HIV/AIDS. At last, we provide a brief discussion on the introduction of violence in the field of HIV/AIDS prevention which, in our opinion, raises important concerns as to how we market so-called "health messages" in this particular field and to what extent we are willing to ensure that these messages are "successfully received."

The Prevention Campaigns

Every year, new HIV/AIDS prevention campaigns are produced by the public sector, the community sector (non-profit organizations), and the private sector (pharmaceutical enterprises, clothing companies, cosmetic brands). Commercial advertising and marketing strategies are commonly used to produce these mass media campaigns and manufacture messages that command attention (an approach also known as social marketing). We believe that the HIV/AIDS prevention campaigns put forward by the public sector in Luxembourg, the community sector in Germany and the private sector in Canada are great examples of social marketing because they were specifically designed to shock people into action. These campaigns were not only produced to remind mass audiences about HIV/AIDS but to persuade them to take up desired (healthy) behaviours such as getting tested for HIV, practising safe-sex, understanding the risks of HIV transmission and seeking more information about HIV/AIDS. What separates them from other prevention campaigns in the field of HIV/AIDS, however, is the extensive (and unforeseen) use of violence to market health messages to the general population. To our knowledge, there is limited information on the development and deployment of these HIV/AIDS prevention campaigns. Nevertheless, we consider that they signal a shift towards new ways of marketing health messages and designing prevention campaigns in the field of HIV/AIDS.

HIV as a Weapon of Mass Destruction

In 2009, the Health Ministry of Luxembourg in collaboration with the Red Cross (Aidsberodung) created a campaign entitled *"Le sida tue toujours, protégez-vous"* (AIDS continues to kill, protect yourself) for the prevention of HIV/AIDSin the general population. This campaign included posters that were diffused widely throughout the country and other communication tools like pamphlets, web banners, radio public service announcements, and advertisement in newspapers and magazines. Overall, the official objectives of the campaign were to raise awareness about the fact that HIV is a deadly disease and to reaffirm the importance of safe-sex practices. Of particular interest to this paper is the poster that was launched on World AIDS Day and created specifically for the general public.[1] This poster includes two different messages that are written in bold white letters and presented on top of a dark canvas. At the top of the poster, the first message reads as follows: "Weapons of mass destruction" (in capital letters). At the bottom of the poster, the title of the campaign is clearly identified: *"Le sida tue toujours,*

---

1   http://www.sante.public.lu/fr/campagnes/sida/2009/sida-journee-mondiale/index.html

protégez-vous" (AIDS continues to kill, protect yourself) along with the logo of the Health Ministry and the Red Cross. Neatly displayed in the middle of the poster are the illustrations of a nuclear bomb, an automatic weapon and a replica of the human immunodeficiency virus (HIV). A clear emphasis is placed on the HIV virus which is illustrated in a different color (red) than the other weapons of mass destruction (white).

AIDS is a Mass Murderer

In 2009, a controversial campaign was launched in Germany by a small AIDS awareness group called Regenbogen e.V. This campaign includes a video, a radio spot and three different posters that were designed to shock people into action. Available on a website that has since been deactivated, the video features a heterosexual couple having unprotected sexual intercourse in a dimly-lit room. Throughout the video, the viewers only see the back of the man's head until the very end, when the face of Adolf Hitler is revealed. Near the end of the video, a message written in bold red letters is presented on top of a dark canvas. It reads as follows: "AIDS is a Mass Murderer" (in capital letters). Based on the images displayed in the video, the viewers come to understand that Adolf Hitler is referred to as a figure of evil and displayed to remind everyone that AIDS is a deadly disease. This campaign also includes posters featuring Adolf Hitler, Saddam Hussein and Joseph Stalin having unprotected sexual intercourse with a woman along with the title of the campaign "AIDS is a Mass Murderer." Unfortunately, there is no way of identifying the official objectives of this campaign due to the fact that its website was deactivated in response to the critics of community-based organisations worldwide and activists in the field of HIV/AIDS.

Take Action

In 2010, the pharmaceutical enterprise Bristol-Myers Squibb (BMS) launched the third phase of the One Life HIV Awareness Campaign. This particular phase of the campaign included a new video entitled "Take Action" that was designed as "a high-impact and emotional 'do something' video to put HIV 'in the face' of at-risk adults in Canada and to encourage them to act."[2] Available on the website of the One Life Campaign and for a broader diffusion in a special package provided by BMS, this video features three intersecting storylines:

- An adolescent is drinking at a party and leaves abruptly without telling his friends. He stops outside to vomit and then climbs a fence to access a public pool. He is suddenly being held under water by an "invisible" person. He fights to free himself and slowly drowns as he continues to be held under water.

---

2   http://www.onelifetolive.ca/take-action-video

- A middle-class woman is giving a hug to a man who appears to be her new boyfriend. She leaves him and starts walking down the street while making sure no one is following her. She proceeds to cross the empty street and is struck with full force by an "invisible" vehicle. She is projected a few feet away from the point of impact and lands on the ground. She breathes heavily and holds her abdomen in pain while staying on the ground. Her face is constricted with pain and her eyes are wide open looking in the empty space.

- A young man is counting money after closing the convenience store he works at. He is standing behind the counter and looks around after hearing noises coming from the back of the store. As he looks down, he is grabbed by an "invisible" person and dragged over the counter. He is then pushed against a glass door refrigerator and falls forward as if trying to escape. He is grabbed for the second time by the "invisible" person and pushed backward as he looks around with fear in his eyes. As the video is about to end, he is punched three times in the face while blood is being spattered on the adjacent walls. Finally, he is kicked multiple times in the abdomen as he is lying on the ground in the foetal position.

This 70 second video unravels in a dark décor and includes a rock soundtrack which viewers can download directly from the One Life Campaign website. Near the end of the video, a message written in bold white letters is presented on top of a dark canvas. It reads as follows: "To those who don't see the danger / HIV is still here / Take action" (in capital letters). Displayed at the end of the video is the logo of the One Life Campaign and a link to the official website. The official objective of the campaign was to reach those who feel invincible or believe HIV/AIDS can only happen to others. As such, it was intended to have an extreme impact and to induce people to reflect on the storylines of three characters from different age groups who "encounter a very dramatic experience, where the danger they face is literally invisible."[2] The final call-to-action message tells viewers that they need to take the necessary actions to protect themselves, understand the risks of HIV transmission, get tested, find out more about HIV/AIDS and seek treatment information.

The posters and videos retrieved from these prevention campaigns were chosen because they introduce new ways of visually and textually representing HIV, HIV transmission and people living with HIV/AIDS. The compelling images and words displayed in these prevention campaigns encouraged us to critically examine the meanings they produce and their overall implications. Using discourse analysis as our method of inquiry, we were able to recognize that these campaigns are embedded in a particular context where new words and images are gradually being introduced to socially construct HIV as a weapon of mass destruction, HIV transmission as a deadly assault, and people living with HIV/AIDS as perpetrators. Such words and images should be situated within a broader discursive production of dangerousness, intentionality, and criminality in relation to HIV/AIDS. We argue that there is a need to look at this particular discourse *in operation* (Weedon 1997) in order to understand whose interests it serves at this particular point in time and how it relates to the ongoing fight against HIV/AIDS. Critical discourse analysis, in the form proposed by poststructuralists, is the best method to undertakethis particular assignment.

Discourse: A Poststructuralist Perspective

In order to explore the concept of discourse, one must turn to written documents, spoken words and/or enacted practices because they are organized in terms of particular discursive positions, most of which make up our "common sense" – a set of meanings that is fixed and widely accepted as true by the general population (Weedon 1997). Articulated in language, this common-sense knowledge of everyday life is derived from the same discourses "that account for and justify the appropriateness of the status quo" (Weedon 1997: 34). In poststructuralism, "the common factor in the analysis of social organization, social meanings, power and individual consciousness is *language*" (Weedon 1997: 21). Language differentiates, it gives meaning to normative behaviours, it teaches us what is socially desirable and undesirable, it dictates communication in ways that are consistent with standards of practice, and it makes up what we are as social beings and how we perceive others (Weedon 1997). According to Lupton (2003: 20), "the poststructuralist concept of *discourse* marries the structuralist semiotic concern with the form and structure of language and the ways in which meaning is established with an understanding that language does not exist in a social vacuum but is embedded in social and political settings and used for certain purposes." From this perspective, the examination of texts is central to an understanding of the different types of discourses that describe and categorize our social and physical worlds (Lupton 2003). As such "all discourses are textual, or expressed in texts, inter-textual, drawing upon other texts and their discourses to achieve meaning, and contextual, embedded in historical, political and cultural settings" (Lupton 2003: 20). In this sense, Williams (2005: 22) defines poststructuralism as "a set of experiments on texts, ideas and concepts that show how the limits of knowledge can be crossed and turned into disruptive relations." This form of experimentation is a key feature of critical discourse analysis and must be undertaken in order to unveil how these texts (both visual and written) are constitutive of social representations, social identities, and systems of knowledge that make up our "common sense."

Poststructuralism agrees with the fundamental principle of structuralism, which stipulates that identities are constructed discursively through external relations of language (Newman 2005). However, it differs from structuralism because it focuses primarily "on the inextricable and diffuse linkages between power and knowledge, and how individuals are constituted as subjects and given unified identities and subject positions" (Barns, Dudley, Harris and Petersen 1999: 3). Concerned with "*de*-constructing the concepts by which we have come to understand the human subject" (Barns et al. 1999: 3), poststructuralism "exposes and interrogates language itself as being both constituted by, and constitutive of, the social reality that it seeks to represent" (Cheek 2000: 40). From this perspective, language becomes a site where the social and the personal are both defined and contested (Weedon 1997). Thus, poststructuralists argue that the social organization of life and the subjectivity of those who participate in it are both products of language (Weedon 1997). In this sense, "subjectivity is produced by a whole range of discursive practices – economic, social and political – the meaning of which are a constant site of struggle over power" (Weedon 1997: 21). Therefore, language is not the expression of a given individuality, but rather the instigator of a sense of self that is socially specific and socially produced by different discourses (Weedon 1997). As a theoretical movement, poststructuralism provides a unique form of deconstructive and analytic approach that coincides with the postmodern condition (Newman 2005). From this perspective, language offers a range of discourses that can be analyzed by scholars to understand relationships between language, power, subjectivity, and the social. Language use, here, is considered as a social practice that needs to be critically examined in order to uncover how it shapes our thoughts, beliefs, actions, behaviours, and interactions (Weedon 1997). Based on words, patterns of words, figures of speech, concepts, values, images, and symbols, poststructuralists can expose how language (as a social practice) functions in both constitutive and transformative ways (Fairclough 1993). Critical discourse analysis is thus useful to undertake such a complex endeavour.

According to Fairclough (1993), critical discourse analysis is concerned with particular discursive events (analysed as texts, discursive practices, and social practices) and how they are shaped by wider structures, relations and processes. Each discursive event, he argues, has "three dimensions or facets: it is a spoken or written language *text*, it is an instance of *discourse practice* involving the production and interpretation of text, and it is a piece of *social practice*" (Fairclough 1993: 136). Based on this complementary framework, there are many ways of reading a discursive event to achieve meaning and understanding that are embedded in a particular social context. Our analysis was informed by this framework which is grounded in poststructuralist theories of language, subjectivity, power and social processes. Through the concept of discursive event, which is a key feature of critical discourse analysis, Fairclough (1993) encourages scholars to examine language (in all its forms) and discursive practices which are socially transformative. The prevention campaigns, as described above, were chosen because they make up a particular instance of language use (or discursive event) and are gradually transforming the prevention discourse as it relates to the field of HIV/AIDS. The extensive (and unforeseen) use of violence in these campaigns encouraged us to critically examine the words and images displayed in the posters and videos, to map the discourse practices involved in the production and interpretation of the messages featured in these campaigns, and to situate the campaigns within a broader social context. Based on our analysis, we argue that the use of violence as a tool to market health messages to the general population ought to be challenged and resisted. In the following segment, we will expand on the use of violence in HIV/AIDS prevention campaigns and the production of new meanings about HIV (as a weapon of mass destruction), HIV transmission (as a physical assault), and people living with HIV/AIDS (as perpetrators). We will also examine how these campaigns contribute to a broader discursive production of dangerousness, intentionality, and criminality in relation to HIV/AIDS. Throughout our analysis, we will also take a closer look at the ways in which these campaigns are pervasively transforming the backdrop of HIV prevention worldwide.

Reframing Dangerousness: HIV as a Weapon of Mass Destruction

Over the past 30 years, the response to HIV/AIDS has been largely shaped by militaristic metaphors of "biosecurity" and warfare (Larson, Nerlich and Wallis 2005, Lupton 2003, Sontag 1989, Waldby 1996). In effect, "warfare analogies, concepts of attack and retreat, triumph and defeat, infiltration and discovery, are drawn upon to describe the machinations of the virus at every level of scale, from microscopic to those of community and nation" (Waldby 1996: 2). The human immunodeficiency virus (HIV) is constructed as the enemy alien whose primary mission is to colonise the human body by invading the immune system and by taking over its chain of commands, starting with the 'commander in chief' identified as the T4–lymphocyte (Waldby 1996). As such, the discourses of virology tend to anthropomorphize the virus by referring to human behaviours and motives when conceptualizing its microscopic activities in the human body (Klein 1994). Providing agency to the viral agent justifies the declaration of war on HIV/AIDS and the deployment of different counteroffensives necessitating legitimate violence – the violence of social, cultural, political and scientific constructions of HIV/AIDS – and the suspension of civil rights (Waldby 1996). In such representations, "the military metaphor has … resonance in western society's discourses on illness and disease because it appeals to the need to mobilize against an emergency, to make sacrifices, to do everything possible to counter a threat to life" (Lupton 2003: 65). Therefore, expanding the battle beyond the virus and onto individuals capable of inflicting 'mass casualties' is marketed as a necessary tactic to contain and eradicate HIV/AIDS. In light of the recent prevention campaign launched by the public sector in Luxembourg, we consider that new tactics are being deployed in the war on HIV/AIDS. It is important to highlight that this campaign is, to our knowledge, the first one to describe the human immunodeficiency virus (HIV) as a weapon of mass destruction – a military term used to denote nuclear, chemical, and biological weapons which are designed to cause death or serious bodily injuries. Hence, we consider that it signals a shift towards new ways of representing HIV and people who are infected with this virus.

It is generally known that weapons of mass destruction (WMD) are designed and intended to cause death or serious bodily injuries through the release, dissemination and impact of radiation, toxic chemicals or biological agents. In the wake of the World Trade Centre attacks, the term "weapon of mass destruction" has broadened to include any means capable of inflicting mass casualties and has become synonymous with terrorism (Bowman 2002). While WMD come in many shapes and forms, they are distinguished from conventional weapons by their potential for proliferation and by the threat they pose to global security. Of particular concern to global security is the threat of highly contagious diseases (biological WMD) which, we argue, may help us understand why and how HIV came to be represented as a weapon of mass destruction. According to Rushton (2010: 245), "the idea that infectious diseases can and should be treated as security threats has gained ground rapidly over the last decade, and the transformation of HIV/AIDS into an issue of international peace and security has been particularly widely discussed." Since the adoption of resolution 1308 by the UN Security Council (July 2000), there has been an important shift in the way we think and speak about HIV/AIDS at a global level. While resolution 1308 was an important milestone in the response to the HIV/AIDS epidemic, Rushton (2010: 510) argues that the "securitization of HIV/AIDS has been far less successful than is often supposed". This suggests that HIV/AIDS is not necessarily considered a threat to international peace and security in other UN bodies. Based on our analysis, we consider that this resolution has had a significant impact *outside* the UN system by producing new meanings about HIV/AIDS worldwide. This phenomenon may not necessarily be reflected in the scientific literature or in UN records (as demonstrated by Rushton 2010) but it is evident in the way prevention campaigns are being designed. As new words and images are gradually being introduced to construct HIV as a weapon of mass destruction, there is a need to situate the prevention campaigns within the broader social context and recognize that efforts to "securitize HIV/AIDS" (Rushton 2010) have actually led to a gradual shift in the prevention discourse.

Perhaps, the most important critique to formulate in response to the prevention campaign put forward by the Health Ministry of Luxembourg is the lack of concern for the socio-cognitive implications of text production and interpretation (Fairclough 1993).What is striking when one examines this prevention campaign is that HIV is positioned alongside weapons of mass destruction used intentionally to kill in times of war or to cause great destruction during terrorist attacks. The term weapon of mass destruction does not exist in a social vacuum – it implies that HIV, as a biological weapon of mass destruction, is intended to cause death or serious bodily injuries and that people living with HIV/AIDS are capable of inflicting mass casualties or committing acts of bioterrorism. As seen earlier, the prevention campaign is specifically designed to raise awareness about the fact that HIV is a deadly disease and to reaffirm that HIV poses a threat to personal (and collective) safety and integrity. As such, the title of the campaign "*Le sida tue toujours, protégez-vous*" (AIDS continues to kill, protect yourself) calls attention to the lethality of the human immunodeficiency virus with a particular emphasis on the representation of the virus as a weapon of mass destruction and the need to 'protect oneself.' Displaying the virus alongside other weapons of mass destruction, this campaign provokes concerns about bodily integrity, safety, intentionality and most particularly, the dangerousness of people living with HIV/ AIDS. Unsurprisingly, then, the use of the term weapon of mass destruction is directly related to the portrayal of HIV as a bioterrorist threat and the position of people living with HIV/AIDS as bioterrorists. Here, it is important to highlight that there is no such thing as a sole depiction of the virus – any representation of the virus in prevention campaigns has important implications for the social relations and practices of people living with HIV/AIDS and the ways in which the HIV/AIDS epidemic is addressed. We argue that the prevention campaign primarily reaffirms the idea that people living with HIV/AIDS are in possession of a harmful device (the virus), one that poses a significant threat to society. If we look at the current context, it becomes apparent that this very idea is being used to incriminate people living with HIV/AIDS under terrorism laws.

In October 2009, Daniel Allen was involved in an altercation in which he allegedly bit his neighbour. Allen was charged with aggravated physical assault as a result of the incident and assault with the intent to maim.[3] In addition, he also was charged with violating a Michigan bioterrorism statute (MCL § 750.200i) based on the allegation he was HIV-positive. This law, which was passed in 2004 by the Michigan legislature in the wake of the World Trade Centre attacks, provides that "a person shall not manufacture, deliver, possess, transport, place, use or release any of the following for an unlawful purpose: (a) A harmful biological substance or a harmful biological device." It is likely that this case was the first of its kind because prosecutors in the United States had never, up to that point, established links between laws designed to stop acts of terrorism (including bioterrorism) and the serological status of a person living with HIV/AIDS.[4] We consider that this case emphasizes the importance of interrogating language as being both constituted by, and constitutive of, the social reality that it represents (Cheek 2000). From this perspective, it is imperative to recognize that the term "weapon of mass destruction" differentiates, it gives meaning to HIV exposure and HIV transmission, it reframes dangerousness, it signals a potential threat to self and an intention to seriously injure or kill others, it dictates practices in ways that are consistent with the meaning of bioterrorism, it shapes how we think and speak about HIV/AIDS, and how we perceive people living with HIV/AIDS. An examination of language as social practice allows us to expose how it shapes thoughts and behaviours. Based on the words and images featured in the prevention campaign entitled "*Le sida tue toujours, protégez-vous*" (AIDS continues to kill, protect yourself), we argue that efforts to raise awareness about HIV/AIDS should not be done to the detriment of people living with HIV/AIDS who are wrongfully represented as bioterrorists and not without consideration for the broader social contexts and the implications on the global governance of HIV/AIDS.

---

3   Amici Curiae Brief in People v. Allen (2010), retrieved from : http://www.lambdalegal. org/in-court/legal-docs/people-v-allen_mi_20100419_amicus-lambda-legal-et-al.html

4   http://michiganmessenger.com/30306/hiv-as-terrorism-case-could-set-legal-precedent

Manufacturing Criminality: People Living with HIV/AIDS as Perpetrators

Prevention campaigns in the field of HIV/AIDS are typically designed to create a state of permanent insecurity with regards to the human immunodeficiency virus and persuade mass audiences to take up desired (healthy) behaviours such as getting tested for HIV, practicing safe-sex, understanding the risks of HIV transmission and seeking more information about HIV/AIDS. In order for these campaigns to be effective, they must create a space of fear where the immediate danger is palpable and the need for action is evident. For this reason, HIV/AIDS prevention campaigns tend to represent the virus as an imminent threat and focus on the importance of making sure that HIV transmission is feared by target audiences who, in response, will be more inclined to adopt desired (healthy) behaviours. As such, fear has wider implication for the ways in which prevention campaigns are designed and how mass audiences consume health messages (Gagnon, Jacob and Holmes 2010). Fear-based prevention campaigns are designed using the same commercial advertising and marketing strategies that serve to promote commercial goods and products (Lupton 1995). The objective of these campaigns, then, is to feature messages that command attention and produce the desired response. In this sense, the deployment of words and images that create a sense of fear and a state of insecurity makes possible the uptake of desired (healthy) behaviours which are introduced as the only way to achieve probabilistic security for oneself. Fear-based HIV/AIDS prevention campaigns have been used in the past, but they have recently resurfaced with a greater focus on the threat posed by HIV (and people living with HIV/AIDS). The prevention campaigns put forward by Bristol-Myers Squibb (BMS) in Canada and Regenbogen e.V. in Germany are striking examples of this phenomenon because they were both specifically designed to shock people into action through the intensification of the threat posed by HIV. We argue, however, that the use of violence in these campaigns is reflective of a particular context where HIV transmission is increasingly being represented as a physical (and potentially deadly and murderous) assault and in which people living with HIV/AIDS are constructed as perpetrators.

In light of the prevention campaigns launched by the private sector in Canada and the community sector in Germany, we consider that new tactics are being deployed to increase awareness about HIV/AIDS. It is important to highlight that both campaigns feature high-impact videos and posters that personify the virus as a "deadly attacker" or "mass murderer". In response to this personification of the virus, it is believed that target audiences will be more likely to express anxiety over the threat of HIV and respond to the impeding menace of HIV transmission. This explains why Bristol-Myers Squibb (BMS) and the creators of the One Life Campaign "felt that it was important to address and dedicate the end message toward those who feel invincible or believe HIV/AIDS can only happen to others." Similarly to the campaign produced by Regenbogen e.V., the combination of the look and feel, the music, the noises and the symbolism are intended to confront, challenge and grab the attention of an audience that is simultaneously accused of being complacent and culpable in the rise of HIV rates in industrialized countries. Both campaigns feature characters that go through a very dramatic experience as they encounter the virus in circumstances where the danger they face is literally "invisible." What is made visible, however, is the violence of the images that are strategically displayed to catch the viewers off guard – whether it be bodies being projected on the ground, beaten, and drowned by an invisible force or women having unprotected sex with evil dictators in a chilling twist of events. What is left unsaid is the fact that these campaigns forcibly shape the ways in which we have come to understand HIV transmission and emphasize the threat posed by people living with HIV/AIDS. Again, it is important to highlight that there is no such thing as a sole depiction of the virus – any representation of the virus contributes to the social construction of people living with HIV/AIDS who, in this case, are portrayed as criminals. We argue that both prevention campaigns are situated within a broader discursive production of dangerousness, intentionality, and criminality in relation to HIV/AIDS – one that needs to be critically examined in light of the increase in the prosecutions of people living with HIV/AIDS.

In recent years, there has been an increase in prosecutions for HIV non-disclosure, HIV exposure and HIV transmission in Europe and North America (UNAIDS 2007). Cases of heterosexual contact remain the focus and this is particularly true of Canada where numerous charges have been laid against people living with HIV for not disclosing prior to having sexual intercourse. Under the Canadian criminal law, a person living with HIV may be guilty of a crime for not disclosing his or her HIV-positive status before engaging in certain activities (Canadian HIV/AIDS Legal Network 2008). A recent report on criminalization in Canada released by the Global Network of People Living with HIV/AIDS and the Canadian HIV/AIDS Legal Network (2010: 2) indicates that as of mid-December 2009, "there had been a total of 96 prosecutions in which a person living with HIV was alleged to have transmitted HIV or exposed a sexual partner to the risk of infection without disclosing HIV-positive status." In 1998, the Supreme Court ruled that a person living with HIV could be found guilty of aggravated assault if he or she did not disclose his or her HIV-positive status and exposed another person to a "significant risk" of HIV transmission (R. v Cuerrier). Since the Cuerrier decision, there has been an increase in prosecutions and an escalation of charges. Possible charges include: assault (five years), assault causing bodily harm (14 years), aggravated assault (14 years), sexual assault (10 years), sexual assault causing harm (14 years) and aggravated sexual assault (life imprisonment) (Canadian HIV/AIDS Legal Network 2008). In numerous cases, HIV-positive individuals "have been charged with one or more of these types of assaults for engaging in unprotected anal or vaginal intercourse without first disclosing their HIV-status" (Canadian HIV/AIDS Legal Network 2008: 5). Here, it is important to highlight that failure to disclose serves as the starting point for these cases because it makes the consent legally invalid which means that the sexual act (whether exposure or transmission as occurred or not during this act) becomes an assault in the eyes of the law. Yet, the law is unclear about what constitutes a "significant risk" of bodily harm. A similar situation is being reported in Europe where there is a significant increase in the prosecutions of people living with HIV/AIDS (UNAIDS 2007).

In light of the current context and the ongoing criminalization of people living with HIV/AIDS worldwide, the implications of the campaigns put forward by BMS and Regenbogen e.V. cannot be understated. The emphasis placed on the metaphors of "AIDS as a deadly attacker" and "AIDS as a mass murderer" contribute to the representation of HIV transmission as a physical (and potentially deadly) assault which, in our opinion, is counterproductive and to a larger extent, damaging to prevention efforts. We argue that the images deployed to support these metaphors are part of a dominant imagery that incriminates, gives a particular significance to HIV exposure and HIV transmission, manufactures criminality, signals a potential threat to self and a definite intention to seriously injure or kill others, shapes practices in ways that are consistent with the interpretation of HIV as a deadly threat, transforms how we think and how we speak about HIV/AIDS, and how we perceive people living with HIV/AIDS. Based on this analysis, we consider that these campaigns have received a lot of attention and were widely criticized because they are pervasively transforming the backdrop of HIV prevention by moving the emphasis away from safe sexual practices and onto the need to ensure personal safety against the threat posed by people living with HIV/AIDS who, we posit, are unjustly represented as perpetrators. This is particularly concerning because safe sexual practices thus become primarily guided by the fear of being viciously attacked or intentionally killed by an HIV-infected perpetrator instead of the motivation to be as healthy as possible as a sexual being. Based on the words and images featured in the prevention campaigns entitled "Take Action" and "AIDS is a Mass Murderer," we argue that efforts to raise awareness about HIV/AIDS must not feed into the wider structures, relations and processes that sustain HIV criminalization – a phenomenon that has a detrimental impact on HIV prevention, testing, treatment and care (Canadian HIV/AIDS Legal Network 2008). Furthermore, we consider that there is a need to examine whose interests are served through these campaigns and how they relate to the ongoing fight to reduce the social burden of people living with HIV/AIDS who are being prosecuted in large numbers based on the sole notion that HIV is a deadly virus.

Final Remarks

In light of our analysis, we believe that as long as commercial advertising and marketing strategies are used to produce mass media campaigns and manufacture messages that command attention, the best-intentioned prevention efforts risk being misplaced and, at worst, health-damaging. In this sense, we consider that the use of social marketing in the prevention domain is a "quick fix" to much larger issues that remain misunderstood and embedded in an array of assumptions that are detrimental to effective health promotion and disease prevention. We argue that the use of social marketing to communicate health concerns raises important matters as to how we market so-called "health messages" in the field of prevention and to what extent we are willing to go to ensure that these messages are "successfully received".

The extensive (and unforeseen) use of violence in the prevention campaigns put forward by the public sector in Luxembourg, the community sector in Germany and the private sector in Canada has important implications in the fight against HIV/AIDS. As such, we encourage health care professionals to question the legitimacy of this violence and to critically examine the outcomes of these campaigns. While they are specifically designed to shock people into action, they undermine HIV prevention efforts and produce new meanings around HIV, new understandings of HIV transmission, and new representations of people living with HIV/AIDS that do more harm than good. It should come as no surprise, then, that these campaigns have been evaluated as far less successful than intended.

It is imperative that we maintain an open dialogue on the issues surrounding HIV prevention and more importantly, on the successes and failures of prevention campaigns. We must remain critical of prevention campaigns that serve as means of propaganda and further increase the social burden of people living with HIV/AIDS. It has been argued that efforts to raise awareness about HIV/AIDS should not be done to the detriment of people living with HIV/AIDS. This is particularly important given that prevention campaigns might evenact as a discursive terrain for the amplification of deviance.

References

Barns I., Dudley J., Harris P. and Petersen A. 1999. Introduction: themes, context and perspectives, in *Poststructuralism, Citizenship and Social Policy*, edited by A. Petersen, I. Barns, J. Dudley, and P. Harris. London: Routledge, 1–24.

Bowman, S. 2002. *Weapons of Mass Destruction: The Terrorist Threat.* CRS Report for Congress. Retrieved from: http://fpc.state.gov/documents/organization/9184.pdf

Canadian HIV/AIDS Legal Network. 2008. Criminal Law and HIV. Info sheets. Retrieved from: http://www.aidslaw.ca/publications/interfaces/downloadFile. php?ref=1318

Fairclough, N. 1993. Critical discourse analysis and the marketization of public discourse: the universities. *Discourse and Society*, 4(2), 133–68.

Gagnon, M., Jacob, J.D. and Holmes, D. 2010. Governing through (in)security: a critical analysis of a fear-based public health campaign. *Critical Public Health*, 20(2), 245–56.

Global Network of People Living with HIV/AIDS and Canadian HIV/AIDS Legal Network. 2010. *Case Study: Criminalization of HIV Exposure in Canada*. Retrieved from: http://www.gnpplus.net/resources/human-rights-and-stigma/item/40–case-study-criminalisation-of-hiv-transmission-in-canada

Klein, M. 1994. Metaphor and the discourse of virology: HIV as human being. *The Journal of Medical Humanities*, 15(2), 123–39.

Larson, B.M.H., Nerlich, B., and Wallis, P. 2005. Metaphors and biorisks: the war on Infectious diseases and invasive species. *Science Communication*, 26(3), 243–68.

Lupton, D. 1994. *Moral Threats and Dangerous Desires: AIDS in the News Media.* London: Taylor & Francis Publishers.

Lupton, D. 1995. *The Imperative of Health: Public Health and the Regulated Body.* London: Sage.

Lupton, D. 2003. *Medicine as Culture.* London: Sage.

Noar, S.M., Palmgreen, P., Chabot, M., Dobransky, N. and Zimmerman, R.S. 2009. A 10–year systematic review of HIV/AIDS mass communication campaigns: have we made progress? *Journal of Health Communication*, 14, 15–42.

Pezeril, C. 2011. Le dégoût dans les campagnes de lutte contre le sida. *Ethnologie française*, 41, 79–88.

Rushton, S. 2010. AIDS and international security in the United Nations system. *Health Policy and Planning*, 25, 495–504.

Sontag, S. 1989. *AIDS and Its Metaphors.* New York: Farrar, Straus and Giroux.

UNAIDS 2007. *International Consultation on the Criminalisation of HIV Transmission.* Retrieved from: http://www.unaids.org/en/media/unaids/contentassets/documents/priorities/20080919_hivcriminalization_meetingreport_en.pdf

Waldby, C. 1996. *AIDS and the Body Politic.* London: Routledge.

Weedon, C. 1997. *Feminist Practice and Poststructuralist Theory.* Cambridge, MA: Blackwell Publishers.

Williams, J. 2005. *Understanding Poststructuralism.* Chesman: Acumen Publishing Limited.

Chapter 10

Bullying in the Workplace: A Qualitative Study of Newly Licensed Registered Nurses[1]

Shellie Simons and Barbara Mawn

Introduction

It has long been acknowledged that some nurses engage in various hostile behaviors toward other nurses, as evidenced by the often repeated expression, "Nurses eat their young." (Bartholomew 2006, Rowe and Sherlock 2005, Meissner 1999). This behavior has been reported predominately in anecdotal stories among nurses and has only recently appeared in the research literature. Bullying in the nursing workplace has been identified in the U.S. and other international research reports.

Various terms have been used to describe the interpersonal hostility that can occur in the nursing workplace including bullying (Quine 2001), horizontal violence (McKenna, Smith, Poole, and Coverdale 2003, Duffy 1995), and verbal abuse (Ferns and Meerabeau 2008, Johnson, Martin, and Markle-Elder 2007). Although the terms are often confused, there are subtle differences that distinguish these behaviors.

Cox (1991) defines verbal abuse as any form of communication that a nurse perceives to be a harsh, condemnatory attack upon him or herself, professionally or personally. Bullying behavior in the workplace is a form of aggression that occurs when an individual perceives negative actions directed at him/her from one or several persons over time with difficulty defending him/herself against these actions (Matthiesen and Einarsen 2001). An incident cannot be categorized as bullying unless there is a power gradient, perceived or actual, between the individuals involved (Zapf and Gross 2001). Bullying is distinct from harassment in that it is not distinguished by sexual or racial motives (Pryor and Fitzgerald 2003).

Bullying differs from horizontal or lateral violence in several ways. Horizontal or lateral violence can occur as a single isolated incident and it occurs without power gradients between the individuals involved, i.e., the interaction occurs between peers in a culture that they share (Duffy 1995). In contrast, bullying is repeated over time (at least six months). Horizontal or lateral violence and bullying do however share common behaviors such as sabotage, infighting, scapegoating, and excessive criticism.

1 From Bullying in the Workplace: A Qualitative Study of Newly Licensed Registered Nurses by S. Simons, and B. Mawn, 2010, *AAOHN Journal*, 58(7), 305–11. Copyright 2010 by the American Association of Occupational Health Nurses. Used with permission.

This descriptive study originates from a survey study that explored workplace bullying among U.S. nurses and the relationship of bullying to intent of the nurse to leave his/her position (Simons 2008). These nurses had compelling stories to tell that exemplified the phenomenon of bullying in the workplace and its impact on the nurse.

Background

Workplace bullying has significant implications for nurses working in the occupational health setting. There is evidence that workplace bullying has profound negative health effects on the individual, thus making this an important issue from an occupational health perspective (Hoel, Faragher and Cooper 2004, Einarsen and Mikkelsen 2003). Considerable economic consequences of bullying to the organization have been confirmed (O'Donnell, MacIntosh and Wuest 2010, Glendinning 2001). In a 2001 study of nurses in the United Kingdom, Quine reported that eight percent of those experiencing bullying had used their sick time to deal with the problem. The direct costs to the employer include a lower quality of work, higher turnover rates and increased absenteeism. The indirect costs are those opportunity costs related to lowered employee commitment, lack of individual discretionary effort, and time spent talking about the problem rather than working. Kivimaki, Elovaino and Vathera (2000) attempted to quantify the cost of bullying to the organization. They studied two Finnish hospitals and estimated that the annual cost related to increased absenteeism as a consequence of bullying was close to £125,000 (approximately $191,489 U.S. dollars).

Recent studies have found that targets of bullying showed a variety of symptoms indicative of post traumatic stress disorder (Balducci, Alfano and Fraccaroli 2009, Tehrani 2004). Kivimaki et al. (2000) found that workplace bullying was associated with a significant increase in the rate of sickness absenteeism. A 2003 study found a strong association between workplace bullying and subsequent depression suggesting that bullying in an antecedent factor for mental health issues (Kivimaki et al.).

In 1976, Brodsky published the seminal work on bullying in the workplace, but it was not until 1990 that Swedish researcher Heinz Leymann (1990) began the systematic study of workplace bullying, conceptualizing it as "psychological terrorization." Recently, studies have been published that explored workplace bullying from an international perspective including those from Australia (Hutchison, Jackson, Vickers, and Wilkes 2006), New Zealand (McKenna, Smith, Poole, and Coverdale 2003), Norway (Nielsen, Matthiesen, and Einarsen 2008), and the United Kingdom (Lewis and Orford 2005).

In the United States, Lutgen-Sandvik, Tracy and Alberts (2007) studied the prevalence of workplace bullying in a sample of workers in a number of industries including health and social services, education and finance. Only a few of the international studies examined the effects of workplace bullying on nurses (McKenna et al. 2003, Quine 2001). More recently, researchers have examined bullying among nurses in the U.S. (Felblinger 2008) but there is still a paucity of research related to bullying among nurses in this country (Lutgen-Sandvik et al. 2007, Lewis 2006, Fox and Stallworth 2005).

Simons (2008) surveyed newly licensed U.S. nurses to measure the frequency and intensity of workplace bullying. The theory of oppressed group behavior served as the theoretical framework for the study (Freire 2000, Fanon 1963).

This researcher mailed 1,000 surveys to a random list of U.S. nurses licensed in the state of Massachusetts. Five hundred and eleven nurses responded. While some studies using postal questionnaires report a response rate as low as ten to twenty percent (Curtis and Redmond 2009), this response rate of 54.4 per cent was higher than the reported average response rate of 49.6 per cent in a recent meta-analysis (Van Horn, Green and Martinussen 2010). The survey utilized the Negative Acts Questionnaire-Revised (Einarsen and Hoel 2001) which asked about 22 items related to bullying and a three item scale which measured intention to leave the job from the Michigan Organizational Assessment Questionnaire (Cammann, Fichman, and Jenkins 1981). In addition, the survey included the definition of bullying and then asked if the respondent had experienced or witnessed bullying at work over the past six months.

The results of the Simons survey revealed that 31 per cent of the sample experienced at least two bullying behaviors on a weekly or daily basis from another nurse over a six-month period based on the criteria in the NAQ-R bullying scale. The data revealed that as bullying scores increased, so did the nurse's intention to leave the organization (Simons 2008). However the survey questions could not ascertain how bullying impacted their intention to leave. At the end of that survey, respondents were offered an open ended section to add any comments related to the topic of bullying One hundred eighty four nurses shared their stories of bullying in their workplace which provided the qualitative data for this article.

Research Design

The purpose of this paper is to present the qualitative findings from a survey study (Simons 2008) that examined workplace bullying among newly licensed nurses. The analysis for the open-ended responses in the survey followed the methods utilized in qualitative description to examine previously undescribed aspects of an experience (Kearny 2001). The Institutional Review Board at the University of Massachusetts Boston approved this study. No names or other identifiers were used in analyzing the results. In appreciation of participation, respondents who completed the survey were eligible for one of five $50 raffles.

Participants

The population of interest was newly licensed nurses in the U.S. Using Benner's (2001) model of Novice to Expert that three years is needed for a nurse to attain competence, the population included registered nurses licensed from 2001–2003 in the state of Massachusetts, graduating from a diploma, associate degree, baccalaureate or a direct entry master's program. Nurse managers and supervisors were excluded from the study. One hundred and fifty-three of 511 registered nurses who responded to the mail survey wrote narratives at the end of the survey that related to bullying. One hundred and thirty-nine wrote of being bullied at work and 14 others wrote of witnessing other nurses being bullied. Respondents were predominately female (92 per cent) with ages ranging from 22–61, and a mean age of 35.8. Forty-three percent of respondents had an associate degree and 37 per cent had a baccalaureate degree in nursing. The remaining 20 per cent had earned a diploma, a baccalaureate or master's degree in another field, or a direct entry master's degree. The majority (85 per cent) were staff nurses. Table 1 reveals a similar demographic pattern among the sub-sample who responded to the open-ended comment section as compared to the sample of entire survey respondents. Seventy-one percent of the nurses who wrote of being bullied reported that they worked in hospitals and 12 per cent worked in nursing homes.

Data Collection

Data were collected using a mailed survey over six weeks utilizing the Tailored Design Method (Dillman 2000). This method consists of specified preparation and distribution of survey materials to increase response rate. As noted, 36 per cent (n=184) of the original 511 survey participants shared their stories related to their personal and witnessed experiences of bullying.

Analysis

The written narratives at the end of the survey were transcribed verbatim and analyzed using content analysis (Sandelowski 2000). Content analysis "refers to the set of techniques that are used to identify patterns, categories and themes in recorded language" (Waltz, Strickland, and Lenz 2005: 239). After reading and rereading the narratives, the transcripts were entered into NVivo 7, a software package for qualitative research. Data reduction was completed by writing in the margins and counting the frequency of similar comments. Two researchers trained in qualitative research, one of whom is an expert in bullying among nurses, independently reviewed the comments to ensure that the stories fit the defining criteria of bullying and then conducted a thematic content analysis making comparisons, noting patterns and explanations. The data were then coded according to themes and patterns that were found. Data saturation was noted by both researchers after analyzing the first 100 responses however all responses were included in the analysis.

Findings

Four themes describing different aspects of bullying were identified from the analysis of the transcripts: structural bullying, nurses eating their young, feeling out of the clique and leaving the job.

Structural Bullying

The term structural bullying was developed by the researchers to represent perceived unfair and punitive actions taken by their supervisors. These included negative actions related to scheduling, patient assignments and workload or use of sick and vacation time. Seventeen nurses wrote of consistently being given an unmanageable workload. For example, one respondent commented:

> The only factor that may cause me to seek another job while still practicing as an RN would be the unsafe staffing situation that exists consistently. Any time the acuity and patient load is so high that patients may be at risk, it creates strife among me and my coworkers.

Others wrote of unfairness related to use of earned time. One wrote: "my manager yelled at me about my sick time in front of six other nurses" while another wrote, "being single with no children, I'm expected to take a holiday and mandatory shifts." A 23-year-old nurse wrote, "my hospital is understaffed and I'm usually the first to be asked to work extra hours or overnight double because "I'm young" and "I don't need a lot of sleep."

Nurses Eat Their Young

Nineteen nurses wrote comments that used the phrase, "nurses eat their young." For example, one respondent commented: "In my first job as an RN, I experienced such extreme hostility; it was like working in a pool with a pack of barracudas that ate their young." Others shared similar stories without using the actual phrase. A new graduate wrote, "Working as a new nurse is scary on its own, Add to this being afraid too ask questions for fear of being ridiculed and now you get one very unhappy nurse."

Similarly, another wrote, "In my first year as a nurse, I saw the majority of senior nurses were much too happy to keep information to themselves and would rather see a new RN fall flat on her face rather than give him or her the information to prevent it."

The concept of nurses "eating their young" was noted by several to begin in the formative years of the respondents' education as a nurse. Several nurses wrote of their negative experiences as student nurses. One commented, "When I was in nursing school, we spent most of our time doing clinical work in a small community hospital. I found so much negativity in this environment that I considered quitting nursing school." Another wrote that, "nursing school was a very different experience. I witnessed many RNs treat my classmates horribly-and that almost prevented me from practicing."

Out of the Clique

Some of the respondents related bullying experiences to their feelings of alienation and not feeling part of the group. These nurses wrote of having difficulty fitting in when they perceived that they were different in any way. Differences may have been related to ethnicity, education or simply because the nurse was not part of that group, being a per diem float or travel nurse.

"During my first pregnancy, because the charge nurse did not like me, I was assigned the most infectious patients (HIV, TB and hepatitis). When I complained, I was ridiculed and told, sorry this is your assignment. When pregnancy complications developed, I was put on light duty but nobody would help me. I was told, do your job or leave."

A 50-year old new graduate wrote, "There were negative behaviors in my first nursing experience which was at a long term care center; clique groups, rumors, sarcasm and nurses not helping me with things I hadn't encountered before. I was left alone with forty patients constantly." A 27-year-old Asian nurse wrote, "My pronunciation and English often gets ridiculed. I am one of the nurses from the Philippines that were hired three years ago."

Leaving the Job

Nurses wrote of leaving their jobs as a result of being targets of bullying behaviors. Some talked of leaving their jobs and others wrote of leaving the profession. The orientation period seems to be a time that newly graduated nurses are particularly vulnerable to bullying. Thirty-eight nurses wrote of negative experiences during the orientation period. A 24-year old staff nurse in the operating room lamented, "During my three months of orientation I was bullied quite often. It was seen as proving yourself to your fellow employees. I was often set up to fail purposely. I considered leaving almost daily."

Another wrote, "This survey allowed me to share my experiences of my first years in the workforce as an RN. I worked in a hospital for ten months. After that experience, I seriously considered never working as a nurse again."

A 28-year-old nurse wrote of her first year, "I currently work in an emergency room but recently left a cardiac floor in the same hospital because of most of the nurses I worked with. The gossip and bullying made me leave. Many other new graduates have left this particular unit as well. The nurse manager was fully aware of the actions and attitudes on her unit but chose not to do much about it. It is a shame that new nurses are treated so badly. Every nurse was a new nurse once!"

Discussion

The qualitative findings in this study served as a method of triangulation for the survey data in the original study. The original study design did not aim to use a mixed-methods approach to examine bullying. At the outset of the study it was not anticipated that 36 per cent of the survey respondents would provide such rich narratives. However, despite these limitations in the original study design, the researchers chose to analyze the rich narratives using qualitative methods in order to share the profound stories of experienced and witnessed bullying among nurses. The four major themes identified from the narratives clarified some of the suffering experienced and witnessed by nurses.

Simons (2008) reported an interesting finding in the original quantitative analysis of the survey in that 31 per cent of the respondents met the criteria for have experienced bullying based on the responses to the NAQ-R scale, while only 21 per cent responded that they had been bullied when asked and given the definition. This suggested a discrepancy in the understanding of the construct of bullying and its impact on nurses' work life. Perhaps some of the nurses had the common perception of bullying as involving verbal taunts as opposed to negative actions by those in positions of power over time. Many of those who shared their stories however reflected an awareness of this aspect of definition. One of the four major themes captured the essence of these stories, structural bullying. Nurses wrote of unfair and punitive scheduling and pressure placed upon them not to use earned sick or holiday time.

The theme of structural bullying has important implications for nursing and occupational health nurses in particular. Nurses need to be aware that this type of subtle bullying such as inequitable patient assignments, shift allocations or vacation allotments needs to be prevented, identified and dealt with fairly. Nurses who feel powerless in the work place need to find their voice and recognize how to identify and resolve this issue and where to seek a remedy. Occupational nurses can serve to provide nursing staff with the knowledge and actions to stop the perpetuation of this process.

The survey questions focused on a descriptive analysis of the prevalence of bullying and its impact on leaving the profession. The two themes identified in the narratives, entitled "nurses eat their young" and "out of the clique" helped to clarify how bullying can emerge in the work setting. The former expression is an unfortunate timeworn expression in nursing that was expressed verbatim by many of the respondents. They experienced and witnessed this phenomenon as nursing students and as newly licensed nurses. In addition, many attributed their experience of bullying to the fact that they didn't quite fit in with the perceived clique. Racial and ethnic differences were identified within this theme as well as other factor such as being pregnant or a float nurse. Implications for nurses in the educational setting as well as occupational health setting are evident in terms of preparing new nurses to address and deal with this potential form of workplace

bullying and educating those in positions of power to learn to prevent it and be aware of its potential impact.

The fourth theme identified in these narratives was related to the perceived impact of bullying on job retention. While the survey tool measured bullying and intention to leave the job, it could not capture the direct impact of bullying and could not control for other factors that would impact leaving the job. Those participants who chose to write their stories commonly discussed the impact of bullying on their choice to leave a job and in some cases, the profession. It is important for occupational health nurses to be aware of the direct impact ion job retention that bullying can have, both in the nursing profession and other job sectors. In the face of such powerlessness, many choose to opt out of the situation and the job. Occupational health nurses can provide a vehicle to educate and support those who are oppressed in the work place.

It is noteworthy that none of the nurses wrote of actions that they employed to ameliorate or eliminate the bullying behavior. With the exception of a one study (Griffin 2004) that tested cognitive rehearsal as a strategy to deal with the negative effects of lateral violence, there is a paucity of research to assist administrators and nurses in occupational health in dealing with this problem that affects all aspects of nursing. Both nursing staff and administrators need to be better educated about bullying so that they can more clearly identify the behavior both in themselves and in others. Future qualitative study designs need to specifically address this aspect of the bullying cycle.

While these qualitative findings shed light on a poorly understood phenomenon, several limitations of this study are identified. The major limitation of this study is that it was not designed originally with the rigor of a qualitative study that includes prolonged engagement in the field, in-depth personal interviews, or an avenue for member checking (Creswell 2007). The authors acknowledge that while the analysis of the data relied on qualitative methods, indeed it was not designed with the standards of a rigorous qualitative study. Creswell suggests that at least two means of validation strategies are incorporated into a qualitative analysis. Two measures used for this analysis included peer review/debriefing by the two authors of this report and the inclusion of data that provided a written rich description that could allow the reader to evaluate whether or not the findings are transferable to nurses in other settings.

A second limitation is that the open-ended section at the survey did not again define bullying or ask for responses related to this definition. However, two researchers independently analyzed the data to ensure that the narratives included in the analysis did meet the criteria. Although the 184 respondents to the open-ended section of the survey were similar in demographics to the entire survey respondent group, it cannot be implied that this group represented all of the survey participants. In addition, another limitation is that the sample was drawn solely from nurses licensed in one state so it is unknown whether these results are typical of nurses in other parts of the country. Self selection bias is a possible limitation to this study in that those with bullying experiences may have been more likely to respond to the survey in the first place and may not represent all newly licensed registered nurses in the U.S.

While additional future survey questionnaires can well serve to document the prevalence and incidence of bullying in varying settings among nurses with diverse levels of experience and education, rigorous qualitative research needs to be conducted to understand the roots of the phenomenon and its impact on nurses. In addition, intervention studies need to be designed to evaluate best practices and policies to improve reporting and reduce the impact and existence of bullying among the nursing workforce.

Conclusion

This survey gave these nurses an opportunity to share their personal stories about workplace bullying. The four themes identified put a new lens on the survey findings and expanded the understanding of bullying among the nursing workforce. A number of recent studies have validated that bullying exists in the workplace of nurses. These studies have shown that bullying is associated with job satisfaction, performance and retention but little has been documented to examine these relationships in depth. Additional research is needed to expand the knowledge about the factors that precipitate this noxious behavior and how to effectively treat and eradicate it.

Occupational health nurses are well positioned to deal with these issues that directly affect the health of the employee. Through research, educational programs, counseling and support occupational health nurses can support and assist targets of bullying through difficult conflict situations. Bullying has been a part of the culture since the beginning of professional nursing that has been tacitly accepted by nurses for too long. We are only just beginning to understand the root of this unfortunate phenomenon. While this study adds to our understanding of workplace bullying among nurses, additional research is needed to fully understand the phenomenon in order to develop effective interventions to ultimately eliminate the behavior.

References

Balducci, C., Alfano, V. and Fraccaroli, F. 2009. Relationships between mobbing at work and MMPI-2 personality profile, posttraumatic stress symptoms, and suicidal ideation and behavior. *Violence and Victims*, 24(1), 52–67.

Bartholomew, K. 2006. *Ending Nurse to Nurse Hostility: Why Nurses Eat Their Young and Each Other.* Marblehead, MA: HCPro, Inc.

Benner, P. 2001. *From Novice to Expert: Excellence and Power in Clinical Nursing Practice.* Upper Saddle River, NJ: Prentice Hall.

Brodsky, C.M. 1976. *The Harassed Worker.* Toronto: D.C. Heath.

Cammann, C., Fichman, M., Jenkins Jr., D., and Klesh, J.R. 1981. Intention to turn over, in *The Experience of Work: A Compendium and Review of 249 Measures and Their Use*, edited by J.D. Cook, S.J. Hepworth, T.D. Wall, and P.B. Warr. New York: Academic Press, 95.

Cox, H.C. 1991. Verbal abuse nationwide, part I: oppressed group behavior. *Nursing Management*, 22(2), 32–5.

Creswell, J. 2007. *Qualitative Inquiry and Research Design: Choosing Among Five Approaches*. Thousand Oaks, CA: Sage.

Curtis, E. and Redmond, R. 2009. Survey postal questionnaire: optimizing response and dealing with non-response. *Nurse Researcher*, 16(2), 76–88.

Dillman, D.A. 2000. *Mail and Internet Surveys: The Tailored Design Method*. New York: John Wiley & Sons.

Duffy, E. 1995. Horizontal violence: a conundrum for nursing. *Collegian Journal of the Royal College of Nursing Australia*, 2(2), 5–17.

Einarsen, S., and Hoel, H. 2001. *The Negative Acts Questionnaire: Development, Validation and Revision of a Measure of Bullying at Work*. Paper presented at the 10th Annual European Congress on Work and Organizational Psychology, Prague.

Einarsen, S., and Mikkelsen, E.G. 2003. Individual effects of exposure to bullying at work, in *Bullying and Emotional Abuse in the Workplace*, edited by S. Einarsen, H. Hoel, D. Zapf, and C.L. Cooper. London: Taylor and Francis, 127–44.

Fanon, F. 1963. *The Wretched of the Earth*. New York: Grove Press.

Felblinger, D.M. 2008. Incivility and bullying in the workplace and nurses' shame responses. *Journal of Obstetric, Gynecologic, and Neonatal Nursing: JOGNN / NAACOG*, 37(2), 234–42.

Ferns, T., and Meerabeau, L. 2008. Verbal abuse experienced by nursing students. *Journal of Advanced Nursing*, 61(4), 436–44.

Fox, S., and Stallworth, L.E. 2005. Racial/ethnic bullying: exploring links between bullying and racisim in the US workplace. *Journal of Vocational Behavior*, 66, 438–56.

Freire, P. *Pedagogy of the Oppressed 2000*. New York: Continuum.

Glendinning, P.M. 2001. Workplace bullying: curing the cancer of the American workplace. *Public Personnel Management*, 30, 269–86.

Griffin, M. 2004. Teaching cognitive rehearsal as a shield for lateral violence: an intervention for newly licensed nurses. *The Journal of Continuing Education in Nursing*, 35(6), 1–7.

Hoel, H., Faragher, B., and Cooper, C.L. 2004. Bullying is detrimental to health, but all bullying behaviors are not necessarily equally damaging. *British Journal of Guidance and Counseling*, 32, 367–87.

Hutchison, M., Jackson, D., Vickers, M.H., and Wilkes, L. 2006. They stand you in a corner; you are not to speak: nurses tell of abusive indoctrination in work teams dominated by bullies. *Contemporary Nurse*, 21, 228–40.

Johnson, C.L., Martin, S.D., and Markle-Elder, S. 2007. Stopping verbal abuse in the workplace. *American Journal of Nursing*, 107(4), 32–4.

Kearny, M. 2001. Levels and applications of qualitative research evidence. *Research in Nursing and Health*, 24, 145–53.

Kivimaki, M., Elovainio, M., and Vahtera, J. 2000. Workplace bullying and sickness absence in hospital staff. *Occupational & Environmental Medicine*, 57(10), 656–60.

Kivimaki, M., Virtanen, M., Vartia, M., Elovainio, M., Vahtera, J., and Keltikangas-Jarvinen, L. 2003. Workplace bullying and the risk of cardiovascular disease and depression. *Occupational & Environmental Medicine*, 60(10), 779–83.

Lewis, S.E. 2006. Recognition of workplace bullying: a qualitative study of women targets in the public sector. *Journal of Community & Applied Social Psychology*, 16, 119–35.

Lewis, S.E. and Orford, J. 2005. Women's experiences of workplace bullying: changes in social relationships. *Journal of Community & Applied Social Psychology*, 15, 29–47.

Leymann, H. 1990. Mobbing and psychological terror at workplaces. *Violence and Victims*, 5, 119–26.

Lutgen-Sandvik, P., Tracy, S.J., and Alberts, J.K. 2007. Burned by bullying in the American workplace: prevalence, perception, degree and impact. *Journal of Management Studies*, 44(6), 837–862.

Matthiesen, S.B., and Einarsen, S. 2001. MMPI-2 configurations among victims of bullying at work. *European Journal of Work and Organizational Psychology*, 10, 467–84.

McKenna, B.G., Smith, N.A., Poole, S.J., and Coverdale, J.H. 2003. Horizontal violence: experiences of registered nurses in their first year of practice. *Journal of Advanced Nursing*, 42(1), 90–96.

Meissner, J.E. 1999. Nurses: Are we still eating our young? *Nursing,* 29(2), 42–4.

Nielsen, M.B., Matthiesen, S.B., and Einarsen, S. 2008. Sense of coherence as a protective mechanism among targets of workplace bullying. *Journal of Occupational Health Psychology*, 13(2), 128–36.

O'Donnell, S., MacIntosh, J., and Wuest, J. 2010. A theoretical understanding of sickness absence among women who have experienced workplace bullying. *Qualitative Health Research*, 20, 439–52.

Pryor, J.B. and Fitzgerald, L.F. 2003. Sexual harassment research in the United States, in *Bullying and emotional abuse in the workplace*, edited by S. Einarsen, H. Hoel, D. Zapf, and C.L. Cooper. London: Taylor and Francis, 79–100.

Quine, L. 2001. Workplace bullying in nurses. *Journal of Health Psychology*, 6, 73–84.

Rowe, M.M. and Sherlock, H. 2005. Stress and verbal abuse in nursing: do burned out nurses eat their young? *Journal of Nursing Management*, 13(3), 242–8.

Sandelowski, M. 2000. Whatever happened to qualitative description? *Research in Nursing and Health*, 23, 334–40.

Simons, S.R. 2008. Workplace bullying experienced by Massachusetts registered nurses and the relationship to intention to leave the organization. *Advances in Nursing Science*, 31(2), E48–59.

Tehrani, N. 2004. Bullying: A source of chronic post traumatic stress. *British Journal of Guidance & Counseling*, 32(3), 357–66.

Van Horn, P.S., Green, K.E., and Martinussen, M. 2009. Survey response rates and survey administration in counseling and clinical psychology: educational and psychological measurement: a meta-analysis. *Educational and Psychological Measurement*, 69, 389–403.

Waltz, C.F., Strickland, O.L., and Lenz, E.R. 2005. *Measurement in Nursing and Health Research (3rd edn)*. New York, NY: Springer.

Zapf, D., and Gross, C. 2001. Conflict escalation and coping with workplace bullying: a replication and extension. *European Journal of Work and Organizational Psychology*, 10, 497–522.

Chapter 11

Sexual Health Nursing Assessments: Examining the Violence of Intimate Exposures

Patrick O'Byrne and Cory Woodyatt

Introduction

Within nursing literature, nurses are often described as *caring* health professionals who almost selflessly provide needed/necessary health services which promote the recovery, and rehabilitation of diverse patients and populations. Nursing practice, in general, is therefore portrayed as a socially beneficial undertaking that fosters the well being of various individuals and groups. In the sexual health domain, specifically, the provision of such care requires that nurses not only undertake physical examinations and specimen collection, but also that they query patents about the types of sexual practices they have engaged in, the places wherein these sexual contacts occurred and/or were arranged, and whether or not condoms or other protective devices were used.

The current explanation about such sexual health assessments[1] is that they help determine the likelihood that a specific patient would or will acquire a sexually transmitted infection (STI). However, when this process is examined using Pierre Bourdieu's idea of symbolic violence and Michel Foucault's writings about discipline, it is possible to suggest, instead, that nurses exercise a form of non-physical violence which imposes a specific worldview when they assess patients' sexual health histories. Indeed, when Bourdieu's and Foucault's work is used as a theoretical starting point for analysis, it is possible to suggest that, by examining and evaluating their patients' sexual histories, nurses engage with their patients according to a pre-established set of standards; they impose a set of ideas upon their patients, and in effect, transform and re-construct their identities. It will thus be argued in this chapter that the sexual health nursing assessment is a symbolically

---

1 For the purpose of this chapter, other activities and tasks that take place during the sexual health assessment, i.e. physical examination, were left out. The assessment itself is a complex process and, often, the subsequent tasks flow from and are often dictated from the risk assessment itself. Regrettably these other tasks are beyond the scope of this paper as symbolic violence relates to the symbolic nature of the assessment and not the physical interaction between nurse and client.

violent process because, as part of undertaking this process, nurses, first, expose the intimate details of their patients' lives and second, force patients to face their previous behaviour and admit to the discrepancies between their personal sexual practices and what is deemed normal.

Symbolic Violence

Bourdieu believed that the principal mode of domination and social control in contemporary Western society shifted from a system of overt coercion to one of symbolic manipulation; that is, a system of symbolic violence. Bourdieu uses this term to mean that symbolic violence is the process of subtly and covertly co-opting groups of people into accepting both the validity and superiority of certain forms of meaning/knowledge and the corresponding distributions of power. Symbolic violence, accordingly, is a gentle and indirect form of force "which is exercised upon a social agent with his or her complicity" (Bourdieu and Wacquant 1992: 167). Without any direct and/or physical form of control and surveillance, most individuals therefore partake in and maintain their own subjugation. Each person maintains the constraints (the walls of a metaphorical prison, that is) that prevent him/her from moving beyond his/her assigned position (Bourdieu and Passeron 1977). The outcome of symbolic violence is that dominant groups maintain their (prestigious) social positioning because each person not only accepts, but also helps preserve, the *status quo* social hierarchy. This applies to people who both benefit and suffer as a consequence of the contemporary social organization (Moore 2004, Bourdieu and Passeron 1977).

Symbolic violence, however, extends beyond processes of inculcating the acceptance and maintenance of uneven distributions of power within the general population; it is also involved in training bodies to correspond with a pre-determined set of standards (Foucault 1977). The main way this happens is through socialization: each person is inculcated to the point that dominant norms and tendencies unconsciously guide and shape his/her behaviour and thinking. According to Wacquant (2005: 316), this process, which is the imposition of symbolic violence, results in an outcome wherein society becomes "deposited in persons in the form of lasting dispositions, or trained capacities and structured propensities to think, feel and act in determinant ways." However, before examining how symbolic violence operates in sexual health nursing practice, an overview of such an assessment will be provided.

The Sexual Health Examination

To guide the sexual health examination, the Public Health Agency of Canada (PHAC) (2008) has provided a detailed set of guidelines. As part of this, nurses are directed to evaluate an individual's risk factors and behaviours according to the following six areas: history of a sexually transmitted infection (STI); knowledge of STIs; relationship status; reproductive health history; psychosocial history; and history of substance abuse. Through this process of data collection, nurses also elicit information about a person's motive for seeking sexual health services (PHAC 2008). More specifically, in undertaking a sexual health assessment, nurses evaluate each patient's current sexual relationship to identify items that may increase a patient's susceptibility to STI/HIV acquisition. Moreover, nurses query patients about previous STI/HIV diagnoses, previous STI/HIV testing, their sexual activities, if they are currently or previously sexually active, and/or if they have any relationship concerns. As part of this, nurses also inquire about patients' sexual orientation, number of different sexual partners, whether their sexual partner(s) is/are/was/were regular or casual, male, female or both. As well, nurses explore the types of sexual contact that patients engage in (i.e., oral, anal, vaginal sex, received and/or performed), and ask about the locations where sexual partners were encountered. Typically, nurses will also engage in discussions about whether or not condoms or other protective barriers were used during these sexual contacts, and if this use was consistent.

The question that remains is what is the symbolically violent component of the aforementioned set of questions which arise from empirical research and which serve to facilitate nurses' interactions with patients in sexual health settings? To answer this question, one needs to examine the attributes that must exist in society for the idea of a sexual health assessment to both occur and be meaningful. Foucault's ideas about training will now be used to describe how the sexual health assessment enforces certain systems of meaning, reproduces existing class divisions, and, in doing so, subjects patients to a symbolically violent process.

Michel Foucault and Training

In his book *Discipline and Punish*, Foucault (1977) described how individuals are rendered docile and compliant in modern-day society. That is, Foucault described how the vast majority of the population is subjected to what Bourdieu called symbolic violence by being inculcated to unconsciously replicate specific power relations without realizing its arbitrary nature. While Foucault (1975) discussed an array of social apparatuses that contribute to this process, in this chapter, it is specifically his work on training, and its three main subcomponents of hierarchical observation, normalizing judgment, and examination, that are of interest. The rationale for selecting these aspects of Foucault's work is the belief that nurses do not develop the systems of social domination and control that subjugate large portions of society, but rather, that they function as the agents within this system who impose symbolic violence at the individual level—in the clinical domain, that is—as a result of rank, knowledge, skill, and technique. The three components of training will now be analyzed and discussed to substantiate our claim that sexual health assessments are symbolically violent.

Hierarchical Observation

The first component of the disciplinary training system that Foucault (1977) identified is hierarchical observation, which is used herein to designate social status or position (that is, the presumed right to observe/assess others). Hierarchical observation thus signals that specific people, at certain times, in identifiable places, have the rank and status to observe others, and that these others should submit themselves to examination by the designated individuals. Consequently, hierarchical observation is one of the key aspects of symbolic violence – as identified by Bourdieu – because it enables certain information, people, and places to be promoted in rank, while others are relegated to inferior positions. For the contemporary social system to operate successfully, the general public must accept these interpretations of power relations and they must do so in a relatively uniform way. Belief in the foundations of the system—which may entail an endorsement of a specific set of power relations—is of primary importance. Otherwise, the current system would have to revert to overt and explicit acts of violence.

As this relates to sexual health assessments and symbolic violence, hierarchical observation relies on four main foundations. The first is the perceived status of scientific knowledge, which can be understood as a key component within the discourse that legitimizes the presumed superiority of certain perceptions about how/why human beings exist, how/why they differentiate, how/why to best correct deviancies that may arise, and how/why these abnormalities arise. Consequently, scientific knowledge is elevated to a dominant status that not only grants it a specific form of priority, but also that obscures other forms of knowledge and consequently captures most people within the dominant mode of thinking. This means that, notwithstanding the various forms of knowledge and knowing which exist, the ones that are labelled as "science" are elevated in rank; these strategies are said to produce the best knowledge and best practices. This perception of science is the first pillar of hierarchical observation: the enforced acceptance of a single mode of thinking and doing.

The second component of hierarchical observation is the current perception of health: what Lupton (1999) calls the "imperative of health." Thus, with a single method of knowledge development and ranking established (i.e., dominant forms of science), hierarchical observation in the sexual health domain operates quite successfully based on the presumption that all individuals are naturally self-motivated toward being healthy (Lupton 1999). This, Lupton argues, amounts to little more than a modern system for ensuring that everyone wholeheartedly submits to specific understandings about human nature and the priority of health (Lupton 1999). Lupton maintains that the current health discourse is nothing more than a control apparatus, however: the regulation of bodies through a variety of methods to compel them to internalize health-improving activities to the point that self-control enables individuals to have power over their health (Lupton 1999). This government of bodies through polymorphous political techniques serves to engage individuals, groups, or communities in the internalization of health-improving behaviours, thus resulting in a greater capacity for self-control while enabling individuals to take control of their own health and to make healthy choices (Lupton 1999). As an outcome, the primacy that is granted to the concept and practices of health lays the foundation for the next two aspects of hierarchical observation: individuals who are worthy of observing others and places wherein such observations appear to naturally take place.

In this context, the third component of hierarchical observation is thus that, to maintain the dominance of scientific knowledge and to properly establish the required parameters for hierarchical observation, certain groups must be invested with specialized education and training. That is, certain groups of workers—who will come to be known as professionals—must become versed in the scientific discourse. The repetitive and stylized immersion of these individuals in particular scientific discourses solidifies the perceptions that they possess increased authority. In other words, after having been educated within designated institutions of power by individuals who are considered experts in their respective fields, nurses have not so much been educated as they have been trained with the basic attitudes and sophisticated ideologies about the dominance and priority of certain fields and ways of knowing. Students, consequently, are invested with the knowledge/information that renders them capable of hierarchical observation, with this capability being recognised and accepted by the general public and other professionals.

The production of health professionals, therefore, builds on the two foregoing pillars: a future nurse must first learn to acquire and decipher scientific information, and second, do so in an effort to help others maintain the imperative of health. The outcome of this system of training is thus the creation of a tacit system of thinking and communicating that is used among members of various kinds of elite communities; individuals who are defined not only by their knowledge, but also by their unique practices, defined and rigid communication styles, and complex network of institutions. As part of this collectivity, nurses therefore reinforce (1) the dominant nature of certain forms of science over others, and (2) the imperative of health as they share an underlying group ideology with other health professionals and the general public.

The fourth and final component of hierarchical observation, at least as it relates to nursing assessments, is the social position and perception of sexual health clinics: because the sexual health clinic is understood as a specified institution of scientific knowledge, this otherwise inert piece of architecture is invested with a form of power that promotes and maintains the hierarchy between the nurse and the client. Indeed, sexual health clinics are sacred places wherein a person can access the agents of science; i.e., the individuals who have learned to interpret and translate text (peer reviewed journal articles) of scientific discourse. A patient's presentation at a sexual health clinic consequently displays his/her complicit acceptance of the hierarchy that renders science and its practitioners superior. The conscious seeking of health transforms from an avoidance of illness into the moral imperative that personal choices should be congruent with ideations about health. Individuals must therefore accept the notion that health is of superior importance that certain ways of understanding health are better than others, and that specific groups of workers (i.e., health professionals) are capable of observing and casting judgment. Consequently, "the self is to style its life through acts of choice, and when it cannot conduct its life according to this norm of choice; it is to seek expert assistance" (Rose 1999: 158).

Examination

With the appropriate social mechanisms in place to ensure the acceptance and execution of hierarchical observation, the second of Foucault's disciplinary techniques, examination, encompasses the means used to inspect and scrutinize individuals (Foucault 1977). In the sexual health domain, by means of the acts of interviewing and/or testing which are described above, the nurse's gaze elicits information which enables the subsequent processes of ranking, correction, and reform to be undertaken (Foucault 1977). In other words, the examination is a ritualized ceremony through which each individual is better understood in relation to their peers—a process which links the formation of knowledge to the exercise of power, and which creates the axis of Foucault's power/knowledge system.

As indicated by Holmes and O'Byrne (2006), the important aspect of this process is not only the precise information that arises from these questions, but also the impact of the method(s) by which nurses elicit this information. For this process to be optimally effective, the in-depth, nurse-patient interaction must unfold in a manner that appears, from the patient-perspective, to be both accepting and acceptable (Holmes and O'Byrne 2006). Nurses, therefore, must not engage in any action that could offend a patient or make him/her feel uneasy during the examination process. This does not mean that questions which induce discomfort cannot be asked; indeed, many of the questions that comprise a sexual health assessment could cause embarrassment. Rather, nurses should pose sexual health-related questions in a way that minimizes the dis-ease of inquiries about disease. A personal, or therapeutic, relationship must develop that enables nurses to gain insight into the sexual practices of each patient (Lupton 1999), and which facilitates the nurse's assessment of each patient. The therapeutic relationship also helps nurses maintain patients' trust so that they will be more susceptible to the ensuing process of normalizing judgement. When constructed as such, the sexual health assessment does not simply inform patients about their STI/HIV statuses; it is also the mechanism that brings people into the light and makes them known.

Normalizing Judgement

Once individuals, who have been vested with social power, (i.e., the right to hierarchical observation) have executed their examinations, Foucault (1977) identified that the third disciplinary technique of normalizing judgement occurs.

Herein, the data which emerge from the examination process are analyzed based on the examiner's expert knowledge. That is, the examiner compares the results of his/her verbal and physical investigation to the dictates of science, and then identifies the areas where a specific individual deviates from group-level norms; this is the process of ranking and training observed bodies. As noted by Bourdieu, the consequences related to a person's performance, whether it is satisfactory or not, no longer focus on physical violence and punishment. Instead, the priority is now to provide corrective and supportive measures that will help individuals enhance or attain satisfactory performances (Foucault 1977). The judgment of a person who poses scientific knowledge and who works to maintain the imperative of health (i.e., an expert who is granted the right to undertake hierarchical observation) allows for the identification and development of corrective strategies and micro-penalties to categorize individuals and their natures, their potentialities, and their level or value (Foucault 1977). In essence, the violent aspects of the sexual health nursing assessment are actualized when normalizing judgment occurs.

This is because, after nurses sort through the myriad of information that they collected, they must develop an appropriate course of action or intervention strategy based on the patient's precise points of deviation. This is the process where nurses provide patients with specific forms of knowledge in an effort to ensure the patient's obedience to the imperative of health. Such topics include safer sex, acceptance of sexuality, contraceptive advice, partner notification, and frequent STI/HIV testing (PHAC 2008). Of particular interest, this corrective strategy, which ultimately subjects a person to the eyes, ears, and mind of sexual health nurses, occurs regardless of the patient's actual STI/HIV outcomes. Unprotected sex is treated as a deviation in itself; the acquisition of an STI or HIV simply validates the expert position and knowledge of the sexual health nurse. At this point, one could thus contend that nurses provide patients with optimal care (if one approaches this process from an imperative-of-health perspective), or they subject patients to symbolic violence as a result of normalizing judgment (if one adopts the perspective of Bourdieu and Foucault).

The specifically violent nature of normalizing judgment is twofold. First, this process co-opts certain patients to undergo a process of self-reflection initiating feelings of guilt, shame, and discomfort. It is symbolically violent method of forcing a person to confront their previous sexual behaviour and misgivings. This can be an embarrassing experience for some patients because they are required to answer confidential and personal questions, to work with the nurse to identify personal practices which are transgressive, and to acknowledge to another person what the imperative of health and dominant science discourses conceptualize as sexual shortcomings (Holmes and O'Byrne 2006). The examination methods employed in health care settings therefore force individuals to be evaluated by a seemingly objective and knowledgeable source. What it also does is subject people to a pre-conceived ideation about what constitutes acceptable sexual behaviour, but it does so without acknowledging the arbitrary nature of these benchmarks.

The second aspect of the sexual health assessment that renders it symbolically violent emerges when nurses give patients corrective and ameliorative suggestions based on the findings of the physical and oral examinations. This is the process wherein nurses counsel patients and provide them with individualized courses of action that address the specific methods by which they can improve/enhance their current states of health (Lupton 1999, Holmes and O'Byrne 2006).

To accomplish such changes, patients are invited, or coerced, with the help of a health professional, to improve their health through behaviour-modification programs and/or therapies (Lupton, 1995). Within the sexual health domain, the sexual health clinic reinforces this process of self-reflection through the engineering of an improved version of the self and of humanity (Lotringer 2007, Rose 1996). Its subtle and symbolically violent role is orchestrated through the continuous efforts that are made to label and correct practices that are considered deviant (in relation to scientific norms) or harmful (in relation to the imperative of health).

Consequently, when comparisons are made between one patient and scientific data, nurses are effectively constructing an overall picture of the patient as "good" or "bad" according to a pre-determined set of norms. Indeed, through routine observations and clinical examinations, nurses use their specialized knowledge to, first, observe clients, and second, base their findings on a set of shared, pre-conceived standards. This enables the nurse to rank clients accordingly and perpetuate a hierarchy between nurse and client that co-opts the client to correct or reform his/her behaviour and reinforce the elevated status of nurses. Taken as a whole, normalizing judgment is a personalization of health information which ensures that individuals understand the implications of the rank they have been assigned.

Infused in these normalizing judgments is a specific language that has been both created and perpetuated by the specialized training and scientific knowledge that pervades nurses, nursing, and general health care practice. Language, in this sense, is used to (1) have patients divulge personal information, (2) empower patients to uphold the imperative of health, and (3) regulate masses and preserve order (Foucault 1990). In the sexual health assessment, data collected from each patient includes, and is not limited to, their sexual practices, sexual preferences, and number of partners—even when some of the importance of some of these questions is uncertain (see O'Byrne, Holmes, and Woodend 2008). For example, patients are often asked when their last sexual contact was, including whether it was with a regular or casual partner.

As per the Public Health Agency of Canada (PHAC) guidelines, motivational interviewing is one strategy that can be used by nurses to enhance "safer sex practices and condom use among patients who may require focused counselling" (PHAC 2008). While the PHAC standards portray this strategy as being in each patients and the entire population's best interest, it is our contention that this strategy is based on the same covert yet powerful system of meaning and language that enables hierarchical observation to occur. For example, in this strategy, patients are asked, "On a scale of one to ten, how confident are you that you (or you and your partner) could always use condoms" (PHAC 2008). If the client responds with a score of eight or more, the PHAC guidelines direct nurses to explore possible barriers that could occur and how the patient might address them. However, if the patient responds with a score of seven or less, the guidelines instruct nurses to ask why the client said X and not lower? Consequently, any score less than seven indicates that the patient is at an elevated degree of susceptibility to STIs/HIV, which necessitates modification (Lotringer 2007), while simultaneously persuading the client to self-reflect on their strengths or their lack thereof. The art of such an exchange encourages the client to listen carefully, conform appropriately, and ultimately submit to the symbolic violence that is subtly contained within this interaction.

Conclusion

Michel Foucault and Pierre Bourdieu have insisted that contemporary society operates using a new form of correction and control. It is an in-depth and subtle strategy that modifies each person, and which no longer relies on overt and spectacular displays of power and violence. Both of the foregoing authors, however, insist that the violent nature of social control has not disappeared; it has simply become less recognizable. Accordingly, when one discusses violence, one must redefine this concept to ensure that it continues to reflect the current social environment. In this context, Bourdieu's ideas about symbolic violence and Foucault's writings about training were used in such a manner to examine the powerful and symbolically violent processes that are involved in, and which occur during, sexual health nursing assessments.

Insisting that sexual health histories are inherently violent transactions forced us to expand our definitions of violence, and not to overlook the profoundly destructive and re-constructive nature of nursing examinations. The conclusion of our assessment was, therefore, that, according to Bourdieu, symbolic violence pervades the sexual health assessment because it forces nurses to rank different lifestyles and practices in relation to one another (Weininger 2004). In conjunction, Foucault's work helps us understand how the status of a lifestyle is a function of its proximity to or distance from the legitimate culture, and that, by examining and judging patients in relation to the legitimate culture, nurses function as social agents who reinforce specific ideas about what is acceptable and appropriate sexual behaviour, or in other words "normal" and "rational" behaviour.

A patient's number of different sexual partners is an example of a question/ category that nurses use to measure people's degree of compliance with the imperative of health and other (religious-based) social mandates about monogamy and procreation; assessments about condom use is a similar strategy. On the whole, the outcome of this process is that nurses enforce and reinforce many of the unequal power balances that define contemporary society, and in turn, construct people's identities based on their abilities to uphold or deviate from the social order. In other words, nurses impose symbolic violence when they compare their patients to, and provide strategies to help their patients be like, the pre-conceived sexual being who refrains from anonymous sexual encounters, has drug-free intercourse, uses condoms consistently, and seeks regular testing without shame (Holmes and O'Byrne 2006). Nurses thus ensure that their patients remain docile citizens who diligently fulfil their social duties, and who are cognizant of how they compare to these dictates (Holmes and O'Byrne 2006).

This aspect of nursing means that nurses, in many clinical domains, find themselves trying to develop or instil codes of behaviour and morality into their patients. While this process is often put forward as a caring process, a sequence of events that involves health promotion and illness prevention, Bourdieu and Foucault's work suggests that caring may be a mask for other socio-political undercurrents. Indeed, under the surface of this caring guise, there is a violent aspect to nursing practice, particularly within the sexual health domain. The sexual health assessment is a personal experience that serves to examine, compare, and normalize each person, one at a time. It involves the divulgence of personal information in an almost confessional interaction, which causes many patients to reflect on how precisely they are following social rules.

As a result of our analysis, we believe that nurses should re-examine and reconceptualise their understanding of caring and nursing practice as it relates to the construction of the self, morality, and patient identity (Winch 2005). In order to provide optimal and quality health care services, nurses should not exclusively focus on definitions of "normal" and "rational" behaviour, but also, should engage in critical self-reflection about the meaning, scope, and nature of nursing practice.

References

Bourdieu, P. 1994. *Raisons pratiques sur la théorie de l'action*. Paris: Seuil.

Bourdieu, P. 2001. *Masculine Domination*. Stanford, CA: Stanford University Press.

Bourdieu, P. and Passeron, J.C. 1977. *Reproduction in Education, Society and Culture*. London: Sage Publications.

Bourdieu, P. and Wacquant, L.J. 1992. *An Invitation to Reflexive Sociology*. Chicago: University of Chicago Press.

Brown, D. 2006. Pierre Bourdieu's "Masculine Domination" thesis and the gendered body in sport and physical culture. *Sociology of Sport Journal*, 23, 162–88.

Davidson, A. Ethics as ascetics, in *The Cambridge Companion to Foucault* edited by G. Gutting. Melbourne: Cambridge University Press, 155–40.

Foucault, M. 1977. *Discipline and Punish*. London: Tavistock.

Foucault, M. 1990. *The History of Sexuality: An Introduction*, Vol. 1. New York: Vintage.

Holmes, D. and O'Byrne, P. 2006. The art of public health nursing: using confession technè in the sexual health domain. *Journal of Advanced Nursing*, 56(4), 430–37.

Lotringer, S. 2007. *Over Exposed: Perverting Perversions*. Los Angeles, CA: Semiotexte.

Lupton, D. 1999. *Risk*. New York: Routledge.

Moore, R. 2004. Cultural capital: objective probability and the cultural arbitrary. British *Journal of Sociology and Education*, 25(4), 445–56.

O'Byrne, P., Holmes, D., and Woodend, K. 2008. Understanding human sexual networks: a critique of the promiscuity paradigm. *Critical Public Health*, 18(3), 333–45.

Public Health Agency of Canada (PHAC). 2008. Canadian Guidelines on Sexually Transmitted Infections. Ottawa: Public Health Agency of Canada.

Rose, N. 1996. *Inventing Ourselves: Psychology, Power, and Personhood*. New York: Cambridge University Press.

Wacquant, L. 2005. 'Habitus', in *International Encyclopedia of Economic Sociology*, edited by J. Becket and Z. Milan. London: Routledge.

Weininger, E. 2004. *Foundations of Bourdieu's classic analysis, in Approaches to Class Analysis*, edited by E.O. Wright, R. Breen, D. Grusky, E. Weininger, A. Sorensen, et al. Cambridge: Cambridge University Press.

Winch S. 2005. Ethics, government and sexual health: insights from Foucault. *Nursing Ethics*, 12(2), 177–86.

Chapter 12

Bullying on the Back-Channels: Everyday Telephone Talk, as a Space for Covert Professional Manipulation

Jackie Cook and Collette Snowden

Introduction

While bullying as a social interaction is widely known and understood within the culture of everyday life, and is further considered to be an increasing practice within the professional workforce (Alexander and Fraser 2004, Bowie 2002, McCarthy and Barker 2000, Budd 1999, Roberts 1983), such practices largely remain hidden from direct public scrutiny. Experiences of bullying, for both victim and perpetrator, are connected to complex issues of self esteem and social shame. Attempts in recent decades to write policies which regulate bullying behaviours within social institutions and workplaces have, this chapter suggests, driven such conduct into even more covert locations and forms of enactment. The use for instance of communicative technologies which are considered 'private' or 'personal' – such as the telephone – makes both institutional scrutiny and research-based analysis harder than ever.

The research reported here suggests that bullying practices within these new spaces of professional interaction (in this case, through both the desktop and personal-mobile telephone) remain concealed. This is in part because of the one-on-one, 'interpersonal' nature of such a communicative relation. Telephone contact enacts the talk-relation as a form of interpersonal 'chat': a friendly, conversational exchange, with each participant securely inside the relative comfort of their known domestic or professional environment at the point of exchange. Paradoxically, this very form of interpersonal 'privacy' permits the deployment of those work-based practices of manipulative control which have evolved within the hierarchies of power built into professional life. Behaviours which Roberts (1983) termed 'horizontal violence' have hardened into 'acceptable' forms of authority; established status; matters of industry-based 'quality control' or productivity assessment; or the expert repertoires of 'collegial' persuasion. When enacted within the relatively limited range of communication relations possible via telephony, these can be brought to bear in very powerful ways, by very skilled practitioners – and can leave the manipulated party with little or no space to manoeuvre.

While power relations within spoken communication – such as telephone talk – have shifted and continue to shift under the conditions produced within, for instance, near-universal mobile telephony and messaging, or the varying patterns of spoken-word contact enabled by Internet applications such as Skype or PODcasting (see especially Castells 2007), the overall outcome is that person-to-person spoken word communication, whether synchronous (in real time) or asynchronous (time-waited recorded messages), has greatly expanded its use. Further, the talk-relations of all telephony are for the most part informally produced - few of us under modernity engage in any sustained educational training in telephone use. The behaviours produced thus rest largely upon the informal, interpersonal speech techniques of everyday social interactions (Eggins and Slade 1997). They are almost always personalised – as any phone user contacted through the 'cold-call' promotional techniques used in telemarketing will know, often to their irritation. As a result they all too often show evidence of the implicit 'rules' of interpersonal talk being used in manipulative ways.

It is this extension of the private modes of everyday conversation into professional life which this research sets out to examine. The researchers suggest that this personalising of the public world of work is however less directed to establishing a comfort zone of familiarity and trust, than a space in which social hierarchies can simultaneously be used to persuade and cajole, and to conceal their very operation. Their claim on the sorts of equitable and collaborative relations more generally felt to exist in social relations of friendship, means that even highly trained and proficient professionals remain vulnerable to manipulation.

To examine power relations within professional exchanges enacted at the level of informal and interpersonal 'private' talk is of course, extremely difficult. Such talk is rarely, if ever, recorded – and in the case of the accelerated levels of outright bullying-talk sought here, unlikely to be offered to researchers. To outline therefore how such talk is produced, and so to analyse how, and why, it works on its victims, this research turns to the case of professional lobbying in the political sphere. The data for our analysis was captured and placed into the public sphere of news reporting, by the Western Australian Corruption and Crime Commission, during telephone tapping in pursuit of a series of allegations of corrupt practice relating to property development, involving a Western Australian ex-politician and former State Premier, identified here simply as 'B'. Subsequently serving a prison sentence in relation to these and other instances of corrupt practice, B had extended his former political power into a career in personalised, one-on-one lobbying, mainly of local government officials and business representatives on planning bodies. Making contact through use of both work and personal-mobile phone calls, he produced sustained pressure on individual decision-makers, working in ways which represent many of the practices reported elsewhere as instances of work-place related bullying – all performed at the level of talk.

Using analytical techniques developed within the Sacksian tradition of Conversation Analysis (Sacks 1984, 1992), this research works to reveal how seemingly casual talk between two individuals can manipulate existing power relations in ways which appear, at least during their enactment, near-impossible to resist. We suggest however that such resistance is in fact possible – and that training in a repertoire of interventions and baffles to such talk, and an understanding of what such a talk-bully is up to, can help reduce instances of successful manipulative conduct in professional settings. Finally, given the ongoing gendering of the workforce in the health professions, and the strong evidence gathered during this particular project on how far such manipulative talk rests on the assertion of powerful forms of masculinity produced with talk (see especially Hutchby 1992, 1996), we suggest that a focus on 'telephone talk' is especially salient in assessing, and learning to resist, bullying behaviours within the health professions. Whether enacted by men or by women – and both are reported in the current bullying literature – an understanding of the ways in which gendered talk patterns can be used to dominate interlocutors can assist in establishing a politics of resistance.

The Social Logic Embedded in Wireless Communication: How to Understand the Back Channels of Telephone Talk

Following on from his definitive study of the 'network society' of digital communications and its various *technologisations* in the 1990s (1996, 1997, 1998), Manuel Castells has proposed the need to study 'the social logic embedded in wireless communication' (2007: 4); a project we take up here, as we work to reveal new spaces of systemic workplace bullying. These are being built, we argue, over ongoing social understandings of what are 'private' interpersonal modes of communications – now disruptively accessible to work-related and coercive forms of use.

In arguing this, we believe that such work also reveals two significant omissions from the Castellsian project, at least as currently conceived. Firstly, while Castells and his co-researchers have been relatively quick to identify the need to re-work descriptions and theorisation of the cabled social networks of the 1990s into the more powerful wireless and mobile forms of connectivity in the twenty-first century, they have not yet fully appreciated what might be termed the 'black' spaces of that connectedness. At the level of practice, research is now needed into establishing which techniques of coercive interpersonal communications might thrive in the mobile-networked mixture of immediacy, intimacy, access, and yet physical and geographic dis-connection. With everyone always accessible, and 'home' space no longer enabling privacy, 'lobbyists' like B are turning more and more to the mobile phone. Secondly, there has been little discussion of how the insights which study of mobile connectivity offers may also prove able to penetrate some of the less easily observable and unanalysed communicative practices evolved through conventional telephony. Such instances include the cases examined here: 'private' phone calls used for manipulative forms of business lobbying. These are, we suggest, common enough in any number of 'professional' workplace exchanges, reflecting the same sorts of power-play interactions and 'peer' pressure.

Castells' new paradigm certainly sets its scope on a wide angle lens, including for instance a socio-political mobilisation, particularly addressed to practices outside formal politics. By this is meant however mostly still a focus on community accessibility to information and issues of citizenship, seeking to maximise civic participation in policy formulation and debate. Here our analysis adds new techniques for the study of such transactions within organised formal politics, but through its informal communications. These we have chosen to call 'the back channels', through which conversations directly influencing both decision-making and the direction of votes occur. What public display of these techniques reveals is just how familiar they are within a very broad range of professional labour. There is, we argue, a well-established 'politics' of lobbying or persuasion within many if not all areas of collegial professional life – and the health professions are in no way exempt. Further: as we will show, the new 'personal' media and the Web 2.0 'social media' experience have, if anything, released these techniques into wider and wider use – without any professional intervention on their modes of operation. More access: less scrutiny – at least in terms of ethical debate, or regulatory critique. Where Castells and his team assert the need to collect, and collect now, those transformations of language under creation in the new networks, we remind researchers of how few examples of actual communicative practice have ever been collected, relating to how conventional audio channels operate. In the field we are examining here, i.e. the politics of land-development lobbying, there has been no primary access for instance to multi-modal communicative forms such as email or SMS – yet. In the health professions, primary data research, since it is subject always – and rightly so – to ethics clearances, has been unable to produce 'natural' data collected from actual instances of collegial transactions. Mediated interpersonal communication always has attached to it that limiting descriptor: 'personal'.

If the Castells study seems however of value to us mostly for what it identifies as deficit within traditional studies of communicative techniques, we also acknowledge that its call for new research directions strengthens our project. It lists the emergence of key trends/categories within mobile connectivity, each of which we recognise as possible motivators for the sheer extremity of some of the communicative behaviours we are witnessing. Together Castells et al. appear to us to be surfacing a new paradigm within communicative culture generally, but one with the capacity to produce some intensely negative outcomes when applied through a 'back-channel' or covert ethics of influence.

Castells et al. list the following characteristics within wireless interconnection:

- Relentless connectivity
- Safe autonomy
- Networks of choice
- Instant communities of practice
- Blurring of the social contexts of individual practice

- Access to the wireless network as a source of personal value, and as a social right
- Recognition of users as the producers of content and services (2008: 119–20).

In telephone bullying, each of these categories is in play. Phone connectivity breaches personal space and professional barriers: no place is safe from intrusion. The interpersonal techniques of phone 'chat' make it difficult to resist the bully's advances: to do so seems churlish. Once connected, the power invested in professional status flattens out, so that workplace proficiency or reputation can all too easily be swept aside. Worse: to resist such access is to cut oneself off from the new status markers of constant social connection – and to appear an unproductive non-player. In turn, each of these features is exploited by the technical talk-performance of the telephone bully. We argue that in our data corpus, all of these qualities interact with practices of covert political lobbying within the field of commercial development, to enhance the personal and interpersonal influence of 'celebrity' professional lobbyists. Our case study relates to the revelation of the phone lobbying practices of ex politician B, in relation to his interventions into land development regulation by local body officers and council members in a beachside development zone near an Australian state capital city. Our analysis of how B uses the interpersonal communication relations enabled by both the workplace landline phone and the personal mobile service reveals the degree to which long-established traditions of one-on-one political conversation in Australia: invoking collegiality, the 'pressure' rules of caucusing, calls on mateship, the 'gender-work' of Australian 'bloke-talk' or hyper-masculine jocularity, skills in commercial negotiation, the reciprocity of formal and informal information sharing, all undergo subtle yet significant intensification when enacted – or even potentially enacted – through the mobile networks and 'the personal phone'.

Threats and Menaces 101: A Short Introduction to the Linguistic Arts of Bullying

Establishing 'friendship' and 'collegiality' in telephone-talk rests on a very small number of conversational strategies – most of them currently very familiar within the training repertoires of 'cold-call' commercial tele-marketing, and producing that oddly jarring note that many householders register when addressed by a total stranger, who then proceeds to inquire solicitously over their health and wellbeing. Most phone calls begin with a short exchange of pleasantries: the sorts of conversational exchange which socio-linguistics calls 'phatic' or 'empty' language, with very little real informational exchange, but a socially necessary preliminary to the launch into the caller's intentions in phoning.

There is a great deal of such ritualised exchange within the talk of Australian mateship, a well-established form of (mostly) male public forms of behaviour and interpersonal address, enacted within spoken language as a particularly weighty or 'up-front' set of practices. It requires for instance constant re-assertion and patrolling of its 'shared' values, reiterating the jovial assumption of common purpose. It builds on an unspoken yet ever-present joint recognition of the need to maintain solidarity, consensus, collegiality, and mutual benefit. All of these are formations held only partly through lexical choice. Talk relations depend less on what is said, than on how it is said. Reinforcing solidarity mean using any or all of a number of recurring talk-techniques.

Over-Sustained Vowels and the Politics of Australian 'Ma-a-a-a-ateship'

A technique brilliantly captured in Casey Bennetto's lyrics for the political cabaret called *Keating! The Musical*, the over-sustained vowel can be used in Australian English to create inclusivity. While a sharply delivered and crisp 'mate!' can for instance imply a none-too-subtle suggestion of discord and disagreement, the drawn out version produces a form of auditory space, into which all addressed can securely enter. In a brilliantly creative extension of the concept, Bennetto imagines Australians sailing together in the 'Maaaateship', an evocation of how 'ma-a-a-a-ates' are defined by techniques of inclusion. Bennetto's creative ear has picked up the cue which shows how far this sort of device is a definer of an identity always nervously under negotiation.

Nor is Bennetto the only user of this technique for the creation of identity-space within language. Australian radio-badlands broadcaster the late Stan Zemanek consistently used the same device to signal to talkback callers that he was inviting them to begin talking as he accessed their call, always over-extending the final word of his cue that he was ready for them to talk: 'And so, let's go to a call – and what do we-e-e-e ha-a-a-a-a-ve he-e-e-e-e-re...' The exaggerated vowel creates an interestingly ambivalent conversational space, in which the power relation however remains firmly in the control of the broadcaster. In CA terms, what Zemanek is doing is offering the caller 'the floor': literally, inviting them to speak. Using the conversational power relativity classically identified by Sacks, Schegloff and Jefferson (1974), this invites the caller to establish the terms of the ensuing discussion: to set the talk agenda by initiating a topic – albeit one for which the broadcaster is already prepared, having been alerted by his production-staff call screeners. He is in danger, in conversational terms, of being forced into the weaker 'going second' position: of having to respond to a caller's initiative, following their logic and reacting to their cues. Professional radio hosts do not however brook any such intervention over their occupancy of the 'P' or 'Power' position within talk-turns. What Zemanek does with his long-drawn vowels is to tease the caller: to seemingly offer the space for occupancy of the 'P' position, yet actually continue to vocalise within that space. Here then the lexis (word choice) runs against the vocalisation (the way in which the words are pronounced) – for while the words seem to invite participation, it is clear that the broadcaster can, and will, reclaim that space at any time.

In an example from our own data, lobbyist B plays out a phone relation with his lobby-target, a 'maaaate' whose identity we will conceal. B uses a talk-initiating strategy which appears, like Zemanek's, to set out from a relatively innocuous position. It seems to be a simple, factual question – but launches from there into altogether deeper waters of influence and intervention:

B: Are you still on that South West Planning Commission?
F: Ah, yeah, yep.
B: Do you take an interest at all?
F: Sorry?
B: Do you take an interest in it at all?
F: I, I'm going down tomorrow morning actually. I get up at six, six o'clock to be there and, uh, unlike the chairman who's only attended two meetings out of the last seven but that's another matter. (laughs)
B: Yeah, well, yeah. I'll tell you what F, um, if I send you an email tonight...
F: Mmhm?
B: ...will you able to access it before tomorrow, before you leave? And I just would like to send you an email with a point of view about dealing with that amendment now and I might just send it to your home one, eh?
F: Okay, yep.

Note how flat and straightforward B's opening sentence is, once the initial 'pleasantries' are over. F has decided that, given the factual and so apparently unthreatening nature of this opening direct question, he can safely answer. He moves from a strategic pause: 'Ah...' to an extended affirmative, leaving thinking time: first a drawn out, semi-provisional 'ye-e-ah' – and only then to the shorter, sharper 'yep' of 'blokey'or all-mates-together hyper-masculine certainty. That 'yep' however remains colloquial, so that together the mix of long and short forms says something like: 'Is there anything more going on in here? – Oh well, you're a mate – so I'll commit'.

But within this talk-relation B is already in total command – a fact which a more alert, or more powerful, talk-respondent would have detected in the flat directness of B's first question. B's second question is designed to crank up both the talk-pressure, and the information flow – and to turn the conversation into the rather muddier waters of exactly what an 'interest' in a Planning Commission might amount to.

B: Do you take an interest at all?
F: Sorry?
B: Do you take an interest in it at all?
F: is immediately ill at ease – in fact, like a rabbit in a spotlight, he literally twists and turns, at first trying to buy time with the open-ended affirmative:
F: Ah yeah ... no.

Then he launches a strategy which is probably designed to suggest that there is no time for him to undertake any intervention for B, but which offers too much incidental narrative detail to act as a powerful resistance. He is gabbling – and all this does is to allow B time to select a much more powerful and direct escalation of his demands.

> F: I, I'm going down tomorrow morning actually. I get up at six, six o'clock to
>   be there and, uh…

F's repetitions and hesitancies: 'I, I'm'; 'six, six o'clock', and his paralinguistic continuers ('uh') extend the space of his talk, just as the overdrawn vowels discussed above do – but here, what is signalled is a form of desperation: a speaker literally stalling for time. He tries to pin the 'matey' relationship back together with a joke about a fellow delegate. F is seeking to re-access the bantering tone of jocularity which he thinks – or hopes –means collegiality, but which B uses instead to dictate consensus. The ploy –inevitably – fails:

> F: Unlike the chairman who's only attended two meetings out of the last seven
>   but that's another matter (laughs).
> B: simply lets it fizzle:
> B: Yeah, well, yeah.

Instead, B now counter-launches a pre-stepped program of direct instructions. These may well be projected as a conditional set of possibilities: "If… then…' but they are already very clearly part of a process in train:

> B: I'll tell you what F, um, if I send you an email tonight…
> F: Mm hm?
> B: Will you able to access it before tomorrow, before you leave? And I just
>   would like to send you an email with a point of view about dealing with that
>   amendment now and I might just send it to your home one, eh?
> F: Okay, yep.

No other answer is possible. F has already conversationally been reduced to the level of para-linguistic continuers: 'Mm hm?' He can in the end only cling to the last pretences of a collegial relation, with his final pseudo-assertive 'yep'.

Setting Up the Conditions: 'Irrealis' and the 'what if?' Scenario

Within that circle of mutual benefit and shared understanding, words powerfully unsaid maintain more power than those spoken. This time the collegial space of shared, matey values, is signalled not so much in over-drawn vowels, as in the 'what if?' imaginative space of future conditional verb tenses. B has now pinned his target into the 'we're mates and agree on everything' position – so now he can move relentlessly into 'so here's what *you* are going to do…'

The strategy of using conditional and future tenses was incisively described by Gaik (1992), who identified it as contributing to what he termed 'irrealis': the opening up of conceptual projection space, used in talk to build a joint vision of what-might-be. Gaik's own work focused on psychological therapy, with irrealis used to diagnose and resolve patient issues – but the technique has also been revealed in the classic study by Montgomery (1986) which showed radio DJs building similar visions with youth audiences. With their lives still largely ahead of them, youth audiences could not be invited into the reminiscence or application into lived experience available to mature listeners, as broadcasters build connection and so interest in discussion topics. Instead, DJs moved to the 'what if' and 'just imagine…' formulae of future and conditional tenses, developing a repertoire of 'how would it be if…' tags which opened up to the imagined future, rather than to the lived past.

Such techniques are of course equally valuable in the art of sustaining menace. A classic Monty Python sketch of the 1960s has two East-End London mobsters sauntering into the office of a Regimental Adjutant. 'That one of your nice new tanks outside, is it? Wouldn't want nuffink nasty to 'happen to that now, would we?' The degree to which the script plays across irrealis and into satire is obvious – but so are all the linguistic techniques of the format, powerfully shifting what is *not* being said to the centre of our awareness.

The phone-lobbyist however will move relatively quickly from this 'mutual-vision' tactic, to one of direct threat. While the delivery may still call upon the bloke-talk repertoires of jokes and colloquial language, it simultaneously makes clear that non-compliance has unpleasant consequences:

> B: Well, mate, I… I, you know, let me just say this to you. I mean, you.. you wouldn't know this, but I'm not a fuckin' good enemy to have, and I don't appreciate it if people aren't up front with me. All he needs to say is, 'B, I don't want to talk to you because of this reason or that reason, or you're fat and bald'. And that's good enough for me.

The Australian Broadcasting Corporation Television (ABCTV) producer Liz Jackson, who compiled a program revealing B's telephone lobbying for broadcast on Channel 2, was able to read back exactly what this means:

> LIZ JACKSON: Rule One – B likes his calls returned.

Gambit by gambit, this extract reveals the strategic pathway from irrealis into menace, and onto direct, unimpeded instruction. B moves first from the linguistic 'continuers' which simply allow him to hold the conversational floor while he gropes for a tactical direction: 'Well, mate, I…I…', to a directive statement only half coloured as a polite request: 'Let me just say this to you.' This is only superficially a formula which is seeking agreement: 'Let me…'. It is closer to the interrogatory barrister's proposition which is trying to force 'the correct' answer: "I put it to you that…' It acts as a 'request' which you will not – cannot – resist. To this extent it is much closer to the US Navy 'Now listen up!' The 'just', rather than signifying 'merely', or 'only this one thing', means something closer to 'I shall say this only once, and you had better hear it the first time'. It signals a shift from the hesitancy of the shuffled continuers and the benevolence of the ongoing claims of mateship, to something altogether larger and of more import.

That B then appears to re-enter the shuffle of inconsequential and phatic continuers: 'I mean, you…' simply buys him time to prepare the king hit. He first hedges it with the conditionality of irrealis: 'you wouldn't know this…' and then implies that you might well be about to find out. The metaphorical fist is already swinging just below the surface of that 'but' introduction: 'but I'm not a fuckin' good enemy to have…'

This is a shared culture of menace, in which both sides know the rules. There is no new information here, but instead the talk is reinforcing a code of conduct. Both sides know that the consequences of rejecting B's 'help' and 'advice' go well beyond 'not appreciating' people who are not 'upfront' with him: who attempt to evade his not-so-euphemised 'conversations'. This time the lightness of the words is counteracted by the heaviness and deliberation of the delivery. The logic is now clear. There is no escape. Prevaricate, lie, or in any way attempt to evade full compliance, and a 'fuckin' bad enemy' will make his non-appreciation felt. Dare to resist: 'B, I don't want to talk to you' –'and that's good enough for me': a good enough reason, that is, to become 'a fuckin' bad enemy'. The formula is – like the insult, 'fat and bald' – heavy in layered and acculturated meaning, and a time-honoured technique of masculine interpersonal aggression. Its claims on straight-forward, 'plain talking' self deprecation are all part of the formula.

Regulating the Flow: Over-Wording, Interrupting, and Directing who is in the Field Addressed

At the other extreme is the shared linguistic pleasure of rituals of 'over-worded' or wittily exuberant play across aspects of category maintenance. Fairclough (1989, 1992) points out that what he terms 'over-lexicalisation' is used when speakers are nervous of the topic under discussion, and their power to control their point of view. As we speak, we patrol issues of concern, through obsessive return to them as topics of our talk, even building patterned language games to help sediment a false confidence in ourselves that we are indeed in control of what we most fear. Bourdieu (1992) has commented in this regard on the powerful social uses of euphemism, arguing that there has been a displacement of physical forms of coercion into linguistic or 'symbolic' contestations of power. While his examples relate to social status and the deployment of formal codes of respect, from pronoun choice to dialect pronunciation, Fairclough has identified over-lexicalisation: allocating too many terms to a single referent, as a 'euphemising' displacement of the speaker's control from the referent itself, to the often bravura use of language used to describe it. In the case of the menacing art of the talk-bully lobbyist, over-lexicalisation appears to invite – but never actually accede to – the interlocutor's powerful co-use of such language. It is a strategy, like Zemanek's drawn-out vowels as he access a caller on-air, which anticipates, and appears to build, collaboration. B is always quick to play along:

> C: P's got a motion coming up today nailing the bloody planners. And she had to bloody ring up A and ask her to support it and who would know what she'll do?
>
> B: I don't fucking believe any of this. They must be mad down there
>
> C: B, there must be something in the fucking water down there, mate.

This is reciprocal talk. The two mirror, and build upon, each other's contributions, shoring up their own – hopefully powerful – consensus and mutual understanding against the evidence of resistant agencies operating elsewhere. Such resistance is, of course, 'mad' – and inherently out of control. Its representatives must be victims of some unconscious control ('something in the fucking water') rather than any planned – or worse: effectively counter-lobbied – set of strategies. To reassure themselves that this is indeed so, B and his interlocutor circle endlessly around the topic, endowing it with far more words than it needs or merits. Add to these more creative elements of speaking-with-menace many other less subtle but equally powerful talk-practices.

Interruption during conversation not only disrupts a speaker's flow of thought and the logic of their argument, but signals the interlocutor's belief that they can – literally – overpower any opposing commentary, or any 'weak' version of the central topic, which they believe they can themselves better represent. Interruption – always by B – is clearly evident in the audio-transcripts of these taped phone-calls used in the ABC TV program made by Liz Jackson. Interruption is not however fully indicated in the text-transcription quoted from here; a further instance of the difficulties of obtaining fully-reported examples of bullying talk. Transcription protocols used in Conversation Analysis (CA) note all instances of successful interruption, as well as the presence of 'over-talking' or attempts at interrupting, a marker of how important breaches of the 'rules' of talk-reciprocity called 'turn-taking' are to CA researchers (see especially Sacks, Schegloff and Jefferson1974). Interestingly, B shows relatively low instances of overt interruption – suggesting a phone-speaker so convinced of his own capacity to control and direct talk, that he is able, as shown here, to let the speaker appear to lead – unaware of just how B is directing the conversational flow.

The use of pronouns, always important as Fairclough shows (1992, 1995), is also worth examining here. They shift here between the powerful 'we' of assumed consensus, to the equally powerful and directive 'you', and even the ultimate assertion of an 'I' who retains the power to judge, to withdraw 'support', and so to punish. The use of first names is very evident – especially when claims are being made upon relationships of mutuality which never in fact existed; at least in the ways or to the levels now being evoked.

When pronouns are used to include and exclude, i.e. to create a clear demarcation between 'us' and 'them', also in play is a talk-based geography or 'deixis' which works to position 'the powerful' within a charmed circle of support. Those outside that circle become a 'they' firmly located in an 'elsewhere' or 'outsider' zone, immediately denigrated and viewed as powerless. Here pronouns are joined by a careful use of consistently patterned prepositions: the grammatical terms used to indicate spatial relations. B for instance constantly alludes to decision-makers – or 'wannabe' decision-makers – who are 'down there'. In this case, this refers to the Southern beachside community whose planning he is attempting to influence – but the formula very effectively builds a hierarchy of power. 'We' – B and his talk-targets - are in powerful contact, at the very centre of things. 'They' – the people to be manipulated and controlled – are cut off from that centre – as B's talk-targets will be, if they refuse to collaborate. 'We' need to have 'you' stay 'in touch' - an interesting formula within telephone talk, where a politics of proximity is so interestingly confused by the synchronous yet distanced exchange of mediated talk.

Conscious and skilled use of all of these 'talk techniques' is what makes lobbyists like B so effective. While such behaviours may appear as if somehow innate or unrehearsed, in fact they have been acquired and polished over many years of professional – in his case political – practice. For most socio-linguistics specialists, these techniques are now seen not to reflect, but to 'perform' and so call into being the types of powerful public presence, business influence and interpersonal self-presentation they were once thought merely to represent (see especially the work of Judith Butler 1997 and in linguistic research, an anthology of articles on gendered talk, edited by Coates1998). While B himself, and others like him, may well deny and laugh off any view that these are deliberate and calculated strategies of conduct, they are also quick to claim efficacy for their 'business' practice, projecting it as a 'results driven' process of professional influence and intervention. In part the success rests on the mystification. The aura which develops around such figures benefits from remaining undefined, and unexamined. Categorise and explain some of these relatively simple techniques, and not only does the field open to competitors, it enables its targets to understand what is happening, and to resist.

There are however other influences at play. Beyond the focus on conversational exchange and techniques of language use, lie what technology analysts call 'the affordances' of the telephone systems primarily used by lobbyists such as B – and increasingly, by professionals in many fields, seeking to extend their power and influence among work colleagues. Telephone talk, undertaken through networks with the enhanced mobility, accessibility and call-capture and management techniques of digital networks, is as ill-understood as a social practice as conversational talk itself. It is the pre-dispositions it carries towards strategic 'mixing' of what Habermas (1987, 1989) would consider private/intimate and public forms of communication, to which this discussion now turns.

Knowing your Place: Building an Awareness of how Telephone Talk Transgresses and Abuses Norms of Public and Private Talk

What we have developed in the conversational analysis undertaken above, is the suggestion that the bullying talk of lobbyists has drawn particular forms of power from its origins within the highly competitive political field. This, in turn, has been built around public forms of hyper-masculine exchange. Its mix of plain-talking (Easthope 1986), sexism, colloquialism and casual profanity, and even a kind of contrived inarticulacy, credential it as a form of egalitarian and therefore 'safe', peer-to-peer 'matey' talk among men. It extends out from and back into the social exchanges of men's public life – and while women can, and do, participate, evidence from this data shows how easily they can be ejected from the powerful 'inner' groups.

How then does this formula cross the public/private social technologisation of the phone – traditionally positioning as a communications device in both an office-business environment, and within the realm of the private? Further: how far have understandings and practices surrounding use of the telephone shifted, as both the desk and the domestic 'home' telephone have been joined by the hand-held 'personal' mobile? What does it mean that phone-lobbyists like B can now 'reach' their targets anytime, and anywhere – and all in a cultural environment which has greatly escalated the imperative to always answer a call: to literally, 'be available'.

Castells, in beginning the theorisation of the new connectedness, calls this 24/7 ubiquitous connection 'mass personal communication' (2008: 119–20). The term aptly encapsulates the paradox of the mobile networks, with their simultaneous offer of 'autonomy', the power to gain connection, and 'security', or enhanced control of 'safe' personal space. Having embraced the use of the mobile phone with huge enthusiasm, we appear far less certain about what it actually 'is', or 'is for'. Instead, connectivity itself has become a form of value: one which is reducing physical forms of social containment, but replacing them with the urge towards constant, and active, participation within the communicative networks.

It is in part this which B exploits: the sense carried by network accessibility that to be somehow excluded from the network is to lose social value. For B, part of the game is to always have his target's phone numbers... especially their personal mobile numbers. The personal mobile allows him to cross all the forms of gate-keeping enacted by layers of switchboards, secretaries and PA 'minders'. Since his previous political prominence guarantees that he can cross most of those barriers anyway, the residual honour of a direct, personal contact generates even more power over his target.

ABC TV:	At the CCC, it was exposed that Minister M had a secret mobile phone for the numerous calls each week to and from B. Not even J was to be told. But the CCC was tapping it.
B:	You don't need anyone else to know you've got the phone mate.
M:	Yep.
B:	Promise me?
M:	Absolutely, done deal.
B:	It's in your own interest.
M:	Yep.

Once again, B is building on mateship, as he projects new commercial benefit founded on long-established loyalties and social ties. All expressed in the typically informal/colloquial registers, the talk-relation enacts the friendship rituals of the personal/wireless networks – forms likely to be destabilised by use on the business phone. The personal mobile is a 'safe', interpersonal form of contact. The very fact that these calls can be made assures both parties that the callers are 'mates'. B is able to take on an overtly paternalistic role: 'Promise me?' M – a Government Minister, with access to whole departments of (protective) public servants, political advisors and lawyers, is brought to complicity with both the influence B is negotiating, and the linguistic registers in which he is exerting that influence. The relation becomes a 'done deal', a neatly clichéd formulation of how much understanding there is between the two. The menace in this conversation – and it is close to overt – lies as much in B's capacity to 'connect with' M as it does with his lobbying skills: he makes it clear that he can, and will, access an otherwise safe personal space.

The cross-over of communicative forms evident here works precisely because of the security expected from private/intimate one-on-one-ness. We have learned that this is the location for the confidential, and the personal. We offer and anticipate confidences and revelations and heightened emotional expressivity on our 'personal' mobile phones. Blokey friendship and jocularity transfer well into this talk-relation, but what of the public-sphere qualities of powerful masculinity and authority? It is the shift from one to the other that pins down B's targets: that gives him purchase on their 'loyalty' and compliance. When a conversation that they assume to be a casual, inter-personal exchange – and which is indeed always initially framed in those terms – slowly or suddenly becomes a vehicle for the exertion of power, few are able to backtrack quickly enough to redefine the relationship. What few have yet realised is that telephone talk has many registers, and many contexts. What social researcher Milroy identified in the 1980s as 'multiplex' social networks, connected simultaneously in multiple ways across multiple groups, cultural analyst Theo Van Leeuwen is beginning to call 'polyrhythmia': an open-ended pulsing of messages through many networks, which he observes as calling forth the free-flowing creativities of jazz or jam-session rock music. While nothing in B's practice illustrates these degrees of creative flow – indeed, his talk-repertoires are, by necessity, limited in scope and resting on well-established formulae – both researchers are clearly observing central experiences within modern, and especially digital/mobile communications.

What B's practice offers is to elevate the interlocutor into powerful forms of public influence, all from within a secure and familiar in-group 'friendship' network, a safe and ongoing space for like-minded support. The talk, so suited to the personal mobile phone, also however reverses its own flow. If it carries the security of one's personal social circles into the contested and competitive spaces of the business or professional office, it can also carry the pressure from the office into the home. Its 24/7 availability is at once a privilege and a pressure. There simply is no down-time, and the sense conveyed that things are constantly in powerful motion in these networks, and that they can switch one's power and influence around in just the same ways, means that one is also open to the same sources of influence and manipulation.

Talking Back: A Politics of Resistance

Above all, the telephone talk-bully understands his own tactics. This is a game played at the level of discourse. It is talk techniques, and not some form of 'in-group knowledge', or social status, or personal 'presence', in play. Understand the rules of the discursive techniques, and you can break the server's game – the most powerful stroke of all being simply refusing to return play: 'I'm stopping *this* conversation, now.' Once inside someone else's talk-game, where they can no longer control play, talk-bullies simply refuse to engage.

What these behaviours alert us to, is the degree to which an awareness of that one feature of talk – its reliance on contextual, situated sets of regulatory behaviours, controlling its flows and preferred techniques – allows talkers to take up the 'P' or 'Power' positions. While a full cataloguing of B's repertoire for instance would require much more detail and broader sampling than attempted here, the major tactics are clear. Draw your interlocutor in to the conversation, by maximising your use of colloquialisms, shared perspectives, 'we' versus 'them' identity inclusion. Make them feel powerful: use heavy doses of prestige formulae: in this case, 'blokey' elements such as obscenity, sexism, the sorts of seeming-inarticulacy which evoke sincerity and authenticity, and the 'plain speaking' public style of the working-man's world. Open the conversational 'floor' to the interlocutor, with drawn-out vowels, and by seeming to invite them to offer their experiences, ideas and suggestions. Maximise the use of 'networks' of affiliation: name drop, to offer access to power, and to guarantee that since I know who you know, we have shared positions on things. Then: move to irrealis. Project a mix of positive and negative scenarios, making it clear that outcome A is preferable to outcome B. Colour outcome B by 'over-wording' its consequences, to sustain its menace. Finally, outline, in directive formulae, what the interlocutor is now going to do – and extract commitment in no-nonsense terms: 'Promise me'.

To resist the technique, is to understand what each stage of the process is designed to achieve – and to refuse participation. B himself, as we have seen, does this at the level of the game itself. He denies his interlocutors the right to name the game in their own terms, and to play it in their own ways. But it is also possible to resist at the tactical level: to block the development of each turn of play, and to reclaim definition of how the conversation will progress. While it is of course always possible to stop a phone call outright: 'I am reporting this call to my supervisor'; 'I do not take calls of this type', doing this is very likely to break a relationship permanently, and is not always possible, or desirable – as talk-bullies fully understand. Beyond that, learning to observe the talk-techniques makes it possible to resist them, and even regain some degree of direction.

Talk which sets out to establish friendship – in this case, matey-ness, can be countered with crisp, factual professionalism. 'How am I? Really busy right now: is there something important, or shall we wait to chat till we meet on some social occasion?'

Interruption: the tacit assertion that somehow the talk-bully's comments are more important than their interlocutor's, should not be contested. To try to regain the ascendancy simply enters the game, and makes it difficult to win. Instead, wait it out. Let the speaker finish their full statement, then summarise and contest: 'You think X, but I think Y – so I won't bother arguing about it.' Summary of another's position is in itself a more powerful act – which is why a talk-bully like B 'invites' their target to express their views on an issue. Summarising, followed immediately by a strongly asserted intention to act: 'so I won't bother arguing...' is difficult to overcome, and signals a formidable opponent.

Counter attempts at 'inclusion' which demand your complicity/compliance, by questioning pronoun use which seems to be including you, or which is building an 'us' versus 'them' position: 'I'm a little confused here: who are you talking about – who is this "we", exactly?' Shift to impersonal modes: not 'Are they deciding this next week? You need my vote then?' but 'So this project is going to be decided next week' – 'People making the decision will want more support.' This lets you deflect full personal engagement, while still getting information: 'More information would be good: is that a possibility?' Avoid the first person. 'It's a possibility' is far less engaged than 'OK I'll think about it.'

Be very alert to 'irrealis' talk and what-if scenarios. If one is used, and seems to imply some form of threat, move back to the impersonal mode, and spell out the consequences: 'So when this happens, X and Y will follow?' The irrealis speaker almost always pulls back to face-saving denials: 'I'm not saying it WILL happen – it's just that IF it happens...' You have taken over the progression and intensification of the circumstances, which the talk-bully uses to pressure their victim. The 'what if' chain of logic has been broken, and once broken, it is very difficult to reconnect.

Above all, what such talk-tactics of resistance require is a clear distinction in the potential target's mind, between what is personal and private 'chat' between friends, and what is a workplace or professional exchange, where necessary information is exchanged and actions planned and agreed upon. While the formulae involved in these two types of talk can, and do, interchange, and can be effectively used in either circumstance, inappropriate use can erode professional relations in a range of ways.

The modern dilemma in this regard arises from not merely our increasing reliance on telephone contact, but on our failure to demarcate the telephone device as being 'for work' or 'for personal use'. The mobile phone, now near universal in its use, carries oral communication into a complex mix of the public and the private, which analysts and theorists are still struggling to define. Once-strict regimes of phone etiquette have dissolved. Workplace access to 'personal' calls is now impossible to regulate. New generations of workers, with life-long mobile phone experience, draw the conversational lines of conduct differently, and appear to admit much broader elements of 'the personal' into 'the public'. Whether this admits more, rather than less, potential for the types of talk-bullying outlined here, remains for researchers to establish. In the meantime, individual decisions on whether to distinguish between work phone and personal phone talk-styles – and knowing which sorts of calls to take on each, and who will have access - can help frame the sorts of call behaviour received.

Conclusion

In healthcare industries in particular, where interpersonal and collegial professional relations are paramount, and where client handover routines demand regular inter-professional contact, knowledge of the techniques of telephone talk can help identify and resist attempts at distorted power relations. Returning to the list of features carried within the new mobile forms of telephone talk in particular, it is now possible to see how far each is influencing the sorts of talk-bullying outlined here. The 'relentless connectivity' of mobile networks and 'personal' phones now exists as an urge exerting powerful psycho-social pressure on individuals, whose sense of self-esteem and social identity appears to be suffering erosion whenever they see themselves as out of contact. The 'safe autonomy' which users feel is offered by the 'personal' phone invites them to both make, and receive, riskier calls than they might otherwise consider. Meanwhile the endless promise that we are building 'networks of choice' as we link into various talk-circles both invites us to 'join' countless sets of activities, and conceals the degree to which this opens us to contact with people well beyond our normal levels of experience or capacity to check. That the 'instant communities of practice' established within such networks and connectedness include participants with very different expectations from our own, and that each 'community' will be exerting a different set of behavioural norms and objectives, has established a level of complexity in our 'social' relations which few are yet able to comprehend. Further: there is a 'blurring' which is, if anything, acting to delay that comprehension. The sense that 'social value' is conferred by network access motivates levels of connection, without in any way encouraging understanding of the consequences, or offering the means of evaluating the activities involved in participation.

Perhaps the most important issue of all lies in the final topic identified by Castells The next phase of this 'relentless connectivity' – the stage at which Castells' 'mass personal media' become re-codified by the recognition that 'content and services' are flowing through these new networks – is going to demand many of the finely-detailed forms of understanding of the communicative practices and technological affordances outlined in this one small instance of modern communication practice. The more we begin to not just manage, but enact our professional lives through these mobile media, the more we are going to need to understand in very acute ways, exactly what we are doing as we interact. The merging of old conventions on 'public' and personal' communication is largely still happening, as we suggest here, on 'the back channels'. It is inaccessible to analysts, and developing a repertoire of behaviours which are effective mostly because of their informality and ill-understood techniques. Such circumstances indicate how far current and future developments of mobile communications media are eroding these distinctions between public and private, front room and back room behaviours, and how many communicative behaviours may depend upon just such forms of confused, 'blurred', and unregulated interpersonal exchange.

References

Alexander, C. and Fraser, J. 2004. Occupational violence in an Australian healthcare setting: implications for managers. *Journal of Healthcare Management*, 49(6), 377–92

Bennetto, C. 2008. *Keating: the Musical!* ABCTV DVD. Madman Entertainment.

Bourdieu, P. 1992. *Language and Symbolic Power*. Cambridge: Polity Press.

Bowie, V. 2002. Defining violence at work: a new typology, in *Violence at Work: Causes, Patterns and Prevention*, edited by M. Gill, B. Fisher, and V. Bowie. Devon: Willan, 1–20.

Budd, T. 1999. Violence at Work: Findings from the British Crime Survey. Health and Safety Executive: London.

Butler, J. 1997. *Excitable Speech: A Politics of the Performative*. New York: Routledge.

Castells, M. 1996. *The Information Age: Economy, Society and Culture; Vol. 1: The Rise of the Network Society*. Oxford: Basil Blackwell.

Castells, M. 1997. *The Information Age: Economy, Society and Culture; Vol. 2: The Power of Identity*. Oxford: Basil Blackwell.

Castells, M.1996. *The Information Age: Economy, Society and Culture; Vol. 3: End of Millennium*. Oxford: Basil Blackwell.

Castells, M., Fernández-Ardèvol, M., Qiu, J.L., and Sey, A. 2008. Mobile communication and society: a global perspective. *Economic Geography*, 84(1), 119–20.

Coates, J. 1998. *Language and Gender: A Reader*. Oxford: Basil Blackwell.

Easthope, A. 1986. *What a Man's Gotta Do: The Masculine Myth in Popular Culture*. London: Paladin.

Eggins, S. and Slade, D. 1997. *Analysing Casual Conversation*. London: Cassell.

Fairclough, N. 1989. *Language and Power*. London: Longman.

Fairclough, N. 1992. *Discourse and Social Change*. Cambridge: Polity Press.

Fairclough, N. 1995. *Critical Discourse Analysis: The Critical Study of Language*. London: Longman.

Fairclough, N. 1995. *Media Discourse*. London: Edward Arnold.

Gaik, F. 1992. Radio talk show therapy and the pragmatics of possible worlds, in *Rethinking Context: Language as an Interactive Phenomenon*, edited by A. Duranti and G. Goodwin. Cambridge: Cambridge University Press, 271–90.

Habermas, J. 1987. *The Theory of Communicative Action, Vol. 2, The Critique of Functionalist Reason*. Cambridge: Polity Press.

Habermas, J. 1989. *The Structural Transformation of the Public Sphere: An Inquiry Into a Category of Bourgeois Society*. Transl. Thomas Burgher and Frederick Lawrence. Cambridge Massachusetts: M.I.T. Press.

Hutchby, I. 1992. The pursuit of controversy: routine scepticism in talk on talk radio. *Sociology*, 26, 673–94.

Hutchby, I. 1996. *Confrontation Talk: Arguments, Asymmetries and Power on Talk Radio*. New Jersey: Lawrence Erlbaum.

McCarthy, P. and Barker, M. 1989. Workplace bullying risk audit. *Journal of Occupational Health and Safety – Australia and New Zealand*, 16(5), 407–17.

Montgomery, M. 1986. DJ talk. *Media Culture & Society*, 8(4), 421–40.

Roberts, S. 1983. Oppressed group behaviour: implications for nursing. *Advances in Nursing Science*, 5(4), 21–30

Sacks, H. 1984. Notes on methodology, in *Structures in Social Action, Studies in Conversational Analysis*, edited by J. Atkinson and J. Heritage. Cambridge University Press, 21–7.

Sacks, H. 1992. *Lectures on Conversation Vols. 1–2*. Oxford: Basil Blackwell.

Sacks, H., Schegloff, E. and Jefferson, G. 1974. A simplest systematics for the organisation of turn taking in conversation. *Language*, 50, 696–735.

Van Leeuwen, T. *Speech, Music, Sound*. [Online]. Available at:http://www.tagg. org/students/Montreal/Tendances/MartineRh/RheaumeLeeuwenAnx2ff. pdf[accessed: June 2011].

PART THREE
Patients' Violence

Chapter 13

Assessment of Risk and Special Observations in Mental Health Practice: A Comparison of Forensic and Non-Forensic Settings[1]

Elizabeth Mason-Whitehead and Tom Mason

Introduction

Special observations in psychiatric practice are, usually, implemented when there is a perceived increased risk of harm being enacted, either to the patients themselves or towards others. In mental health settings, this type of observation can be distinguished from more general observations by their level of intensity by which they are embarked upon, and the closeness to the individual who is being observed. Other terms and phrases used, some colloquially, include 'close observations', 'maximum observations', 'continuous observations', 'constant observations', 'precautionary observations', 'one-to-one observations', and so on (Jones and Jackson 2004, Bowers and Park 2001). There is usually a distinction drawn between the levels of observations in terms of the required closeness by which the person undertaking them should be to the person being observed. If the patient is perceived to be at-risk from, say, command hallucinations instructing them to pull out their eye, it is clear that the observing nurse(s) must be very close to the patient to prevent a sudden surge to enucleate. Alternatively, if the patient is considered to be a threat towards assaulting others, it may be more appropriate to observe them from several feet away rather than encroach upon their personal space and provoke an attack. These levels of close observations are known by various gradations. For example, the Standing Nursing and Midwifery Advisory Committee (1999) defined four levels of observations: level 1, general observations; level 2, intermittent observations; level 3, within eyesight; and level 4, within arm's length. For the purposes of this paper we will employ the term special observations to include all such variations above and beyond the general observations undertaken on an everyday level in psychiatric practice. Special observations are predominantly undertaken as an alternative to seclusion and/or restraining techniques, either as a precursor to them or in supplanting them. However, their efficacy as a therapeutic intervention is largely a neglected area of investigation.

Background of the Study

There are three basic levels of secure psychiatric services in the UK forensic mental health system: (i) the high security psychiatric hospitals, known as the special hospitals of Ashworth, Broadmoor, and Rampton serving England and Wales, and Carstairs serving Scotland; (ii) the medium secure units, of which there are approximately 40 throughout the UK, which tend to be smaller in size than the special hospitals, and, as the name suggests, they are also of a lesser security; (iii) the low secure units, which are fewer in number but a fast-growing element of the service, and these constitute the lowest level of security within the forensic system. Taken as a whole, the forensic psychiatric system aims to work in harmony with the transfer of patients through the services in relation to risk assessment and security needs. However, in reality the transfer of patients can be difficult, time-consuming, and 'politically' motivated. Furthermore, all levels of secure provision tend to have a tense relationship with both local and national media outlets with numerous public inquiries, internal and external enquiries, judicial reviews and police investigations peppering a somewhat chequered history. Deaths of patients while in forensic psychiatric care under physical restraint (MacAttram 2005), in seclusion (CAPT 1998/2005) and following the administration of medicine (Prins 1993) are all too frequent. This all serves to produce a cultural cauldron in which forensic psychiatric practice must be employed in response to the values, norms, and standards of competing personal and professional ethical frameworks. With such internal, as well as external, pressure assessing patients for appropriate levels of risk is most assuredly a risky business (Vinestock 1996).

Literature Review on Special Observations and Assessment of Risk

The literature on assessment of risk and special observations pivots on who initiates the procedure and for what reasons. The authority to initiate special observations varies from organization to organization (Bowers and Park 2001). Although dated, Goldberg's early work remains highly relevant to today's issues on the use of special observations. Goldberg (1987) collected 48 policies on the use of special observations and claimed that in two-thirds of them the nursing staff were given the authority to initiate a special observations procedure. However, this author also stated that the authority to terminate the observations was less clear with most referring to a decision by a psychiatrist and little has changed today. Hodgson et al. (1993) reported that the medical staff stated that they were more involved in the decision to initiate and terminate than other disciplines and this was supported by Childs et al.'s (1994) study. This latter study reported that even when nurses are empowered with the authority to initiate a special observations policy, it was more often at the behest of the medical staff. Duffy (1995) reported that although, in his study, it was medical staff who had the authority to initiate and terminate the procedure, it was usually at the suggestion of the nursing staff.

In a later paper, Jones and Jackson (2004) claimed that both the decision and the intensity of the observations should be determined by a multidisciplinary team and undertaken via a risk assessment. Langenbach et al. (1999: 30) reported that the junior doctor most made the decision to initiate observations and the levels it should be operated at. Following this, it was 'made by a team, either between staff nurse and junior doctor, on occasion on a ward round, between nursing staff and consultant, or junior and senior doctors'.

The Standing Nursing and Midwifery Advisory Committee (1999) practice guidance believes that the risk assessment should be based on (i) current mental state; (ii) current assessment of risk; (iii) specific level of observation to be implemented; (iv) clear directions regarding therapeutic approach; and (v) timing of next review. Precise details within the literature regarding what exactly is being perceived as presenting a risk is difficult to ascertain. However, in broad terms, Cardell and Pitula (1999) claimed that the special observations were employed to prevent suicide, while others claimed that they were predominantly employed for the prevention of self-harm (Langenbach et al. 1999). These latter authors also reported other reasons for close observations as danger to self or property, risk of absconding and danger to others.

Again, in broad terms Phillips et al. (1977) reported that special observations were predominantly employed on three distinct groups of people. The first group comprised of those suffering from schizophrenia, who are younger, male, and non-English speaking immigrants. The second group were depressed patients with suicidal ideation and the third group were predominantly female with personality disorder, and had behavioural problems as well as suicidal intent. Tardiff (1981) claimed that other forms of emergency measures, such as seclusion, restraint, and medication also accompanied special observations, and that patients were more likely to be depressed. Goldberg (1989) found that the patients under special observations in this study were suicidal, agitated, and suffering from a psychosis. Lamdan et al. (1996) claimed that their patients were more likely to have special observations if they were younger, single, have a substance abuse history, and have a personality disorder. Langenbach et al. (1999) reported that special observations were more frequently used on involuntary patients, admitted outside of normal office hours, who had not been referred by their general practitioner and who were unmarried.

Goldberg (1989: 194) reported that of the 80 patients in his study, 46 (58 per cent) were male and 54 (42 per cent) were female. Ninety per cent (72) were white while 9 per cent (7) were black. 'Thirty (38 per cent) were married; 29 (36 per cent) single; nine (11 per cent) were divorced; and six (8 per cent) were widowed'.

In conclusion, there is a paucity of studies pertaining to the use of special observations in the literature; however, it can be said that this is growing with concerns regarding the issues raised within the published material reviewed. There is currently no published work on the use of special observations in forensic settings and it was felt apposite to undertake a small comparative study between forensic and non-forensic settings.

Hypotheses

From the foregoing literature review, it became apparent that there were two main questions that needed to be addressed and that these concerned, first, the factors being assessed in the formulation of risk assessment and, second, the differences between psychiatric settings. Therefore, the following two hypotheses were formulated.

Hypothesis One: There will be a consistency across forensic and non-forensic psychiatric settings in relation to the factors being assessed in perceiving patients as requiring special observations. The null hypothesis is that there would be no consistency across psychiatric settings.

Hypothesis Two: There will be statistically significant differences between the weighting attached to the factors being assessed in perceiving patients as requiring special observations between forensic and non-forensic psychiatric settings. The null hypothesis is that there would be no statistical significance between forensic and non-forensic groups.

Method

The method employed involved a two-pronged approach. First, nursing staff ($n = 60$) were asked to undertake a rank ordering of factors that they considered to be the most important in undertaking a risk assessment of psychiatric patients requiring special observations. Second, primary nurses ($n = 30$) were requested to score a Likert scale referring to the extent to which the 10 major factors identified from the rank ordering are present in those being placed on special observations.

Population

In two phases, nursing staff were asked to undertake the rank ordering of factors and undertake an assessment, within 24 hours, of patients who had been placed on special observations. The nursing staff was all registered mental nurses with over 12 months of experience operating as primary nurses in their particular psychiatric setting. The three settings chosen were: (i) a medium secure forensic psychiatric unit; (ii) a low secure forensic psychiatric unit; and (iii) a non-forensic unit in a general psychiatric hospital. The medium secure unit is a locked, state-of-the-art, purpose-built secure unit while the low secure forensic unit comprises of a locked ward within a general psychiatry facility. The non-forensic unit is an open ward with general psychiatric facilities. The wards catered for a range of conditions, including acute psychoses usually associated with drug misuse, generally comparative in clinical conditions but with the forensic units patients having interfaced with the law at one level or another.

Data Collection

Data were collected until 10 patients on each of the three settings had been assessed and rated. Nursing staff were requested to rank-order the ten major factors that caused concern in relation to the assessment of risk leading to special observations being required. From this they were then requested to score the presence of those factors in relation to their severity in terms of risk assessment. The scoring was on a 7–point Likert scale from mild to extremely severe. The medium secure unit collected their ten patients within four months, the low secure unit within seven months, while the non-forensic unit took almost a year to collect their numbers.

Data Analysis

The data were tabulated and rank-ordered for frequencies and percentages. The scores across the three groups were analysed using **anova** (one-way); a prior linear contrast was used to test the direction of any difference between groups. The **anova** test is used when one variable needs to be tested under three or more conditions and when different subjects are used in each condition. However, **anova** can only inform us of a difference in scores while the Jonckheere Trend Test was applied to provide a statistical measure of the strength and direction of any differences.

Ethics

Ethical approval was sought via various internal management groups and clinical teams and as the study only involved nursing staff, it was not necessary to approach the Local Research and Ethics Committee. Participation was entirely voluntary and full confidentiality was maintained as no record of nursing staff names was recorded. The raw data were kept in a locked cupboard in a locked room until placed on computer under password, and then it was destroyed. The Data Protection Act was adhered to.

Results

The results from the rank ordering of factors revealed the ten major elements from each of the three settings and these differed slightly depending on area. The three-site rank ordering can be seen in Table 13.1 with the merging of the three sites into a grand total rank order.

Table 13.1   Ten Major Risk Factors in Rank Order

Medium secure		Low secure		Non-forensic		Total	
Factors	**Scores**	**Factors**	**Scores**	**Factors**	**Scores**	**Factors**	**Scores**
Assault	182	Assault	180	Suicidal intent	178	Assault	538
Threat of assault	174	Threat of assault	176	Assault	176	Threat of assault	486
Suicidal intent	156	Self-injury	144	Threat of suicide	156	Suicidal intent	446
Self-injury	130	Threat of self-injury	132	Threat of assault	136	Self-injury	388
Threat of self-injury	106	Suicidal intent	112	Self-injury	114	Threat of self-injury	316
Verbal abuse	88	Verbal abuse	82	Threat of self-injury	78	Verbal abuse	170
Provoking others	62	Depression	66	Depression	58	Depression	168
Depression	44	Tense	46	Agitation	38	Tense	70
Tense	24	Agitation	28	Hallucinations	22	Agitation	66
Anxiety	12	Destroying property	14	Anxiety	8	Hallucinations	22

Ten primary nurses from each of the three sites were requested to score the extent of presence of these grand factors in relation to their patients being placed on special observations. One-way anova (unrelated) was carried out using spss and the following statistical results were identified. This was followed by a Jonckheere Trend Test to give strength and direction to any differences noted (see Table 13.2).

Table 13.2   Anova and Jonckheere Values

Factors	Anova	*P* values	Jonckheere	*P* values
Assault	$F_{2,27} = 7.4$	$P \leq 0.01$	S = 48	$P \leq 0.05$
Threat of assault	$F_{2,27} = 6.8$	$P \leq 0.01$	S = 46	$P \leq 0.05$
Suicidal intent	$F_{2,27} = 5.1$	$P \leq 0.25$	S = 44	$P \leq 0.05$
Self-injury	$F_{2,27} = 7.6$	$P \leq 0.01$	S = 51	$P \leq 0.05$
Threat of self-injury	$F_{2,27} = 9.6$	$P \leq 0.001$	S = 65	$P \leq 0.01$
Verbal abuse	$F_{2,27} = 9.8$	$P \leq 0.001$	S = 68	$P \leq 0.01$
Depression	$F_{2,27} = 3.2$	NS	S = 22	NS
Tense	$F_{2,27} = 2.7$	NS	S = 18	NS
Agitation	$F_{2,27} = 2.7$	NS	S = 18	NS
Hallucinations	$F_{2,27} = 2.7$	NS	S = 21	NS

The results would indicate that there is a statistically significant difference between the forensic and non-forensic areas in relation to the factors of assault, threat of assault and self-injury ($P \leq 0.01$), suicidal intent ($P \leq 0.25$), and a stronger relationship pertaining to the threat of self-injury and verbal abuse ($P \leq 0.001$) leading to special observations. The remaining factors did not reveal any statistical differences.

Discussion

The rank ordering of factors to test hypothesis one showed that there was a consistency of items revealed to be important in the assessment of risk in relation to special observations. This consistency was apparent across both forensic and non-forensic sites. Table 13.1 shows that the first two major risk elements included actual assault and threat of assault across all sites scoring 538 out of a possible 600 (89 per cent) and 486 out of a possible 540 (90 per cent), respectively. Unsurprisingly, assault and threat of assault are considered of highest concern in psychiatric settings, both forensic and non-forensic, but it should be remembered that they are also of greatest concern in many other areas of health care (Mason and Chandley 1999). While assault is a direct and acute infringement on the victim's personal well-being and physical integrity, the threat of assault can have a more chronic impact on their psychological and emotional well-being through long-term stress (Gournay and Carson 1997). In Table 13.1, it is interesting to note that the next three major risk factors in the rank ordering refer to the physical integrity of the patient – another form of assault, in terms of suicidal intent 446 out of a possible 480 (93 per cent), self-injury 388 out of a possible 420 (92 per cent), and threat of self-injury 316 out of a possible 360 (88 per cent). These risk factors suggest a great deal of concern in psychiatric nursing and are a source of stress that creates tension in nursing staff in these environments (Gournay and Carson 1997). If we now note the sixth rank-ordered factor in Table 13.1, that is, verbal abuse, we can report that the top six major risk factors in the rank order in both forensic and non-forensic settings involve assault or threat of assault on both staff and/or patient. Finally, in Table 13.1, we can see that the final three items in the top-10 risk factors refer to what may be viewed as psychiatric symptomatology: depression 168 out of a possible 240 (70 per cent), tenseness 70 out of a possible 180 (40 per cent), and agitation 66 out of a possible 120 (55 per cent).

In terms of the results of this study it, perhaps, is not surprising that if such levels of threat, to self or others, is perceived as high risk then it will be those at the clinical interface, that is, the nurses who are likely to initiate special observation procedures. As is noted, this is usually embodied in official policy (Duffy 1995, Goldberg 1987). However, it is open to debate whether this should be standard practice as it may be that nurses in such stress-perceived environments may be over-reacting. Research in forensic units in relation to stress has clearly shown that they are higher stressful environments than their counterparts in non-forensic units (e.g. Gournay et al. 1997). It can be argued that a more objective, or detached, observer should be more closely involved in the decision to initiate special observations (Langenbach et al. 1999, Childs et al. 1994, Hodgson et al. 1993). In any event, from the nurses' perspective they perceive themselves under threat irrespective of whether other disciplines have the same outlook (Kirby and Pollock 1995, Robinson 1994). Thus, in terms of hypothesis one, the evidence from this study supports the consistency across forensic and non-forensic settings in relation to the risk factors being perceived by nurses. The null hypothesis is therefore rejected. However, this does not give us any indication if there is any difference in the strength of perception in regard to the risk factors.

The results from the statistical tests do provide evidence regarding this latter point and indicate that those nurses from the forensic settings scored the risk factors significantly higher than their counterparts in a non-forensic setting. Forensic psychiatric nursing has been concerned with identifying if it has a unique body of knowledge or sphere of operations that distinguish it apart from general psychiatric nursing. However, the evidence from this study, although examining only a narrow aspect of practice, on special observations suggests that the two settings (forensic and non-forensic) are similar in the identification of risk factors, but that there is a difference in the scores relating to the nurses' perceptions of the risk factors leading to the implementation of special observations. This finding has some support in the literature from Robinson and Kettles (1998). These authors have long been concerned with the issues explored in this paper and whose early work indicated that forensic nurses perceived their work to be similar to that in non-forensic nurse settings, but that the 'forensic' element appeared to be a question of 'more than' than in non-forensic settings. Unfortunately, this 'more than' was not elucidated beyond a general perception by the nurses. Notwithstanding this, Robinson and Kettles provided an early indication of this forensic nurses intensity of perceptions. Later, Kettles et al. (2004) identified nine main reasons for placing patients on special observations with three referring to safety, self-harm attempts and self-harm thoughts. They also reported that the highest use was for 'symptoms' and this ranged from hopelessness, paranoid delusions, and suicidal intent to illicit drug use and agitation. This research is useful to us in our work as they conclude 'implications for mental health nursing practice include the way that the variation between staff in the way that evidence is used (or not used) and the issue about making judgements from the evidence needs to be more fully explored'.

From the statistical analysis, there is strong evidence that the forensic psychiatric nurses perceive the patients placed on special observations as significantly more at risk of harm to self or others on the first tabulated rank-ordered six factors. However, in relation to the latter four risk factors there were no statistical significant differences. This may be due to the forensic patients actually being more dangerous or violent, or it may be due to a false perception of the nurses. It is fair to say that those patients requiring compulsory admission and the provision of secure services do so because they are deemed to be a higher risk than those who do not. There is an academic and clinical industry on the risk assessment of forensic psychiatric patients (e.g. Prins 1995, Bjorkly 1994, Steadman et al. 1993, Monahan 1984) and irrespective of the accuracy, or otherwise, of their instruments and procedures it is axiomatic that those requiring higher levels of security are at more risk of harming others. Therefore, hypothesis two is supported in that forensic nurses scored the risk factors significantly higher in relation to harm to self or others, but that it is not supported in the risk factors relating to depression, tenseness, agitation, and hallucinations. It would appear that more research is needed in relation to the assessment of psychiatric patients. This is supported by Dennis (1997) who argued for a systematic nursing assessment and outlined two useful assessment processes for (i) patients who threaten to abscond; and (ii) patients requiring a decrease in levels of observations.

Barker and Cutliffe (1998) went further and argued against the high use of special observations and called for a more incisive analysis of clinical risk and an increased need for engagement with the patient. This is supported by others (Bowles and Dodds 2002, Bowles et al. 2002, Dodds and Bowles 2001). A further development was outlined by Kettles and Bryan-Jones (1998) who were concerned regarding the high use of special observations and argued for a computer-modelling approach to marrying nursing resources with clinical need.

Limitations to the Study

There are several limitations to this study and these can be briefly stated as: first, the small number of participants involved at the study sites make generalizability difficult, and to address this more sites ought to be included in any future research; second, a method needs to be designed that will analyse other factors in the assessment of patients requiring special observations such as organizational requirements, policy demands, litigation, and blame culture, as this current study did not attempt this; third, we did not include participants from other disciplines and a multidisciplinary approach is crucial as they are involved in both the initiation and termination of special observations; finally, we did not analyse the patients' characteristics and this, in a larger study, would provide clearer evidence of the relationship between risk assessment and clinical need.

Conclusions

This study highlighted a similarity of identified risk factors by nurses across both forensic and non-forensic psychiatric settings using a rank-ordering technique. However, statistically significant differences were found between forensic and non-forensic nurses who scored patients higher on factors associated with risk to harming themselves or others. This intensity of the nurses' perceptions appears to be related to the forensic patients appearing as more dangerous and/

or violent to self or others. The forensic group were more likely to use special observations for these factors than their counterparts in the non-forensic group. This has implications for training nursing staff who work in the forensic psychiatric settings who clearly need high levels of skills and competencies in risk assessments and clinical engagement of those patients who are deemed to require special observations.

References

Barker, P. and Cutliffe, J. 1998. Clinical risk: a need for engagement not observation. *Mental Health Practice*, 2(8), 8–12.

Bjorkly, S. 1994. The scale for the prediction of aggression and dangerousness in psychotic patients (PAD): a prospective pilot study. *Criminal Justice and Behavior*, 21(3), 341–56.

Bowers, L. and Park, A. 2001. Special observation in the care of psychiatric in-patients: a literature review. *Issues in Mental Health Nursing*, 22, 769–86.

Bowles, N. and Dodds, P. 2002. The use of refocusing in acute psychiatric care. *Nursing Times*, 98(22), 44–5.

Bowles, N., Dodds, P., Hackney, D., Sunderland, C. and Thomas, P. 2002. Formal observations and engagement: a discussion paper. *Journal of Psychiatric and Mental Health Nursing*, 9, 255–60.

CAPT (19982005). *Take-Downs That Kill.* [Online]. Available at: http://www.psych-health.com.hartford.htm [accessed: 10 March 2005].

Cardell, R. and Pitula, C.R. 1999. Suicidal inpatients' perceptions of therapeutic and non-therapeutic aspects of constant observation. *Psychiatric Services*, 50(8), 1066–70.

Childs, A., Thomas, B. and Tibbles, P. 1994. Specialist needs. *Nursing Times*, 90(3), 32–3.

Dennis, S. 1997. Close observation: how to improve assessments. *Nursing Times*, 93(24), 54–6.

Dodds, P. and Bowles, N. 2001. Dismantling formal observation and refocusing nursing activity in acute inpatient psychiatry: a case study. *Journal of Psychiatric and Mental Health Nursing*, 8(2), 183–8.

Duffy, D. 1995. Out of the shadows: a study of special observation of suicidal psychiatric in-patients. *Journal of Advanced Nursing*, 21(5), 944–50.

Goldberg, R.J. 1987. Use of constant observation with potentially suicidal patients in general hospitals. *Hospital and Community Psychiatry*, 38, 303–305.

Goldberg, R.J. 1989. The use of special observation in general hospitals. *Journal of Psychiatry in Medicine*, 19, 193–201.

Gournay, K. and Carson, J. 1997. *Stress in Mental Health Professionals and its Implications for Staff Working with Forensic Populations: Review, Critique and Suggestions for Future Research*. London: Section of Psychiatric Nursing, Institute of Psychiatry, King's College.

Hodgson, C.M., Kennedy, J., Ruiz, P., Langenbach, M., Moorhead, S. and Junaid, O. 1993. Who is watching them? A study of the interpretation of the observation policy in a mental health unit. *Psychiatric Bulletin*, 17, 478–9.

Jones, J. and Jackson, A. 2004. Observation, in *Acute Mental Health Nursing*, edited by M. Harrison, D. Mitchell and D. Howard. London: Sage, 162–84.

Kettles, A. and Bryan-Jones, J. 1998. Computer modeling for patient observation. *Nursing Standard*, 12(19), 43–46.

Kettles, A., Moir, E., Woods, P., Porter, S. and Sutherland, E. 2004. Is there a relationship between risk assessment and observation level? *Journal of Psychiatric and Mental Health Nursing*, 11, 156–64.

Kirby, S. and Pollock, P. 1995. The relationship between a medium secure environment and occupational stress in forensic psychiatric nurses. *Journal of Advanced Nursing*, 22, 862–7.

Lamdan, R.M., Ramchandani, D. and Schindler, B. 1996. Constant observations in a medical-surgical setting: the role of consultation–liaison psychiatry. *Psychosomatics*, 37(4), 368–73.

Langenbach, M., Junaid, O., Hodgson-Nwaefulu, C.M., Kennedy, J., Moorhead, S.R. and Ruiz, P. 1999. Observation levels in acute psychiatric admissions. *European Archives of Psychiatric and Clinical Neuroscience*, 249(1), 28–33.

MacAttram, M. 2005. *Rocky Bennett Report Sidelined as Minister Refuses to Admit NHS is Institutionally Racist*. [Online]. Available at: http://www.blink. org.uk.proxy.bib.uottawa.ca/pdescription.asp [accessed: 10 March 2005].

Mason, T. and Chandley, M. 1999. *Managing Violence and Aggression: A Manual for Nurses and Health Care Workers*. Edinburgh: Churchill Livingstone.

Monahan, J. 1984. The prediction of violent behaviour: toward a second generation of theory and policy. *American Journal of Psychiatry*, 141(1), 10–15.

Phillips, M., Peacocke, J., Hermanstyne, L. et al. 1977. Continuous observation, part 1: who needs it? *Canadian Psychiatric Association Journal*, 22(1), 25–28.

Prins, H. 1993. *Report of the Committee of Inquiry into the Death in Broadmoor Hospital of Orville Blackwood and a Review of the Deaths of Two Other Afro-Carribean Patients: Big, Black and Dangerous*. London: SHSA.

Prins, H. 1995. Risk assessment and management in criminal justice and psychiatry. *Journal of Forensic Psychiatry*, 7(1), 42–62.

Robinson, D. 1994. A chance to bridge the gap: a strategy for research and development in the special hospitals. *Psychiatric Care*, 1(3), 97–101.

Robinson, D. and Kettles, A.M. 1998. The emerging profession of forensic nursing: myth or reality. *Psychiatric Care*, 5(6), 214–18.

Standing Nursing and Midwifery Advisory Committee 1999. *Mental Health Nursing: Addressing Acute Concerns*. London: Department of Health.

Steadman, H.J., Monahan, J., Robbins, P.C. et al. 1993. From dangerousness to risk. assessment: implications for appropriate research strategies, in *Mental Disorder and Crime*, edited by S. Hodgins. Newbury Park: Sage, 39–62.

Tardiff, K. 1981. Emergency control measures for psychiatric inpatients. *Journal of Nervous and Mental Disease*, 169(10), 614–18.

Vinestock, M. 1996. Risk assessment: a word to the wise. *Psychiatric Treatment*, 2, 3–10.

Chapter 14

Policing Pornography in High-Secure Care: The Discursive Construction of Gendered Inequality

Dave Mercer

Introduction

The chapter focuses on clinical management of sexual media in the context of a rehabilitative environment for the treatment of detained sexual offenders diagnosed as personality disordered. It is based on the findings of research undertaken in the Personality Disorder Unit [PDU] of a high-secure mental health service in the United Kingdom. The aim was to explore how forensic nurses, and mentally disordered sex offenders, constructed accounts of pornography and offending (Mercer 2010). In the UK this is a vexed issue for treatment providers, attracting professional and political criticism (Fallon et al. 1999).

Empirical inquiry has been undertaken in the behavioural sciences to establish a relationship between pornography and male sexual violence (Diamond 2009), but the topic remains controversial. Arguably, the value of this work is questionable in terms of forensic practice, where healthcare staff are required to make decisions about the suitability of certain materials for client consumption. This chapter outlines a discourse analytic approach to exploring pornography as a healthcare issue, with the research question, and data collection, located in the practice setting. The hybrid role of forensic nurse, as agent of security and advocate of therapy, means they occupy a pivotal position in policing sexual media; acting as gatekeepers of all that enters secure environments, and searching out what is not approved.

Discussion is sympathetic to the idea of forensic nursing as a discursive-practice (Perron et al. 2005, Holmes 2002). It is suggested that the talk of forensic nurses, and offender-patients, illustrates how individuals position themselves in relation to dominant institutional, and ideological, discourses about sex and sexual offending. Central themes are concerned with the way pornography is defined in a secure hospital, and searching strategies enacted as part of nursing practice. It is concluded that performative language of male staff and patients contribute to the cultural texturing of a masculine and sexist world that marginalises female nurses, mediates the otherness of inmates, and contradicts therapeutic ideals.

Situating Pornography as a Concern in Secure Healthcare

Pornography, as an issue worthy of professional consideration, has received scant attention in the nursing press. An early claim that the nursing profession, and healthcare staff, ought to engage with the issue of pornography (Orr 1988) was grounded in a set of concerns arising from service provision. These focused on sexually violent content, objectification of women, representations of nursing roles, workplace harassment, and gendered inequities in NHS career structures. Latterly, Regan (2005) drew attention to the blatantly sexist portrayal of nurses in a high-profile advertisement campaign. Psychiatric nursing literature, likewise, reveals few references to either health risks associated with pornography consumption, or perceptions of educators toward possible effects (Drake 1994). When pornography does receive meagre coverage, it is typically a newsworthy response to disciplinary action, against individual nurses, resulting from criminal actions and/or professional misconduct (Castledine 2002).

The emergence of forensic nursing as a discrete area of practice highlights pornography as a clinical dilemma, repositioning academic questions in the clinical domain (Mercer 2000, Mercer and McKeown 1997). Here, pornography is approached from the perspective of ethical nursing practice, where the decision to restrict certain items can be interpreted as positive therapeutic intervention, or breach of the human rights of offenders. Few effective policy statements have been formulated, but access to pornography by detained patients has long been recognised (Duff 1995). Nursing staff, in particular, play an important role in monitoring sexual media in secure facilities, and assessing what constitutes 'clinically inappropriate' material, but lack guidance in undertaking this role.

Kingston and colleagues (2009) explore individual differences in pornography-use in relation to offender treatment. Noting theoretical diversity, and definitional difference, they distinguish between 'pornography' as a commodity designed to sexually arouse the user, and 'embedded sexual media'. The latter includes a diverse range of mediated imagery, particularly televised entertainment that, if not sexually explicit, can influence desire and behaviour. Clinical-psychological research in a high-secure hospital (Steward and Follina 2006) reviewed empirical evidence on behavioural effects of violent media in relation to developing policy for forensic practice. Timely as this attention might be, discussion rehearses methodological problems identified in the next section of this chapter, where factors such as imprecise terminology and validity compromise generalisation. In contrast, contributions to the pornography debate can be understood as disciplinary knowledges, and related discourses, worthy of exploration and analysis (Jensen 1998, Dines et al. 1998).

High-secure services in England and Wales have recently undergone radical restructuring. For much of its history, the special hospital system of England and Wales was centrally managed alongside the prison service. Nursing staff were required to sign the Official Secrets Act, and were usually members of the Prison Officers Association [POA]. In the late 1980s and early 1990s a series of structural changes and professional developments impacted on the hospitals and their workforce. There were incremental attempts to bring these institutions within the National Health Service [NHS] framework of policy and provision (Deacon 2004). Reorganisation emphasised individualised care (Mason and Chandley 1992) and embraced a philosophy of therapeutic engagement, in part evidenced by the introduction of 'relapse prevention' type sex-offender treatment programmes [SOTP] pioneered in the US (e.g. Marshall et al. 2005, Marques et al. 2005, Marshall and Serran 2000, Cowburn and Wilson 1992, Laws 1989).

Public and political outrage greeted the publication of the *Fallon Inquiry into the Personality Disorder Unit at Ashworth Special Hospital* (Fallon et al. 1999) which was framed within an organisational failure to take the subject of pornography seriously. The report was a direct response to allegations made by a former PDU patient about organised paedophile activities in the hospital, including grooming/ photographing a child, trading children's underwear, pornography, drugs/alcohol misuse, and financial irregularities (Warden 1999). The appointment of an inquiry panel by the Secretary of State to investigate these claims represented the most recent investigation in the troubled history of the secure system (e.g. Blom-Cooper et al. 1992, NHS Advisory Service 1988, Boynton 1980).

Pornography and Sexual Violence: Theory and Ideology

Published literature relating to pornography constitutes a diverse body of work with a long tradition (Cocks 2004, Hunt 1993, Kendrick 1987). Concerns about the societal effects of pornography have prompted its recognition as a global public health issue (Perrin et al. 2008). This section, though, briefly reviews only material pertaining to *sexual media* and *sexual harm*. It is difficult to disentangle the epistemological traditions that construct an intellectual engagement with pornography, making it difficult to define materials in any universal way. Ideas about pornography are historically and culturally constructed (Semonche 2007, Vadas 2005) provoking debate in moral philosophy, politics and policy, alongside a range of academic disciplines; typically, a contested topic area attracting polarised and ideologically located critiques. Though much behavioural science research into harmful effects of pornography grew out of feminist scholarship, sharing a common interest in 'harm', philosophical approaches differ markedly (Fukui and Westmore 1994, Fisher and Grenier 1994). In the UK pornography has been dealt with under the Obscene Publications Act [OPA] embracing a notion of indecency, whereas a broadly feminist critique has focused on exploitation and demanded legislative reform (Itzin 1992).

Conflicting debates about pornography, within the sexual-political arena of the women's movement, make it rash to suggest a unified feminist perspective (Cowan 1992), with tensions between a liberal feminist emphasis on gendered discrimination and the radical variant of patriarchal oppression (Millett 1969). Understanding rape as the exercise of power, rather than an extreme expression of sexuality, Brownmiller (1975) placed violence against women centre stage in political activism. Like rape, pornography became a male cultural invention, without any female equivalent, where there could be no sexual equality (Dworkin 1981). The campaign slogan coined by Morgan (1980) articulated this with enraged clarity: 'Theory and practice, pornography and rape'. The idea of 'degradation' in filmic presentations of violence, bondage and female submission fostering rape-supportive attitudes in male viewers became a persistent focus of research studies (Golde et al. 2000, Cowan et al. 1988, Russell 1988).

The massive growth, and commercial success, of 'cyber-porn' is a relatively recent development within the pornography industry, with Internet access rivalling travel and business sites in popularity (Stack et al. 2004), where an estimated 85–90 per cent of users of electronic-mail and Net tools are male (Kramarae and Kramer1995). Addictive use of Internet pornography, as masturbatory stimulus, has been clinically diagnosed as a variant of 'pathological sexuality' (Fitzpatrick 2008, Stein et al. 2001). Particular concern has been expressed about visual depictions of real, or simulated, rape, where women who initially reject sexual attention eventually respond to the ill treatment of their aggressors. Gossett and Byrne (2002) comment on ease of access, range of choices, and interactive options that enable viewers to 'see through the eyes' of the rapist and manipulate content. Beyond examples such as pornography, or analysis of narrative accounts of convicted rapists (Kellett 1995), it is contended feminist scholars and discourse analysts consistently fail to present sexist discourse as 'hate-speech' (Lillian 2007). In this context, the standard test of 'obscenity', as items that shock prevailing community standards, is impossible to operationalise where there is no local community (Spencer 1999, Wallace and Mangan 1996).

Evidence of a relationship between pornography and sexual crime is based upon diverse forms of data, from macro-level analyses of crime rates, (Gentry 1991, Court 1984, 1976) to individual victim testimony (Everywoman 1983). Bauserman (1996) reviewed correlational research with regard to the experience of sex offenders and pornography compared to non-offenders, sex crime rates and circulating pornography. Findings did not support the argument that sexually explicit materials contributed to sex crime, but a 'minority of offenders' reported using pornography prior to, or during, offending. Experimental research into harmful effects of pornography usually focuses on two discrete categories of sexually explicit materials [SEM], the 'violent' and 'non-violent' (Check and Guloien 1989). Consistently, behavioural science studies have linked the use of these kinds of pornography to sexual aggression and negative attitudes toward women. Disagreement exists between researchers, though, as to what has been 'proved', particularly in the longer-term (Dines, Jensen and Russo 1998). Donnerstein and colleagues (1987) argue that only pornography combining sex and violence can be shown to be harmful, and then only in terms of immediate effects. A third grouping, the 'erotic', depicting consensual and mutually pleasurable sexual relations, did not produce similar results. In North America the experimental studies of Malamuth and colleagues, over an extended time period (e.g. Malamuth and Huppin 2005, Malamuth and McIlwraith 1988, Malamuth et al. 1977) have combined clinical and theoretical strands. This body of work has attempted to develop objective assessment techniques, for the treatment of rapists, which take account of feminist theorising about pornographic media promoting gender hatred. Incorporating an 'exposure-arousal-fantasy-behaviour' process to explain sexual violence, attention is given to disinhibitory conditioning resulting from prolonged exposure to pornographic depictions of sexual aggression.

If pornography emerged as a 'problem' of 'sexual revolution' in the 1960s, boundaries of singular interpretation and categorisation have been eroded by unprecedented cultural change in terms of a mediated, or sexualised, society (Beaver 2000, McNair 1996, Plummer 1995). Change in the sexual marketing of 'men's magazines' has witnessed the emergence of weekly publications with titles such as *Zoo* and *Nuts*, interpreted as a chic replacement for 'soft-porn'. Exploring the discursive construction of male heterosexuality in 'lifestyle' weeklies, Attwood (2005: 97) noted the re-cycling of traditional signifiers of masculinity, described as 'tits and ass and porn and fighting'. Without denying some connection between pornography and violence against women, the 'effects' debate that has dominated feminist discourse is seen as damaging, over-investing in messages rather than the medium, and reifying a set of images as a-historical and unchanging (Attwood 2004, Wilkin 2004, Boyle 2000). Ciclitira (2004), noting the dissatisfaction of women with the anti-porn movement, equating it with 'anti-sex', comments on the way 'interactive sex entertainment' opened a technological space for women to produce and distribute non-profit pornography to explore sexual desire and identity. From this perspective, social-scientific research is seen as a product of constructing pornography through definition, exploring links between 'low culture texts' and 'effects'; where pornography as 'outlaw discourse' signifies a range of social ills and anxieties. An ethnographic shift is recommended, with attention directed from 'pornography' to 'pornographies', in terms of the reader, text, and context (Benwell 2005, Wilkin 2004, Attwood 2002, Boynton 1999).

Philosophy and Method: Critical Inquiry in an Institutional Setting

The high-security hospital system represents a unique cultural environment (Richman and Mercer 2000, Richman and Mason 1992, Richman 1989) with a distinct patient population. Critical reports have identified institutionalised sexism (Blom-Cooper et al. 1992) and pornography (Fallon et al. 1999) as problematic. Gaining access to carceral institutions means negotiation, at a series of levels, with embodied power relations that can obstruct, impede or attempt to control the research agenda (Mercer 2009, Scraton and Moore 2005). There have been few attempts by researchers to access accounts of incarcerated sexual offenders regarding the specific issue of pornography. Exceptions include pioneering work undertaken in the USA by Scully (1990) and Jensen (1998) prioritising the narrative voices of inmate populations. The project reported in this chapter acknowledged early critical analysis of gendered talk in custodial settings (Scully and Marolla 1985, 1984) while adopting a contemporary interest in discourse analysis as a technique in researching gender violence (Skinner et al. 2005).

A focus on pornography, as it is spoken about by the subjects/agents of forensic psychiatry, required a methodology that located language within a critique of power and singular knowledge claims (Rolfe 2000). A discourse analytic design (Potter and Wetherell 1987) shifted the research agenda from experiment to experience in exploring how pornography was discussed in relation to the nursing management of sexually violent men with a master status of personality-disorder. Further, personality disorder (Pilgrim 2001) and pornography (Hardy 2008) are contested categories, where theoretical insights from constructionist theory have utility. Academic and professional attention has recently shifted toward critical analysis of therapeutic discourse in sex offender treatment programmes (Auburn 2005), and understanding how masculinities are constructed through language (Cowburn 2006). Based upon the guidance of Kvale (1996), respondent interviews, with nine patients and eighteen nurses, were seen as co-constructed accounts, rather than a search for facts, situating respondent talk in the hospital environment. Transcribed data was coded and analysed with attention to variability within accounts, and the way respondents used language to position themselves within the institutional culture of the hospital.

Drawing on research findings, the next section explores nursing staff definitions of pornography, as concept and construct, and how these related to accounts of sexual offending; respective sets of discourses that informed the management of sexual media on the wards.

Talking About Pornography: Men's Knowing and Women's Experience

A discursive repertoire that constructed pornography in the context of the secure psychiatric ward was characterised by gender division and discrimination. Male talk about pornography, whether nurse or patient, was confident and informed. It was an understanding rooted in the experience of being a man and living in a masculine culture. A collective discourse about sexual media defined pornography in terms of content and function, where there was little recourse to external reference points; 'men talking about porn' could be likened to 'men talking about sex':

> pornography I would say…this is obviously off the top of my head…I wouldn't say it's like a definition from the *Oxford English Dictionary*…but I'd say pornography is…a stimulus somebody uses for…to gain sexual pleasure (male nurse 2).

Pornography had the power to 'name' (Dworkin 1981), and for male respondents it named arousal, pleasure and orgasm through the textual and visual depiction of sexual acts. Pornography was, commonly, described in terms of imagery, such as photographs or films, with a singular focus on male masturbation, so that consumption was defined as a product of sexual frustration and sexual release:

> I suppose it's any sort of literature [long pause] images [long pause] that might stimulate arousal in an individual [break] yeah the main function…I suppose another function could be relief from sexual sort of frustration (male nurse 9).

Discussions referred, in general, to solitary sexual activity, but constructed broader sexual and social relations, where gender inequality was fundamental to definitions of pornography. Generic terms like 'nudity' or 'intercourse' were associated with a way of looking *at* women's bodies, or doing something *to* women's bodies. Male respondent talk about pornography in the treatment setting was framed by experiences from the world outside, and spoken about as entertainment, aphrodisiac, or surrogate for heterosexual intimacy; a replacement for women who were referred to as 'the real thing'. If pornography defined male pleasure, and sex was seen as healthy, it became normalised within discourses about male sexuality. Any awareness of critical debate was subsumed within an all embracing idea about gratification:

> whatever underlying meanings pornography may have…whatever feminists may read into pornography…whatever misogynists may read into pornography…I think the underlying and the most basic principle of pornography…is that it's there for your sexual gratification (patient 7).

Men were able to easily categorise different types of sexual products with recourse to a distinction between 'hard' and 'soft-core' materials, connoting an unthinking awareness of what each offered a male audience. The former suggested depictions of sexual acts, while the latter denoted anatomical detail. Portrayals of non-consensual sex, as a staple of hardcore pornography, meant rape could be incorporated within discussions about male sexual pleasure:

> I've always considered pornography like hard core to be videos or [pause] books [pause] depicting [pause] the full sexual act within…in explicit terms [break] I think the hard core…to me some of it depends on whether it looks like the woman is consenting to what is going on (.) 'cos you see some porn stuff where it might [long pause] some of it looks like little more than rape to be honest and it all seems to be there just from the man's point of view…for the man's pleasure and the women are just there to be…well the woman's just a sex object really (male nurse 15).

Men were familiar with a range of titles such as *Mayfair* or *Penthouse*, employing colloquial slang, like 'girly books', to communicate a taken-for-granted domain that conferred a mandate to exploit women; one that, if distasteful to some, was too commonplace to question. In this sense, pornography contributed to the demarcation and texturing of male space, offering a template for sexual-social relations that legitimated the inferior treatment of women:

> there's people order *The Sun* [newspaper] and things like that and you've got page three and all this kind of thing [pause] but I'm talking about graphic detail...legs open...vaginas seen...typical girly magazine type thing...*Fiesta*... all that kind of thing (patient 6).

> on the one extreme you've got the subordination of women in pornography [pause] that's a legalised form of pornography [break] I think by and large people...in a majority accept that that type of pornography is going to subordinate women [pause] some people may not like it [pause] but they watch it (patient 7).

Subordinate positioning of women was embedded in men's accounts of pornography, and the graphic display of women's bodies featured in talk about workplaces characterised by a masculinist ideology. For the patient group, displaying pornography asserted masculinity and signalled sexual orientation in an environment with limited sexual opportunities. Alternatively, it could be interpreted as a strategy for concealing aspects of the sexual-self that could incur sanctions in a densely macho environment:

> maybe it's trying to make a statement that I am heterosexual (.) maybe a guy who's in the closet and he's really gay...but he doesn't want his mates to know will put it up...maybe guys who are really heterosexual and do fancy women wanna make that statement that I do...and she's got great tits or whatever...she's got a great arse (patient 9).

If pornography defined male pleasure, men's talk defined the ward as male territory. In the context of the institutional culture, respondents talked about efforts to restrict the display of sexual images as an invasion of their rights. It was not unusual for comparisons to be made between the hospital wards and other masculine environments, such as the factory-floor, signalling a shared value-system of sexist and exploitative practices:

> if it's in the privacy of their own room and that [pause] their room's not really any different to...you can go in any sort of work hut in the country and they've got pictures like page three (.) I mean the factory I used to work in before I went into nursing...there was...our dining room was like plastered with page three out of the *Sun* [newspaper] and stuff like that (.) look in the newspaper..and you see all this stuff and you don't...I don't even bother looking at it anymore y'know it's just a picture of a woman with her boobs out (male nurse 15).

Patients who took part in the study shared social histories characterised by childhood abuse and chaotic parenting. Most had encountered criminal justice agencies at an early age, and circulated within the transcarceral network (Menzies 1987) for their entire lives. Talking about initial exposure to pornography, they described it as a unifying feature of youth detention, secure services and the prison system. Learning about sex was devoid of intimacy, and gratification was divorced from emotion. Pornography, as educative, exploitative and pervasive featured as a discursive repertoire that might explain sexual violence, and offer mitigation:

> you could have full blown sex going on in the picture...and the more y'know... lads buy pictures off each other...they put them on their walls and of course they masturbate to all these pictures...all these acts and all that (.) and if you're in prison or you're in institutions throughout your life then...with these pictures always available and very few females around anyway to fantasise on...people use pornography to fantasise on (patient 9).

Detained men spoke about pornography and offending in terms of an obsessive relationship that developed over time. Dominant and aggressive themes that characterised films and magazines in their collections were attributed with the power to negate external influences, and normalise abusive acts:

> and I was obsessed with it...I had a vast collection [long pause] and after a while I started to think right [pause] that's what normal relationships are [break] away from the pornography when I was in normal social settings I used to think...I bet she wants a good one...things like that y'know [pause] I may not have even spoken to the person (patient 7).

> the fantasy...was so real that I was actually in the picture...I was that person... that offender [pause] and a couple of times I masturbated and ejaculated but [pause] to some degree that pulled me back from actually doing the real thing [break] it pulled me back from actually doing the real thing...but [pause] it wasn't the excitement...it wasn't as exciting as the real thing...it wasn't y'know [pause] and the more and more and more it preyed on me mind [pause] was gradually...the catalyst that was taking me towards...i.e. actually offending against females [pause] and in many of me offences...committed..it's similar to...scenes that I've seen either on television or magazines (patient 6).

Discussing pornography as a clinical/therapeutic issue, male respondents made scant reference to how this might relate to female nurses in the hospital. Rather, they were described in a dichotomised discourse that constructed them in terms of, either, passive domesticity or provocative sexuality. In contrast, female nurses lacked a vocabulary that enabled them to talk, with understanding, about pornography. Their talk was hesitant and questioning, accompanied by appeals for reassurance, and attention directed at sex as a component of romantic relationships. Their accounts were organised as a personal narrative, and pornography did not fit within the conventional structure of a 'story':

> I think it's...magazines...films...I think that's mainly...really how I see it...
> films and magazines about sexual...relationships betwee [unfinished] which can
> be male and male...female and female or males and females (.) usually quite
> graphic aren't they? They're usually...very graphic...very sexually explicit...
> no story line (female nurse 4).

Pornography had significance, or meaning, only in relation to women's professional
role in the hospital, often depicted as a threat. Their accounts revealed the uniquely
gendered nature of experiences, and personal anecdote illustrated abusive uses
of pornography, by patients, to harass and intimidate female nurses. One woman
spoke about needing to ask junior male colleagues to assess the appropriateness
of a pornography magazine, delivered in the mail, for one of the patients. The
reported interaction indicated how sex, status and professional roles collated into
a gendered dynamic, where sexual representations of the female body could only
be known through a male gaze:

> I suppose it depends what sort of [pause] a knowledge you have of these things
> (.) so this magazine came the other day and...I opened it and I looked and I was
> quite mortified to be honest...but that's me being judgmental isn't it? [pause]
> because it was very graphic of...women's [pause] bodily parts...and I said to a
> couple of the lads [male nurses] that were in the office with me oh god look at
> this I said tell me if that's ok...so they had a look and they said oh yeah that's
> soft porn (female nurse 11)

This respondent also talked about the traumatic experience of undertaking a search
of a patient bedroom, where sexually explicit images were prominently displayed.
This was compounded by the assertion that the man in question had previously
made offensive sexual requests. Discourse, in this account, worked to reconcile
a situation where the professional identity of the nurse was compromised by a
sexualised repositioning; vulnerability and powerlessness exacerbated by the
failure of a male colleague to demonstrate any awareness of her distress:

> I was absolutely shocked by it all and I tried not to make a big issue out of it
> because I didn't want the patient to feel that he'd shocked me (.) but I found
> it really offensive...and I felt that the [male] staff I was with should have
> acknowledged the impact it had...would have on me (.) and he was quite
> dismissive of it all as if it was ok [pause] but he [the patient] was an untreated
> sex offender...and I couldn't understand why we'd condone anybody having
> pictures...around his room...and if he did have them...to be on show [pause]
> and I've had great difficulty with that (female nurse 11).

Despite insensitivity, to the feelings of female colleagues, men on the nursing shift
were consulted for guidance regarding the suitability of sexual media for patient
consumption, where male knowledge invested them with expertise. The following

section develops these ideas further, exploring how talk about pornography as a risk factor in the macho culture, diminished women, generally, and marginalised female nurses in particular.

Constructing Risk in a Gendered World: Collusion and Game-Playing

A focus on performative aspects of language afforded some understanding of life in a high-security hospital, where nursing staff and patients lived alongside each other, in close confinement, for many years. The ward was constructed as the lowest tier of a rule-structured, hierarchical, organisation. Each set of respondents positioned themselves, symbolically, as alienated from more powerful managers and clinicians. Notwithstanding mutual antagonism between 'keeper' and 'kept', nursing staff and patients, reminiscent of Goffman (1961, 1963), maintained relations by deploying a repertoire and vocabulary of manageable fronts. Within the institutional culture of the hospital this manifested in a 'tradition of toughness' (Morrison 1990) that privileged physicality. Male nurses talked about the ward population as belonging to a 'family', where different versions of the self would be enacted according to formal, and informal, contexts that comprised a typical day. Transcending roles and status, it was suggested men on the ward, at points in time, cohered around common interests expressed through male language. In the evening, when other professionals who were described as 'outsiders' departed, it was suggested the social fabric of the ward changed; when two groups of men chatted casually about sport, sex and women – metaphors of masculinity:

> families stick together and I had...I do see that the...on a lot of wards that the staff and the patients are a kind of...they are an entity in their own right (.) and they are looking out for one another as well...and that's always been the case y'know...patients will look out for staff...they'll look out for staff...particularly if they value them (male nurse 14).

> and what people don't see is...sort of after five o clock at night we're sat there...very often in small groups talking about...values we share...about the hospital...about football...about women (.) about those types of...things that men talk about [break] I call it lad's talk (male nurse 1).

In these accounts, female nurses were notably absent. This was reflected in the way women members of the nursing team spoke about their experience of working in a male dominated setting. Collectively, women talked about feeling invisible and prioritised a discourse about gendered discrimination, powerlessness, injustice, and a deprecating diminution of being:

you do see it all the time…it's very [pause] it's very old boy networkish [pause] as a woman in here sometimes you can feel that you're the…little girl…you can see quite a lot of that (female nurse 7).

It was suggested specific duties, such as serving food or tidying up, were routinely allocated to female nurses as part of an ideology of domesticity that defined 'women's work'. These tasks were scathingly referred to as 'girly jobs', in the same way men used the term 'girly mags' as shorthand for pornographic publications. They drew attention to the way particular qualities, signifiers of femininity, were ascribed to women, where a sexual division of labour and overwhelming sense of hopelessness caricatured life in a 'man's world':

> we're seen very much as a decorative [pause] thing and…we're here to smooth the waters (.) 'cos…men mightn't act out as much if women are there (.) our role is very much…played down…it's a man's world here…promotion prospects are very poor because we're not seen to be…in charge enough…to have enough… power…physical…or whatever…patients see us very much as a token role as well (.) and there are jobs that are seen to be girly jobs (female nurse 11).

In this milieu, risk was spoken about as an institutional, and interactional, product that had little anchorage in the clinical business of mental health care. Longevity of staff-patient contact sustained the idea that risk assessment derived chiefly from 'knowing' particular individuals; an informal assessment of actions and events that was accredited to 'gut instinct'. A recurrent theme in male nursing discourse extended this idea beyond familiarity, or proximity, to suggest survival depended on identifying and adopting idiosyncratic traits that typified a diagnosis of personality disorder:

> I've known people in here longer than I've known people outside [pause] it's incredible [break] so when it comes to assessing the risk that they pose…that [laughter] longevity of experience goes a long way in determining whether… whether or not you believe seriously that they're gonna do something which is a risk (male nurse 17).

> I would say there's an art to working with PD's [pause] I suppose you almost have to be one yourself…well you certainly have to understand enough to be able to be one [long pause] there's…always got [unfinished] the PD's generally… will always…it's part of their nature…they will always try and get one over on somebody [pause] there's always something going on…and it's a case of knowing what's going on…and knowing when to stop it [pause] and when not to (male nurse 6).

Male nurses talked about learning to think, and act, in a way that constructed their role around conflict and competition. Ultimately, this was expressed as an assertion of psychological, rather than physical, power to outwit or out-manoeuvre the patient in a game-playing strategy to master control of the environment:

> sometimes it does them no harm to be talked to and to feel threatened by you (.) but not physically threatened (.) they're…threatened because [pause] this sounds mad but it's as though you're one little bit ahead of them…you know what they're planning…you know what they're thinking (male nurse 16).

Contextual transactions of risk meant that the patient population were subjected to continual scrutiny, where slight variation in daily rituals invoked cause for concern and invited increased vigilance. Informal observations expressed in lay language, it was suggested, filtered into the discourse of the multi-professional care team, where they became reified in clinical documents, assuming the status of fact:

> that's what gets written into the clinical notes on a very frequent basis [pause] he's doing…he's perhaps sitting in a peculiar place in the day room…he's now stalking the females on the ward…he's sat on a seat where he can view through the mirrors and the doors of the ward and the reflections on the ward…people in various activities…and really he could just be sat there reading a book…so we become hypersensitive…and then that becomes…that goes into the clinical notes…and those become real risks (male nurse 1).

'Fantasy' assumed a central position in male nurse's talk about sexual dangerousness, and female staff, like pornography, became emblematic of threat. In the same way male staff talked about watching patients, they also watched female nurses. This revealed a contradictory set of discourses, where women represented, both, a positive counter-balance to aggressive masculinity and an innate sexual nature that needed checking. The frequent suggestion that women colleagues were vulnerable, and needed protection, was interwoven with a discourse about sexuality and risk:

> women are to be really aware of their own sexuality and how they present themselves really [pause] I mean to be honest I've never come across a female staff on any of the wards I've worked on who've like dressed inappropriately… they might have skirts too short or [pause] too tight I mean it's just as well… some of the fuckin' male staff [laughs] some of the male staff on here (male nurse 15).

> they do defuse [pause] certain volatile situations [pause] because they're non-threatening aren't they? But by and large they're not…they tend to like…to want to defuse the situation rather than having a macho…approach to things [break] but on the other side [long pause] the way some of them dress [pause] a bit provocatively [pause] can only fuel certain peoples…fantasies (patient 7).

The final section will explore how pornography was policed on the wards of the institution, the key part played by nursing staff, and broader implications of gendered language in practice. It will be noted how the othering of female staff, and detained sexual offenders, merged in the production of a discursive distance that precluded female nurses from any dealings with the sexual domain and diminished their professional agency.

Nursing Practice as Policing: Searching and Surveillance

It was noted earlier how shared male discourse enabled men to talk about 'sex' and 'pornography' in terms of sexual pleasure, language-use that extended to discussions about sexual violence. The concept of 'motivation' figured prominently in the way nurse respondents talked about pornography and offending; where fantasy was part of the sexual lives of 'normal men', demarcated by an ability to exercise restraint based on personal morality. Detrimental effects were described as a consequence of the user, rather than the material. Pornography became a resource to stimulate the viewer, with pre-existing intent shaping the outcome of the experience. What was referred to by one nurse as a 'bloody bizarre porno film' was invested with different meanings in relation to the context in which it was watched:

> I think offenders use pornography to put themselves in the mood to offend (.) i.e. to stimulate themselves to go out and get [unfinished] but I think the desire comes before the pornography...not the other way around [pause] the same as [pause] a normal man [pause] will use pornography to put himself in a sexual mood [pause] and even married couples will use pornography [pause] watch it together to get in the mood [pause] for normal sex [pause] it might be a bloody bizarre porno film (male nurse 6).

Talking about an actual rather than imagined offence, one patient attempted to separate the *sexual* from the *violent* components of his raping and killing a young girl, where identifying with 'higher-status' violent crime, as enjoyable, reduced the offence to an unfortunate by-product, failing to delineate between rape and sex. Distancing himself from individuals with a primary interest in rape allowed him to discriminate between types of offenders and types of sexual offences. A moral codification of sex-crime related to the futility of trying to rehabilitate 'gross' offenders, and demarcated the decent and deviant perpetrator. The serial rapist was described as repugnant, set apart by number and severity of offences. In contrast to men seen as beyond redemption, other offences could be understood as the product of context and circumstance; the *average rapist* and the *average rape*. A differentiation between offenders that normalised acts of sexual aggression against women:

I'm not talking about a gross rapist like er...somebody that does twenty rapes and...mutilates them...something like that...fuck that! What you do with them I don't...pull the plug on 'em I think...probably lock 'em up...I'm talking about most people who what I call rape a woman...in the average circumstances... right? [pause] They're redeemable in my book (patient 3).

One nurse mobilised a similar set of discourses to discriminate between men who had raped adult women, and those who had offended against children. The latter had a pariah status in the hospital which made them a specific target in nurses policing of sexual imagery. Using a hackneyed rape myth about certain women who 'asked for it' permitted the respondent to construct child sexual abuse as a crime planned and controlled exclusively by the perpetrator. In contrast, only extreme violence, such as 'beating the victim to death', placed the allegation of rape beyond question:

if you talk to someone and they go 'Ah she asked for it...short skirt on...she was pissed...she was all over me...she said no but she got it' [pause] now against children...they've gotta plan it (.) it's not the children's...it's not the child's act...it's their act and their control" [pause] I think with adults...a rape on females...and unless y'know...they don't beat them to death 'She was a woman...she knew him' [pause] they can justify (.) but you can't [pause] justify that with a child (male nurse 10).

These discursive repertoires, about sex and sexual offending, had powerful implications when male respondents talked about treatment and management of pornography within the hospital. In short, male staff and patients engaged in a 'game-playing exercise' with regard to engagement with the ideal of the SOT programme; male nurses were reluctant to participate in therapeutic sessions and actively discouraged female nurses from any kind of rehabilitative work with sexual offenders; and policing pornography focused on 'paedophile' offenders who were institutionally constructed as the personification of 'deviant' sexuality' and totally resistant to change.

Though male respondents illustrated their accounts with conventional ideas about pornography as a discrete product, nursing search strategies assumed an entirely contextual dimension; where there was a marked tension between the discourse of control (prohibited items) and that of treatment (clinically inappropriate items). At the time when the research was undertaken, institutional restrictions – referred to as a 'blanket ban' – meant that all forms of commercial sexual media had been confiscated from the wards; with exceptional cases requiring care-team approval. Male respondents talked about pornography within a larger commentary about organisational change, described in terms of increased control and regulation. There was uncertainty about whether pornography represented an issue for clinical teams or security staff. Implementation of measures to restrict pornographic materials was described as having sanitised the environment of almost all materials pertaining to the sexual, which equated to 'pictures of women'. One patient who had been detained in the secure-hospital system for twenty five years claimed levels of security had increased significantly, and attributed the control of pornography as an aspect of these changes:

> never seen any of it here...I've never seen any pornography whilst I've been here...no mild porn...I've never seen anything of the kind (patient 9).

> well you can't have it [pornography] you're not allowed to have it [break] security says you can't have it (patient 2).

The unit had a set of guidelines for managing 'pornography/clinically unsuitable material', but these were seldom discussed by staff or patients. For nurses who did introduce this document into their accounts it functioned as a linguistic device to construct the hospital as a bureaucratic, rule-driven, organisation with which they felt little affinity. The nursing role was about imposing 'rules' and minimising 'risk' in a *blame*-culture, not a *therapeutic*-culture:

> there's a comfort zone for shall we say the hierarchy [pause] I don't know what to call them...they make these decisions (.) there's a comfort zone... risk is that if they don't get it [pornography] they [the patients] won't do it...do y'know what I mean? And 'We're covered' y'know [pause] 'We said they can't have it...now if they do something without it that's y'know their problem' (male nurse 16).

> I've often thought that it's a bit silly [pause] not allowing it [commercial pornography] when it is freely available [pause] but I can understand too that [pause] the hospital has to maintain an element of control [pause] in the words of the hospital management...in order to reduce as much as possible any risks (male nurse 17).

These accounts introduced a central dilemma in the institutional management of pornography that was interwoven throughout the study findings. Where pornography represented a malleable artefact of male imagination, it was both an adjunct to healthy sexuality and indicator of deviant sexual interest; any meaningful interpretation of imagery in relation to risk was sacrificed to a crude duality between normal and abnormal men, and pornography became a neutral category with the potential for use or abuse. From this perspective, male nursing staff saw little justification for withholding sexual materials from patients with non-sexual categories of offence, while uncritically accepting the application of restrictions to the 'sex offender':

> if you've got arsonists and [pause] robbers...thieves...y'know...anything that's not rela [unfinished] any offence that is not related to...of a sexual nature..that patient can apply to have pornographic magazines...and material to use in a

masturbatory..reasons (.) and my view of it is that they will be allowed to have it because they haven't got that sexual offending behaviour...history (male nurse 5).

No longer a recognisable commodity, pornography became a product of deviant sexual imagination, manufactured through the corruption of day to day imagery. On the wards of the PDU, mundane and innocuous items were reclassified in terms of the perceived relationship between an image and the offending history of the viewer. Commonly cited examples, intimated as forms of virtual abuse, focused on the potential for children's clothing catalogues [Argos] and television programmes to be converted into erotica. Representations of the schoolgirl, in a series of classic comedy films were comparable to 'porno' or a 'blue movie':

> the *Argos* catalogue becomes...becomes...a problem for us because while it isn't offensive...in legal terms...it is very definitely them getting off on the *Argos* catalogue...children's programmes on the TV are a problem because they're getting off on those kids (.) now if those kids...those kids aren't...aren't aware of them getting off on them but it's still an image...of a real kid and you don't know what that's fuelling (male nurse 1).

> [in St Trinian's films] running round with pig-tails..women...short skirts... flashing their knickers...flashing their bra (.) my God to a...to a paedophile it's gotta be heaven for them hasn't it? It's gotta be a blue movie...it's gotta be porno for them (male nurse 10).

One patient respondent who had talked about sexually offending against young girls endorsed the removal of pictures of 'kids' from the ward environment, making reference to supplements included in the Sunday newspapers. Issues of topical interest such as fashion, eating disorder, or teenage pregnancy assumed an additional dimension when it was implied that pictures were taken from the magazine to be used as a source of sexual stimulation:

> sometimes they may have a feature on kids clothing [pause] they might be doing an issue on teen pregnancies [pause] teen anorexics or whatever [pause] and I'm not saying the images are sexually explicit...but [long pause] I have seen on occasions when people have taken these pictures out...of magazines and sidled off down their rooms with them (patient 7).

Another patient spoke about staff adopting an almost fanatical approach in searching out, and removing, images of children, where cultural or intellectual distinctions between art, erotica, and pornography had been eroded; with images appraised only in terms of their possible effects on the viewer. The description of staff using scissors to cut out newspaper articles evidenced the visceral assumption that *particular pictures* could result in *particular behaviours*, and that these largely related to paedophile offenders:

> Pictures of children and other aspects have been cut out of various magazines
> (.) there was a lady did an exhibition not long back…a photographic artist…
> of female…male and female children…I don't know if you recall it? Yeah…
> well a lot of the Sunday magazines covered that [art exhibition] in depth (.) well
> you was getting the newspaper orders and the Sunday magazines and they was
> coming down but you was going like that [indicates difficulty to read] and there
> was squares cut out of the magazines…somebody had sat up there…just sat
> there and just gone systematically through the magazines (patient 6).

It might be that, for some patients, pictures of children could be invested with erotic meaning, but stark censorship represented a crude attempt to sanitise the environment of any sexual cues, and exert *external control* over what patients might look at, as if this equated with an *internal control* of what they might think.

Concluding Remarks

This chapter has identified a series of context-specific issues relating to the hospital where data was collected, but the findings might have relevance for the management of pornography in other secure mental health services. The results of the study emphasise that there are no simple solutions to complex problems. Decision-making about sexual offenders accessing sexual materials rely on specific definitions and agreed criterion, while pornography, broadly, evades easy classification. Approaching the issue from a discursive perspective, shifts attention from pornography as discrete commodity, and permits understanding of how mediated images texture the treatment environment.

The reported study contributes new knowledge to a growing body of critical social research conducted in the English high-security hospital system. Previous discourse analytic inquiry (Stowell-Smith and McKeown 1999) explored race as a central construct in diagnosing psychopathy through textual analysis of psychiatric reports. An ethnographic study (Chandley 2007: 139) investigated the concept of temporality for those who live and work on the wards, suggesting social relations were more 'gracious' and 'respectful' than critical literature indicated. Their view of the world amalgamated into a single culture, with its own stock of shared knowledge, beliefs and norms, an assertion echoed in this chapter. But, if there is a degree of similarity, there is a distinct difference that relates to gendered aspects of ward culture.

Other constructionist work (Warner and Wilkins 2004, Warner 1996) has drawn attention to the 'invisibility' of women patients in high-secure care, concealed within a 'general male story', but the voices of female staff working in high-security hospitals remain unheard. This chapter goes some way toward redressing the silence, acknowledging institutional inequalities. The dominant culture that has been described is inimical to the ideals, and goals, of therapeutic work with sexual offenders. Values of the SOT programme understand sexual offending as abusive *behaviour* rather than *sickness* (e.g. Mann 2004), where therapy seeks to change how offenders construct victims through thought and language. In contrast, talk rooted in the culture of the hospital reinforced rigid, stereotypical, assumptions about sex/gender, and a sex-specific division of labour.

This critical commentary does not lend itself to the language of evidence-based practice. It did not begin with an easily defined problem, and has not concluded with a neatly packaged solution. In nurse and patient accounts, the concept of pornography emerged as a way of talking about injustice, discrimination and exploitation. Debate about the danger of sexual images, by those who view them, has to take place alongside discussion about the damage of secure hospitals, for those who live and work within them.

References

Attwood, F. 2005. 'Tits and ass and porn and fighting': male heterosexuality in magazines for men. *International Journal of Cultural Studies*, 8(1), 83–100.

Attwood, F. 2004. Pornography and objectification: re-reading the picture that divided Britain. *Feminist Media Studies*, 4(1), 719.

Attwood, F. 2002. Reading porn: the paradigm shift in pornography research. *Sexualities*, 5(1), 91–105.

Auburn, T. 2005. Narrative reflexivity as a repair device for discounting 'cognitive distortions' in sex offender treatment. *Discourse and Society*, 16(5), 697–718.

Bauserman, R. 1996. Sexual aggression and pornography: a review of correlational research. *Basic and Applied Social Psychology*, 18(4), 405–27.

Beaver, W. 2000. The dilemma of Internet pornography. *Business and Society Review*, 105(3), 373–82.

Benwell, B. 2005. 'Lucky this is anonymous': ethnographies of reception in men's magazines: a 'textual' approach. *Discourse and Society*, 16(2), 147–72.

Blom-Cooper, L., Brown, M., Dolan, R., and Murphy, E. 1992. *Report of the Committee of Inquiry into Complaints about Ashworth Hospital*. Cm 2028. London: HMSO.

Boyle, A. 2000. The pornography debates: beyond cause and effect. *Women's Studies International Forum*, 23(2), 187–95.

Boynton, J. 1980. *Report of the Review of Rampton Hospital*. Cmnd 8073. London: HMSO.

Boynton, P.M. 1999. 'Is that supposed to be sexy?' Women discuss women in 'top shelf' magazines. *Journal of Community and Applied Social Psychology*, 9, 449–61.

Brownmiller, S. 1975. *Against Our Will: Men, Women and Rape*. New York: Simon & Schuster.

Castledine, G. 2002. Professional misconduct studies, case 77, child pornography: interim suspension of a nurse who videoed children at play. *British Journal of Nursing*, 11(16), 1055.

Chandley, M. 2007. Ashworth time, in *Inside Ashworth: Professional reflections of institutional life*, edited by D. Pilgrim. Oxford: Radcliffe.

Check, J. and Guloien, T. 1989. Reported proclivity for coercive sex following reported exposure to sexually violent pornography, non-violent pornography and erotica, in *Pornography: Research advances and policy considerations*, edited by D. Zillman and J. Bryant. Hillsdale, N.J.: Lawrence Erlbaum.

Ciclitara, K. 2004. Pornography, women and feminism: between pleasure and politics. *Sexualities*, 7(3), 281–301.

Cocks, H.G. 2004. Saucy stories: pornography, sexology and the marketing of sexual knowledge in Britain, c. 1918–1970. *Social History*, 29(4), 465–84.

Court, J. 1976. Pornography and sex crimes: a re-evaluation in the light of recent trends around the world. *International Journal of criminology and Penology*, 5, 129–57.

Court, J. 1984. Sex and violence: a ripple effect, in *Pornography and Sexual Aggression*, edited by N. Malamuth and E. Donnerstein. London: Academic Press.

Cowan, G. 1992. Feminist attitudes toward pornography control. *Psychology of Women Quarterly*, 16, 165–77.

Cowan, G., Lee, C., Levy, D., and Snyder, D. 1988. Dominance and inequality in X-rated video cassettes. *Psychology of Women Quarterly*, 12(3), 299–311.

Cowburn, M. 2006. Constructive work with male sex offenders: male forms of life, in *Constructive Work with Offenders*, edited by K. Gorman, M. Gregory, M. Hayles, and N. Parton. London: Jessica Kingsley.

Cowburn, M. and Wilson, C. 1992. The underlying framework: research, theory and values, in *Changing Men: A Practice Guide to Working with Adult Male Sex Offenders*, edited by P. Lowenstein. Nottinghamshire Probation Service. Nottingham, England.

Deacon, J. 2004. Testing boundaries: the social context of physical and relational containment in a maximum secure psychiatric hospital. *Journal of Social Work Practice*, 18(1), 81–97.

Diamond, M. 2009. Pornography, public acceptance and sex related crime. *International Journal of Law and Psychiatry*, 32, 304–14.

Dines, G., Jensen, R., and Russo, A. (eds). 1998. *Pornography: The Production and Consumption of Inequality*. London: Routledge.

Donnerstein, E., Linz, D., and Penrod, S. 1987. *The question of Pornography*. New York: The Free Press.

Drake, R.E. 1994. Potential health hazards of pornography consumption as viewed by psychiatric nurses. *Archives of Psychiatric Nursing*, 8(2), 101–106.

Duff, A. 1995. Pornography and censorship: the problems of policy formation in a psychiatric setting. *Psychiatric Care*, 2(4), 137–40.

Dworkin, A. 1981. *Pornography: Men Possessing Women*. London: Women's Press.

Everywoman. 1983. *Pornography and Sexual Violence: Evidence of the Links*. The complete transcript of public hearings on ordinances to add pornography as discrimination against women: Minneapolis City Council, Government Operations Committee, December 12th and 13th 1983. London: Everywoman.

Fallon, P., Bluglass, R., Edwards, B., and Daniels, G. 1999. *Report of the Committee of Inquiry into the Personality Disorder Unit, Ashworth Special Hospital*. Cm 4194. London: HMSO.

Fisher, D. and Grenier, G. 1994. Violent pornography, antiwoman thoughts, and antiwoman acts: in search of reliable effects. *The Journal of Sex Research*, 31(1), 23–38.

Fitzpatrick, J. 2008. Internet addiction: recognition and intervention. *Archives of Psychiatric Nursing*, 22(2), 59–60.

Fukui, A., and Westmore, B. 1994. To see or not to see: the debate over pornography and its relationship to sexual aggression. *Australian and New Zealand Journal of Psychiatry*, 28(4), 600–606.

Gentry, C.S. 1991. Pornography and rape: an empirical analysis. *Deviant Behavior: An Interdisciplinary Journal*, 12, 277–88.

Goffman, E. 1961. *Asylums: Essays on the social situation of mental patients and other inmates*. Harmondsworth: Penguin.

Goffman, E. 1963. *Stigma: Notes on the Management of Spoiled Identity*. Harmondsworth: Penguin.

Golde, J.A., Strassberg, D.S., Turner, C.M., and Lowe, K. 2000. Attitudinal effects of degrading themes and sexual explicitness in video materials. *Sexual Abuse: A Journal of Research and Treatment*, 12(3), 223–32.

Gossett, J.L. and Byrne, S. 2002. 'Click here': a content analysis of Internet sites. *Gender and Society*, 16(5), 689–709.

Hardy, S. 2008. The pornography of reality. *Sexualities*, 11(60).

Holmes, D. 2002. Police and pastoral power: governmentality and correctional forensic psychiatric nursing. *Nursing Inquiry*, 9(2), 84–92.

Hunt, L. 1993. *The Invention of Pornography: Obscenity and the Origins of Modernity, 1500–1800*. New York: Zone Books.

Ignatieff, M. 1978. *A Just Measure of Pain: The Penitentiary in the Industrial Revolution, 1750–1850*. New York: Columbia University Press.

Itzin, C. 1992. *A briefing for MPs and MEPs on Evidence of Pornography Related Harm and a Progressive New Approach to Legislating Against Pornography Without Censorship*. Violence, Abuse and Gender Relations Research Unit. Bradford, England.

Jensen, R. 1998. Using Pornography, in *Pornography: The Production and Consumption of Inequality*. London: Routledge.

Kellett, P. 1995. Acts of power, control and resistance: Narrative accounts of convicted rapists, in *Hate Speech*, edited by R.K. Whillock and D. Slayden. London: Sage.

Kendrick, W. 1987. *The Secret Museum: Pornography in Modern Culture*. Harmondsworth: Viking Penguin.

Kingston, D.A., Malamuth, N.M., Fedoroff, P., and Marshall, W.L. 2009. The importance of individual differences in pornography use: theoretical perspectives and implications for treating sexual offenders. *Journal of Sex Research*, 46(2–3), 216–32.

Kramarae, C. and Kramer, J. 1995. Legal snarls for women in cyberspace. *Internet Research: Electronic Networking Applications and Policy*, 5(2), 14–24.

Kupers, T.A. 2005. Toxic masculinity as a barrier to mental health treatment in prison. *Journal of Clinical Psychology*, 61(6), 713–24.

Kvale, S. 1996. *Inter-views: An Introduction to Qualitative Research Interviewing*. London: Sage.

Laws, D.R. 1989. Relapse prevention: The state of the art. *Journal of Interpersonal Violence*, 14(3), 285–302.

Lillian, D.L. 2007. A thorn by any other name: sexist discourse as hate speech. *Discourse and Society*, 18(6), 719–40.

Malamuth, N. and Huppin, M. 2005. Pornography and teenagers: the importance of individual differences. *Adolescent Medical Clinics*, 16(2), 315–16.

Malamuth, N.M. and McIlwraith, R.D. 1988. Fantasies and exposure to sexually explicit magazines. *Communication Research*, 15(6), 753–71.

Malamuth, N.M., Feshbach, S., and Jaffe, Y. 1977. Sexual arousal and aggression: recent experiments and theoretical issues. *Journal of Social Issues*, 33(2), 110–33.

Mann, R. 2004. Innovations in sex offender treatment. *Journal of Sexual Aggression*, 10(2), 141–52.

Marques, J.K., Wiederanders, M., Day, D.M., Nelson, C., and van Ommeren, A. 2005. Effects of a relapse prevention program on sexual recidivism: final results from California's Sex Offender Treatment and Evaluation Project (SOTEP). *Sexual Abuse: A Journal of Research and Treatment*, 17(1), 79–107.

Marshall, W.L., Ward, T., Mann, R.E., Moulden, H., Fernandez, Y.M., Serran, G., and Marshall, L.E. 2005. Working positively with sexual offenders: maximising the effectiveness of treatment. *Journal of Interpersonal Violence*, 20(9), 1096–114.

Marshall, W.L. and Serran, G.A. 2000. Current issues in the assessment and treatment of sexual offenders. *Clinical Psychology and Psychotherapy*, 7, 85–96.

Mason, T. and Chandley, M. 1992. Nursing models in a special hospital: cybernetics, hyperreality and beyond. *Journal of Advanced Nursing*, 17(11), 1350–354.

McNair, B. 1996. *Mediated Sex: Pornography and Postmodern Culture*. London: Arnold.

Menzies, R.J. 1987. Cycles of control: the transcarceral careers of forensic patients. *International Journal of Law and Psychiatry*, 10(3), 233–49.

Mercer, D. 2010. *A Discourse Analysis of Staff and Patient Accounts of Pornography in a High-security Hospital*. Faculty of Health and Life Sciences, University of Liverpool [unpublished].

Mercer, D. 2009. Research in state institutions: a critical issue for forensic nursing. *Journal of Forensic Nursing*, 5, 107–108.

Mercer, D. 2000. Pornography and practice: the misfortunes of therapy, in *Forensic Mental Health Care: A Case Study Approach*, edited by D. Mercer, T. Mason, M. McKeown, and G. McCann. Edinburgh: Churchill Livingstone.

Mercer, D. and McKeown, M. 1997. Pornography: some implications for nursing. *Health Care Analysis*, 5(1), 56–61.

Millett, K. 1969. *Sexual Politics*. London: Hart-Davis.

Morgan, R. 1980. Theory and practice: pornography and rape, in *Take Back the Night: Women on Pornography*, edited by L. Lederer. New York: William Morrow.

Morrison, E.F. 1990. The tradition of toughness: a study of non-professional nursing care in psychiatric settings. *Image Journal of Nursing Scholarship*, 22(1), 32–38.

NHS Hospital Advisory Service. 1988. *DHSS Social Services Inspectorate Report on Services Provided by Broadmoor*. HAS-SS1–88. Sutton: NHS HAS.

Orr, J. 1988. The porn brokers. *Nursing Times*, 84(20), 22.

Perrin, P.C., Madanat, H.N., Barnes, M.D., Carolan, A., Clark, R.E., Ivins, N., Tuttle, S.R., Vogeler, H.A., and Williams, P.N. 2008. Health education's role in framing pornography as a public health issue: Local and national strategies with international implications. *Promotion and Education*, 15(1), 11–18.

Perron, A., Fluet, C., and Holmes, D. 2005. Agents of care and agents of the state: bio-power and nursing practice. *Journal of Advanced Nursing*, 50(5), 536–44.

Pilgrim, D. 2001. Disordered personalities and disordered people. *Journal of Mental Health*, 10(3), 253–65.

Plummer, K. 1995. *Telling Sexual Stories: Power, Change and Social Worlds*. London: Routledge.

Potter, J. Wetherell, M. 1987. *Discourse and Social Psychology: Beyond Attitudes and Behaviour*. London: Sage.

Regan, M. 2005. Virgin's nurses and the public image of nursing. *Nursing Philosophy*, 6, 210–12.

Richman, J. 1989. *Psychiatric Ward Cultures Revisited: Implications for Treatment Regimes*. Paper presented to the British Sociological Association Annual Conference, 1989.

Richman, J. and Mason, T. 1992. Quo vadis the special hospitals? in *Private Risks and Public Dangers*, edited by S. Scott, G. Williams, S. Platt, and H. Thomas. Aldershot: Avebury.

Richman, J. and Mercer, D. 2000. Rites of purification: the aftermath of the Ashworth Hospital inquiry of 1992. *The Journal of Forensic Psychiatry*, 11(3), 621–46.

Rolfe, G. 2000. *Research, Truth and Authority: Postmodern Perspectives on Nursing*. London: Macmillan.

Russell, D.E.H. 1988. Pornography and rape: a causal model. *Political Psychology*, 9(1), 41–73.

Scraton, P. and Moore, L. 2005. Degradation, harm and survival in a women's prison. *Social Policy and Society*, 5(1), 67–78.

Scully, D. 1990. *Understanding Sexual Violence: A Study of Convicted Rapists.* London: Routledge.

Scully, D. and Marolla, J. 1985. 'Riding the bull at Gilleys': convicted rapists describe the rewards of rape. *Social Problems*, 32(3), 251–63.

Scully, D. and Marolla, J. 1984. Convicted rapists' vocabulary of motive: excuses and justifications. *Social Problems*, 31(5), 530–44.

Semonche, J.E. 2007. *Censoring Sex: A Historical Journey Through American Media.* Plymouth (UK): Rowman and Littlefield.

Sim, J. 2002. The future of prison health care: a critical analysis. *Critical Social Policy*, 22(2), 300–322.

Skinner, T., Hester, M., and Malos, E. 2005. *Researching Gender Violence: Feminist Methodology in Action.* Devon: Willan Publishing.

Spencer, J. 1999. Crime on the Internet: its presentation and representation. *The Howard Journal*, 38(3), 241–51.

Stack, S., Wasserman, I., and Kern, R. 2004. Adult social bonds and use of Internet pornography. *Social Science Quarterly*, 85(1), 75–88.

Stein, D.J., Black, D.W., Shapira, N.A., and Spitzer, R.L. 2001. Hypersexual disorder and preoccupation with Internet pornography. *American Journal of Psychiatry*, 158(10), 1590–94.

Steward, J.H. and Follina, F. 2006. Informing policies in forensic settings: a review of research investigating the effects of exposure to media violence on challenging / offending behaviour. *The British Journal of Forensic Practice*, 8(2), 31–46.

Stowell-Smith, M. and McKeown, M. 1999. Race, psychopathy and the self: a discourse analytic study. *British Journal of Medical Psychology*, 72, 459–70.

Vadas, M. 2005. The manufacture-for-use of pornography and women's inequality. *The Journal of Political Philosophy*, 13(2), 174–93.

Wallace, J. and Mangan, M. 1996. *Sex, Laws, and Cyberspace: Freedom and Censorship on the Frontiers of the Online Revolution.* New York: Henry Holt.

Warden, J. 1999. Ashworth report confirms problems with special hospitals. *British Medical Journal*, 318, 211.

Warner, S. 1996. Special women, special places: women and high security mental hospitals, in *Psychology discourse practice: From Regulation to Resistance*, edited by E. Burman. Bristol: Taylor & Francis.

Warner, S. and Wilkins, T. 2004. Between subjugation and survival: women, borderline personality disorder and high security mental hospitals. *Journal of Contemporary Psychotherapy*, 34(3), 265–78.

Wilkin, P. 2004. Pornography and rhetorical strategies – the politics of public policy. *Media, Culture and Society*, 26(3), 337–57.

Chapter 15

Warning – this Job Contains Strong Language and Adult Themes: Do Nurses Require Thick Skins and Broad Shoulders to Deal with Encounters Involving Swearing?

Teresa Stone and Margaret McMillan

Introduction

Swearing is used to express deep emotional feelings so it is not surprising that nurses encounter it because they connect with people at their most vulnerable. Perhaps more surprising is the frequency with which nurses are the target. This chapter will explore the complexities of the offensiveness of bad language in the workplace, whether nurses would benefit from becoming "thick skinned and broad shouldered" to counter the impact, or if some other method might more successfully deal with the emotional effect and assist them to cope with this sometimes "extreme behaviour with presence and attunement" (Delaney 2009a).

Swearing is a complex issue and an understanding of its causes and effects will assist nurses to deal with it. Three kinds of factors affect swearing: neurological (including the cerebral cortex, which governs speech comprehension and production, and subcortical systems, which regulate emotional reactions); sociocultural (including gender, cultural background, taboo, law and etiquette and degree of formality); and psychological (including age, coping style, religiosity and moral reasoning) (Jay 1999).

Swearing as a research topic has been largely ignored by academics and has not been discussed in the nursing context, despite the insight to be provided into "discourses of power and gender, social, group formation and maintenance, the acquisition of linguistic competence in young children, and . . . psychological and neurological disorders" (Burns 2008: 61). Even rarer is discussion of the positive aspects of swearing, or its impact on the victims.

Definition

Swearing will here be defined, following and building on Andersson and Trudgill's (1990) definition of swearing, as those words which: (a) refer to something that is taboo, offensive, impolite, or forbidden in the culture; (b) can be used to express strong emotions, most usually of anger; (c) may evoke strong emotions, most usually of anger or anxiety; (d) include the strongest and most offensive words in a culture – stronger than slang and colloquial language; and (e) may be used also in a humorous way and can be a marker of group identity.

Discussion of swearing invariably involves the concept of taboo: the greater its potential to offend, the more likely is a word to be considered a swearword (Beers Fägersten 2000). Some words are deemed offensive precisely because they broach taboos – "norms whose violation can be expected to provoke inflexible, disgust-related responses" (Gutierrez and Giner-Sorolla 2007). Freud (1919) understood taboo as a conscious external prohibition against the fulfilment of powerful unconscious desires, and probably the earliest form of conscience. According to the psychoanalytic perspective, offensive words refer to parts of the body, secretions or behavioural patterns that arouse sexual desire, trigger deep memories, revive incestuous conflict, and provoke trauma (Arango 1989). Thus a lust for violence and murder underlie the murder taboo, suggested Weibart (2010), who believed we have a strongly ambivalent attitude: we yearn to break taboos but at the same time are afraid of doing so, hence the fascination. Swearing is, like the abject, "both disgusting and irresistible, outraging and fascinating" (Holmes, Perron, and O'Byrne 2006: 308, Kristeva 1982). Taboos form the boundary between the allowed and the forbidden: in language, between the obscene and the acceptable or sacred (Werbart 2010).

In Western society taboos attach to functions such as bodily waste, sex, religion, ethnic groups, food, dirt, and death – frequently objects or acts too private to be shared (Abel and Buckley 1977), and what are thought of as taboo terms are avoided because their use in particular social contexts is regarded as distasteful. The decreasing role of religious institutions has been accompanied in Christian societies by the diminishing power of the taboo associated with religious terms (Wajnryb 2004: 97). From religion, body parts and sexuality, association has moved to personal vilification, tabooed in the current political climate when based on looks, mental and physical capacity, and sexual preference (Butler 2003), race, and age.

Swearwords are often described as being unpleasant or ugly-sounding, as though people imagine a real connection between the "actual physical shape of the words and their taboo sense" (Burridge 2002: 161). They believe "that words are able, in and of themselves, to corrupt" (Gray 1993: 316); because of the perceived relation between morality and physical cleanliness we behave as if a moral stain is actual physical dirt (Zhong and Liljenquist 2006).

While the assumption that swearing is invariably negative and is morally wrong pervades the literature on both swearing and verbal aggression, swearwords may have a role also in affirming friendships, establishing relationships, intensifying humour and signalling comfort with fellows. It can be a badge of membership (Dessaix 2003), and is a powerful method of rebellion against the prevailing culture. Swearwords communicate emotions more powerfully and succinctly than any other words (Jay and Janschewitz 2007), and have the advantage of "guaranteeing maximum attention" (Morris 1998: 187). Mercury (1995: 29) used a striking example to show that omitting swearwords can weaken or change meaning: "this shirt is made of shitty material" is rich in connotative meaning when compared with the sanitised version, "this shirt is made of poor quality material." The same is true of attempts to censor the expression of emotion; nurses and patients may need to employ taboo language to convey the ineffable depths of their experience. The force of the speaker's emotional reaction is not conveyed when swearwords are replaced with euphemistic equivalents. Nurses might use swearwords to describe strong emotional reactions about patients, just as patients who have experienced abuse or psychiatric symptomatology beyond normal experience might resort to these words to describe their feelings.

Swearing can constitute a "pat on the back" – the boss may swear or employ a slang expression as a friendly gesture (Andersson and Trudgill 1990). Context is vital: the same words, "shit", "fuck", "bullshit", can express negative feelings and also positive ones such as amazement and delight (Kidman 1993). Winters and Duck (2001) stated that swearing could be an indication that the speaker was relaxed, and might also express sympathy or friendliness. A more recent finding however was that chief executive officers when lying are more likely to swear (Zakolyukina and Larcker 2010).

An exhaustive list of words that could be considered swearwords is impossible to devise, let alone a set of words that would be taboo in every culture: "the English language is rife with creative ways of depicting sexual or excretory organs or activities, [and] new offensive and indecent words are invented every day" (Cameron 2010).

Attitudes to Swearing

Many people, including nurses, disapprove of swearing, seeing it as representing a decline in moral standards or as a sign of limited education (Burns 2008) and public use provokes intense reactions. Others have equally strong but opposing opinions, typified by the witness for the defence in 1960 trial *Regina* v. *Penguin Books* over D.H. Lawrence's book, *Lady Chatterley's Lover:* "probably to the Crusaders, mere words were potent and evocative to a degree we can't realise." The evocate power of so-called obscene words must have been very dangerous to the dim-minded, obscure violent natures of the Middle Ages… In the past, man was too weak-minded, or crude-minded, to contemplate his own physical body and physical functions, without getting all messed up with physical reactions that overpowered him… It is no longer so. Culture and civilisation have taught us to separate the reactions (Rolph 1961: 78).

Swearing is frequently headline news and tension often arises between protests about bad language and freedom of speech. The furore over U2's Bono who said on the 2003 Golden Globe awards night, "this is really, really, fucking brilliant" resulted in a statement by the USA Federal Communications Commission that"the 'F-Word' is one of the most vulgar, graphic and explicit descriptions of sexual activity in the English language.. The tens of thousands of emails, calls and letters that poured in to the Commission opposing this broadcast are telling of the sexual connotation and offensiveness of that word" (FCC 2004). The appeal court, however, ruled that banning the fleeting use of expletives ran contrary to the First Amendment of the US Constitution which protects free speech (Allen 2010). In their judgement the Court commented: "sex and the magnetic power of sexual attraction are surely among the most predominant themes in the study of humanity since the Trojan War. The digestive system and excretion are also important areas of human attention. By prohibiting all 'patently offensive' references to sex, sexual organs, and excretion without giving adequate guidance as to what 'patently offensive' means, the FCC effectively chills speech" (United States Court of Appeals 2010).

National differences in offensiveness were highlighted in Tourism Australia's disastrous campaign, "Where the bloody hell are you?", when the UK's Advertising Standards Authority clamped down on television advertising and requested that swearwords not be used in future tourism promotions. Scott Morrison, Managing Director of Tourism Australia, saw the phrase as "a uniquely Australian invitation that harks back to the days when Paul Hogan threw a shrimp on the Barbie", but the word "bloody" ranks 27th on the British Broadcast Advertising Clearance Centre's list of offensive words that may not appear in advertisements (Deutsche Presse-Agentur 2006). Other countries such as Canada had difficulty with "bloody" but also with "hell" used as an expletive; in Singapore the swearwords were deleted completely, but the advertisement was allowed to run in full in the USA and New Zealand despite protests from lobby groups.

The UK media regulator Ofcom recently updated guidelines on language, saying their research indicated more public acceptance of swearing (Laughlin 2010). Despite racial and ethnic words' having become perhaps the most taboo in contemporary society (Wachal 2002), Ofcom ruled that "loony", "nutter", "mental", "lezza", "poof" and "queer" can be used at any time of day, while "fuck" remains unacceptable before a nine pm watershed (Laughlin 2010).

An Australian magistrate recently ruled that being called a prick was what a policeman should expect and therefore dismissed a charge of offensive language, inviting criticism that he was confusing what was to be expected with what was to be tolerated (Bolt 2010). The judgement provoked outrage from the NSW Police Association, concerned that their authority on the street would be undermined and pointing out the contextual differences: "It's a very different situation for a police officer doing his job to have language directed at him in a very offensive way as opposed to hearing language in the street"(Remfrey in Kozaki 2010). Similarly a lawyer's opinion was that telling a policewoman to "fuck off" was not obscene because it had become part of everyday language and was "not interpreted by anyone in the literal sense of the word" (O'Gorman in AAP 2010); ironically the newspaper report redacted the phrase to "f--- off." The lawyer advised the proper way to deal with the situation would be to say, "Please stop the language" and walk away, instead of "laying charges of public nuisance like confetti at a wedding." This view is typified by Justice Kirby's comment, quoted at the beginning of this chapter, that public officials are expected to be "thick skinned and broad shouldered in the performance of their duties."

Swearing: our Research

Using a mixed methods approach Stone (2009) set out to explore the extent of swearing in three contrasting health care settings, the implications of swearing for a therapeutic encounter and the impact of swearing on nurses. The study findings suggested that swearing in a range of health contexts is both widespread and under-reported.

Frequency

Questionnaires completed by 107 nurses working in adult mental health, paediatrics and child and adolescent mental health focused on nurses' experiences of swearing, an exploration of the association between personal attributes of nurses such as their own use of swearing, which may affect this interaction, and the effect on them of swearing. The methodology has been described in detail elsewhere (Stone, McMillan, and Hazelton 2010, Stone, McMillan, Hazelton, and Clayton 2010). Of the respondents 39 were male and 68 female, 15 worked in a paediatric setting, 40 in child and adolescent mental health, and 52 in adult mental health. Twenty-nine per cent of nurses reported being sworn at one to five times per week and 7 per cent "continuously". Nurses in mental health settings reported experiencing higher rates of patient and carer swearing than did paediatric nurses; however, caution should be exercised in interpreting this result because of the small number of paediatric respondents. Comments from nurses on the question of frequency showed that this figure varied greatly over time, from one shift to the next and from one patient to the next. Other nurses found it difficult to recall the number of times they had been sworn at by patients or carers. A typical comment was: *I honestly can't remember; it is often like water off a duck's back,* whilst one comment suggested a conscious avoidance of being sworn at: *Usually do night duty for this reason.* The authors have heard from many nurses that they changed jobs because they could not cope in previous clinical positions with the high levels of swearing.

There is no comparable research into the frequency of swearing in healthcare settings. The results of other frequency studies are contradictory. A study based on covert recordings of speech samples of college students found that swearwords accounted for 1 per cent of the words used (Jay 1992). Reported frequency of swearing differs depending upon source of data and research methodology. Recent perceptions of increase, for example by Wachal (2002), may have been based on misinterpretation of less inhibited swearing as indicating greater frequency because actual frequencies are not easy to verify (Harris 1990). Comparing data on swearing on college campuses in 1986 and in 1996, Jay (1999) concluded that the swearing lexicon was "remarkably stable", and that most swearing involved the use of a small set of words repeated frequently (e.g., "fuck", "shit", "hell", "Jesus", "goddamn", "damn" and "God"). Rarely spoken were more offensive words such as "cocksucker", "cunt", or "nigger". The main difference was that the rates of females' swearing in public had increased. A frequency analysis conducted in the UK revealed that taboo words were used most frequently by males of all ages, and by both sexes aged less than 35, and that social class did not affect the use of swearwords (Rayson, Leech, and Hodges 1997).

Distress

It was noteworthy that the majority of nurses in our study, asked to rate how distressing it was to be sworn at in several different situations, found each scenario to be highly distressing; 40–50 per cent rated all situations at the highest level of distress the instrument would allow, and 25 respondents indicated high levels for all (Stone et al. 2010). Reported as most distressing was being sworn at by a patient's relatives or carer, which rated higher than swearing associated with threats or physical violence. A significant gender difference showed in total distress scores, with female nurses recording higher scores than did male nurses.

The amount of distress felt is likely to be related to context: whether or not the nurse takes it personally; the level of personalisation and offensiveness; the religious views of the nurse; the nurse's own vulnerabilities; and the degree to which the language is embedded in the context of the nurse's life. Luck, Jackson and Usher (2007) found that in personalised verbal aggression, as when their appearance or manner was attacked, nurses felt emotional distress, whereas they were not so affected when perceiving themselves to be merely symbols for the "system" and the aggression to be not intended personally (2007: 5). Further, the impact of swearing was shown to be contextual – when it did not have the intent of personal harm it was not experienced as "verbal violence". Several nurses reported feeling distressed or upset as a result of swearing which in most cases was caused by frustration arising, for example, from denial of liberty for patients being restrained, or admitted to a psychiatric hospital. Frequently the presence of others appeared to add to the feeling of distress: An example of the extremes of human behaviour with which nurses have to deal was recounted by one nurse:

> An 11 year old boy with a burnt hand from putting a banger in a cat's rectum was becoming very vocal when I did his dressing saying… 'You're not fucking touching me… Fuck off bitch and leave me alone.' I was upset that his mother didn't attempt to intervene or chastise. I wasn't personally affronted but I was sad to hear this from an 11 year old to people who were trying to help him.

Impact

The impact on nurses covered a wide range of emotions: anger and annoyance, fearfulness, surprise, weariness, distress, indifference, disgust and repellence, and being sad, wounded, embarrassed and uncomfortable. A few nurses reflected on their practice and what might have prompted the swearing.

Nurses described strong affective responses to swearing:

> I HATE it – it really impacts on me now – makes me shake. I feel less clear thinking.
>
> Distressed, disgusted, embarrassed, fearful for safety of staff, upset for other patients/parents/visitors who were subjected to this outburst.

A major affective response to swearing was fearfulness, the intensity ranging from "petrified" to "a little apprehensive" or "tense". Nurses referred to being concerned about their safety, feeling vulnerable, and anxious about future interactions with the patient. The strongest affective response appeared to be produced by contextual dissonance: surprise caused by swearing "in a public place," in a paediatric unit, by a fellow staff member; or misinterpretation of an intervention – for example, a nurse who "reached to touch someone who was distressed and anxious" and was told, "don't fucking touch me." Three respondents described feeling tired and weary when swearing was prolonged – on two occasions over several hours. Other reported reactions were being disgusted and repelled, in one case by a patient who told the nurse: "you stupid bitch – I'm going to follow you home and piss in your milk and kill your dog, you f...ing white c.t and on and on," – evoking disgust related not only to the violation of sexual and possibly racial taboos but also to food and excretory-related taboos.

Most instances of feeling hurt and wounded involved a strong sense that it stemmed from the discrepancy between the care the nurse perceived s/he had invested in the patient and the patient's or carer's lack of appreciation of that care:

> My patient has cancer and refused treatment. As she was found to be able to make that decision we were treating palliatively. Others present: patient and her husband. Daughter of patient [Female, mid-late 30s] said that I was an incompetent fuckwit who was unable to fucking do anything fucking right and would I go get some other stupid bitch nurse who might at least want to keep patients alive. Then she said she was going to take her mother out of this cunt of a place.

It is theorised that the greater the emotion and resources invested in a patient, the more hurtful it is to be sworn at in a situation where gratitude or appreciation is due, resulting in a gap between expectation and outcome. Remaining professional during incidents which produce such a strong affective response takes a great deal of insight and effort by the nurse to avoid a reactive response, and thus widen the therapeutic distance between patient and nurse. The discrepancy here is emphasised by the high degree of taboo of the words directed at the nurse in the presence of the patient and her husband.

For a significant minority of nurses indifference seemed to be the predominant emotional response, typically epitomised by one nurse: "didn't bother me. If you are offended by being sworn at you are in the wrong job."

Nurses' caring responses were affected by these strong emotional reactions – their beliefs about swearing, negative social value-judgement about the swearer, perceived association between verbal and physical aggression, discrepancy between what was felt to be "deserved" and the way they were treated; for example, several comments about the appropriateness of swearing or its management appeared to indicate that patients or their carers were viewed as culpable for the behaviour.

Context and Offensiveness

Several respondents noted the importance of context in assessing offensiveness, and the vast difference between being *sworn at* and swearing used in conversation:

> I don't mind swearing in a general context – everyday conversation. But aggressive swearing really changes the meaning like "I have a sore cunt" is O.K, "You are a cunt" is very different.

Illustrating Ross's (1962: 34) view that obscenity can be a variable concept, depending not only upon who is speaking the words but also to whom and when and where. Context, including context of care, the patient's psychopathophysiology, and the broader societal context, clearly is a crucial moderator of both effects and perceptions of swearing.

Respondents were asked to rate 24 listed words for offensiveness: the mean offensiveness rating was 1.24 (N= 106, SD= 0.67) where 0: "not offensive at all," 1: "a little offensive," 2: "moderately offensive," 3: "very offensive," and 4: "extremely offensive." Three words, "cunt", "fuck", and "motherfucker", were rated as significantly (p<0.5) more offensive than other words, indicating that sexually based swearwords were regarded as more offensive than profanity or blasphemy. A second group also rated as highly offensive: "slut", "fuckwit", and "paedophile". The swearword whose use was most frequently cited by nurses was "fuck".

Nurses' responses revealed strong feelings about words they considered to be offensive: in all cases the word singled out for special mention was "cunt".

> I don't use the "C" word or blasphemy.
> "Cunt" is a word which I have always found offensive in any context.
> "Cunt" is the worst word ever, if a man ever called me that word I would never speak to him or have anything to do with him again.

Swearing's "in-group" role was evident in responses from nurses asked about their own usage of swearwords with colleagues: only four (4 per cent) replied never and 16 per cent replied often. Nearly half the respondents reported never using swearwords with patients, a further 42 per cent only rarely. About two-thirds reported the same frequency for swearing with colleagues as with social swearing, and 19 per cent less with colleagues than socially; 17 per cent reported more frequency with colleagues than socially, contrary to Jay's (1992) studies which showed that most people swear more in a social setting.

Interventions

The limited range of interventions described in response to patient swearing suggests that many nurses feel powerless and at a loss when confronted by it (Stone 2009). At worst they failed to explicate the encounter or consider ethico-moral-legal dimensions and duty of care. It is likely that such high levels of swearing-related distress threaten to overwhelm coping abilities, and possibly trigger non-therapeutic interventions. At one end of the spectrum nurses attempted either to placate or to ignore the patient: at the other they employed coercive interventions. One commented, "I don't deal well with yelling and/or confrontation," perhaps epitomising the apparent unease which for the majority inhibited assertive intervention, as evidenced by large numbers who withdrew or ignored the behaviour because of having no other way of responding. In contrast, some did not intervene because they found it understandable in the context of the patient's mental state. Nurses mostly described interventions which avoided active engagement; in only one case was there an attempt to confront the patient, in that instance a reminder about the "no tolerance" policy. In all other incidents attempts were made to placate or ignore the behaviour before resort to coercion.

Swearing and Healthcare

The contemporary view is that swearing can act as an intensifier of aggression, and also as a portent of impending physical aggression, perhaps a signal to others about one's state of mind (Burns 2008), and indeed Stone et al.'s (2010) study showed it was rare for physical violence to occur without verbal aggression in mental health care inpatient settings. In the past swearing was viewed as a substitute for physical aggression, enabling the expression of a strong emotional state in symbolic form instead of actual violence (Jay and Janschewitz 2007). The theory that swearing helps you let off steam or release tension featured in Stone's (2009) study in relation to nurses' attitudes towards swearing: "if they're swearing they're not usually fighting." The association between swearing and physical aggression is critical to nursing practice: if patient swearing is a substitute for physical aggression, nurses would be well advised to ignore it or even encourage it, but if it is a precursor of physical aggression then nurses should take proactive steps to avert a more serious incident.

A prominent feature of Laskiwski and Morse's ethnographic study (1993) of quadriplegic and paraplegic patients in a Canadian spinal cord unit was the amount of swearing, the most frequent users being males in their late adolescence to mid-thirties; conversational swearing was common but it was used also to express anger and frustration. The researchers concluded that swearing had five main functions: (a) to maintain personal space; (b) to maintain the camaraderie of the group; (c) to release emotions; (d) to create personal space; and (e) to build facades. Swearing was a badge of membership and patients new to the group, even if they began as non-swearers, adopted the common language; it served to release overwhelming emotions, both positive and negative, and cover up feelings of insecurity. The authors noted also that crying was a socially unacceptable emotional release for adult males in Canadian society, as it would be in Australian society, and swearing was the acceptable means for the group to express strong emotions.

Also relevant to a healthcare context is the finding that swearing is a common response to pain (Stephens, Atkins, and Kingston 2009), and in comparison with not swearing it increased pain tolerance, increased heart rate, and decreased perceived pain. When using swear words men held their hands in iced water 30 per cent longer than when using words such as "brown", "square", or "wooden". Women were able to tolerate the iced water submersion 44 per cent longer when saying swear words. The researchers hypothesised that the observed pain-lessening effect might have occurred because swearing induces a fight-or-flight response and nullifies the link between fear of pain and pain perception.

Swearing may bring to the fore underlying systemic cultural issues. Indigenous Australians are charged with 15 times as many language offences as would be expected given their proportion in the community (Muehlmann 2008, Heilpern 1999), but Aboriginal Australians use swearwords differently and may not recognise them as offensive. Health service policies which rigidly mandate Zero Tolerance for swearing whatever the context potentially discriminate against minority or traditionally disadvantaged groups.

It is clear that the majority of the nurses in our study were distressed and offended by being sworn at and necessarily could not follow the legal advice to "just walk away." The danger of repeatedly being subjected to this type of verbal onslaught is that nurses themselves can become emotionally exhausted, unfeeling, and attempt to protect themselves from stress by withdrawing from and becoming impersonal towards patients (Maslach, Schaufeli, and Leiter 2001); indeed general hospital staff who suffered frequent verbal aggression also displayed significantly higher levels of emotional exhaustion than those less exposed to it (Winstanley and Whittington 2002). How nurses are to be helped to remain open to their clients in the face of offensive language is a challenge which will be discussed later in the paper.

Mind the Gap: Models of Therapeutic Intent

A theme emerging from Stone's study (2010) was the moral evaluation of patients by nurses. A belief that swearing is morally reprehensible and requires some form of punishment will clearly produce negative repercussions for the therapeutic relationship, although prevention of a patient's swearing may be of no therapeutic value at all. Preparedness to put up with swearing or verbal aggression appeared to depend on the extent to which the behaviour was thought to be excusable. According to the attributions made about the cause of swearing, nurses' empathy appeared to be reduced or neutralised when patients were seen to be responsible for their own distress. Hoffman (2000) also found that the observer was sympathetic about distress when the cause was beyond the person's control. The result may be discrimination between excusable and inexcusable patients, and some being labelled as difficult (Johnson and Webb 1995). Holmes et al. (2006: 310) noted that "the marginalized and despised, those individuals portrayed as polluting and threatening, always provoke intense reactions, and when this polluting identity is associated with so-called transgressive practices, the intensity of these reactions is exacerbated"; a similar process seems to have occurred in this study.

The implications for therapeutic intervention begin with nurses' attributions as to the causes of aggression. Patient aggression was most often viewed as being due to factors intrinsic to the patient, some of which triggered moral evaluation (individual characteristics including age, gender, diagnosis, and substance misuse), termed by Duxbury (2002) an *internal model*. The underlying philosophy behind the internal model of causation is consistent with the biomedical model, which provides justification of medical treatment for aggression, and also frees the nurse from individual responsibility (Hahn et al. 2006).

A nurse's ability to monitor his or her own reactions to patients is imperative in establishing and maintaining a therapeutic relationship (Austin, Bergum, and Goldberg 2003).Parameters for achieving optimal therapeutic intention will be influenced by the potential for particular incidents to become catalysts for a drift towards limited therapeutic connection (Holder and Schenthal 2008). Contemporary nursing environments are so complex, dynamic, and reactive that nurses may feel overwhelmed and boundary slippage ensue, which can happen in many different ways; particular conditions or circumstances such as stress may increase the likelihood of further complications.

Implicit in the concept of boundaries (Figure 15.1) is the notion of non-therapeutic practice in terms of over- and under-involvement. Appropriate boundaries ensure safe connection between nurse and patient, based on the patient's needs (Holder and Schenthal 2008). It is suggested here that swearing may limit the likelihood of maintaining or achieving therapeutic practice and initiate a situation more reflective of under-involvement. Optimal therapeutic engagement results from nurses' empathic behaviours and judgements, considered responses and comprehensive assessment of the emotional status of patients (Figure 15.1). A patient's swearing might trigger negative counter-transference reactions leading to

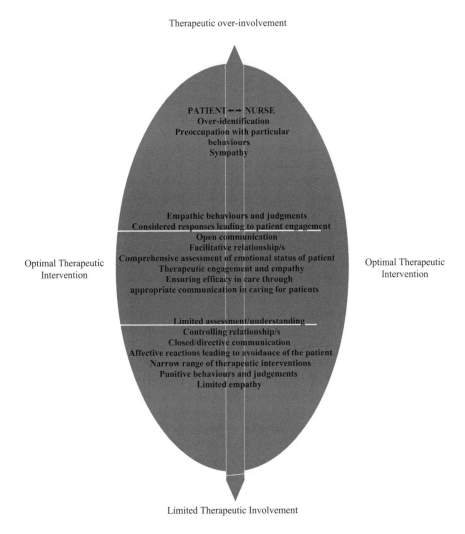

Therapeutic over-involvement

PATIENT → NURSE
Over-identification
Preoccupation with particular
behaviours
Sympathy

Empathic behaviours and judgments
Considered responses leading to patient engagement
Open communication
Facilitative relationship/s
Comprehensive assessment of emotional status of patient
Therapeutic engagement and empathy
Ensuring efficacy in care through
appropriate communication in caring for patients

Limited assessment/understanding
Controlling relationship/s
Closed/directive communication
Affective reactions leading to avoidance of the patient
Narrow range of therapeutic interventions
Punitive behaviours and judgements
Limited empathy

Optimal Therapeutic
Intervention

Optimal Therapeutic
Intervention

Limited Therapeutic Involvement

**Figure 15.1   A Model of Therapeutic Intervention in Response to Verbal
Aggression and Swearing**

un-therapeutic practice: nurses sometimes cannot move beyond their affective responses
to episodes of swearing which could produce disengagement, avoidance of the patient,
a narrow range of therapeutic interventions and punitive behaviours and judgements.
In addition swearing by nurses might represent a "boundary transgression" – that is,
an intentional or unintended infringement of the established limit of a professional
relationship – unless the nurse used carefully-chosen words with therapeutic intent.
Nurses are expected to guide and coordinate therapeutic communication, observe
professional boundaries and implement appropriate therapeutic action.

Nurse-patient Interaction

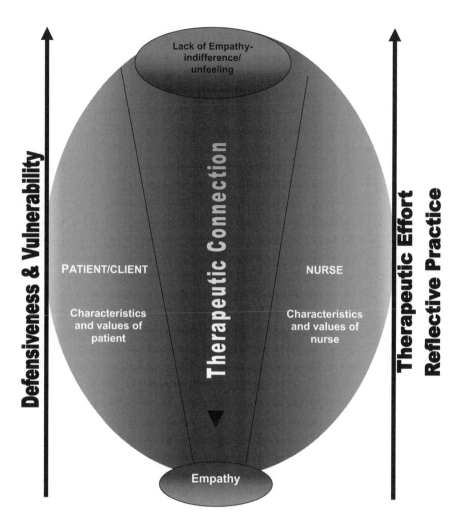

Figure 15.2   Mind the Gap: A Model of Potential Therapeutic Distance between Nurse and Patient

Figure 15.1 provided clarity in relation to swearing by patients, that therapeutic engagement and empathy were essential to understanding the dynamic, and a second set of concepts was proposed which expands on the first (Figures 15.2 and 15.3) and places these processes at the centre of the model. Empathy is the capacity to understand another person's subjective experience from within that person's frame of reference (Bellet and Maloney 1991), and encompasses both affective and cognitive domains (Stueber 2008). Crucial in this context is the notion that empathic arousal precedes helping behaviour and has been found also to reduce aggression (Hoffman 2000). Swearing by patients has consequences for nurses' empathic feelings: the extent to which expression of empathy can be enhanced or diminished depends on both patient's and nurse's personal characteristics, the nurse's appraisal of both the situation and the patient, ability to reflect upon the clinical situation, and inclination to invest therapeutic effort by putting into effect appropriate and constructive responses.

Given that we concluded empathy and engagement are at the heart of the nurse-patient relationship, Figure 15.2 was developed to illustrate how that relationship may be affected by a patient's swearing. It is easier for nurses to establish and maintain an optimal therapeutic connection with patients when nurse and patient have not too dissimilar characteristics and values. The therapeutic relationship benefits because most people empathise more with people with similar needs and concerns (Hoffman 2000); however certain characteristics of the nurse or patient have potential to create a therapeutic gap between them, leading to a sense of otherness and increasing vulnerability for the patient. Nurses must be mindful of factors triggering their affective responses, and expend greater therapeutic effort in order to bridge this gap.

Figure 15.3 illustrates some of the triggers identified in Stone's (2009) study that may affect nurses' responses to patients and their ability to empathise, and therefore impair the quality of the therapeutic connection. They may include strong affective responses (high levels of distress or anger) and ultimately perhaps emotional blunting/burnout. In terms of the gap, nurses may have to acknowledge existing beliefs and mind sets such as that swearing is invariably negative and is morally wrong; that certain characteristics of a patient may lead to negative social evaluation/judgement by the nurse; and the perceived association between physical aggression, verbal aggression, and swearing and therapeutic pessimism. Additionally discrepancies between what is felt to be deserved and what is received by nurses can create therapeutic distance. Context plays a crucial role in the level of word offensiveness, and they both mediate the impact of swearing. An internal model of causation for aggression may contribute to creating therapeutic distance between the nurse and patient.

Towards a Resolution

Nurses deal with deformity, disfigurement, diarrhoea and other leakages of the human body, and their work exposes them to experiences which challenge the clean and proper body and can lead to fear and anxiety (McCabe 2010), but can we deal with "verbal filth"? There is no complete prescription for coping with swearing in all its expressions and complexities to optimise patient outcomes and ensure physical and psychological safety for the nurse, but what follows is a discussion of possible approaches.

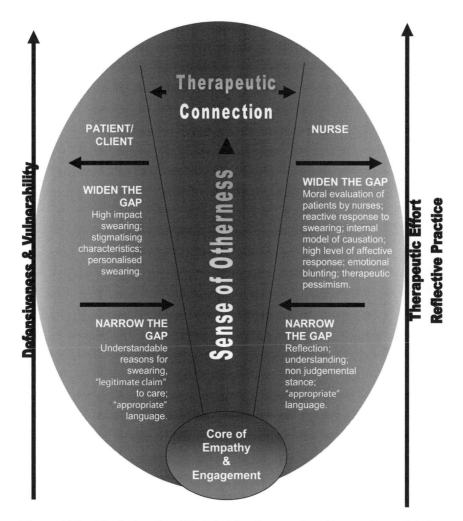

Figure 15.3   Mind the Gap Model: The Factors Leading to Potential for Creation of Therapeutic Distance between Nurse and Patient

Many of the interchanges reported in our study attack self-esteem by frightening, ridiculing, invading space, withholding politeness and keeping silent, or failing to act where politeness is expected (Culpeper, Bousfield, and Wichmann 2003: 1555). These attacks and the high levels of swearing negatively affect empathy and may result in nurses' distancing themselves from patients. Distancing in the form of passive types of behaviour (withdrawing, wishing the situation would go away, being silent, and blaming oneself) was observed in Rowe and Sherlock's (2005) study when nurses attempted to deal with verbal aggression from colleagues. It is likely that teaching nurses assertive conflict management would benefit their relations with both patients and colleagues. Nurses could substitute many therapeutic strategies, including de-escalation techniques, with the aim of calming distressed patients and redirecting them into constructive problem solving (Wand and Coulson 2006).

In managing patient swearing nurses need to appraise their rehabilitative, long-term therapeutic goals. They must "re-cognise" and manage their immediate negative emotional responses, and prevent their emotions from overtaking the thinking parts of their brain (Beauregard, Levesque, and Paquette 2004): If nurses block all feeling – becoming "thick skinned" – they may not be able to maintain a therapeutic connection with the patient.

Dealing with swearing in a helpful, salutary, constructive, and patient-focused way demands a clinical understanding of the behaviour so that nurses distinguish between swearing as a sign of underlying distress or as a precursor of more serious aggression. Many nurses carefully differentiated between swearing and "swearing *at*", thus recognising when swearing was the customary manner of self-expression. It is this distinction that is important in guiding practice: to treat these two behaviours similarly is to risk overreaction to the first and to underestimate the impact of the second. Patients and carers swear for many reasons and in many cases nurses are dealing with people at the extremes of experience, which it could be argued might warrant this type of language. When very distressed it is likely that we suffer an impoverished emotional lexicon which could lead to swearing. Although there is a legitimate cause to feel anxious about swearwords intended to intimidate or hurt, there is no clinical reason to treat swearwords used in other ways as a threat, despite our finding that nurses regard the literal use of such words as being as offensive as their use in anger. Treating this behaviour in the same way may cause disadvantage through nurses' distancing themselves or acting punitively towards patients whose use of such words implied no intent of harm and posed no threat to the nurse's safety or authority.

Jay's (2006) views about parents' reactions to a child's swearing might apply also to adults. When patients swear and are punished for doing so, instead of dealing with the situation that led to the swearing nurses are effectively reinforcing the behaviour. Jay believed this happens for two reasons: first that an extreme response to a word alerts the patient to its power; and secondly that the cause of the swearing is not addressed. Nurses have the responsibility of guiding therapeutic reactions, and their responses should be empathic and not reactionary: what is optimal is that they deal with the swearing as a sign of underlying distress rather than emotionally reacting to the linguistic content; in other words moving from symptom to understanding.

As Delaney (2009b) described the skills needed to cope with affective disregulation in children, so nurses need to read patients' affect, step in, and help them to understand and dampen down emotions, maintaining a positive tone with appropriate and matching body language to reduce the sense of threat. Though it may be hard, the first step is to learn not to personalise what is said: see the swearing not as a personal affront but instead as the patient's way of communicating emotions (Castillo 1978). It is important to remain calm and use "I" statements rather than pointing out the patient's inappropriate behaviour. Anecdotal evidence suggests that, if patients are using swearwords to recount a story, asking them to tell the same story without swearwords can reduce the negative emotional affect of what is said and assist the patient to use constructive problem solving skills.

Use of Swearwords in a Therapeutic Way

On many occasions nurses themselves reported thoughtfully using swearing to fulfil several complex relational functions. The ability to adapt verbal communication style to ensure effective therapeutic communication is an attribute of a skilled clinical practitioner. Questions that may be useful to promote reflection on the appropriateness of swearing with patients include:

> Were swearwords used in a consciously therapeutic way in order to benefit the patient?
> Does language fall within policy and ethical guidelines?
> How does this use of language appear to the patient and others?
> Was the goal or expected outcome for the interaction met?
> Has the language the potential to destroy the professional relationship?
> May the language cause harm to the patient?
> Does the language represent a sexual boundary violation?
> Did the language occur because of stress, loss, or trauma suffered by the nurse?
> inspired by Holder and Schenthal (2008)

Preparation for Practice

How are we to train clinical staff to deal with these issues? Usually training involves safely mimicking actions, yet when we talk formally about verbal aggression we generally sanitise the content by euphemism (the f-word), clinical terminology (defecatory adjectives), and obfuscation (objectionable utterances). Yet raw language carries a much more powerful emotional content. Authenticity also is essential: training in prevention and management of aggression is an important part of preparing clinicians for difficult aspects of their role in order to preserve the therapeutic relationship and maintain staff and patient safety. Nursing scenarios frequently leave out important aspects such as florid, destabilising, erratic and distasteful expressions. A good example of why authenticity is difficult to achieve involved a local heath service trainer in New South Wales Australia in 2001, realistically enacting a situation to illustrate methods of prevention and management of aggression; staff participants were learning how to respond in a measured way to verbal abuse: a human resources manager, unaccustomed to encountering such events, interrupted the proceedings and complained about the language used.

The need to maintain verbal hygiene and avoid offending anyone while confronting the realities of clinical experience leaves clinicians ill equipped to deal with everyday practice. We would contend that education and training must include the full spectrum of actuality, such as extreme language, in order to better understand, monitor and moderate our responses. We must prepare our workforce to cope with incidents that are beyond the range of normal human experience.

Conclusion

Just as the physically unclean side of nursing is overlooked in academic literature (Holmes et al. 2006), so is the dirty, dangerous and "disgusting" language of swearing. Hospitals and health facilities reflect contemporary society, dealing now with chronic debilitating illness and multiple psycho-pathologies, and are expected to absorb and treat the victims of society's system failures. They are no longer safe havens and realistically cannot ever achieve a "zero" verbal aggression state. Our response therefore must equip clinicians and nurses to manage swearing, to stay protected without retreating or becoming therapeutically blocked. Nurses need to develop an other-directed model to include awareness of greater complexity underlying the behaviour, and look beyond it to attempt helpful, thoughtful, emotion-centred interactions which build and do not damage the therapeutic relationships.

References

AAP. 2010. Swearing not obscene. *Newcastle Herald*, 7 August.

Abel, E.L. and Buckley, B.E. 1977. *The Handwriting on the Wall: Toward a Sociology and Psychology of Graffiti*. Connecticut: Greenwood Press.

Allen, N. 2010. US court throws out strict television profanity rules. *The Daily Telegraph UK*, 14 July.

Andersson, L. and Trudgill, P. 1990. *Bad language*. Oxford: Blackwell.

Arango, A.C. 1989. *Dirty Words: Psychoanalytic Insights*. New Jersey: Jason Aronson.

Austin, W., Bergum, V., and Goldberg, L. 2003. Unable to answer the call of our patients: mental health nurses' experience of moral distress. *Nursing Inquiry*, 10, 177–83.

Beauregard, M., Levesque, J., and Paquette, V. 2004. Neural basis of conscious and voluntary self-regulation of emotion,in *Consciousness, Emotional Self-Regulation and the Brain*, edited by M.Beauregard. Philadelphia: John Benjamin Publishing.

Beers Fägersten, K.A. 2000. A Descriptive Analysis of the Social Functions of Swearing in American English. University of Florida Press.

Bellet, P.S. and Maloney, M.J. 1991. The importance of empathy as an interviewing skill in medicine. *JAMA*, 266, 1831–32.

Bolt, A. 2010. Judging by magistrate's words, this is a swearing-in ceremony. *Herald Sun*, 5 May.

Burns, M.C. 2008. Why we swear: the functions of offensive language. *Monash University Linguistics Papers*, 6, 61–9.

Burridge, K. 2002. *Blooming English*. Sydney: ABC Books.

Butler, S. 2003. *Vulgar Language*. [Online: ABC]. Available at: www.abc.net.au/wordmap/rel_stories/swearing.htm.

Cameron, M. 2010. *Who Gives a Fleeting F#@*!*[Online: Gazette of Law and Journalism]. Available at: http://www.glj.com.au/76–Category?cat=179.

Castillo, G. 1978. Language arts and emotionally disturbed children. *Classmate*, 8, 14–18.

Culpeper, J., Bousfield, D., and Wichmann, A. 2003. Impoliteness revisited; with special reference to dynamic and prosodic aspects. *Journal of Pragmatics*, 35, 1545–79.

Delaney, K.R. 2009a. *Neuroscience and Neuro-Imaging: Useful Bridges for Attuning to the Mind*. ACMHN International Conference. Sydney: Two to Tango.

Delaney, K.R. 2009b. Reducing reactive aggression by lowering coping demands and boosting regulation: five key staff behaviors. *Journal of Child and Adolescent Psychiatric Nursing*, 22, 211–19.

Dessaix, R. 2003. *Swearing*. [Online: Radio National: Lingua Franca]. Available at: www.abc.net.au/rn/arts/ling/stories/s1154074.htm.

Duxbury, J. 2002. An evaluation of staff and patient views of and strategies employed to manage inpatient aggression and violence on one mental health unit: a pluralistic design. *Psychological Medicine*, 9, 325–37.

FCC. 2004. *Complaints Against Various Broadcast Licensees Regarding their Airing of the Golden Globe Awards Program FCC 04-43*. [Online: Federal Communications Commission]. Available at: http://hraunfoss.fcc.gov/edocs_public/attachmatch/FCC-04-43A1.pdf.

Freud, S. 1919. *Totem and Taboo*. London: Pelican.

Gray, P. 1993. Oaths and laughter and indecent speech. *Language and Communication*, 13, 311–25.

Gutierrez, R. and Giner-Sorolla, R. 2007. Anger, disgust, and resumption of harm as reactions to taboo-breaking behaviors. *Emotion*, 7, 853–68.

Hahn, S., Needham, I., Abderhalden, C., Duxbury, J., Halfens, R.J.G., and Feans, J.G. 2006. The effect of a training course on mental health nurses' attitudes on the reasons of patient aggression and its management. *Journal of Psychiatric and Mental health Nursing*, 13, 197–204.

Harris, R. 1990. Lars Porsena revisited, in *The State of the Language*, edited by C.Ricks and L. Michaels. Berkeley: University of California Press, 411–21.

Heilpern, D. 1999. Judgement: Police v Shannon Thomas Dunn Dubbo Local Court. *Alternative Law Journal*, 24, 238–42.

Hoffman, M. 2000. *Empathy and Moral Development*. Cambridge: Cambridge University Press.

Holder, K.V. and Schenthal, S.J. 2008. Watch your step: nursing and professional boundaries. *Nursing Management*, 38, 24–30.

Holmes, D., Perron, A., and O'Byrne, P. 2006. Understanding disgust in nursing: abjection, self, and the other. *Research and Theory for Nursing Practice: an International Journal*, 20(4).

Jay, T.B. 1992. *Cursing in America: A Psycholinguistic Study of Dirty Language in the Courts, in the Movies, in the Schoolyards, and on the Streets.* Philadelphia: John Benjamins Publishing Company.

Jay, T.B. 1999. *Why we Curse: A Neuro-Psycho-Social Theory of Speech.* Philadelphia: John Benjamins Publishing.

Jay, T.B. and Janschewitz, K. 2007. Filling the emotion gap in linguistic theory: commentary on Potts' expressive dimension. *Theoretical Linguistics*, 33, 215–21.

Johnson, M. and Webb, C. 1995. Rediscovering unpopular patients: the concept of social judgement. *Journal of Advanced Nursing*, 21, 466–75.

Justice Kirby. 2004. *Coleman vs Power.* [Online: High Court of Australia]. Available at: http://www.ipsofactoj.com/international/2005A/Part03/int2005A%2803%29–014.htm.

Kidman, A. 1993. *How to do Things with Four-Letter Words: A Study of the Semantics of Swearing in Australia.*[Online: Thesis submitted to the University of New England 1993. Available at: www.gusworld.com.au/nrc/thesis/intro.htm.

Kozaki, D. 2010. *Storm Over Student's Police Insult Surprising: Lawyer.* [Online: ABC News]

Laskiwski, S. and Morse, J.M. 1993. The patient with spinal cord injury: the modification of hope and expressions of despair. *Canadian Journal of Rehabilitation*, 6, 143–53.

Laughlin, A. 2010. *Ofcom: Public Relaxed on TV Swearing.* [Online: Didigital Spy]. Available at: http://www.digitalspy.co.uk/broadcasting/news/a224937/ofcom-public-relaxed-on-tv-swearing.html.

Luck, L., Jackson, D., and Usher, K. 2007. Innocent or culpable? Meanings that emergency department nurses ascribe to individual acts of violence. *Journal of Clinical Nursing*, 1–8.

Maslach, C., Schaufeli, W.B., and Leiter, M.P. 2001. Job burnout. *Annual Reviews Psychology*, 52, 397–422.

McCabe, J. 2010. Subjectivity and embodiment: acknowledging abjection in nursing, in *Abjectly Boundless: Boundaries, Bodies and Health Work*, edited by T.Rudge and D. Holmes. Farnham: Ashgate, 213–26

Mercury, R. 1995. Swearing: a bad part of language; a good part of language learning. *TESL Canada Journal*, 13, 28–36.

Morris, D.B. 1998. *Illness and Culture in the Postmodern Age.* Berkeley: University of California Press.

Muehlmann, S. 2008.Spread your ass cheeks: and other things that should not be said in indigenous languages. *American Ethnologist*, 35, 34–48.

Rayson, P., Leech, G., and Hodges, M. 1997. Social differentiation in the use of English vocabulary: some analyses of the conversational component of the British National Corpus. *International Journal of Corpus Linguistics*, 2, 133–52.

Rolph, C.H. 1961. *The Trial of Lady Chatterley: Regina v. Penguin Books Ltd.* Reading: Cox and Wyman.

Ross, H.D. 1962. Use of obscene words in psychotherapy. *Archives of General Psychiatry*, 6, 31–9.

Rowe, M. and Sherlock, H. 2005. Stress and verbal abuse in nursing: do burned out nurses eat their young? *Journal of Nursing Management*, 13, 242–8.

Stephens, R., Atkins, J., and Kingston, A. 2009. Swearing as a response to pain. *NeuroReport*, 20, 1056–60.

Stone, T.E. 2009. Swearing: impact on nurses and implications for therapeutic practice. PhD thesis University of Newcastle.

Stone, T.E., McMillan, M., and Hazelton, M. 2010. Swearing: its prevalence in health care settings and impact on nursing practice. *Journal of Psychiatric and Mental health Nursing*, 17, 1365–2850.

Stone, T.E., McMillan, M., Hazelton, M., and Clayton, E.H. 2011. Wounding words: swearing and verbal aggression in an inpatient setting. *Perspectives in Psychiatric Care*. DOI: 10.1111/j.1744-6163.2010.00295.x

Stueber, K. 2008. *Empathy*. [Online: Stanford University]. Available at: http://plato.stanford.edu/entries/empathy/

United States Court of Appeals. 2010. *United States Court of Appeals*. [Online: United States Court of Appeals]. Available at: http://www.techdirt.com/articles/20100713/12185410195.shtml.

Wachal, R. 2002. Taboo or not taboo: that is the question. *American Speech*, 77, 195–206.

Wajnryb, R. 2004. *Language Most Foul*. Crows Nest: Allen and Unwin.

Wand, T. and Coulson, K. 2006. Zero tolerance: a policy in conflict with current opinion on aggression and violence management in health care. *Australasian Emergency Nursing Journal*, 9, 163–70.

Werbart, A. 2010. *Our Need of Taboo: Pictures of Volence and Mourning Difficulties.*[Online:Institute of Psychotherapy, Stockholm]. Available at: http://www.human-nature.com/free-associations/werbart.html.

Winstanley, S. and Whittington, R. 2002. Anxiety, burnout and coping styles in general hospital staff exposed to workplace aggression: a cyclical model of burnout and vulnerability to aggression. *Work and Stress*, 4, 302–15.

Winters, A.M. and Duck, S. 2001. You ****!: swearing as an aversive and a relational activity. in *Swearing as Social Behavior*, edited by R.M. Kowalski. USA: American Psychological Association, 59–77.

Zakolyukina, A.A. and Larcker, D.F. 2010. *Detecting Deceptive Discussions in Conference Calls.*[Online: Stanford University]. Available at: https://gsbapps.stanford.edu/researchpapers/library/RP2060%20&%2083.pdf.

Zhong, C. and Liljenquist, K. 2006. Washing away your sins: threatened morality and physical cleansing. *Science*, 313, 1451–52.

Chapter 16

Prison Nursing: Managing the Threats to Caring

Elizabeth Walsh

Introduction

> It was a gated room. There was a gate at the door, but, but it's important. I was having an argument with him [the prisoner-patient], well, he was arguing with me and I was not so much arguing as trying to put my point across and there was all these other prisoners watching and standing at the door. He walked away and eventually backed down a bit...you have to rely on your own skills to deal with them as sometimes there aren't any other officers. I mean, if it got too bad, I would just press the alarm bell (Prison Nurse in Walsh 2007).

According to Lemmergaard and Muhr (2009: 35) 'a growing number of service workers are experiencing physical assaults, threatening behaviour, and verbal abuse whilst on duty'. They note that abusive behaviour is having a significant impact on nursing homes, day care centres, the police and in hospitals. Indeed, violence and aggression in nursing are noted in general hospitals (Zampieron et al. 2010, Winstanley and Whittington 2002); care settings for people with dementia (Rodney 2000) and in mental health settings (see Bonner and Wellman 2010, Bowers et al. 2009, Finfgeld-Connett 2009). From the literature, we can also see that violence and aggression is not just perpetrated by the patient. Patient's relatives and work colleagues are also identified as perpetrators (see Zampieron 2010). The impact of violence and aggression in health care settings is significant to the overall well-being of the nurse, their relationship with the patient and with the organisation. In this chapter, we concentrate on the potential impact of violence and aggression on the well being and practice of the prison nurse, and provide a framework through which it can be understood and consequently, managed.

The quote that opens this chapter comes from an experienced prison nurse, detailing an incident where they were in conflict with one of their prisoner patients during the administration of medication. It demonstrates three main issues which we will explore throughout the course of this chapter. Firstly, the aggression facing prison nurses on a daily basis, often with an audience of other prisoner patients; the way in which prison nurses must rely on both their own interpersonal skills and the custodial systems in place to manage aggressive behaviour; and the potential impact of aggressive behaviour on nursing care in prison. For the purposes of this chapter, the concept of aggression is defined as 'hostile or violent behaviour or attitudes' (Concise Oxford Dictionary 2008) and as such, literature pertaining to both violence and aggression has been included where deemed appropriate.

Context

At the time of writing, there are over 85,000 prisoners detained in prisons in England and Wales (Ministry of Justice 2010), all of whom are entitled to the same standard of health care as they would be able to access outside of prison, in the community. Nurses caring for these prisoners are employed by both the private and public sectors. Prison, by its very nature, necessitates a climate of security and discipline, provided predominately by discipline officers. However, the nurse working within this culture also has a responsibility to support the security and order of the establishment, therefore, nurses often have to adopt a dual role, that of both carer and custodian.

A prison can be viewed as a community in its own right. Consequently the health needs of the offender population in prison are wide and varied, requiring nursing skills from all branches of nursing: child for young offenders, learning disability, mental health and adult. Services provided to prisoners include primary care, inpatient care, outpatient care for long term conditions through a variety of nurse led clinics, mental health care, health screening and health promotion. Therefore nurses working in prison require skills and competencies in a wide range of areas from mental health to physical nursing, to skills and competencies in custodial care and security.

Of note here is the high prevalence of mental health and substance misuse need amongst prisoners (see HM Inspectorate of Prisons 2007). A recent report to consider and review the experience of people with mental health problems and people with learning disabilities in the criminal justice system noted both the high prevalence of mental health problems amongst offenders and the impact of the custodial environment itself on mental health (Bradley 2009). High rates of mental health issues amongst prisoners necessitate all nurses working in prison to possess skills in mental health care, and given the wide ranging inter professional team caring for prisoners, skills in interprofessional working. Discipline staff work closely with prisoners, providing custodial care and are a key part of the interprofessional team in a prison. It is vital that in ensuring consistent, high quality care, that health care staff work closely with their discipline colleagues. Although mental health care is a priority for many in prison, there are also significant physical health needs prevalent amongst the prisoner population, both acute and longer term chronic conditions (see Condon et al. 2007). The physical nursing skills required of nurses have been likened to those of practice nursing (Freshwater et al. 2002).

Although the physical and mental health needs of prisoners have been mentioned, de Viggiani (2007) notes the importance of considering the 'structural determinants of health' on prisoner health and suggests that 'as agencies of disempowerment and deprivation, prisons epitomise the antithesis of a healthy setting' (de Viggiani 2007: 115). Although we have considered the impact of prison on prisoner health and resultant health needs, of note here, is the potential frustration for the nurse in trying to provide a climate of care, and the possible conflict with their own professional values and attitudes to caring.

In their Point of Care review paper with the Kings Fund, Goodrich and Cornwell (2008: 3) note that 'the tension between the intended moral and ethical purpose of care and the inevitable day-to-day difficulties of retaining that purpose at the point of care is a shared dilemma of all in health care'. Although it is recognised that resource constraints and operational difficulties are key to this shared dilemma in the wider health community, this is particularly evident in the practice of the prison nurse, where the competing priorities of care and security provide particularly difficult challenges for nurses, both professionally and sometimes personally. Indeed, the constraints of providing care in a prison setting are well documented in the literature (see Walsh 2005, Weiskopf 2005). Willmott (1997) concludes that nurses working in prison must adjust their responsibilities and expectations without losing sight of their professional attitudes and values. Others suggest that in order to work within the prison culture, nurses caring for prisoners must adopt an ethical approach to caring, where 'Ethical caring, as a response set, represents a conscious effort to find a way to do the right thing, for the right reasons' (Maeve and Vaughan 2001: 53). Maroney (2005: 159) identifies the 'ever present struggle to find the balance between the health care needs of the prisoner and the security limitations of the institution'. It is this struggle between caring and custody, working within an interprofessional team with a dominant discourse of security which underpins the practice of prison nurses.

The Prison Nurse Patient Relationship

Although much of the discourse surrounding the challenges of prison nursing is located in the caring custody debate, they are also linked to the nature of the patient and subsequent nurse patient relationship.

In a study of 287 nurses working in American correctional facilities, Flanagan and Flanagan (2001) explored some of the differences between working both inside and outside of prison. One of the key distinctions reported in this study is the nature of the patients with participants describing them as 'difficult, manipulative, aggressive and demanding' (Flanagan and Flanagan 2001: 75). They continue to note that many of the respondents in their study expressed the view that prisoners utilised malingering for secondary gain. Norman and Parrish (2002: 15) suggest that 'many of the clients with whom prison nurses work may present specific challenges with regard to manipulative behaviours that can be designed to compromise and undermine the essence of nursing care'. I am not suggesting that all prisoner patients feign illness for secondary gain nor are they all aggressive and violent; however, the prison nurse must be alert to this possibility and have the appropriate skills to manage it effectively in the pursuit of high quality health care provision. As Burrow (1993: 23) states, 'The forensic nurse must exercise a benign scepticism. This is not to say that a patient's wishes are not to be entertained, but that an awareness should exist that they may be actively exploited to undermine the integrity of security procedures and gain some personal advantage'.

Work undertaken for a doctoral thesis (Walsh 2007) notes three main prisoner-patient specific impacts on the nurse patient relationship in adult male prisons: aggression, manipulation and the patient's offence. Nurses in this study reported the perceived increase in aggressive and angry prisoners, using aggression to manipulate and achieve their own goals:

> The prisoners are coming in, their way of doing things, dealing with people is to do it aggressively and get angry. It's almost becoming the norm. It's expected that a prisoner will get aggressive and angry if they don't get what they want.. Prisoners don't really respect staff anymore. Prison Nurse in Walsh (2007)

When this nurse was questioned about the impact this approach has on staff, they replied:

> Its stressful, yeah, it's very tiring. It's tiring being confronted with aggression all day.

Prison nurses are therefore not only dealing with the day to day stresses of caring for patients, but they are caring for patients located in a disciplinary environment, where the use of aggression can be a common way to express feelings. If we return to the quote at the beginning of this chapter, what is striking is the way in which the prison nurse remarks 'if it got too bad'. It appears as though there is some acceptance that aggressive behaviour is part of the fabric of the prison nurses' role; that 'bad' is acceptable, but that 'too bad' would require access to external management (the alarm bell). In the wider nursing literature, this wide acceptance of aggressive behaviour as integral to nursing practice is supported by McLaughlin et al. (2009) who note the underreporting of verbal aggression as a consequence of being seen as just part of the job.

It is important to consider the impact of not only actual, witnessed violence and aggression, but also the impact of the *ever present threat* of violence and aggression on the well-being of the prison nurse. Indeed, violence and aggression facing prison officers working within the same environment as the prison nurse, is noted to be a significant source of occupational stress (see Finn 2000, Triplett and Mullings 1996). For the prison nurse, 'stress arises from a correctional environment that fosters isolation, aggression, violence and manipulative behaviour' (Galindez 1990 cited by Flanagan and Flanagan 2002: 284). Antai-Otong (2001) notes the way in which psychiatric nurses are often on their guard against potential aggression, which entails high autonomic nervous system arousal and subsequent high levels of energy, contributing to cumulative stress reactions. However, in addition to this constant threat of aggression and violence, the prison nurse must contend with other organisational constraints on practice, and the resultant stress caused by them. This continued, chronic threat of aggression, impacts on the practice of nursing in prison, and consequently on the mental well-being of the nurse as they cope with the management of both their professional identity in the custodial setting and their own personal emotions. In Walsh (2007), the impact of this manipulative and aggressive behaviour by prisoner patients on the prison nurse is explored through the lenses of emotional labour and emotional intelligence.

Emotional Labour

Prison nurses are subjected to high levels of emotional labour in the course of their practice, resulting in significant consequences for their mental well being (Walsh and Freshwater 2009). Emotional labour is defined by Hochschild (1983: 7) as 'the management of feelings to create a publicly observable facial and bodily display'. Mann (2004: 208) reports three components to emotional labour: 'the faking of emotion that is not felt, and/or the hiding of emotion that is felt and the performance of emotion management to meet expectations within the work environment.' In the context of the prison nurse working in an environment where the threat of aggression and violence are ever present, and indeed sometimes physically carried out, the need for the regulation of emotions is significant to both provide quality nursing care and maintain a safe environment.

In Walsh (2007) and Walsh (2009), a framework is proposed that illustrates the emotional labour of prison nurses. This framework demonstrates the relationships that the prison nurse engages in, which cause significant levels of emotional labour. There are three external relationships: with colleagues, with the organisation and with the prisoner patient. In addition, a fourth, more internal relationship is proposed, that which the nurse has with themselves. This is referred to as the intra-personal relationship. The framework is illustrated in Figure 16.1 below.

The framework above demonstrates the three main external relationships that the prison nurse engages in. In this framework, the prisoner patient operates from two perspectives, that which is 'expected' and that which is 'as self'. This dual activity can also be seen in the interaction with the prison nurse's colleagues (other nurses, prison officers and members of the interprofessional team). These two facades of both prisoner patients and colleagues necessitate high levels of emotional labour for them too. If we return to the definition of emotional labour from Hochschild (1983: 7) 'the management of feelings to create a publicly observable facial and bodily display', we can see that prisoner patients engage with it, where they may for example have to present a tough exterior within the prison culture, and for prison officers, where they too must ensure a professional

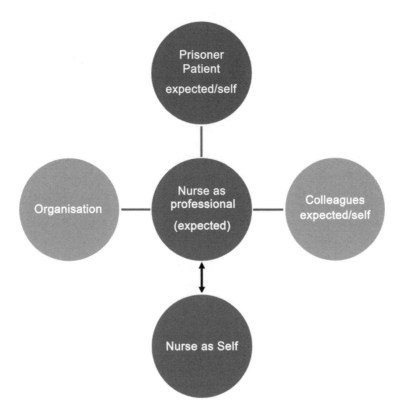

Figure 16.1   A Framework for the Emotional Labour of Prison Nurses

display. Emotional labour is required to meet the objectives of the organisation within which the prison nurse works, however, the requirements of the organisation may also provide challenges to caring (e.g. the care custody dilemma discussed earlier). The prison nurses' role therefore, entails having a working relationship with their colleagues, the organisation and their prisoner patients through which all parties engage in high levels of emotional labour, including colleagues and prisoner patients.

The Intrapersonal Relationship

What is of interest here, however, is the impact that these relationships have on the relationship the nurse has with themselves. This is termed the intrapersonal relationship. Nurses must engage in emotional labour to present themselves as professionals. However, what they often feel privately about their patients, their colleagues and the institution within which they practice, may be very different to how they are expected to present themselves as professionals to their patients, colleagues and employers. It is the often contradictory feelings that emerge internally for the nurse, which cause tension and discomfort, and which are a result of emotional dissonance. The emotional labour and subsequent high levels of emotional dissonance experienced by the prison nurse has a significant impact on their mental wellbeing (Walsh and Freshwater 2009). If we return to the nature of caring in an environment where caring and custodial philosophies conflict (colleagues and organisation), and where there is an ever present threat of violence and aggression (prisoner patient), we can see that the potential dissonance for the nurse is significant.

However, it is not only the concept of emotional labour which is pertinent to this discussion. In order for the prison nurse to manage these high levels of emotional labour effectively, the successful use of emotional intelligence is imperative.

Emotional Intelligence

According to Mayer et al. (2001) there are four components to emotional intelligence: the ability to manage emotions, understand emotions, use emotions to facilitate thought, and be accurate in perceiving the emotions of others. In the management of both actual and threatened violence and aggression, high levels of emotional intelligence are vital to ensure the early detection and safe management of a threatening situation. Indeed, Chapman et al. (2009) note that the ability to predict a violent or aggressive event early will enable strategies to be used to de-escalate the situation and promote a positive outcome.

If we consider Mayer et al.'s four components of emotional intelligence through the lens of violence and aggression, it is clear that ability across all four is vital for both management and prevention. Prison nurses must be able to *manage their emotions* as displaying fear or irritation with patients in the prison setting can fuel further violence and aggression and has the potential to portray the prison nurse as vulnerable. In her work exploring the work and lives of prison officers, Crawley (2004) draws attention to the fear felt by prison officers and the ways in which they manage it. Some officers in her study noted the potential for fear to be 'crippling' but noted that to be unable to manage it would prevent them from undertaking their duties.

Prison nurses must be able to *understand emotions*, and be accurate in their reasoning about emotions in both themselves and their prisoner patients. Acceptance that a feeling of apprehension or anxiety is appropriate in a potentially aggressive situation is vital if the nurse is then to be able to address it. Conversely, the ability to understand exactly why a prisoner patient may be getting frustrated and exhibiting aggressive behaviour will assist in developing correct strategies to manage the situation. The ability to be able to *use emotions to facilitate thought* and to *accurately perceive the emotions of others* allows the prison nurse to react appropriately, with insight into how their own emotions may affect their responses. Waddington et al. (2005) in their discussions of workplace violence, highlight the way in which people engaged in violent and aggressive acts apportion different meanings to them. For example, they suggest that in the prison setting, what would be viewed as innocuous in the outside world, may be worthy of a violent or aggressive response in prison culture. The nurse working in prison needs to understand the culture within which they are working, and the potential emotional responses of prisoner patients in the context. For example, a simple, polite greeting to mark a special occasion such as Christmas or a birthday may be met with hostility when such occasions may remind prisoner patients that they are incarcerated. The importance of emotional intelligence in the detection, management and prevention of violence and aggression in prison health care settings cannot be underestimated.

If we consider the concepts of emotional labour and emotional intelligence as they pertain to the practice of the prison nurse working in an environment where violence and aggression are both actual and constantly perceived as a threat, the implications for the mental well being of the nurse are significant when added to the other challenges that impact on their practice i.e. the competing philosophies of caring and custody, and the nature of the nurse -prisoner patient relationship. If emotional intelligence is the key to both managing emotional labour and dealing effectively with the perceived threat and actual incidents of violence and aggression, it would appear that the development of emotional intelligence in prison nurses should be a fundamental part of their education and development, especially in the management of violence and aggression.

In Walsh (2007), Clinical Supervision was successfully employed as a framework to provide regular opportunities for prison nurse participants to engage in facilitated reflection on practice in order to develop their own emotional intelligence, nursing practice and to obtain support. Clinical Supervision is defined as 'regular protected time for facilitated, in-depth reflection on clinical practice. It aims to enable the supervisee to achieve, sustain and creatively develop a high quality of practice through the means of focussed support' (Bond and Holland 1998: 77). This definition makes use of the model proposed by Proctor, in which it is suggested that clinical supervision has three main functions: normative (ensuring quality and standards), formative (enabling learning from experience), and restorative (providing support and increasing self awareness). The value of clinical supervision to staff working in the prison setting can be seen on many levels: for the development of emotional intelligence to effectively manage potential/actual aggression; to support the mental well being of the prison nurse working in this environment, and to provide space to reflect on standards of care to challenging prisoner patients.

Critical Incident Debriefing and Post Incident Reviews

Given earlier discussion highlighting the significant levels of emotional labour for prison staff and need for emotional intelligence to manage it, the value of clinical supervision as a *supportive* space for facilitated reflection is of particular interest to our discussion in the care of actual and potentially violent and aggressive prisoner patients. However, although clinical supervision is offered as a mechanism to support staff and promote mental well being, alternative forms of support are available to prison nurses, and indeed all prison staff involved in aggressive/ violent incidents in the form of post incident support and debriefing.

In her paper exploring critical incident stress debriefing for psychiatric nurses, Antai-Otong (2001) states that a critical incident is 'a powerful and overwhelming event that lies outside the range of usual human experience'. She continues to identify the way in which critical incidents 'exhaust one's usual coping mechanisms, resulting in psychological distress and disruption of normal adaptive functioning' (Antai-Otong 2001: 127), and can result in feelings of fear, anxiety and depression. Debriefing following a critical incident is now common in many high risk occupations, prisons included. The main goals of debriefing are to 'mitigate the impact of the traumatic event on victims, and to accelerate the recovery process' (Mitchell et al. 2003: 46). Debriefing supports those involved to verbalise distress and ground the experience in appropriate reality hence facilitating suitable coping mechanisms. However, Bonner and Wellman (2010) question the value of post incident support in the form of traditional incident debriefing for psychiatric nurses following experience of aggression and violence at work. They note that as debriefing entails the need to relive traumatic events very soon after they have occurred, there is potential to expose those involved to those feelings and fears for a second time, leading to further distress. Bonner and Wellman identify a lack of useful guidance for practice concerning the most appropriate post incident interventions to support staff and state that 'less serious incidents, for example, where injury has not occurred, are not routinely reviewed…and post incident support is missed' (Bonner and Wellman 2010: 36). Debriefing and more formal organisational support usually occurs *after* a traumatic incident. No one would dispute that incidents of violence and aggression are traumatic for all involved, however, managing the situation from the perspective of having immediate debriefing/support post incident does not address the stress associated with chronic, ongoing *threat* of aggression facing prison nurses, help with the resultant impact on mental well-being in the long term or explore the effect this has on practice, and ultimately patient care. From experience, the view that working with aggressive behaviour is considered to be part of the nurses role (see McLaughlin et al. 2009), has led practitioners to seeking support from their colleagues and peers.

Peer Support

Informal support is regularly accessed by prison staff from each other in the form of 'ad hoc' peer support. Indeed, in the work we have undertaken to develop and implement clinical supervision and reflection in prison health care settings (see Walsh and Dilworth 2010), a rallying cry of 'we do that already' can regularly be heard when staff are introduced to the concept of structured reflection on practice. What we have found that actually occurs in practice is a more informal approach to reflection, usually during rest breaks, that focuses on the more negative experiences and difficulties facing prison nurses in their daily practice, and has support rather than transformation at its centre. A paper that explores the coping mechanisms of nurses who have experienced trauma in the workplace (Niiyama et al. 2009: 8) suggests that 'a ruminating coping strategy that continually involves talking about the event to somebody else presumably contributes to the persistence of traumatic stress rather than to recovery'. This is congruent with the arguments against formal debriefing raised earlier in our discussion concerning involvement in actual violence and aggression. However, if we are to consider a coping strategy for managing the impact on mental well being of *non physical aggression* and the ever present *threat* of violence and aggression, is informal discussion and rumination amongst peers useful in managing the associated stress and its impact on well being and practice? I would suggest that formal reflection on practice, through facilitated, protected time with an experienced colleague allows the practitioner to transform their thinking and practice based on reflection from many perspectives. If this support is offered regularly, rather than just at times of extreme stress e.g. after a traumatic event, nurses can support their mental well being whilst simultaneously developing alternative strategies to manage violent and aggressive behaviour. Clinical supervision is proposed as a useful mechanism to achieve on-going support and development of practice.

Clinical Supervision in Prison Nursing

Recent work has been undertaken to develop and implement clinical supervision in prison health care settings (see Walsh and Freshwater 2009) and more latterly to develop reflective practice for staff working with prisoners along the offender pathway, encompassing police custody, through to court, prison and then on into the community (see Walsh and Dilworth 2010). Of interest to this chapter is its potential effectiveness in supporting prison nurses wellbeing and developing their practice, in the care of actual and potential violent and aggressive prisoner patients. We have already considered Bond and Holland's definition of clinical supervision as 'regular protected time for facilitated, in-depth reflection on clinical practice. It aims to enable the supervisee to achieve, sustain and creatively develop a high quality of practice through the means of focussed support' (Bond and Holland 1998: 77). However, there are others who place different emphasis on its purpose. Lyth (2000) asserts that 'clinical supervision is a support mechanism for practising professionals within which they can share clinical, organizational, developmental, and emotional experiences with another professional in a secure, confidential environment in order to enhance knowledge and skills. This process will lead to an increased awareness of other concepts including accountability and reflective practice' (Lyth 2000: 728). From these definitions, we can see that clinical supervision affords the practitioner, regular, protected time to reflect on their practice and develop it, whilst gaining support in a safe and confidential space.

Given the way in which clinical supervision supports nurses, promotes the maintenance of standards and encourages experiential learning to take place through reflection on practice, its potential to be highly beneficial to the nurse faced with the ever present threat of aggression and occasional actual violence, is significant. It is through the function of experiential learning and reflection on practice that the nurse can develop emotional intelligence, which has been clearly demonstrated as key to managing both aggressive prisoner patients and the impact of the emotional labour undertaken.

Clinical supervision provides an on-going, sustainable approach to the management of emotional labour through the supportive function; the development of emotional intelligence from the formative function, and the maintenance of high standards of practice through the normative function. All of which are vital in predicting aggressive situations, managing them, and indeed managing the resultant impact on the mental well being of the prison nurse.

Theory into Practice

In order to place the theoretical perspectives into context we return to the words of the prison nurse introduced at the very beginning:

> It was a gated room. There was a gate at the door, but, but it's important. I was having an argument with him [the prisoner-patient], well, he was arguing with me and I was not so much arguing as trying to put my point across and there was all these other prisoners watching and standing at the door. He walked away and eventually backed down a bit...you have to rely on your own skills to deal with them as sometimes there aren't any other officers. I mean, if it got too bad, I would just press the alarm bell (Prison Nurse in Walsh 2007).

By viewing the experience this nurse has shared through a more supervisory lens rather than a purely supportive one, we can see how it can be explored to promote sense making and a transformed perspective.

This nurse explains the context, a gated room. They note the importance of telling us about this gate as it paints a picture for us which is common to the practice of prison nurses. Barriers that separate health care staff from their patients. In the words of this nurse, the gate is important to acknowledge. It allows us to understand the physical barrier present between nurse and patient, but perhaps more importantly, provides us with an understanding of the security apparatus that surrounds nursing practice in prison. For this nurse, the gate may provide a sense of security, that they and their medications are safe from a group of people deemed to be a risk. Alternatively, the gate could promote a sense of 'them and us' between the nurse and patients. This feeling between a nurse and their patients could be contrary to the way in which the nurse feels nursing should be, thus resulting in emotional labour and making sense of the dissonance felt in the intrapersonal relationship.

The nurse notes that they were having an argument, and then corrects themselves, stating that they were trying to 'discuss', whereas the prisoner patient was 'arguing'. For me, this illustrates the dissonance in the intrapersonal relationship that the nurse is having with themselves. Perhaps they felt like arguing, indeed, in their recollection of events perhaps this appeared like an argument, but in presenting themselves as a professional, it should be relayed as a discussion. Again, we are seeing an example of emotional labour.

The nurse then continues to tell us that there was an audience of prisoners, observing this interaction. Not only does this nurse have their own prisoner patient to care for, but they are also being scrutinised by others who might not only be looking to support their fellow prisoner, but who might also be waiting to see if the nurse exhibits any weakness or unprofessionalism on which they can draw for the purposes of manipulation at a later date. The nurse at the gate knows this is what might be happening. They also know that the situation could escalate and become more aggressive. Again, this nurse illustrates our earlier theoretical discussion of emotional intelligence, understanding that they need to draw on their own skills in managing the situation.

At the end of the statement, the nurse tells us that 'if it got too bad, I would just press the alarm bell'. There is some security for the nurse in knowing that there is an alarm bell that can be pressed to summon help. This knowledge could provide some comfort for them in this situation, perhaps allowing them a clearer mind in order to manage it effectively. Alternatively the presence of an alarm bell could serve to promote the ever present underlying custodial perspective on practice. The gate and the alarm bell are representations of the disciplinary apparatus that surround prison nurses and their practice. The impact of this apparatus on prison nursing practice and ultimately, recognition of it, can be explored through clinical supervision.

Clinical supervision can assist in managing the stress generated by this event, enable the nurse to reflect on their actions, learn from them, and indeed, allow the nurse time to consider how they might manage the situation differently next time. Facilitated reflection on the event within a clinical supervision session would enable the nurse to consider all facets of the incident, and indeed, support them to crystallise learning, explore alternative ways of dealing with the situation should it arise again, and generally help make sense of what has happened.

However, experience in prison nursing suggests that the incident discussed above is a common occurrence which prison nurses manage on a daily basis. Without regular clinical supervision through which to reflect, the impact of the significant levels of emotional labour on the mental well being of the nurse will not be recognised until the nurse has reached breaking point. Critical incident reviews and debriefing have a place in managing the effects of aggressive and violent prisoners, but only tend to be utilised when there is a crisis or incident. Ad hoc peer support also has its place in supporting prison nurses facing aggressive prisoner patients, but can lack the transformational potential of regular clinical supervision.

Conclusion

In this chapter, we have considered the context within which prison nurses practice and how aggressive behaviour from prisoner patients can affect the nurse patient relationship, with consequential affects on the mental wellbeing of the nurse through impact on the intrapersonal relationship i.e. the relationship the nurse has with themselves. Having explored the intrapersonal relationship through the lens of emotional labour, we have seen the importance of emotional intelligence in managing the effect of violent and aggressive prisoner patients, on both practice and the mental wellbeing of the nurse. We have explored the use of critical incident debriefing, post incident reviews and informal peer support as mechanisms through which nurses often manage the feelings and emotions generated by trying to care for aggressive prisoner patients. However, an alternative mechanism is proposed in the form of *regular* clinical supervision, as a way to support, develop and reflect on practice in a professionally appropriate manner, leading to the effective management of the dissonance caused in the intrapersonal relationship and the transformation of nursing practice in the face of challenging conditions.

References

Antai-Otong, D. 2001. Critical incident stress debriefing: a health promotion model for workplace violence. *Perspectives in Psychiatric Care*, 37(4), 125–32.

Bond, M. and Holland, S. 1998. *Skills of Clinical Supervision for Nurses*. Buckingham: Open University Press.

Bonner, G. and Wellman, N. 2010. Post incident review of aggression and violence in mental health settings. *Journal of Psychosocial Nursing*, 48(7), 35–40.

Bowers, L., Allan, T., Simpson, A., Jones, J., Van Der Merwe, M., and Jeffery, D. 2009. Identifying key factors associated with aggression on acute inpatient psychiatric wards. *Issues in Mental Health Nursing*, 30, 260–71.

Bradley, K. 2009. *The Bradley Report*. London: Department of Health.

Burrow, S. 1993. The role conflict of the forensic nurse. *Senior Nurse*, 13(5), 20–25.

Chapman, R., Perry, L., Styles, I., and Combs, S. 2009. Predicting patient aggression against nurses in all hospital areas. *British Journal of Nursing*, 18(8), 476–83.

Condon, L., Hek, G., and Harris, F. 2007. A review of prison health and its implications for primary care nursing in England and Wales: the research evidence. *Journal of Clinical Nursing*, 16, 1201–1209.

Crawley, E. 2004. *Doing Prison Work*. Devon: Willan Publishing.

Finfgeld-Connett, D. 2009. Model of therapeutic and non-therapeutic responses to patient aggression. *Issues in Mental Health Nursing*, 30, 530–37.

Finn, P. 2000. *Addressing Correctional Officer Stress*. Washington DC: National Institute of Justice.

Flanagan, N.A. and Flanagan, T.J. 2001. Correctional nurses' perceptions of their role, training requirements and prisoner health care needs. *Journal of Correctional Health Care*, 8, 67–85.

Flanagan, N.A. and Flanagan, T.J. 2002. An analysis of the relationship between job satisfaction and job stress in correctional nurses. *Research in Nursing & Health*, 25, 282–94.

Freshwater, D., Walsh, L., and Storey, L. 2002. Developing leadership through clinical supervision. *Nursing Management*, 8, 10–13.

Goodrich, J. and Cornwell, J. 2008. *Seeing the Person in the Patient*. The Point of Care Review Paper. London: Kings Fund.

HM Inspectorate of Prisons. 2007. *The Mental Health of Prisoners: A Thematic Review of the Care and Support of Prisoners with Mental Health Needs*. London: HMIP.

Hochschild, A. 1983. *The Managed Heart*. London: University of California Press.

Lemmergaard, J. and Muhr, S.L. 2009. Treating threats: the ethical dilemmas of treating threatening patients. *The Service Industries Journal*, 29(1), 35–45.

Lyth, G.M. 2000. Clinical supervision: a concept analysis. *Journal of Advanced Nursing*, 31(3), 722–9.

Maeve, M.K. and Vaughn, M.S. 2001. Nursing with prisoners: the practice of caring, forensic nursing or penal harm nursing? *Advances in Nursing Science*, 24(2), 47–64.

Mann, S. 2004. People-work: emotion management, stress and coping. *British Journal of Guidance and Counselling*, 32(2), 205–21.

Maroney, M.K. 2005. Caring and custody: two faces of the same reality. *Journal of Correctional Health Care*, 11, 157–69.

Mayer, J.D., Salovey, P., Caruso, D., and Sitarenios, G. 2001. Emotional intelligence as a standard intelligence. *Emotion*, 1(3), 232–42.

McLaughlin, S., Gorley, L., and Moseley, L. 2009. The prevalence of verbal aggression against nurses. *British Journal of Nursing*, 18(12), 735–9.

Ministry of Justice. 2010. *Prison Population and Accommodation Briefing*. [Online]. Available at: www.hmprisonservice.gov.uk[accessed: 15 October 2010].

Mitchell, A., Sakraida, T.J., and Kameg, K. 2003. Critical incident stress debriefing: implications for best practice. *Disaster Management & Response*, 1(2), 46–51.

Niiyama, E., Okamura, H., Kohama, A., Taniguchi, T., Sounohara, M., and Nagao, M. 2009. A survey of nurses who experience trauma in the workplace: influence of coping strategies on traumatic stress. *Stress & Health*, 25, 3–9.

Norman, A. and Parrish, A. 2002. *Prison Nursing*. Oxford: Blackwell.

Proctor, B. 1986. Supervision: a co-operative exercise in accountabiliy, in *Enabling and Ensuring*, edited by M. Marken and M. Payne. National Youth Bureau and Council for Education and Training in Youth and Community Work, Leicester, UK.

Rodney, V. 2000. Nurse stress associated with aggression in people with dementia: its relationship to hardiness, cognitive appraisal and coping. *Journal of Advanced Nursing*, 31(1), 172–80.

Triplett, R. and Mullings, J.L. 1996. Work related stress and coping amongst correctional officers: implications from organisational literature. *Journal of Criminal Justice*, 24(4), 291–308.

de Viggiani, N. 2007. Unhealthy prisons: exploring structural determinants of prison health. *Sociology of Health & Illness*, 29(1), 115–35.

Waddington, P.A.J., Badger, D. and Bull, R. 2005. Appraising the inclusive definition of workplace violence. *British Journal of Criminology*, 45, 141–64.

Walsh, E. 2007. *An Exploration of the Emotional Labour of Prison Nurses*. Unpublished PhD Thesis, Bournemouth University.

Walsh, E. and Dilworth, S. 2010. *Developing Sustainable Reflective Practice in Offender Care*. A report for Offender Health, Department of Health. Leeds: University of Leeds.

Walsh, E. and Freshwater, D. 2009.The mental well-being of prison nurses in England and Wales. *Journal of Research in Nursing*, 14(6), 553–64.

Walsh, L. 2005. Developing prison health care through reflective practice, in *Transforming Nursing through Reflective Practice*, edited by C. Johns and D. Freshwater, 2nd Edition. Oxford: Blackwell.

Weiskopf, C. 2005. Nurses experience of caring for inmate patients. *Journal of Advanced Nursing*, 49(4), 336–43.

Wilmott, Y. 1997. Prison nursing: the tension between custody and care. *British Journal of Nursing*, 6(6), 333–6.

Winstanley, S. and Whittington, R. 2002. Anxiety, burnout and coping styles in general hospital staff exposed to workplace aggression: a cyclical model of burnout and vulnerability to aggression. *Work and Stress*, 16(4), 302–15.

Zampieron, A., Galeazzo, M., Turra, S., and Buja, A. 2010. Perceived aggression towards nurses: study in two Italian health institutions. *Journal of Clinical Nursing*, 19, 2329–341.

Chapter 17

The Mentally Ill and Civil Commitment: Assessing Dangerousness in Law and Psychiatry

Cary Federman

Introduction

The purpose of this chapter is to provide a general overview to the problem of dangerousness, the mentally ill, and civil commitment. Dangerousness usually refers to persons who are in danger of hurting themselves or others. Dangerousness, though an ambiguous term in law and psychiatry, has both civil and a criminal components. Dangerousness is applied in criminal cases to those who have committed certain violent acts and appear willing to do so again. "Future dangerousness testimony is the major means of persuading the sentencing jury that a convicted defendant poses a threat to society and thus merits the death penalty" (Beecher-Monas, 2003: 412). Dangerousness in civil law, that is, for the purpose of commitment to a psychiatric hospital, is less easily defined, mostly because the purpose of hospitalization is treatment, not punishment. Dangerousness has no scientific meaning, that is, as a disease or disorder. Yet medical professionals will assert that someone is dangerous based on his or her behavior and not on any particular disease. Or, they may suggest that the person has a disease or disorder, but with the notation: not otherwise specified (NOS), meaning that the disease or disorder does not meet the standard criteria. Dangerousness, however, is not a medical condition.

Because dangerousness is both a problem of criminal justice and a problem for the health professions, I would like to provide those in the health professions with a foundation for understanding dangerousness as it is understood and described by legal professionals. There is not enough communication between the law and the health sciences on the issue of dangerousness and the mentally ill. The deleterious effects of this lack of cross-fertilization can be seen in the debates in the popular and academic press over the meaning of "insanity," a legal term with no basis in the natural sciences. Yet it is a term that those in health professions must deal with on a regular basis. Despite these controversies, I do not intend this chapter to be a comprehensive analysis of the problem of dangerousness. But I have tried to be thorough regarding the ideas that constitute dangerousness.

Insanity

There is a world of difference between "mental illness" and "insanity" and the way the health professions and the law regard it and its connection to dangerousness. The creation in Britain of the McNaughtan rules in 1843, which continue to govern insanity cases in the United States (often in a modified and truncated form), focused not on the various mental diseases from which one could suffer, but on the act of violence itself, and therefore on the level of dangerousness emitted by the criminal.

> [T]o establish a defense on the ground of insanity, it must be clearly proved that, at the time of the committing of the act, the party accused was laboring under such a defect of reason, from disease of the mind, as not to know the nature and quality of the act he was doing; or, if he did know it, that he did not know he was doing what was wrong (West 1979: 75).

The McNaughtan rules stress cognition not volition, and therefore punishment not psychiatric care is the solution to the criminal's problems. Despite the acknowledgment of various psychological states within the rules, the underlying theme of the McNaughtan rules is the level of violence and the status of the victim, and not the status of the defendant's mental capacity. Arizona used to have a law that largely tracked the McNaughtan rules.

> A person is not responsible for criminal conduct if at the time of such conduct the person was suffering from such a mental disease or defect as not to know the nature and quality of the act or, if such person did know, that such person did not know that what he was doing was wrong (Rozelle 2007: 34).

But after a public outcry over a state court finding that a criminal defendant was not guilty by reason of insanity, Arizona modified its law regarding insanity defenses. It now states:

> Under current Arizona law, a defendant will not be adjudged insane unless he demonstrates that "at the time of the commission of the criminal act [he] was afflicted with a mental disease or defect of such severity that [he] did not know the criminal act was wrong." (*Clark* v. *Arizona* 2006: 743)

Arizona also prohibits the submission of evidence, at a trial, of a defendant's mental disorder "short of insanity… to negate the *mens rea* element of a crime" (*Clark* v. *Arizona* 2006: 745). The United States Supreme Court upheld this law in 2006.The result was that Arizona sentenced a seventeen-year old schizophrenic to life in prison for shooting and killing a police officer, even though he believed that "'aliens' (some impersonating government agents) were trying to kill him and that bullets were the only way to stop them" (*Clark* v. *Arizona* 2006: 745).

The case of Eric Michael Clark provides us with an opportunity to understand how lawyers, politicians, and the public equate mental illness with dangerousness (Austin et al. 2008, Buchanan 2008, Addison and Thorpe 2004, O'Mahoney 1979). Of the approximately two million adults in jails and state and federal prisons in the United States, about 10 to 15 percent have been diagnosed with "severe mental illness" (Lamb et al. 2004: 108). While it is true that the mentally ill are more likely than the non-mentally ill to be incarcerated (Gagliardi et al. 2004: 134), this does not mean that the mentally ill are more dangerous than the non-mentally ill. According to a study published in the *Archives of General Psychiatry*,

> patients discharged from psychiatric facilities who did not abuse alcohol and illegal drugs had a rate of violence no different than that of their neighbors in the community. Substance abuse raised the rate of violence both among discharged psychiatric patients and among non-patients. However, a higher portion of discharged patients than of others in their neighborhoods reported having symptoms of substance abuse, and – at least when they first got out of the hospital – substance abuse was more likely to lead to violence among discharged patients than among non-patients (Grohol 1998).

In the United States, Canada, Australia and in Europe, the number of prisoners with mental illnesses continues to grow (Council of Europe 2009, Rogers 2008, Canadian Mental Health Association 2005, Harcourt 2003). According to Human Rights Watch, "More than half of all prison and state inmates [in the United States] now report mental health problems, including symptoms of major depression, mania and psychotic disorders" (Human Rights Watch 2006). Does this mean that the mentally ill are more likely than the non-mentally ill to commit violent acts? There is no direct correlation between mental illness and the potential for violence. However, because "[o]ffenders think differently than non-offenders" (Morgan et al. 2009: 2), there is reason to suspect that offenders have a tendency to think about unlawful behavior more than non-offenders, and for a variety of reasons, both neurological and behavioral, may be unable to resist the temptation once the thought occurs. Nevertheless, it is worth mentioning that other factors besides the cognitive have contributed to the rise of the mentally ill in prisons.

Bernard Harcourt (2003) and Steadman et al. (1984) suggest that there may be a significant correlation between the deinstitutionalization of mental hospitals in the 1960s and 1970s and the surge in incarceration rates during the 1980s and 1990s that would account for the increase in mentally ill prisoners. It is possible, in other words, that in the past, those with mental disorders would have been confined to mental institutions, whereas now they are not, and are therefore more exposed to crime. Similarly, Fellner (2006: 394) argues that the "tough on crime" policies of the 1980s and 1990s, which stressed both drug interdictions and non-violent street crime, have contributed to the rise of the mentally ill in prisons. Diamond et al. (2001) suggest that mental illness also appears as a consequence of the longer sentences prisoners have been receiving since the 1980s, as older prisoners are more susceptible to mental disorders than younger prisoners (Malcolm 1988). Race is also a factor in the rise of the mentally ill in prisons. African-Americans and Hispanics, two groups that are disproportionally represented in American prisons, tend to be more at risk than whites for mental disorders (Diamond et al. 2001). African-Americans and Hispanics also tend to be diagnosed with serious mental disease rather than more mild forms, such as depression (Baker 2001), which could account for the higher rates of mental illness in prisons.

Whatever factors may have caused the increase in mentally ill prisoners, we do know one thing for sure. The mentally ill are more likely than the non-mentally ill to confess to crimes committed (*People* v. *Connelly* 1985) and to confess to crimes they did not commit (*Arizona* v. *Bravo* 1988). As Richard Leo has written, "individuals with certain personality traits and dispositions are more easily pressured into giving false confessions" (Leo 2008: 198). In one study of 40 prisoners released because of DNA testing, "Seventeen or forty-three percent ... who falsely confessed were mentally ill, mentally retarded, or borderline mentally retarded" (Garrett 2010: 1064).

In *The Insanity Offense*, E. Fuller Torrey, an influential advocate for the forced treatment and confinement of the mentally ill who display dangerous tendencies or commit acts of violence, writes: *"Conservatively, it seems reasonable to predict that 5 to 10 percent of individuals with severe psychiatric disorders will commit acts of serious violence each year"* (Torrey 2008: 143). Torrey tells us that among the 400,000 seriously mentally ill in the U.S. who are also homeless or incarcerated is a subset of about 40,000 who "have proven to be dangerous" (Torrey 2008: 6). For this reason, Torrey sees the mentally ill primarily as a problem of the administration of justice. He is a particular critic of the Lanterman-Petris-Short Act, which restricted (in California) involuntary psychiatric hospitalizations to a maximum of seventeen days, unless the patient could be shown to be "imminently dangerous" (Torrey 2008: 28–31, Karasch 2002, *Court of Appeal (Calif.)* v. *Rodney M.* 1996: 516).

Torrey's advocacy work on behalf of civil commitment for the mentally ill reveals the deep divide over the perception of the mentally ill as dangerous, as unworthy of rights. But it also shines a light on the inability of lawyers and health professionals to define dangerousness and predict it. Both among the public and public officials, the view persists that the mentally ill are dangerous and that the dangerous are mentally ill.

Civil Commitment

A case in point that blurs the distinction between dangerousness and mental disorder is the sexual predator law in Kansas that allows the state to commit a person convicted of a sex crime, and who has fulfilled his prison sentence, to a psychiatric hospital following the end of his prison sentence. Kansas defines a sexual predator as follows:

> any person who has been convicted of or charged with a sexually violent offense and who suffers from a mental abnormality or personality disorder which makes the person likely to engage in the predatory acts of sexual violence (*Kansas v. Hendricks* 1997: 352).

Supreme Court Justice Clarence Thomas, writing for the majority in *Kansas v. Hendricks*, the Supreme Court case that upheld Kansas's civil commitment statute, stated that "A 'mental abnormality' was defined, in turn, as a 'congenital or acquired condition affecting the emotional or volitional capacity which predisposes the person to commit sexually violent offenses in a degree constituting such person a menace to the health and safety of others'" (*Kansas v. Hendricks* 1997: 352). The language suggests that sexual offenders may be mentally ill, but acknowledges that they are not, in an effort to reinforce the idea that criminals are responsible for their actions and not mentally ill.

The purpose of civil commitment statutes is further confinement. Civil commitment statutes do not apply, for example, to habitual check forgers, only to sex offenders. The concern is future dangerousness of a particular kind. Treatment is not the purpose of civil commitment statutes, even though the criminal, now an ex-felon, is about to become a patient. "In practice, states provide inadequate treatment services and make it exceedingly difficult for committed persons to obtain release from civil commitment. Rather than enable the offender to overcome his sexual deviancy, treatment often engenders further confinement by providing the prosecution with incriminating records" (Miller 2010: 1208).

Kansas, in fact, did not try to "treat" Hendricks while he was in prison. As Justice Thomas admitted, Kansas's treatment of Hendricks while in prison was "meager" (*Kansas v. Hendricks* 1997: 367). And yet, despite the problems civil commitment statutes raise regarding defining and predicting dangerousness, "Twenty-one states and the federal government have civil commitment schemes that provide for the further confinement of sex offenders after they have completed their prison sentences" (Miller 2010: 2093). The underlying assumption is that sexual predators are preternaturally dangerous and have incurable urges. Dangerousness is always in remission (*Washington State v. Klein* 2005: 110). Thus, forty-four states, with different degrees of mandatory obligations on the part of the mentally ill and doctors, have laws that require "courts to order certain individuals with brain disorders to comply with treatment while living in the community" (Treatment Advocacy Center, Kamins 2010: 34). In fact, whatever one might say about the efficacy of these acts and their humanitarian impulses, these laws, by and large, do not require that the mentally ill person be declared mentally incompetent before action is taken. Of the twenty states that have civil commitment statutes that provide for having someone civilly committed after serving a criminal sentence, fifteen provide jury trials, but only ten require "proof beyond a reasonable doubt" (Miller 2010: 2128). These laws, then, are controversial for a number of reasons regarding the civil rights of mentally ill individuals (Swanson 2010, Flug 2003, Watnick 2001), but primarily because it is not clear how health professionals are able to determine who is potentially dangerous to others. The law treats the mentally ill as criminals (Slovenko 2000).

While "[a]ssessments and predictions of dangerousness permeate every stage of the criminal justice, juvenile justice, and mental health systems" (Zenoff 1985: 562), trained health professionals have no more power over determining a person's dangerousness than criminologists, economists, lawyers, philosophers, sociologists or statisticians. One might expect, given the medical problems that inform dangerousness, that health professionals might have pride of place in determining who is dangerous, as they would seem to have the best understanding of mental illness and its consequences (*Estelle* v. *Smith* 1981, *Addington* v. *Texas* 1979). To be sure, a psychiatric assessment of dangerousness can weigh heavily on a jury's determination that the defendant should never be released from prison, or upon release, sent to a psychiatric hospital. Ultimately, jurors decide the meaning of dangerousness.

What seems like a medical problem is in fact administrative, not moral or philosophic. By administrative, I do not mean to suggest that the assessment of dangerousness is free of political considerations, that is, that there is a neutral understanding of the term that all disciplines can appreciate and accept. Nor do I mean to imply that the assessment of dangerousness is purely bureaucratic, that is, that it has a fixed meaning, established by law or a commission and codified in a manual that would enable health and criminal justice professionals to diagnose dangerousness, much like the *Diagnostic and Statistical Manual* does with mental disorders; it does not.

In its administrative sense, dangerousness mostly means an assessment of future danger, based on a number of important factors that take into consideration behavior and neurological abnormalities, and which can be isolated and valued. In law, for example, dangerousness is assessed by a person's age, the history of violence in the person's life, his socio-economic background, the nature of the offense, and any assortment of concepts that influence behavior, including the stability of his family, family income, and living arrangements. A Texas Court of Criminal Appeals has held that jurors are allowed to consider the following in their determinations of dangerousness:

> 1. the circumstances of the capital offense, including the defendant's state of mind and whether he or she was working alone or with other parties; 2. the calculated nature of the defendant's acts; 3. the forethought and deliberateness exhibited by the crime's execution; 4. the existence of a prior criminal record, and the severity of the prior crimes; 5. the defendant's age and personal circumstances at the time of the offense; 6. whether the defendant was acting under duress or the domination of another at the time of the offense; 7. psychiatric evidence; and 8. character evidence (*Keeton* v. *Texas* 1987: 61).

These factors, however, are extremely difficult to render accurately for a determination of future dangerousness in both law and medicine. Indeed, many scholars versed in law, medicine, and the social sciences have critically evaluated the use of assessments of dangerousness in the courtroom and found such assessments unscientific and biased (Texas Defender Service 2004, Slobogin 1984, Diamond 1974).

The assessment of danger has become the management of risk; the unknown must answer for itself. Homicidal mania, Michel Foucault writes, "is the danger of insanity in its most harmful form" (Foucault 1990: 135) because it is the physical manifestation of a hitherto hidden disorder. Unknown disorders lead to motiveless crimes, the sudden eruption of crime and madness "which no intelligibility explains" (Foucault 2003: 121). Motiveless crimes pose too many problems for the law. For this reason, the unknown entity (dangerousness) gets named (risk) and becomes a manageable problem within the criminal justice system (Rose 2002).

Dangerousness, therefore, in its administrative or managerial sense, is determined by choosing between statistical and clinical methods of the assessment of dangerousness, but always with an eye on the administration of criminal justice (Underwood 1979). Clinical methods are largely subjective and not the preserve of psychiatrists or psychologists. Clinical assessment could involve anyone in the health professions with training in mental health. The assessment of dangerousness relies on the presumed expertise of trained clinicians in human behavior to evaluate the possibility that the patient may, at one point in the future, return to a life dedicated to violence (Skeen and Monahan 2011).

> Statistical methods, on the other hand, are specified in advance, and so is the rule for combining them to produce a score for each applicant. This score must be convertible into an estimate of the applicant's expected performance. This method of making predictions is often called statistical prediction, because statistical techniques are generally used to generate the rule from an analysis of prior cases to measure the accuracy of the rule in describing those prior cases, and to decide whether the rule should be used to predict results in future cases (Underwood 1979: 1420–21).

Under a statistical analysis of dangerousness, there is a preconceived notion of what constitutes danger. Certain character traits and behaviors get valued as potentially more dangerous than other traits. But these assessments do not confine their understanding of dangerousness to biological problems, such as bipolar disorder, which may increase one's potential for violence (Feldmann 2001: 128). They allow for enough ambiguity – somewhere between scientific certainty and common sense – so that jurors will regard these factors with a degree of certitude (*Addington* v. *Texas* 1979: 233). In other words, to criminal lawyers and the public, the qualities of dangerousness have the aura of scientific fact. But what they really are are "shorthand expression[s] for predicting criminal behavior" (Zenoff 1985: 566), divorced from the methodologies of scientific inquiry.

Medical Dangerousness

This is not to say that there is such a thing as dangerousness in the medical literature or that civil commitments make scientific sense, only that if an assessment of dangerousness determines future confinement, then dangerousness ought to be scientifically verifiable. But dangerousness, like insanity, is a term of legal art, not medicine. There is no particular or peculiar mental or physical disorder that leads to violence or dangerousness, though frontal lobe damage does diminish one's ability to resist desires and therefore may lead to criminal activity. Moreover, "a variety of neurotransmitter and hormonal influences have been implicated in violence and aggression. Serotonin is of particular interest in the study of violence" (Feldmann 2001: 124). Such studies have revealed, for example:

> that serotonin exhibits inhibitory control over both affective and predatory aggression. Low levels of cerebrospinal fluid (CSF) 5-hyrdoxy-indole-acetic acid (5-HIAA), a serotonin metabolite, were found in depressed patients who had a history of violent suicide attempts, but not in patients with non-violent suicide attempts (Feldmann 2001: 125, LaHue et al.1999, Takahashi et al. 2011).

To be sure, any link between serotonin and violence remains controversial, as does any apparent link between violence and biological phenomena in general (Popova 2008, Krakowski 2003). Indeed, the sources of violence remain deeply mysterious, and wedded to both biological explanations and to personal, social, and economic factors (Rafter 2008, Fink 1938). The larger point to make here, however, is that the scientific community has long regarded violence as a biological problem, even when it could not locate the source of the violence within the body, specifically, the brain, of the offender or patient (*Roper* v. *Simmons* 2004). But it has tried, over the years, despite the law's hold on the meaning of violence, to control the solution.

Phillippe Pinel and his student, Jean-Etienne Esquirol, are credited with discovering the psychopath. Among those they sought to help, first at the Bicêtre and then at the Salpêtrière, were those they believed to be suffering from *manie sans délire*, or mania without delusion. The manifestations of mania without delirium were obsessive thoughts and compulsive behavior that could, potentially, erupt into personal violence. The problem was that the patients with these thoughts had no physical manifestations of illness (Pinel 1806). Were they *morally* insane? Isaac Ray, the noted early nineteenth-century American alienist and proponent of moral insanity, wrote: "In the normal mind the idea of crime is associated with those of injury and wrong; can we then impute crime where there is neither intention nor consciousness of injury?" (Ray 1838: 98). The problem seemed moral, but the suspicion was that it was either biological or willful.

By the end of the nineteenth century, the location in the brain of a violent predisposition had not been found, but the idea of moral insanity or mania without delirium was under attack. Most neurologists argued that moral insanity was willful depravity, not organic brain disease. Dr. John Gray, the superintendent of the Utica asylum in upstate New York, and a man of deeply conservative and moral convictions, believed that the brain could not be diseased unless the body was (Prichard 1973 [1837], Gray 1882), a view that forced neurologists in the twentieth century to look more carefully at the brain as the source for behavior.

In truth, it was not as though those arguing for moral insanity were ready to cut the dangerous loose to live among the population (Scull 1993, Doerner 1981). Regardless of the medical assessment of moral insanity, those deemed morally insane were always considered potentially dangerous, as they lacked the requisite inner strength to resist the impulse toward violence (Rosenberg 1989). It is not surprising, therefore, that the idea of mania without delirium travels through moral insanity to the sexual psychopath laws of the early twentieth century (Federman et al. 2009, Freedman 1987, Morris 1986) and then to psychopathy, a disorder with no particular biological symptoms, but whose hallmark trait is antisocial behavior.

The second edition of the *Diagnostic and Statistical Manual* (published in 1968) defined psychopaths as exhibiting a combination of antisocial traits that amounted to something more than a mere description of behavior, but something less than a full-fledged disease of the nervous system. Psychopaths are: "unsocialized, impulsive, guiltless, selfish, and callous individuals who rationalize their behavior and fail to learn from experience" (Hare 2003: 189). The DSM does not consider psychopathy a mental disease with an organic etiology, and Robert Hare, a psychologist and prominent psychopathy analyst, is adamant that psychopathy is not a biological disorder. He believes that there are no treatments for psychopaths, just punishment (Hare 1999). The real concern, then, with defining psychopathy, present in Pinel's time as well, is with the law (Goldstein 1987). That is, because psychopaths are not mentally ill, they deserve to be held responsible for their actions (Cleckley 1964, Gray 1882).

Non-organically based psychopathy, however, remains controversial within the neuroscientific community. The current belief, among neuroscientists, is that the brain causes crime (Anckarsater et al. 2009). Neuroscientific studies of the brains of prisoners increasingly show a connection between a problem within the brain and the resultant bad behavior (Teplin 1990). Among those working on the connections among the brain, the nervous system, and behavior, psychopathy, they hold, if it means to be scientific, must be located within the brain itself (Anckarsater 2006, Siever 2003). Neuroscientists reject any definition of psychopathy as rooted in non-biological factors, such as free will (Hare 1999: 22). The brains of psychopaths are diseased, they argue, although the technology is not ready to reveal exactly where in the brain these dangerous impulses lie. But if someone is acting without regard for others and expresses no remorse or guilt, it is possible, say neuroscientists, that the psychopath has a faulty amygdala, which affects learning and provides responses to fear (Blair 2003). Other possible scientific explanations for dangerous behavior may be related to frontal lobe damage (Pincus 2001).

The movement to define dangerousness in a more structured manner, that is, as emanating from within the criminal body rather than as something willful, is part of a more general movement to define dangerousness through statistical analyses, as risk. Like psychopathy, this movement has its roots in the late nineteenth century. The Belgian statistician, Adolphe Quetelet, argued that crime rates were predictable and that "the guilty are only the instruments" of society (Beirne 1993: 156). As these instruments remained stable over time, the assessment of those instruments was Quetelet's primary concern. Similarly, the nineteenth-century Italian doctor and criminologist, Cesare Lombroso, devised numerous classifications, based on body types, to assess dangerousness and determine a criminal's life course (Lombroso 1891, 1911). And the English criminologist and statistician Charles Goring sought to make the assessment of danger more exact by using advanced statistical techniques (Goring 1913). Dangerousness, then, has always had a statistical component to it; risk has always been a part of dangerousness.

What we are seeing now, however, is a greater reliance on statistical models to further the goals of punishment and deterrence, at the expense of rehabilitation and other, less harsh forms of confinement (Rose 2002). At the core of dangerousness as risk is the requirement that individuals govern themselves, hold themselves responsible for all of their actions, and assume responsibility for what they have done, even if their state of mind is diseased or disordered. As François Ewald argues, "The principle of responsibility relies on a method of managing causality that makes it possible to devise self-regulation of conduct and activities" (Ewald 2002: 275). It does not take into account mental states.

Dangerousness, then, remains confined by the goals it seeks to foster. The inability of the medical profession both to isolate the source or sources of violence and to accurately assess the potential for danger has enabled dangerousness to find a home within the legal profession, where the criteria for dangerousness are lower than what one would find in scientific analyses. The law attaches dangerousness to the rationally dangerous. Thus, the Supreme Court has declared, in a case involving a defendant who established his insanity in a court of law, and therefore was absolved of criminal responsibility, that:

> when a criminal defendant establishes by a preponderance of the evidence that he is not guilty of a crime by reason of insanity, the Constitution permits the Government, on the basis of the insanity judgment, to confine him to a mental institution until such time as he has regained his sanity or is no longer a danger to himself or society (*Jones* v. *US* 1983: 370).

Legal Dangerousness

Precisely because the law frames dangerousness's meaning as the potential to harm others and oneself, and allows for regarding mental illness as dangerous (*Jones* v. *US* 1983: 368), it deeply influences the health professions' and the public's understanding of it. Consequently, in this section, I will provide an overview of how the law understands dangerousness.

In *Foucha* v. *Louisiana*, the Supreme Court held:

> [T]he State must establish the grounds of insanity and dangerousness permitting
> confinement by clear and convincing evidence. Similarly, the State must
> establish insanity and dangerousness by clear and convincing evidence in order
> to confine an insane convict beyond his criminal sentence, when the basis for his
> original confinement no longer exists (*Foucha v. Louisiana* 1992: 86, *O'Connor*
> v. *Donaldson* 1975, *Humphrey* v. *Cady* 1972, *Baxstrom* v. *Herold* 1966).

Terry Foucha was found guilty of "aggravated burglary" and the illegal discharge
of a weapon (*Louisiana* v. *Foucha* 1990: 1138). He pleaded not guilty and
requested a sanity inquiry. The trial court found Foucha not guilty by reason of
insanity. Louisiana law requires all those found not guilty by reason of insanity to
be committed to a mental facility. The court noted "that he is a menace to himself
and others" (*Louisiana* v. *Foucha* 1990: 1139). After a request for temporary
release, a panel of doctors recommended that Foucha be released. That decision
was later overturned. The state relied on a medical report that found that Foucha
"continues to be a menace to society" (*Louisiana* v. *Foucha* 1990: 1141).

> When a person has been committed after pleading not guilty by reason of insanity,
> the burden is upon the committed person to prove that he can be released without
> danger to others or to himself. "Dangerous to others" means the condition of a
> person whose behavior or significant threats support a reasonable expectation
> that there is a substantial risk that he will inflict physical harm upon another
> person in the near future. "Dangerous to self" means the condition of a person
> whose behavior, significant threats or inaction supports a reasonable expectation
> that there is a substantial risk that he will inflict physical or severe emotional
> harm upon his own person (*Louisiana* v. *Foucha*, 1990: 1140).

Foucha took his claims to the United States Supreme Court. The Court was
divided over the question of whether Louisiana could continue to hold a person in
a psychiatric hospital based on a finding of dangerousness even though the person
did not suffer from mental disease. Although it held that as Foucha was no longer
mentally ill, and he must be released, "the plurality opinion merely emphasized
that the Louisiana statute was lacking in the procedural protections necessary for
continued confinement." Therefore, "it is still possible for an insanity acquittee
to face continued commitment based solely on dangerousness" (Dallett 1993:
169–70).

What is most important in the *Foucha* case is the recommendation by
doctors in the Louisiana hospital where Foucha was confined to continue
Foucha's confinement based on a finding from a doctor "that defendant 'remains
combative, agitated, and psychotic'" (*Louisiana* v. *Foucha* 1990: 1141). But no
doctor diagnosed Foucha as psychotic. The supreme court of Louisiana wrote
that defendant's "'main diagnosis is Antisocial Personality Disorder,' but there

was 'never any evidence of mental illness or disease since admission.' The panel did not discuss whether defendant was dangerous" (*Louisiana v. Foucha* 1990: 1141). The decision to continue to hold Foucha was not based on any diagnosed mental disease. The *Diagnostic and Statistical Manual* does not classify Antisocial Personality Disorder (or psychopathy) as an organic mental disease. It is considered a "cluster B" conduct disorder and is not curable. Those with ASPD are, in a sense, psychopaths, persons who willingly participate in bad behavior (on the distinctions between ASPD and psychopathy, see Black 1999, Hare 1999, Serin 1996).

It seems clear from the state and Supreme Court opinions that the decision to continue Foucha's commitment was not based on any real assessment of his potential for future harm to himself or to others. Rather, his guilt and crime played a large part in deciding what to do with him. According to Justice Sandra Day O'Connor, "It might therefore be permissible for Louisiana to confine an insanity acquittee who has regained sanity if, unlike the situation in this case, the nature and duration of detention were tailored to reflect pressing public safety concerns related to the acquittee's continuing dangerousness" (*Foucha* v. *Louisiana* 1992: 87–8). In fact, according to the supreme court of Louisiana, the lower courts in Louisiana had relied on the medical reports of two doctors, both of whom believed that Foucha was dangerous to himself and to society.

> [A]t the time of the hearing there was no evidence of psychosis or neurosis and defendant was in "good shape" mentally. However, defendant previously had a drug-induced psychosis. If defendant was released, that psychosis could reassert itself. Dr. Ritter further testified that defendant's record at the facility showed recurrent problems. Defendant has been involved in altercations with other patients. Within the two months before the hearing, he had been sent to the maximum security section because of an altercation with another patient. Defendant's "attitude had been …extremely paranoid," as well as arrogant and threatening. Dr. Ritter refused to say that defendant would not be a danger to others or to himself. The parties stipulated that if Dr. Medina were to testify, his testimony would be essentially the same. Under the circumstances, we are unable to say that the trial court abused its discretion in finding that defendant did not prove that he could be released without danger to others or to himself under La.Code Crim.P. art. 657 (*Louisiana* v. *Foucha* 1990: 1141).

The controversy over Foucha's dangerousness – that is, whether it was determined scientifically or by more politically-driven concerns, such as public safety – reveals more than an administrative split between doctors and lawyers regarding assessment. Dangerousness is its own term. Like retribution, it does not refer to anything outside itself. It is an "absolute theory" (Merle 2009: 4). The perception of dangerousness determines whether one is ill or not.

Conclusion

Dangerousness is a vital part of the administrative understanding of justice, where justice is understood to contain moral principles but not necessarily to operate exclusively on those principles. Other less-elevated principles, such as expediency, efficiency, redundancy, and clarity also matter. Dangerousness, that is, the potential for danger that one carries within, usually because of a prior dangerous act, is very difficult to define, and is not the preserve of any one conception or discipline.

The problem with dangerousness is that it is an amphibian. It lives in two worlds, the legal and the medical, but it is at home in neither. Yet jurors give excess weight to medical pronouncements of dangerousness (*Estelle* v. *Smith* 1981: 459–60). As Eugenia La Fontaine has argued, "jurors are more likely to rely on the psychiatrist who is one hundred percent certain of his opinion than the psychiatrist who simply states that such predictions are unreliable" (La Fontaine 2002: 231). And as the Texas Defender Service has noted (Texas Defender Service: 2011: xv), the use of doctors in jury trials related to non-medical questions, such as dangerousness, is given a lot of weight by jurors in their determinations of guilt and potential dangerousness.

The assessment of dangerousness is a problem, then, particularly for health professionals. Dangerousness itself is not an offense. It "*is not an illness*. It is not a symptom" (Foucault 1990: 191). But it is treated as such, not just by lawyers but by psychiatrists, too, and jurors fall in line. They respond affirmatively to the judge's question: is this man dangerous? But neither psychiatrists nor jurors can answer that question, so they translate a lack of remorse into a lack of responsibility, and a lack of responsibility means the criminal is dangerous. The circular nature of dangerousness, and the problems it creates for mentally ill offenders, requires health professionals to pay special attention when confronted with such instances.

References

Addison, S.J. and Thorpe, S.J. 2004. Factors involved in the formation of attitudes towards those who are mentally Ill. *Social Psychiatry and Psychiatric Epidemiology*, 39, 228–34.

Anckarsater, H., Radovic, S., Svennerlind, C., Hoglund, P., and Radovic, F. 2009. Mental disorder is a cause of crime: the cornerstone of forensic psychiatry. *International Journal of Law and Psychiatry*, 32, 342–7.

Anckarsater, H. 2006. Central nervous changes in social dysfunction: autism, aggression, and psychopathy. *Brain Research Bulletin*, 69, 259–65.

Austin, W.J., Kagan, L., Rankel, M., and Bergum, V. 2008. The balancing act: psychiatrists' experience of moral distress. *Medicine, Health Care and Philosophy*, 11, 89–97.

Baker, F.M. 2001. Diagnosing depression in African Americans. *Community Mental Health Journal*, 37(1), 31–38.

Beecher-Monas, E. 2003. The epistemology of prediction: future dangerousness testimony and intellectual due process. *Washington & Lee Law Review*, 60, 353–416.

Beirne, P. 1993. *Inventing Criminology: Essays on the Rise of Homo Criminalis*. New York: State University of New York Press.

Black, D. 1999. *Bad Boys, Bad Men: Confronting Antisocial Personality Disorder*. New York: Oxford University Press.

Blair, J.R. 2003. Neurobiological basis for psychopathy. *British Journal of Psychiatry*, 182(1), 5–7.

Buchanan, A. 2008. Risk of violence by psychiatric patients: beyond the actuarial versus clinical assessment debate. *Psychiatric Services*, 59(2), 184–90.

Canadian Mental Health Association. 2005. *Criminalization of Mental Illness*. [Online]. Available at: www.cmha.bc.ca/files/2-criminalization.pdf [accessed: 2 May 2011].

Cleckley, H. 1964. *The Mask of Sanity*. 4th edn. St. Louis: C.V. Mosby.

Council of Europe. 2009. *Annual Penal Statistics*. [Online].Available at: http://www3.unil.ch/wpmu/space/space-i/annual-reports/[accessed: 2 May 2011].

Diamond, B. 1974. The psychiatric prediction of dangerousness. *University of Pennsylvania Law Review*, 123, 439–52.

Diamond, P., Eugene W.W., Holzer III, C.E., Thomas, C., and des Anges Cruser. 2001. The prevalence of mental illness in prison. *Administration and Policy in Mental Health*, 29(1), 21–40.

Dallett, R. 1993. Foucha v. Louisiana: the danger of commitment based on dangerousness. *Case Western Reserve Law Review*, 44, 157–94.

Doerner, K. 1981. *Madmen and the Bourgeoisie: a Social History of Insanity and Psychiatry*. Oxford: Oxford University Press.

Ewald, F. 2002. The return of Descartes's malicious demon: an outline of a philosophy of caution, in *Embracing Risk: The Changing Culture of Insurance and Responsibility*, edited by T. Baker and J. Simon. Chicago: University of Chicago Press, 273–301.

Federman, C., Holmes D., and Jacob, J.D. 2009. Deconstructing the psychopath: a critical discursive analysis. *Cultural Critique*, 72, 36–65.

Feldmann, T. 2001. Bipolar disorder and violence. *Psychiatric Quarterly*, 72(2), 119–29.

Fellner, J. 2006. A corrections quandary: mental illness and prison rules. *Harvard Civil Rights-Civil Liberties Law Review*, 41, 391–412.

Fink, A.E. 1938. *Causes of Crime: Biological Theories in the United States, 1800–1915*. New York: A.S. Barnes & Company.

Freedman, E. 1987. Uncontrolled desires: the response to the sexual psychopath 1920–1960. *Journal of American History*, 74(1), 83–106.

Flug, M. 2003. No commitment: Kendra's Law makes no promise of adequate mental health treatment. *Georgetown Journal on Poverty Law and Policy*, 10, 105–29.

Foucault, M. 2003. *Abnormal: Lectures at the College de France, 1974–1975*. New York: Picador.

Foucault, M. 1990. The dangerous individual, in *Michel Foucault: Politics, Philosophy, Culture: Interviews and Other Writings, 1977–1984* edited by L. Kritzman. London: Routledge, 125–51.

Foucault, M. 1990. Confinement, psychiatry, prison, in *Michel Foucault: Politics, Philosophy, Culture: Interviews and Other Writings, 1977–1984*, edited by L. Kritzman. London: Routledge, 178–210.

Gagliardi, G.J., Lovell, D., Peterson, P.D. and Jemelka, R. 2004. Forecasting recidivism in mentally ill offenders released from prison. *Law and Human Behavior*, 28(2), 133–55.

Garrett, B. 2010. The substance of false confessions. *Stanford Law Review*, 62, 1051–1118.

Goldstein, J. 1987. *Console and Classify: The French Psychiatric Profession in the Nineteenth Century*. Cambridge: Cambridge University Press.

Goring, C. 1913. *The English Convict: A Statistical Study*. London: H.M. Stationery Office.

Gray, J. 1882. The Guiteau trial. *Journal of Insanity*, 38(3), 303–448.

Grohol, J. 1998. *Dispelling the Myth of Violence and Mental Illness*. [Online]. Available at: http://psychcentral.com/archives/violence.htm [accessed: 2 May 2011].

Harcourt, B. 2003. The shaping of chance: actuarial models and criminal profiling at the turn of the twenty-first century. *University of Chicago Law Review*, 70(1), 105–28.

Hare, R. 2003. Psychopaths and their nature: implications for the mental health and criminal justice systems, in *Psychopathy: Antisocial, Criminal, and Violent Behavior*, edited by T. Millon, E. Simonsen, M. Birket-Smith, and R. Davis. New York: Guilford Press, 188–212.

Hare, R. 1999. *Without Conscience: the Disturbing World of the Psychopaths Among Us*. New York: Guilford Press.

Human Rights Watch. 2006. *U.S.: Number of Mentally Ill in Prisons Quadrupled*. [Online]. Available at: http://www.hrw.org/en/news/2006/09/05/us-number-mentally-ill-prisons-quadrupled [accessed: 2 May 2011].

Kamins, B. 2010. New criminal justice legislation. *New York State Bar Journal*, 82, 30–34.

Karasch, M. 2003. Where involuntary commitment, civil liberties, and the right to mental health care collide: an overview of California's mental illness system. *Hastings Law Journal*, 54, 493–523.

Krakowski, M. 2003. Violence and serotonin: influence of impulse control, affect regulation, and social functioning. *Journal of Neuropsychiatry and Clinical Neuroscience*, 15(3), 294–305.

Lacey, N. 1988. *State Punishment: Political Principles and Community Values*. London: Routledge.

LaFontaine, E. 2002. A dangerous preoccupation with future danger: why expert predictions of future dangerousness in capital cases are unconstitutional. *Boston College Law Review*, 44, 207–24.

Lahue, L., Ruiz, J., and Clarke, P. 1999. Serotonin: what role has it in the making of a Rotten apple. *Journal of Police and Criminal Psychology*, 14(2), 20–28.

Lamb, R.H., Weinberger, L.E., and Gross, B.H. 2004. Mentally ill persons in the criminal justice system: some perspectives. *Psychiatric Quarterly*, 75(2), 107–26.

Leo, R. 2008. *Police Interrogation and American Justice*. Cambridge: Harvard University Press.

Lombroso, C. 1891. *Physiognomy of Anarchists*. [Online]. Available at: http://www.spunk.org/library/humour/sp001494/physiog.html [accessed: 2 May 2011].

Lombroso, C. 1911. *Crime: Its Causes and Remedies*. Boston: Little and Brown.

Malcolm, J. 1988. Aged inmates pose problem for prisons. *New York Times*. 24 December.

Merle, J. 2009. *German Idealism and the Concept of Punishment*. Cambridge: Cambridge University Press.

Miller, J. 2010. Sex offender civil commitment: the treatment paradox. *California Law Review*, 98, 2093–2128.

Morgan, R.D., Fisher, W.H., Duan, N., Mandracchia, J.T., and Murray, D. 2010. Prevalence of criminal thinking among state prison inmates with serious mental illness. *Law and Human Behavior*, 34, 324–34.

Morris, G.1986. The supreme court examines civil commitment issues: a retrospective and prospective assessment. *Tulane Law Review*, 60, 927–53.

O'Mahoney, P.D. 1979. Attitudes to the mentally ill: a trait attribution approach. *Social Psychiatry*, 14, 95–105.

Pincus, J. 2001. *Base Instincts: What Makes Killers Kill?* New York: Norton.

Pinel, P. 1806. *A Treatise on Insanity*. London: Sheffield.

Popova, N.K. 2008. From gene to aggressive behavior: the role of brain serotonin. *Neuroscience and Behavioral Physiology*, 38(5), 471–5.

Prichard, J.C. 1973 [1837]. *A Treatise on Insanity and Other Disorders Affecting the Mind*. New York: Arno Press.

Rafter, N. 2008. *The Criminal Brain: Understanding Biological Theories of Crime*. New York: New York University Press.

Ray, I. 1838. *A Treatise on the Medical Jurisprudence of Insanity*. Boston: Little and Brown.

Rogers, D. 2008. Out of sight, out of mind: mentally ill in Queensland correctional centres. *Queensland Law Student Review*, 1(2), 88–100.

Rose, N. 2002. At risk of madness, in *Embracing Risk: The Changing Culture of Insurance and Responsibility*, edited by T. Baker and J. Simon. Chicago: University of Chicago Press, 209–37.

Rosenberg, C. 1989. *The Trial of the Assassin Guiteau: Psychiatry and Law in the Gilded Age*. Chicago: University of Chicago Press.

Rozelle, S. 2007. Fear and loathing in insanity law: explaining the otherwise inexplicable Clark v. Arizona. *Case Western Reserve Law Review*, 58, 19–58.

Scull, A. 2003. *The Most Solitary of Afflictions: Madness and Society in Britain, 1700–1900*. New Haven: Yale University Press.

Serin, R.C. 1996. Violent recidivism in criminal psychopaths. *Law and Human Behavior*, 20(2), 207–17.

Siever, L. 2003. Neurobiology in psychopathy, in *Psychopathy: Antisocial, Criminal, and Violent Behavior*, edited by T. Millon, E. Simonsen, M. Birket-Smith, and R. Davis. New York: Guilford Press, 231–46.

Sites, B. 2007. The danger of future dangerousness in death penalty use. *Florida State University Law Review*, 34, 959–996.

Skeem, J. and Monahan, J. 2011. Current directions in violence risk assessment. *Current Directions in Psychological Science*, 20, 38–42.

Slobogin, C. 1984. Dangerousness and expertise. *University of Pennsylvania Law Review*, 133, 97–174.

Slovenko, R. 2000. Civil commitment laws: an analysis and critique. *Thomas M. Cooley Law Review*, 17, 25–51.

Steadman, H.J., Monahan, J., Duffee, B., Hartstone, E., and Robbins, P.C. 1984. The impact of state mental hospital deinstitutionalization on United States prison populations, 1968–1978. *Journal of Criminal Law & Criminology*, 75(2), 474–490.

Swanson, J. 2010. What would Mary Douglas do? A commentary on Kahan et al., cultural cognition and public policy: the case of outpatient commitment laws. *Law and Human Behavior*, 34, 176–85.

Takahashi, A., Quadros, I.M., de Almeida, R.M.M., and Miczek, K.A. 2011. Brain serotonin receptors and transporters: initiation vs. termination of escalated aggression. *Psychopharmacology*, 213, 183–212.

Texas Defender Service. 2004. *Deadly Speculation: Misleading Texas Capital Juries with False Predictions of Future Dangerousness*. [Online]. Available at: www.texasdefender.org [accessed: 2 May 2011].

Treatment Advocacy Center (kendra's law.org). [Online]. Available at: http://www.treatmentadvocacycenter.org/index.php?option=com_content&task=view&id=1488&Itemid=260[accessed: 2 May 2011].

Underwood, B. 1979. Law and the crystal ball: predicting behavior with statistical inference and individualized judgment. *Yale Law Journal*, 88, 1408–1448.

Watnik, I. 2001. A constitutional analysis of Kendra's law: New York's solution for treatment of the chronically mentally ill. *University of Pennsylvania Law Review*, 149, 1181–1228.

West, D.J. and Walk, A. 1977. *Daniel McNaughton: His Trial and Aftermath*. Kent, United Kingdom: Headley Brothers, Ltd.

Zenoff, E. 1985. Controlling the dangers of dangerousness: the ABA standards and beyond. *George Washington Law Review*, 53, 562–607.

Cases

Addington v. Texas, 441 U. S. 426 (1979).
Arizona v. Bravo, 158 Ariz. 364, 762 P.2d 1318 (1988).
Baxstrom v. Herold, 383 U.S. 107 (1966).
Clark v. Arizona, 548 U.S. 735 (2006).
Court of Appeal v. Rodney M, 50 Cal.App.4th 1266, 58 Cal.Rptr.2d 513 (1996).
Estelle v. Smith, 451 U.S. 454 (1981).
Foucha v. Louisiana, 504 U.S. 71 (1992).
Humphrey v. Cady, 405 U.S. 504 (1972).
Jones v. United States, 463 U.S. 361 (1983).
Kansas v. Hendricks, 521 U.S. 346 (1997).
Keeton v. Texas, 724 S.W.2d 58, 61 (Tex. Crim. App. 1987).
Louisiana v. Foucha, 563 So.2d 1138La. (1990).
O'Connor v. Donaldson, 422 U.S. 563 (1975).
People v. Connelly, 702 P.2d 722, Colo. (1985).
Roper v. Simmons, 125 S.Ct. 1183 (2004). Brief of the AMA.
Washington State v. Klein, 156 Wash.2d 103, 124 P.3d 644 (2005).

Chapter 18

Working in a Violent Environment: The Pitfall of Integrating Security Imperatives into Forensic Psychiatric Nursing

Jean Daniel Jacob

Introduction

Historically, the development of a "scientific criminology" corresponds to a shift in emphasis away from the deviant act and towards the deviant individual (Mercer and Mason 1998). Since the nineteenth century, criminal law has been highly influenced by the emergence of *the criminal* as an object of investigation and a focal point in the determination of punishments (Foucault 1978). Somehow, this movement from the crime to the criminal has generated a conceptual gap—that is, establishing "the criminal as existing before the crime and even outside of it" (Foucault 1978: 252)—a gap with which experts in the field of law continue to struggle. Precisely at the moment when the criminal's actions cannot be explained or understood rationally, the judicial machine ceases to function and the penal system must turn to psychiatry for answers (Chauvaud 2009). In a complex analysis of what transpires between the act of reasoning (or lack thereof) and the action itself, medico-legal expertise has developed a technical-knowledge system considered to be scientifically accurate in the identification of mad or bad individuals (Federman, Holmes and Jacob 2009). In other words, criminal acts have become the responsibility of experts (such as psychiatrists and nurses) who can determine the sense beneath the act, measure the danger of an individual and establish the necessary intervention (i.e., indefinite hospitalization) to counter potential dangers (Foucault 1978). The work of Rose (1998), who problematizes the new associations established between public risk and the priority of public safety, echoes the introduction of psychiatry into the field of law. Forensic psychiatry now holds the authority to evaluate "those who are thought to pose a risk to society on the basis not so much of what they have done, but of what they might do" (Rose: 184). As the introductory quote would suggest, if Charles Manson (the leader of a U.S. cult responsible for serial murders, including that of actress Sharon Tate) had been identified as an "at risk individual," and had been indefinitely hospitalized under the potential risk that he embodied, history might have been different.

The inherent assumption that medicine may have a role to play in the assessment and treatment of mentally ill offenders is an important element in the medicalization of risk and its clinical management. In effect, the introduction of the psychiatric expertise in the field of law, and more precisely the management of risk with a specific population (mentally ill offenders), has had a ripple effect in many para-medical disciplines, including nursing. The introduction of psychiatry in the field of law has prompted health authorities the world over to construct special institutions designed to contain and treat those detained under medico-legal jurisdiction (Kettles and Woods 2006). In this case, the ripple effect mainly revolves around the enhanced security measures that are associated with these institutions which influence the provision of health services (including mental health); that is, within these institutions, health care professionals, and especially nurses, must constantly attempt to marry therapeutic and security imperatives (Holmes 2001a, 2001b, 2005, Peternelj-Taylor 2004, Mason 2002, Burrow 1998). The complex association between the prison and the hospital proves to be difficult to the extent that nurses must provide care while concurrently ensuring social control/security (Holmes 2005); a role which often includes the daily management of potential dangers (perceived or real) embodied by the inpatient population. As a result, the need to safeguard and maintain personal and group safety becomes a perceptible variable in nurse-patient interactions, since fear is considered to be evocative of caregivers' self-protective interventions (Whittington and Balsamo 1998).

The issue presented here may not necessarily revolve around actual violence but rather the perceived risk that a population poses to nurses. If a higher risk of violence in forensic psychiatry is not evident, it is nonetheless perceived as so (Mason, Coyle and Lovell 2008). According to Mason, Lovell and Coyle (2008), the condition of working in a potentially violent environment induces a somewhat chronic fear, even if stressful situations only periodically spill into acute states of actual violence. This perception of threat or fear is what differentiates the forensic psychiatric environment from traditional hospital settings (medical or surgical units). In this area of practice, where the patient population is believed to be dangerous and is kept at a distance, the perceived risk of violence and the need for personal safety reconfigure nurse-patient interactions (Whittington and Balsamo 1998).

The objective of this chapter is to expand on the effects of nursing work in potentially violent environments and explore its repercussions on nursing practice. In order to do so, I will present results obtained from a qualitative research undertaken in a Canadian medium secure forensic psychiatric unit. These results highlight the power dynamics at play within the nurse-patient relationship and the integration of the security discourse into nursing practices. This understanding of the relationship between nurses and patients requires that violence be examined within the context of the total institution (Goffman 1990) where power dynamics reconfigure the way nursing care may be provided (Holmes 2005, Holmes and

Federman 2003, Whittington and Balsamo 1998).The research design has been described elsewhere (see Jacob and Holmes 2011).

From Therapy to Security

As a general statement, how we deal with threatening experiences varies from one person to another (Lazarus and Folkman 1984). In this sense, our behavirous are considered to be enacted in reaction to the demands and contraints of our environment, and will vary depending on our appraisal of the situation. However, our reflection may bring us to question how the environment itself modulates our actions (Lemert and Branaman 1997). By asking this question, it is then possible to explore the taken for granted assumptions that guide what we may consider as "naturally" occuring behaviours. We are in a position to ask what elements of an environment make it possible for differences between individuals, such as gender, to be of significant importance in the way we conduct ourselves in the face of threatening events. It also allows us to explore how individual responses are governed by culturally mediated constructs "that instruct people as to how they should respond to threats to their security" (Furedi 2006: 20). According to Furedi (2006: 20), the "conversion of a response to specific circumstances is mediated through cultural norms that inform people about what is expected of them when confronted with a threat and how they should respond and feel". In other words, the way forensic psychiatric nurses deal with violence and threatening situations is enmeshed in a specific set of values and beliefs that are often shared within a group and enacted through specific procedures and practices (Schein 2004). These procedures and practices are in themselves the product of a unique context that support their occurence. Understanding the forensic psychiatric institution then becomes an important variable if we wish to understand the way forensic psychiatric nursing practice may be exercised.

The work of Erving Goffman (1990) on asylums helps us examine the fundamental nature of forensic psychiatric institutions. His sociological analysis positions the psychiatric institution outside of its therapeutic rationalization, supposing that we can break away from the particularities of the psychiatric culture of cure and identify common characteristics between the institutional management of mental illness and the general mandate of other social institutions such as schools, monasteries, prisons, hospitals, and so on (Castel 2002). By doing so, it is then possible to explore how certain types of social structures empirically represent unifying components (Castel 2002). Goffman's (1990) analysis of what he refers to as "total insitutions" looks beyond institutional discourses that theoretically support particular practices in order to situate each institutional discourse within a wider frame of reference, one that transcends individual justifications and acknowledges the common determinants of social institutions (Castel 2002). Goffman's work is beneficial because it helps identify the gap that resides between the therapeutic rationalization of the forensic psychiatric institution and its much larger institutional objective of social control (Foucault 1995).

In short, Goffman (1990) posits that each individual who enters a total institution – such as the forensic psychiatric institution – does so with an imported or domestic culture, one that is shaped by life experiences and social structures. For nurses, this may represent a professional culture resulting from academic training and hospital based practice (Goffman 1990). At any point in time, this culture is what constitutes the frame of reference that consolidates the individual's identity (Goffman 1990). However, even with the best intentions (therapeutic rationale), the institution will not substitute its own culture with each individual's presenting culture. The total institution suppresses previously consolidated external identity, and imposes its own internal frame of reference. According to some authors (Holmes and Federman 2006, Holmes 2005, Perron Holmes and Hamonet 2004), this imposed culture is problematic to the extent that it modifies nursing ideals of care and presents an important paradox (care vs custody) that threatens the existence of nursing practice.

In our research, the cultural paradox imposed by the institution was one that juxtaposed nursing practice and security imperatives. To some extent, security has always been an important aspect of psychiatric ward environments (forensics and others) (Kindy, Petersen and Pakhurst 2005, Cleary and Edwards 1999). Psychiatric nurses must assume the security of their units as well as the safety of its residents (Moylan 1996). However, the difficulty associated with this responsibility is evident in the production of seemingly opposite social mandates: to provide care but also to ensure social control. Goffman (1990) articulated this paradoxical pitfall of caring while having to enforce regulations that then poses a threat to this very caring process. As with the results of this research, nurses discussed the difficult integration of security imperatives into nursing care. Often set at opposing ends of a continuum, these opposite mandates created practical dilemmas for nurses, who may become preoccupied by one practice (security measures) over the other (nursing care).

> I think it causes conflict internally within people's minds, and differing opinions in terms of approaches to treatment plans and things. I think the conflict inside is that you can become a little preoccupied with the security and the legalistic aspects of it. And that has an impact on the care and treatment you can provide as well. So reconciling those two is difficult. (Informant 3)

Working with patients who are considered to be at risk of violence forces nurses to incorporate a secure mind-set into their practice; with some nurses actually identifing with the role of a correctional officer, a way of thinking that they have adopted in response to their awareness of the potential for dangers in their line of work.

> I think we are up there with corrections; I think we are similar to corrections. But because we are in a mental health system, we handle ourselves differently. But we have to be a correctional officer, so we are geared...; yes, you would have to say it is dangerous, because we are geared to not allowing weapons or potential weapons, so you have to think like that. So obviously we think like that, because it can be dangerous ... and over the years, we have had some really bad people and really dangerous people. (Informant 15)

In essence, not only do security and nursing care coexist, but one also needs to be present for the other to take place. Coupled with institutional demands, the perception of being safe must be present if nurses want to apply therapeutic principles. If security cannot be achieved, then nursing care becomes difficult to exercise.

> There are situations where security will trump what is a treatment focus as well. ...We know that, every day, it is therapeutic to take these patients outside, ...get them off the unit, get some sunlight, socialize a bit, move around a bit outside. But we need two staff to be a part of that. We want to re-enforce that the yard needs to be searched beforehand, and because of competing demands, sometimes that cannot be. "I am sorry, we do not have the staff today to be able to go out and search the yard and take two of us down with you guys." So unfortunately, that therapeutic opportunity cannot happen because of security issues. So that is a struggle. You realize the meaningfulness of taking this group outside; yet there are security considerations as well. (Informant 3)

One could argue that security management is far from being a nursing role. In effect, when the nurse interprets a threatening or challenging situation, it is supposed that he/she can choose to avoid (flight) or to engage (fight) in the situation (Whittington and Balsamo 1998). However, due to institutional functioning and their professional role, nurses are often put in a position where they must *act* in certain threatening situations that are not always related to mental illness in order to provide both a safe and therapeutic environment; thus, avoiding a threatening situation may not always be possible, and nurses must act regardless of their emotions. Therefore, the notion of control as both a clinical obligation and a way to present oneself was an important aspect described by the participants. In addition to being confronted by a threat, nurses must also remain in control of the threatening situation (or at least appear to be).

> In that situation. ... You knew that if you flinched you were going to lose the control of the situation. ... If you allow that, you lose control of the situation. (Informant 11)

Interestingly, in this research, the violent encounter was not always described as an immediate element. Nurses are also forced to interact with the potential threat that becomes pervasive with an awareness of the patient's history. While immediate interactions may not be threatening, the thought of the patient's past behaviour may very well be.

> I cannot tell you that I would not be guarded. You know, it depends on the crime. Like I said, there are horrific crimes out there. I think I try hard, and I think I am successful at trying not to show this patient that I know what he did and I am afraid. (Informant 13)

As such, being able to control and act as though one is in control remains a valued psychiatric skill. Nurses have a distinct identity that revolves around the management of the self (calm and controlled) as well as the control of the unstable situation. In other words, nurses reject their own sensibilities about the threatening situation in favour of a professional persona or "front" (Jacob, Gagnon, and Holmes 2009). *Being fearless*, therefore, becomes part of a group dynamic.

> One of my first experiences, when I went there, I was really afraid. The first day we had a client who was self-abusive and he would start to have flashbacks and he would pound himself. And I thought, I cannot let staff here think that I am afraid to get involved. So I started down the hall. … Of course, I was working with a whole new group of people. …I thought I had to prove myself. I was not comfortable to say I was afraid. (Informant 5)

This control described by participants necessitates that nurses need to assert authority in different situations. These situations may include phsyciatric crisis but also the need to enforce social order. In effect, nurses must portray themselves as an authoritative/controlling figure to enforce social order. The institution imposes social dynamics and certain rules of functioning that nurses must implement and enforce. If patients do not adhere to these rules, then the situation becomes a control issue for nurses, who must deploy authoritative actions, and, possibly, generate confrontational altercations. Evidently, the central relationship that exists between the staff and patients is one of surveillance and control (Goffman 1990). Echoing the works of Goffman, participants in this research evoked the danger associated with having dual responsibilities of care and social control. The danger implicated with this dual role mainly revolves around one imperative becoming more important than the other. Having to act in violent situations (psychiatric or other) produces an identity that reinforces authority and control, thus making it possible for gendered qualities to surface and predominate in the work environment. In this respect, the results from this research concur with Morrison's (1990) conclusions regarding the frequently observed and documented development of macho cultures in psychiatric settings. Such findings would also concur with Holmes' (2005) depiction of forensic psychiatry as a milieu that promotes the "virilization" of nursing care, in which feminine attributes are somewhat repressed. In these circumstances, it is possible to question whether the management of violence defines the forensic psychiatric hospital as an institution of control rather than therapy; or to put forward that having to manage violence makes it difficult for nurses to practice as the focus of interventions is tainted by security imperatives.

If the works of Goffman (1990) has helped us understand staff-patient relationships within the forensic psychiatric institution, it remains, however, incomplete. Goffman's (1990) analysis is essential to understand the inner structure and the internal functioning of psychiatric institutions. The works of French philosopher Michel Foucault, on the other hand, harmonizes Goffman's description of internal functioning with the analysis of macro structures and practices, thus positioning the psychiatric institution within a broader strategy of social control (Lagrange 2003). While Goffman problematizes the internal processes of what he refers to as "total institutions," Foucault seeks to understand how certain techniques of power, closely linked to social and political structures, are exercised in the management of individuals (Hacking 2004, Lagrange 2003). Hence, Foucault's (1995) analysis of institutions can be seen as an extension of Goffman's micro-sociologic description of total institutions. Foucault's (1995) perspective explores human action and interactions in light of power and its exercise over individuals. As part of his work, Foucault's insight on power relations implies that technologies of government, as means for the control of conducts, are exercised to modify personal characteristics in order to influence social and personal actions (Holmes and Gastaldo 2002). If Goffman's meticulous ethnographic work helped us understand the culture of asylums, then Foucault (1995) re-inscribed human interactions within a political analysis or "microphysics of power" (Gordon 1991: 3). As such, the following will explore the Foucauldian power/knowledge dynamics "designed to observe, monitor, shape and control the behaviour of individuals" (Gordon 1991: 3).

Inpatient Violence: Revisiting the Imbalance of Power

In forensic psychiatry, very rarely do we consider patients as exercising power over nurses. That is, power relations are often portrayed as uni-directional, from the nurse to the patient. Such a perception relies heavily on traditional conceptions of power that define it as belonging to a small group of people who occupy a position of legitimate authority at the heart of an organization, and impose their decisions upon others (Perron, Fluet and Holmes 2005). However, a closer look at nurse-patient interactions may reveal that power is actually distributed more equally than thought. In this sense, there are instances where patients exercise power over nurses, notably through the use of violence. Patients may be conceptualized as exercising power over the nurse inasmuch as they evoke a physical or psychological threat that forces nurses to reconfigure their practice to include self-preservation rationales (Whittington and Balsamo 1998). As the participants in this research explained, having to manage violence involves a power struggles between patients and nurses, wherein the loss of control puts the patient in a position of authority.

> I had a patient come at me…he was probably from me to you, beet red. He was a personality disorder, screaming mad at me because I confined him. […]And I was sitting there. I mean you have to think, "If I show anything, then I lost." So you just have to be firm. …You just have to remain in control and remain firm. I mean, sometimes you have to show one side. You may fear inside, but you are not going to show that to him because you cannot. …
> Q: What happens if you do?
> A: You lose control and you cannot. (Informant 11)

Not unlike the results of this research, nurses attempt to regain control over the distribution of power by effectively using space, regulation of time and therapeutic intervention (Johnson and Delaney 2006, Holmes 2005). In effect, nurses in this research described interventions directed at the self, the patient and the environment to diminish the threat embodied by patients (Jacob and Holmes 2011). According to Foucault (1995), this relation of power is one of discipline, whereby nurses develop techniques that meticulously control the operations of the body, assuring the constant subjection of its forces, and imposing upon patients a relation of docility-utility (Foucault 1995). Through constant coercion and management of time, space, actions and therapeutic regimens, nurses are able to *produce* docility (Foucault 1995). In effect, a Foucauldian analysis of power suggests that subtle strategies of government serve a distinct productive function, one that seeks to generate forces, make them grow and order them (Rabinow 1984). In terms of the nurse-patient interaction, violence may be seen as emerging out of struggle between power and resistance. Violence will either erupt from patients attempting to exercise power over nurses or, similarly, erupt from nurses attempting to regain control over patients when subtle techniques of power have failed to maintain order.

Evidently, it is imperative that we conceptualize how practices of violence relate to the concept of power if we wish to understand the effects of violence on nursing practice. Without a doubt, violence has oppressive characteristics whereby "it is the way in which violence acts on the body that makes it oppressive" (Mason 1999: 121). Influenced by a Foucauldian conception of power, Mason asserts that the oppression of violence is found in the ability of the act itself to constraint individuals. In other words,

> it engenders an imperative to constantly negotiate physical safety by managing certain aspects of oneself. […] In this way, the perceived risk of violence exerts a subtle governing influence over those who directly experience it, and those who believe they might (Mason 1999: 22).

We must be careful, however, in the interpretation of such a statement. Violence is depicted here as an instrument of power that acts upon individuals for the sole purpose of oppression. We must not understand violence as a synonym of power whereby violence is considered to be a repressive vehicle of power. According to Mason (1999), violence must be conceptualized as an instrument of power. Therefore, violent acts represent one strategy among others that nurses and/or patients may employ to exercise power.

In effect, understanding violence as an instrument of power enables us to expand on its productive effects. In this research, the negotiation between physical safety and management of the self was not described by nurses in terms of its oppressive effects, but rather in the way it justified and created interventions to counter possible victimization. The threat of violence that patients embodied forced nurses to produce interventions to contain and control this threat. In this sense, the interplay between power and violence has overt productive effects. The question remains, however, how does violence produce these effects? We posit, much like Mason (1999), that productive effect of violence lies in the possibility that power not only *acts upon* individuals, but also *through* them as subjects of power. Grounded in Foucauldian thought, this notion of subjectification supposes that there is a production of knowledge and discourses regarding forensic psychiatric patients and nurses, and that these knowledge and discourses will influence practices and shape identities. What we *know* about violence can work itself *into* our bodies to shape the way we understand forensic psychiatric care. Following Mason's (1999) reasoning, violence marks forensic psychiatric nurses with undesirable statements about their vulnerability to violence; that is, with the idea that to be a forensic psychiatric nurse is to be "in danger" of violence. Consequently, perpetrators of violence also represent a subject position that poses a danger to others (Mason 1999). These representations come to infiltrate the process of *subjectification* through which we understand what it means to be a forensic psychiatric nurse. This knowledge system about violence works its way into the way nursing practice may be exercised in forensic psychiatry and, in the process, produces new practices, discourses and identities. As Holmes (2005) points out, nurses are subjects of power to the extent that they incorporate discourses of social control into their practice and use technologies of "government" in order to control mentally ill individuals. In our research, defining the patient population as violent proved to be important in the production of nursing roles to manage violent patients; that is, the effects of violence on nurses created divisive roles that had more to do with security than with nursing care.

Managing Violent Bodies

During the interviews, some of the participants highlighted personal characteristics that were believed to be important to work in forensic psychiatry. These characteristics, which include being laid-back, very strong, forthcoming with directions, and able to "hold one's ground" and stand up to patients in tough situations, often carry connotations of masculinity, and define the way nurses present themselves in the workplace. These attributes are further situated within a context that was described as having at its core a strong male culture, in which weaknesses are masked and masculine attributes may prevail over feminine/emotional attributes, a phenomenon described as a form of masculinization.

> I just see a typical strong male culture, which I think is a good thing. ... it is funny, I wonder if the females become a little masculinized in an environment like this. ... not in terms of their physical features but in terms of their interpersonal. (Informant 3)

According to the participants, there was a particular importance for having a male nursing presence on the wards. Some tasks are required to be gender specific. For example, a male patient who has committed an offence against children will most likely be accompanied in the community by a man to ensure proper supervision. Participants also described specific dynamics that exist within their practice and revealed that gender is a central element of forensic psychiatric nursing, especially in potentially violent situations. As such, participants described a predominantly male positioningas a figure of authority and protection.

One of the gendered implications was described in terms of *presence*. Men are considered to have an effect on both the patients and the general ward dynamics.

> It is not so much that he could do more than us or we could not handle it ... It just keeps that level down a little bit. (Informant 11)

> As far as psychiatric crisis and those types of things, I think that there is probably less because there are males in the environment. If there is all females in the environment, and the female is trying to provide an intervention, and the larger male patient chose not to participate or needed to be restrained because of dangerous behaviour...then it would be different in this world. The males actually help settle those types of things. (Informant 9)

As these next participants explain, men are summoned in violent situations, but also enforce a degree of docility simply by being present on the ward.

> Not just on forensics, but in the whole psychiatric setting. Anytime there is a problem, men are summoned to the problem, moreso than women. Even though there is a policy in the hospital that there is no gender specifics, that is just in writing. Because there definitely is. And if you are a man with any kind of size, too, you are definitely getting called. And you are going to go in and you are going to be the ones with the hands on the violent patient; or put people in seclusion; or hold them down for needles. Very seldom do you have women doing it. Which is fine. I mean, me as a man, I would rather do that than put a

woman in jeopardy. And I think in the patient's eyes, too. I do not know for sure, but I think that when they see men coming, I think they are a little more nervous. You know: "I do not have much of choice here. There is a few men coming. I should cooperate." Whereas if it is women, I think they feel they have more control. (Informant 8)

There is a lot less horseplaying. ...like a big guy trying to bully the little nurse and trying to use his size to intimidate her to get what he wants. That does not happen so much if there are five guys on. (Informant 4)

The physical contribution of men in this environment is practically unavoidable, particularly in times of threat. This physical contribution is usually needed in times of imminent threat. The gendered representations are very divisive: women usually take on securityroles (preparing the needle, preparing the seclusion room, making sure other patients are not in the way), while men tend to confront and control violent patients.

Usually when a patient was acting out, they went to a quiet room, time-out type situation. So the males kind of handled the actual handson and the women kind of got everything organized. (Informant 5)

If you know how to handle yourself, it is not going to matter so much your gender; not as much anyway. I mean, it still matters, you are not going to be getting too far if you put a 4½-foot-tall female staff that weighs maybe 100 pounds against a 300–pound six-foot-six guy. That just is not going to happen. But you know, as a rule, there is a bit of a difference; again it depends on who they are. (Informant 1)

Participants did not discuss a division of roles, but, rather,assumed gendered expectations. Given a violent situation, male presence provides a protective connotation. Men are described as being larger, stronger and more inclined to be called upon in these situations. When it comes to controlling a man of any size, then one must "match force with force".

I will tell you something... nine times out of ten, if there is verbal escalation or there is potential for violence, it is always the men that get called. And I agree with it, and I disagree with it, because I have had instances where some female nurses have started arguments with patients...and then she would come to me, asking me to go talk to him while he is all agitated. ...I mean, I could defuse the situation, but there is potential for violence. But I will be the first guy to stand there to help out, too, you know. ...There is an expectation and there always has been. And, not being the big macho guy, but I would jump in over any women here. It is just basics. I mean men are stronger than women. Well, most men. But I would take a punch before I watched one of my female co-workers take a punch. It is just a guy thing. ...It is kind of an unwritten rule and it always has been. And like...some guys disagree with it, but most guys just accept it. (Informant 4)

In a psychiatric crisis, it goes to the macho-ism or the male dominant society, that males will push the females aside and lead the intervention when it becomes physical and violent. ...If you are thinking of an intervention where it has to get to control, then you need to match the force with force. If you have someone who is physically fit, 200 pounds, then you need to have a presence that can manage that. ...that would probably be males versus a 100–pound attractive female that is not physically fit or someone who may be obese. (Informant 9)

As we can see, male and female nurses fulfilled a number of prescribed roles that are presented in the form of "taken for granted" assumptions. This can be interpreted as a reflection of "natural differences" that are rationalized in terms of a necessity (Stobbe 2005). The affinity of male nurses for work in forensic psychiatry revolves around their gender attributes of providing (in part) authority and protection. In such cases, biologicaldifferences between men and women are evoked in the exercise of power. By embodying authority, male nurses are believed to create a degree of docility on the units. What is important, however, is to question if forensic psychiatric nursing practice essentially needs men to function or is it the structure of the environment that make it possible for gendered differences to be of any particular importance. The answer to this question, we believe, is the latter. Being a man or a woman should not affect one's ability to exercise one's professional role. However, introducing security imperatives forces nurses to emphasize other qualities that may not be distributed evenly between genders. How we define nursing practice as being at the frontline and managing violent behaviours in forensic psychiatry reconfigures what it means to be a nurse in this setting. Evidently, it shapes nursing practices and identities.

In this research, both men and women described taking on security guard roles. However, a distinction was made between being security-minded, which affects all staff, and being assigned the actual physical role associated with security.

Not all the time, like being a guy, you do feel like being a guard sometimes; or the heavy; or the big brother kind of thing where you have to lay down the law. (Informant 4)

Although some women may be able to adopt a role of protection, it is usually assigned to men (not necessarily in an official capacity). In other words, the results obtained in this research indicate that the managment of violence in forensic psychiatry produces new practices, disourses and identities. A division is created between nurses, where some individuals embody the security role while others are protrayed as beying more therapeutic. Interestingly, this division was also presented as having penetrated the experience of patients where the authoritative presence generally associated with men was described in terms of a perceived threat. The division in roles is, therefore, embeded in social intereactions en enacted in practice. The male presence is associated with a security/defensive position, while a female presence may not elicit the same effect.

> Generally, I think, as a female we tend to be able to talk people down a lot more effectively than the male staff. With the male staff, even the staff that are not confrontational, when a client is agitated they see the male and they start posturing and they do not want to be seen as the lesser man. Whereas when a female comes into the picture, if their approach is not confrontational, they can often defuse the situation very quickly and effectively, simply because they are not threatening to the male patient. (Informant 2)

The particular structure of the forensic psychiatric institution reinforces that being a male or female will shape the way nursing care is conceptualized and practiced. Working with a patient population that is considered to be at risk of violence and impliying that nurses should be responsible for the management of this risk encourages the creation of a divisive role – some nurses embody the role of the 'security guard' in order to facilitate the caring process of other nurses.

Final Remarks

Many authors have described the difficult articulation of therapy and security imperatives associated with nursing care in forensic psychiatry (Peternlej-Taylor 2004, Holmes 2001a, Holmes and Federman 2003, Mason 2002, Burrow 1998, Peternelj-Taylor and Johnson 1995). Our analysis suggests that nurses find themselves enmeshed in a matrix of power relations forcing them to assimilate discourses of security and violence into their practice. Nurses are subjects of the insitution to the extent that they intergrate discourses of violence into their practice and develop ways to counter possible victimization and in the process, distance themselves from nursing ideals of care. As such, the results from this research would suggest the impossibility of defining nursing practice outside of the specific context in which it is exercised and the population that is cared for. Working with a threatening population within a secured facility will inevitably create new power dynamics between groups. As this research confirmed, such a difficulty is often associated with the overriding need to assure security in order to facilitate nursing care. Consequently, the difficult integration of nursing practice in the forensic environment may be reflective of complex system of functionning; one that situates therapeutic imperatives as functioning within the forensic institution but never outside of it. In other words, nursing practice in forensic psychiatry is never exercised outside of an overriding security discourse. This may help us

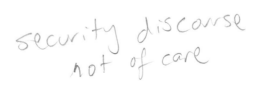
security discourse
not of care

understand the constant struggle to balance therapeutic ideals of care with security imperatives.

References

Burrow, S. 1998. Therapy versus security: reconciling healing and damnation, in *Critical Perspectives in Forensic Care: Inside Out*, edited by T. Mason and D. Mercer. London: Macmillan, 171–97.

Castel, R. 2002. Présentation, in *Asiles: Étude sur la Condition Sociale des Malades Mentaux*, edited by E. Goffman.Paris: Editions de Minuit, 7–35.

Chauvaud, F. 2009. Leçons sur la « souveraineté grotesque ». Michel Foucault et l'expertise psychiatrique, in *Folie et Justice : Relire Foucault*, edited by P.Chevallier and T. Greacen. Toulouse: Éditions Érès, 49–66.

Cleary, M. and Edwards, C. 1999. Something always comes up: nurse-patient interaction in an acute psychiatric setting. *Journal of Psychiatric and Mental Health Nursing*, 6, 469–77.

Federman, C., Holmes, D. and Jacob, J.D. 2009. Deconstructing the psychopath: a critical discursive analysis. *Cultural Critique*, 72, 36–65.

Foucault, M. [1975] 1995. *Discipline & Punish*. New York: Vintage Books.

Foucault, M. 1978. About the concept of the dangerous individual in 19th century legal psychiatry. *International Journal of Law and Psychiatry*, 1, 1–18.

Furedi, F. 2006. *Culture of Fear Revisited*. Fourth edition. London: Continuum.

Goffman, E. [1961] 1990. *Asylums. Essays on the Social Situation of Mental Patients and Other Inmates*. New York: Anchor Books.

Gordon C. 1991. Governmental rationality: an introduction, in *The Foucault Effect*, edited by G. Burchell, C. Gordon, and P. Miller. Chicago: University of Chicago Press, 1–51.

Hacking, I. 2004. Between Michel Foucault and Erving Goffman: between discourse in the abstract and face-to-face interaction. *Economy and Society*, 3(33), 277–302.

Holmes, D. 2001a. Articulation du contrôle social et des soins infirmiers dans un contexte de psychiatrie pénitentiaire (Unpublished doctoral dissertation). University of Montreal, Canada.

Holmes, D. 2001b. From iron gaze to nursing care: mental health nursing in the era of panopticism. *Journal of Psychiatric and Mental Health Nursing*, 8(1), 7–15.

Holmes, D. 2005. Governing the captives: forensic psychiatric nursing in corrections. *Perspectives in Psychiatric Care*, 41(1), 3–13.

Holmes, D. and Federman, C. 2003. Constructing monsters: correctional discourse and nursing practice. *International Journal of Psychiatric Nursing Research*, 8(3), 942–62.

Holmes, D. and Federman, G. 2006. Organisations as evil structures, in *Forensic Psychiatry: Influences of Evil*, edited by T. Mason. Totowa: Humana Press Inc.

Holmes, D. and Gastaldo, D. 2002. Nursing as means of governmentality. *Journal of Advanced Nursing*, 38(6), 557–65.

Jacob, J.D. and Holmes, D. 2011. Working under threat: fear and nurse-patient interactions in a forensic psychiatric setting. *Journal of Forensic Nursing*, 7(2), 68–77.

Johnson, M.E. and Delaney, K.R. 2006. Keeping the unit safe: a grounded theory study. *Journal of American Psychiatric Nurses Association*, 12(1), 13–21.

Kettles, A.M. and Woods, P. 2006. A concept analysis of forensic nursing. *The British Journal of Forensic Practice*, 8(3), 16–27.

Kindy, D., Petersen, S., and Parkhurst, D. 2005. Perilous work: nurses' experiences in psychiatric units with high risks of assault. *Archives of Psychiatric Nursing*, 19(4), 169–75.

Lagrange, J. 2003. Situation du cours, in *Le pouvoir psychiatrique*, by M. Foucault, Cours au Collège de France 1973–1974. Paris: Gallimard, Seuil, 352–72.

Lazarus, R.S., and Folkman, S. 1984. *Stress, Appraisal, and Coping*. New York: Springer.

Lemert, C. and Branaman, A. 1997. *The Goffman Reader*. Malden: Blackwell Publishing.

Mason, G. 1999. *The Spectacle of Violence. Homophobia, Gender and Knowledge*. London: Routledge.

Mason, T. 2002. Forensic psychiatric nursing: a literature review and thematic analysis of role tensions. *Journal of Psychiatric and Mental Health Nursing*, 9, 511–20.

Mason, T., Coyle, D. and Lovell, A. 2008. Forensic psychiatric nursing: skills and competencies: II clinical aspects. *Journal of Psychiatric and Mental Health Nursing*, 15, 131–9.

Mason, T., Lovell, A. and Coyle, D. 2008. Forensic psychiatric nursing: skills and competencies: I role dimensions. *Journal of Psychiatric and Mental Health Nursing*, 15, 118–30.

Mercer, D. and Mason, T. 1998. From delivery to diagnosis: the painful birth of forensic psychiatry, in *Critical Perspectives in Forensic Care: Inside Out*, edited by T. Mason and D. Mercer. London: Macmillan, 9–30.

Moylan, L. 1996. Relationship between the nurse's level of fear, anger and need for control, and the nurse's decision to physically restrain the aggressive patient (Unpublished doctoral thesis). Ann Arbor Michigan: Adelphi University.

Perron, A., Holmes, D., and Hamonet, C. 2004. Capture, mortification, dépersonnalisation: la pratique infirmière en milieu correctionnel. *Journal de Réadaptation Médicale*, 24(4), 124–31.

Peternelj-Taylor, C. 2004. An exploration of othering in forensic psychiatric and correctional nursing. *Canadian Journal of Nursing Research*, 36(4), 130–46.

Peternelj-Taylor, C. and Johnson, R.L. 1995. Serving time: psychiatric mental health nursing in corrections. *Journal of Psychosocial Nursing*, 33, 12–19.

Rabinow, P. 1984. *The Foucault Reader*. New York: Pantheon Books.

Rose, N. 1998. Governing risky individuals: the role of psychiatry in new regimes of control. *Psychiatry, Psychology and Law*, 5(2), 177–95.

Whittington, R. and Balsamo, D. 1998. Violence: fear and power, in *Critical Perspectives in Forensic Care: Inside Out*, edited by T. Mason and D. Mercer. London: Macmillan, 64–84.

Index